The Beatitudes through the Ages

The Beatitudes *through the* Ages

~

Rebekah Eklund

WILLIAM B. EERDMANS PUBLISHING COMPANY

GRAND RAPIDS, MICHIGAN

Wm. B. Eerdmans Publishing Co.
4035 Park East Court SE, Grand Rapids, Michigan 49546
www.eerdmans.com

Published 2021
Printed in the United States of America

27 26 25 24 23 22 21   1 2 3 4 5 6 7

ISBN 978-0-8028-7650-8

Library of Congress Cataloging-in-Publication Data

Names: Eklund, Rebekah Ann, author.
Title: The Beatitudes through the ages / Rebekah Eklund.
Description: Grand Rapids, Michigan : William B. Eerdmans Publishing
    Company, 2021. | Includes bibliographical references and index. | Summary:
    "A reception history of the Beatitudes, from the first century to the present
    day"—Provided by publisher.
Identifiers: LCCN 2020046893 | ISBN 9780802876508 (hardcover)
Subjects: LCSH: Beatitudes—Reader-response criticism.
Classification: LCC BS2575.52 .E39 2021 | DDC 226.206—dc23
LC record available at https://lccn.loc.gov/2020046893

For Angie

CONTENTS

FOREWORD

Older Catholic commentaries on the Gospels are often deposits of tradition. Aquinas's *Catena Aurea* is exclusively a catena of excerpts from earlier commentators and theological authorities. Cornelius à Lapide's endlessly fascinating work, known in English as *The Great Commentary*, is almost as much a discussion of previous writers as it is a discussion of Matthew, Mark, Luke, or John. Juan Maldonado's *Commentarii in quatuor Evangelistas* is much the same: rare is the page that does not engage with Tertullian, Hilary, Jerome, Ambrose, Augustine, Chrysostom, or some other church father.

The Protestant Reformers and their immediate descendants, when writing commentaries, engaged in a different pursuit. Given their severe criticism of Catholic tradition and their belief in *Sola Scriptura*, their exegetical works do not pay obeisance to those who came before them.

Indeed, in many respects their commentaries are attempts to overcome the predominant history of interpretation, such as the once-common use of Matthew 5:26 ("you will never get out until you have paid the last penny") as a prooftext for purgatory, or the use of 16:18 ("you are Peter, and on this rock I will build my church") to establish papal primacy. The early Protestants are not beholden to the authoritative past.

Calvin is here typical. He does, in his commentary on the Synoptic Gospels, occasionally refer to "interpreters" or "some" or "others." Their names, however, are unimportant, and they do not steer his judgments. Calvin's goal is to understand what he thinks of as the plain sense of the text, and earlier interpreters are, for this task, not so important.

This sidelining of predecessors recurs in many later Protestant commentaries. Matthew Poole's *Annotations upon the Holy Bible* and Johann Albrecht Bengel's *Gnomon novi testamenti* are famous examples. So too Matthew Henry's very different Nonconformist work. Yet it was inevitable that Protestants would eventually produce their own exegetical tradition. Thus their nineteenth-century commentaries are full of references to G. B. Winer, F. Schleiermacher, W. M. L. De Wette, D. F. Strauss, H. A. W. Meyer, and A. Tholuck, just as their twentieth- and twenty-first-century commentaries regularly cite J. Wellhausen, J. Weiss, W. Wrede, R. Bultmann, M. Dibelius, E. Lohmeyer, C. H. Dodd, and J. Jeremias. None of these names, however, takes one very far into the exegetical past.

The Protestant rejection of Catholic tradition was only one reason so many exegetes came to pay scant heed to premodern interpretive traditions. Also crucial, beginning in the eighteenth century, was the advent of historical-critical methods. Those methods led to new questions that seemed to make the old interpreters, for so many purposes, obsolete. What did they know? It is not that commentaries from the nineteenth and twentieth centuries altogether forget Origen, Aquinas, and others who wrote before J. S. Semler and J. D. Michaelis. Yet commentators outside the historical-critical stream typically remain of marginal import. The implicit demotion is reflected in the indices to some commentaries, indices that include "Modern Authors" but not "Ancient Authors," or "Modern Literature" but not "Ancient Literature."

The same self-centered constriction was part of my training in biblical studies in graduate school. The history of interpretation played next to no role in my classes. The dominant assumption was that the great bulk of interpretive wisdom lay in my own century. I was not asked to make the acquaintance of any commentator or New Testament critic before David Friedrich Strauss. My education trained me to investigate the New Testament and what lay behind it, not to investigate what came later, at least until modern times. I do recall a professor once telling me that Origen was "important." He failed, however, to elaborate, and he certainly did not ask me to read him.

Happily, things have changed since I left graduate school. *Wirkungsgeschichte* (history of influence or effective history) and *Rezeptionsgeschichte* (reception history) have become familiar enterprises within the guild. It is true that some contemporary commentators betray no acquaintance with anything written before 1900 or thereabouts. But their day, all signs indicate, is passing.

Why things have changed I am unsure. Part of the reason likely lies in the anxiety that traditional historical criticism may be nearing its useful end. Many or even most of our debates are, if one knows the history of the discipline, re-runs of earlier debates, and the returns seem ever smaller (as regrettably do the subjects in many dissertations). So the desire to defeat boredom plays a role here. So too does the postmodern proclivity to be self-conscious, self-critical, self-reflexive, to become cognizant of our own social location and biases and recognize how both affect what we do. To discover what interpreters in other times, places, and contexts did with the biblical texts cannot but help us to gain perspective on the presuppositions and activities of our own time, place, and context.

Yet another factor that has led to the history of interpretation receiving renewed attention is a desire to erase the heavy line often drawn between what a text meant when it first appeared and what it might mean for people today. The library shelves are full of commentators from the last two hundred years who are shy of making any theological, spiritual, or pastoral points. The history of interpretation is a way of reintroducing questions about theology and application, because application and theology were, before the advent of modern historical criticism, the heart and soul of all commentaries.

This, then, is the larger setting for Rebekah Eklund's *The Beatitudes through the Ages*. It is a delightful and learned exposition of the *Wirkungsgeschichte* and *Rezeptionsgeschichte* of the Beatitudes. Before reading it, I vainly fancied that I knew something about the history of the interpretation of Matthew 5:3–12. This volume has humbled me, leaving me cognizant of how little I really know. I did not, before reading Professor Eklund, know that some octagonal baptisteries are inscribed with the Beatitudes because many, including Gregory of Nyssa, have counted eight beatitudes. I did not know of the long exegetical tradition of linking the Beatitudes with the traditional seven gifts of the Holy Spirit. I did not know that the idea of "meekness" as a weakness or deficiency first became prevalent in the eighteenth century. I did not know about that artistic tradition that displays the Beatitudes in the shape of a cross. I did not know that a significant number of premodern exegetes understood "inherit the earth" (Matt 5:5) to refer to receiving resurrected bodies. It would be an affront to say that Eklund has done her homework. She has rather become our teacher.

If Professor Eklund's remarkably wide-ranging work is valuable because it has much to teach even the most learned, it has additional virtues. One is that it helps us to overcome the ever-present conceit that the new—which conveniently includes the work we just happen to be doing in the present—is always better so that the old is obsolete. But interpretation of the biblical text is not like computer technology. The new is not always the best, and it should not lead us to neglect the old. If they do not already know this, readers of this book will soon be convinced.

I am delighted that Professor Eklund draws no line between the exegetical past and the exegetical present. All voices—which includes not only commentators, theologians, and historians but also preachers and devotional writers—

from manifold times and places, and from all Christian groups, mainstream and nonmainstream, speak at once. Although unusual, this strategy is an improvement upon the commentaries that, while they highlight the history of interpretation, still leave the impression that it is a sort of entertaining add-on, something exegesis proper can ignore without loss. The history of interpretation, however, is vital. In the right hands, such as those of Professor Eklund, it unfolds the logical alternatives in a text. It reveals that, while the options for application are infinite, there is a finite number of plausible exegetical moves.

Consider, as illustration, the meaning of "the poor in spirit" (Matt 5:3). What do these words mean? The beatitude does not interpret itself, nor has the evangelist Matthew courteously added annotations. So all we are left with is the words—and the history of their interpretation. The latter, if expounded thoroughly, reveals the decisions we inevitably face. Drawing upon Eklund's discussion, here they are:

(1) "The poor in spirit" refers to
    (a) the humble or pious; or
    (b) those detached from wealth; or
    (c) those who are oppressed or dispossessed.
(2) If it refers to (c), the oppressed or dispossessed, this can mean
    (d) the despondent or miserable in general; or
    (e) those living in poverty.
(3) If it means (e), those living in poverty, then it can refer to
    (f) all those living in poverty or
    (g) the righteous who are living in poverty.
(4) If it refers to (g), the righteous who are living in poverty, then it can designate
    (h) those in voluntary poverty; or
    (i) those in involuntary poverty.

This sort of outline is implicit throughout Eklund's work, and for this serious exegetes are in her debt.

A further asset is that while Eklund faithfully notes the reasons typically given for this or that interpretation, it is not her primary goal to adjudicate between alternatives. She nowhere, to be sure, discourages others from making the attempt; that is, she does not deny that we can often muster evidence for thinking that the evangelist or a first-century audience more likely than not thought along one line rather than another. But she clearly appreciates how hard it is to make definite decisions, in large part because she knows the extent to which the Beatitudes are indeterminate, open-ended. Matthew's Gospel nowhere clarifies the meaning of "inherit the earth" (5:5) or "see God" (5:8). The text, then, inevitably requires one to fill in the blanks, and this in turn allows for multiple possibilities. Professor Eklund reminds me of the old Baptist commentator John Gill, who could regularly list multiple interpretive options and then refuse to decide among them, because he found some truth in all of them.

Beyond being a boon for exegesis, this book is a treasure of sermonic possibilities. It holds much that is not on the pages of the commentaries that typically line the shelves of pastors' offices. So if one is looking for fresh thoughts for preaching, they are here in abundance. Furthermore, interpretation and application are, for Eklund, not separate things. Here she stands in line with the misnamed precritical exegetes. The latter were consistently interested in how one might enter into the Beatitudes and bring them to life. Like them, Eklund is not a disinterested observer.

At one point in her introduction, Professor Eklund writes: "For me, past interpreters have been great company—enlivening, passionate, and sometimes completely surprising. They've challenged me to examine my own assumptions and biases, to consider and reconsider how I relate to the Beatitudes and indeed to God, to see things I would never have otherwise noticed." After finishing *The Beatitudes through the Ages*, readers will be able to say much the same thing about their experience with it.

—*Dale C. Allison Jr.*

ACKNOWLEDGMENTS

No book is a truly solo endeavor, and this one took a village. My editor, James Ernest, planted the seed of the idea for this book and then patiently nurtured it into existence. Along the way, I consulted a number of other scholars. Among the many who lent a hand with particular topics, special thanks to Marion Taylor and Joy Schroeder (women interpreters), Heather Vacek (more women interpreters), Fritz Bauerschmidt (all things medieval), Ian Boxall (the Beatitudes in art, and the reception history of Matthew more broadly), Derek Olsen (monastic interpretations), Matt Moser (Dante), Remi Chiu (musical settings), Anton ten Klooster (Aquinas), and Stephen Chester (Reformation theology). Fritz Bauerschmidt generously translated a few paragraphs of medieval Latin for me when I got stuck.

My colleague John Kiess asked, "Why does it matter?" and helped me to articulate the framing questions that drove the book from beginning to end. Other generative conversation partners included Ben Quash, Brent Laytham, and Trent Pomplun. John Kiess, Pete Jordan, Steve Fowl, Chuck Eklund, Sam Wells, and Susannah Ticciati generously read drafts of chapters and gave enormously helpful advice.

Loyola University Maryland provided invaluable support through their Summer Research Grants and the Loyola Dean's fund. Thanks to Loyola's generosity, I spent several weeks researching and writing at Tyndale House in Cambridge. I'm grateful to my fellow residents at Tyndale House for their encouragement and support, as well as the assistance of staff at the Tyndale House and Cambridge University Library. Librarians at the British Library in London and the Library of Congress in Washington, DC, also provided quick and cheerful help.

I worked on several chapters during the faculty writing retreats sponsored by the Office of Academic Affairs at Loyola; many thanks to them for the time, the space, and the free food. Colleagues in the Junior Faculty Symposium gave insightful feedback on a very early draft of the introduction and chapter 1.

I'm deeply grateful to the friends and family who traveled with me during the years I spent researching and writing this book. My dad Chuck and step-mom (*styvmor*) Caroline provided constant loving support. Sisters and brothers at Faith Christian Fellowship, especially my community group, kept me centered in the gospel. Colleagues and friends at Loyola brainstormed with me, sharpened my ideas, and cheered me on from beginning to end. Baltimore Pacemakers, especially Bob Hilson and Cynthia Evans, often asked me "How's that book coming?" and then put up with my explanations during long Saturday morning runs.

Weiyi Mu and Martin Camper graciously endured my rambling pontification on the Beatitudes over many long dinners. Fritz, Maureen, and Denis welcomed me into their family. Mel Curless shared my home on and off, providing companionship and sous-chef assistance during the years this book came into being. Finally, the loving friendship of Angie Karr has sustained me for over forty years. This book is for my friends, and especially for her.

ABBREVIATIONS

ACW	Ancient Christian Writers
ANF	*Ante-Nicene Fathers*
AThR	*Anglican Theological Review*
BDAG	Bauer, Walter, Frederick W. Danker, William F. Arndt, and F. Wilbur Gingrich, *Greek-English Lexicon of the New Testament and Other Early Christian Literature.* 3rd ed. Chicago: University of Chicago Press, 2000 (Bauer-Danker-Arndt-Gingrich)
BGBE	Beiträge zur Geschichte der biblischen Exegese
BZ	*Biblische Zeitschrift*
CBQ	*Catholic Biblical Quarterly*
CD	*Church Dogmatics*
Cels.	*Contra Celsum (Against Celsus)*
cols.	columns
Conf.	Conference
DSD	*Dead Sea Discoveries*
EBR	*Encyclopedia of the Bible and Its Reception.* Edited by Hans-Josef Klauck et al. Berlin: de Gruyter, 2009–
Eth. nic.	*Nicomachean Ethics*
FC	Fathers of the Church
GOTR	*Greek Orthodox Theological Review*
Gos. Thom.	Gospel of Thomas
HWV	Handel Werke Verzeichnis
Hom. Lev.	*Homiliae in Leviticum (Homily on Leviticus)*
Hom. Num.	*Homilae in Numeros (Homily on Numbers)*
HTR	*Harvard Theological Review*
HvTSt	*Hervormde teologiese studies*
ICC	International Critical Commentary

IEJ	*Israel Exploration Journal*
IKaZ	*Internationale katholische Zeitschrift*
ill.	illustrator
Int	*Interpretation*
JBL	*Journal of Biblical Literature*
JBMS	*Journal of Book of Mormon Studies*
JR	*Journal of Religion*
JSNT	*Journal for the Study of the New Testament*
JTI	*Journal of Theological Interpretation*
LCC	Library of Christian Classics
LCL	Loeb Classical Library
LNTS	The Library of New Testament Studies
LXX	Septuagint
MT	Masoretic Text
n.d.	no date/not determined
NICNT	New International Commentary on the New Testament
NIGTC	New International Greek Testament Commentary
NTS	*New Testament Studies*
NPNF[1]	*Nicene and Post-Nicene Fathers*, Series 1
NPNF[2]	*Nicene and Post-Nicene Fathers*, Series 2
PG	Patrologia Graeca [= *Patrologiae Cursus Completus*: Series Graeca]. Edited by Jacques-Paul Migne. 162 vols. Paris, 1857–1886
PL	Patrologia Latina [= *Patrologiae Cursus Completus*: Series Latina]. Edited by Jacques-Paul Migne. 217 vols. Paris, 1844–1864
RB	*Revue biblique*
rev. ed.	revised edition
RevExp	*Review and Expositor*
RTAM	*Recherches de théologie ancienne et médiévale*
SBLSP	Society of Biblical Literature Seminar Papers
Serm. Dom.	De sermone Domini in monte (Sermon on the Mount)
SP	Sacra Pagina
SVTQ	*St. Vladimir's Theological Quarterly*
TD	*Theology Digest*
TDNT	*Theological Dictionary of the New Testament*. Edited by Gerhard Kittel and Gerhard Friedrich. Translated by Geoffrey W. Bromiley. 10 vols. Grand Rapids: Eerdmans, 1964–1976
TDOT	*Theological Dictionary of the Old Testament*. Edited by G. Jo-

	hannes Botterweck and Helmer Ringgren. Translated by John T. Willis et al. 8 vols. Grand Rapids: Eerdmans, 1974–2006
TNTC	Tyndale New Testament Commentaries
WBC	Word Biblical Commentary
WUNT	Wissenschaftliche Untersuchungen zum Neuen Testament
ZKunstG	*Zeitschrift für Kunstgeschichte*
ZTK	*Zeitschrift für Theologie und Kirche*

INTRODUCTION

In the mid-nineteenth century, the famous Chinese rebel Hong Xiuchuan, leader of the Taiping Rebellion, was inspired by the Gospel of Matthew in general and by the Beatitudes in particular. He called his kingdom Taiping Tianguo (the Great Peace Kingdom of Heaven). Shortly after conquering the city of Nanking, he erected in the city a Monument of the Beatitudes, inscribed with Matthew's Beatitudes (Matt 5:3–10). He did so in order to declare "that the blessings Jesus announced in the Sermon on the Mount had now been fulfilled in his kingdom."[1]

The Beatitudes, it turns out, are everywhere—even (once upon a time) on a stone monument in China (the monument was later destroyed by imperial troops). They are the faces of seven women in medieval manuscript illuminations. They feature in poems and Nobel Peace Prize speeches. They pop up in debates over pacifism and poverty, the nature of heaven and the meaning of righteousness. They have contributed to Christology and to character ethics and to the nuclear disarmament movement.

While working on this book, I experienced for myself the claim that the Beatitudes contain the whole gospel: studying them led me into explorations of divine and human agency, the beatific vision, the hesychast controversy, the doctrine of the image of God, the role of grace in human goodness, the significance of poverty and wealth, the relation of the emotions to the moral life, and the nature of prayer. Even the proverb "patience is a virtue" comes from a poem about the Beatitudes! (Patience, it turns out, is the virtue of the persecuted in the eighth beatitude.)[2]

1. John Y. H. Yieh, "Jesus as 'Teacher-Savior' or 'Savior-Teacher': Reading the Gospel of Matthew in Chinese Contexts," paper delivered at The Society of Biblical Literature, November 2008, https://www.sbl-site.org/assets/pdfs/Yieh_TeacherSavior.pdf, 4. See also Thomas Jenner, *The Nanking Monument of the Beatitudes* (London: William Clowes & Sons, 1911).

2. The Gawain-Poet's poem "Patience" opens with the famous line "Patience is a virtue" and then links patience to the eighth beatitude; Gawain-Poet, *Complete Works: Patience, Cleanness,*

For two thousand years, the Beatitudes have stood at the very heart of Christian teaching. They might be the most commented-upon biblical text in history. They've long been seen as a compressed form of the whole of Jesus's teaching.[3] If Scripture interprets Scripture, many have believed that the Beatitudes hold the key. So I decided to set out to see what kind of a key people in the past have thought it was. In other words, I decided to do a reception history.

―

Reception history: what is it and why do it?

A reception history, or a history of interpretation, is an exploration of a text's "effects" as it has traveled through history. This is asking a broader question than what the text has "meant" throughout history. It's interested in what effect the text has had on individual readers, on communities like churches and towns, and on societies—and what effect those communities have had, in turn, on the texts and their readers. How has a text like the Beatitudes functioned when it has been read by particular people, in specific social contexts, at certain points in history?

One of the architects of this approach was philosopher Hans-Georg Gadamer (1900–2002). Because Gadamer was German, there are two German terms to consider here; both are difficult to wrestle into English. The first is *Wirkungsgeschichte*, which is sometimes translated "reception history," but more precisely means something like "the history of a text's effects." For New Testament scholar Markus Bockmuehl, this definition points to the two-

---

Pearl, Saint Erkenwald, Sir Gawain and the Green Knight, trans. Marie Borroff (New York: Norton, 2011), lines 1, 11, 27–28.

3. For example, Augustine saw the rest of the Sermon on the Mount as an expansion of each beatitude—Matt 5:21–24 commented on "the poor in spirit"; Matt 7:13–23, on the peacemakers. For each section, see Augustine, *Commentary on the Lord's Sermon on the Mount: With Seventeen Related Sermons*, FC 11 (Washington, DC: Catholic University of America Press, 2001), 1.9.22–10.28; 1.11.29–32; 1.12.33–36; 1.13.1–18.55; 1.19.56–23.80; 2.1.1–22.76; 2.23.77–25.86. Modern scholars have attempted their own schemes for matching beatitudes with content in the subsequent Sermon—e.g., Jacques Dupont, *Les évangélistes*, vol. 3 of *Les Béatitudes* (Paris: Gabalda, 1973), 3:316–20; H. Benedict Green, *Matthew, Poet of the Beatitudes* (Sheffield: Sheffield Academic, 2001), 256–61; Warren Carter, *What Are They Saying About Matthew's Sermon on the Mount?* (New York: Paulist, 1994), 36–42; and Ulrich Luz, *Matthew 1–7*, trans. James E. Crouch, Hermeneia (Minneapolis: Fortress: 2007), 173.

way street (so to speak) between the biblical text and its readers: "Rightly understood as the history of the text's effects (and not merely its 'reception'), *Wirkungsgeschichte* speaks of how Scripture has interpreted us, the readers."[4] That is, says Bockmuehl, not only do *we* read Scripture, seeking understanding, but Scripture "reads" us; it exegetes (draws meaning from) our lives, in all the particularities of our specific contexts. (This reveals Bockmuehl's understanding of Scripture as a *living* Word. One could also say that the Holy Spirit exegetes us through our reading of Scripture.)

The second term is *wirkungsgeschichtliches Bewusstsein,* or "historically effected consciousness."[5] This is, in short, both the consciousness (or understanding) that is effected (brought into being) by history, and the awareness of one's own understanding being thus effected.[6] That is to say, I understand the Beatitudes in the context of a particular historical location (time, place, language, culture); I cannot understand the Beatitudes in the abstract, apart from those contexts.

The practical upshot of this approach, for my purposes, has to do with what a text "means." For a long time in modern biblical scholarship, the gold standard was "authorial intention"—a text means what its author intended it to mean. Confidence in that standard began to wane as some scholars became less certain about their ability to pin down exactly what an author did intend for his (or her) text to mean. Attention shifted to the author's context: perhaps a text means whatever it meant to its original audience.

This approach also captures the two hundred-(or so)-year division of labor between biblical scholars and theologians: the biblical scholars' job was to establish what a text meant (in its original context) and the theologians then worked on what it might mean in the present. For Gadamer, however, texts exceed both the intentions of their author and the meaning(s) those texts had in their original context.[7]

---

4. Markus Bockmuehl, "New Testament *Wirkungsgeschichte* and the Early Christian Appeal to Living Memory," in *Memory in the Bible and Antiquity,* ed. Loren Stuckenbruck, Stephen C. Barton, and Benjamin G. Wold (Tübingen: Mohr Siebeck, 2007), 343.

5. Hans-Georg Gadamer, *Truth and Method,* rev. ed. (London; New York: Continuum, 2004), 299; see also Robert Evans, *Reception History, Tradition, and Biblical Interpretation: Gadamer and Jauss in Current Practice* (London: Bloomsbury T&T Clark, 2014), 3.

6. Gadamer, *Truth and Method,* xv. In Gadamer's words, it is "at once the consciousness effected in the course of history and determined by history, and the very consciousness of being thus effected and determined" (Gadamer, *Truth and Method,* xxx).

7. Gadamer, *Truth and Method,* 296, 396. In addition to Gadamer and Luz, I've been influenced by Rowan Williams, "Historical Criticism and Sacred Text," in *Reading Texts, Seeking Wisdom,* ed. David F. Ford and Graham Stanton (Grand Rapids: Eerdmans, 2003), 217–28; Ben

Following Gadamer, some modern biblical scholars dismiss the division between biblical scholars and theologians as artificial. A text's "meaning" cannot be confined to its original context any more than it can be limited to its author's intention. Scripture, after all, is a living Word. For German biblical scholar Ulrich Luz, for example, the idea that texts go beyond their author's intentions is not a threat but a sign of the text's abundance. The biblical text, Luz insisted, must be able "to speak, time and again, to new people in new situations and to be interpreted in new ways in their lives."[8] (In a more theological key, one might say that the Holy Spirit must be able to speak *through* the text in new ways to new readers of that text.) Luz was one of the first to make reception history a significant part of a modern biblical scholar's investigations.

Dale Allison was another: "The history of interpretation shows us how readings always change because readers are always changing."[9] Luz and Allison helped pave the way for New Testament scholars to take seriously premodern interpretation. Around the same time, historian David Steinmetz and others were arguing that modern scholars had too long neglected the insights of the premodern past, wrongly dismissing them as eisegesis (reading into the text) rather than true exegesis (drawing meaning out of the text). Steinmetz's landmark essay was boldly titled, "The Superiority of Pre-Critical Exegesis."[10]

This book isn't trying to make a case for the *superiority* of premodern readers (or for the superiority of modern readers!). But it is very interested in what they had to say, because they help to show us how Scripture speaks "to new people in new situations," which might help us likewise to see how

---

Quash, *Found Theology: History, Imagination and the Holy Spirit* (London: Bloomsbury, 2013); Dale C. Allison Jr., "The History of the Interpretation of Matthew: Lessons Learned," *In die Skriflig* 49, no. 1 (2015): Art. #1879, http://dx.doi.org/10.4102/ids.v49i1.1879; Ellen T. Charry, *By the Renewing of Your Minds: The Pastoral Function of Christian Doctrine* (Oxford: Oxford University Press, 1997); and Sandra M. Schneiders, *The Revelatory Text: Interpreting the New Testament as Sacred Scripture* (Collegeville, MN: Liturgical Press, 1999).

8. Ulrich Luz, "Reflections on the Appropriate Interpretation of New Testament Texts," in *Studies in Matthew*, trans. Rosemary Selle (Grand Rapids: Eerdmans, 2005), 276.

9. Dale C. Allison Jr., *Studies in Matthew: Interpretation Past and Present* (Grand Rapids: Baker Academic, 2005), 61. Friedrich August Tholuck (1799–1877), a German Protestant scholar, also demonstrates deep familiarity with premodern interpreters in his 1869 commentary on the Sermon on the Mount, *Commentary on the Sermon on the Mount*, trans. R. Lundin Brown (Edinburgh: T&T Clark, 1869).

10. David C. Steinmetz, "The Superiority of Pre-Critical Exegesis," *Theology Today* 37, no. 1 (1980): 27–28.

Scripture might speak to us today, in our own situations. The Beatitudes won't mean for us what they meant for, say, Reformer Katharina Schütz Zell, but how she wrestled with them might show us in turn how to wrestle with them. Past interpretations can help us explore the potential boundaries of what the Beatitudes might mean for us today, illuminating dead ends and penciling in some guard rails.

Allison again: "Although we may be grateful that the plain sense of a text usually guarantees some stability of meaning across the centuries, we may be equally grateful that such stability does not prevent the ceaseless and creative reapplication of the Scriptures, from which we can bring forth treasures new as well as old."[11]

The limits and possibilities of "meaning"

Allison's observation about the "plain sense of a text" leads to another important guideline. Texts don't merely mean whatever the reader brings to them. As Sandra Schneiders claims, "Although there is potentially an unlimited number of valid interpretations for a given text, not all interpretations are valid, and some valid interpretations are better than others."[12] But where do these boundaries lie, and how might we identify them in relation to the Beatitudes? How do we judge whether this interpretation is "better" than that one? I tend to object when my students use the word "better" to make claims. Better for whom? Better in what way, exactly?

Here's one example. When I teach the book of Revelation, I insist to my students that the beast in Revelation 13 is *not*, contrary to some websites, the United Nations. It would be easy to say that this isn't true because the author obviously didn't intend to equate the two. But I've cut that argument out from under my feet. If the book of Revelation can exceed its author's intention and its original context, then why *can't* the beast represent the UN? Let me suggest a few possible guidelines, all of which can (more or less) be boiled down to one word: context.

---

11. Allison, *Studies in Matthew*, 62.

12. Schneiders, *The Revelatory Text*, 164. Susan Schreiner makes a very similar claim in Susan E. Schreiner, *Where Shall Wisdom Be Found? Calvin's Exegesis of Job from Medieval and Modern Perspectives* (Chicago: University of Chicago, 1994), 17.

Historical context

The Beatitudes were spoken—and later recorded—in a particular language, at a particular time and place, and in particular religious, cultural, and sociopolitical contexts.[13] Understanding as much as we can about those particularities helps to root the Beatitudes in the historical age of their "birth," as it were. This knowledge can help to provide a baseline, a place at which to begin, when considering their function or meaning, because they first functioned there before they functioned anywhere else.

In the first century, to return to my earlier example, Revelation's beast was the Roman Emperor. Now, this doesn't mean that all valid applications must be directly analogous to this original symbolism. But an application that is wildly *dis*-analogous should give us pause. Interpreting the book of Revelation "responsibly" (as Michael Gorman says) also involves identifying the genre of Revelation, since reading well typically involves understanding what genre we are reading.[14] Because all genres are historically conditioned—"comedy" means something different to Dante and to Tina Fey—understanding as much as we can about what a first-century apocalypse *is* means understanding how an apocalypse (and a first-century epistle) might have functioned for its hearers. This provides an anchor, a starting point, from which to begin.[15]

The Beatitudes' original contexts exert a gentle pull on the centrifugal movement of meaning—a centripetal counterbalance, if you will. The original context doesn't *determine* meaning; as Luz proposed, "It would be a mistake to reject as illegitimate everything that is exegetically not justified in the forum of the biblical text. It is rather part of the biblical texts' own power that they themselves are able to open up new dimensions in new people."[16] (The beast in Revelation 13 doesn't

---

13. See, e.g., Markus Bockmuehl, *Seeing the Word: Refocusing New Testament Study* (Grand Rapids: Baker Academic, 2006), 57–58.

14. Michael J. Gorman, *Reading Revelation* (Eugene, OR: Cascade, 2011).

15. Trevor Hart uses the metaphor of an anchor used by rock climbers to secure a rope in a rock face to explain the tension between "determinacy and indeterminacy in language"; precisely because of this tension, language is "a tool of sufficient flexibility to plot a world of experience which is never the same twice, open-ended and complex. We might liken it to a rope fixed securely to a point on a rock face, on the other end of which a climber hangs and skips across the rock, skillfully exploring its contours. Without the firm anchor the task of moving out beyond is an impossible one; but the point of mooring the rope in this way is precisely to allow such movement to occur" (Trevor Hart, "Imagination and Responsible Reading," in *Renewing Biblical Interpretation*, ed. Craig Bartholomew, Colin Greene, and Karl Moller [Cumbria, UK: Paternoster; Grand Rapids: Zondervan, 2000], 329).

16. Luz, *Matthew 1–7*, 197.

signify *only* the Roman Emperor.) But Luz added, "the original meaning of the text" should be a conversation partner with these new dimensions.[17] (How is the United Nations like and unlike the Roman Emperors?) The term "conversation partner" is helpful here. A conversation partner, unlike a dictator, doesn't have veto power over a new and different meaning. But it does have a voice.

This means, of course, that interpretations that push against the grain of the original context are not by definition inadmissible.[18] But on what grounds might we admit them?

The wider context of Scripture

In the next chapter, we'll look at how the narrative contexts of Matthew and Luke might shape how we hear and understand the two versions of the Beatitudes. For example, the gospel contexts press us to hear the Beatitudes in light of Jesus's identity (as the authoritative speaker of the Beatitudes) and in light of the end of the story (the empty tomb, the risen Jesus).

We might also ask if a reading coheres with the whole of Scripture. Does an interpretation of a beatitude, even if it obviously wasn't possible in the beatitude's original context, resonate with the witness of the Old and New Testaments? Of course, that witness is enormously complicated, diverse, and in some cases stands in significant tension with itself. Nonetheless, premodern readers were convinced that both Old and New Testaments ultimately bear unified and harmonious witness to the triune God. And I take it, in all its complexity, as the primary way that God has spoken—the foremost of God's gifts to God's people. A new interpretation might resonate with a key theme elsewhere in Scripture, even while it fails to cohere with what might have been possible in the text's original context. But how do we decide what counts as "a key theme"? Another way to parse the same question is to apply what Jesus called the two greatest commandments (Matt 22:34–40). Does an interpretation lead to greater love of God and greater love of neighbor? This brings us to the final criterion.

---

17. Luz, *Matthew 1–7*, 197.

18. See the friendly debate between Walter Moberly and Susannah Ticciati in R. W. L. Moberly, "Theological Thinking and the Reading of Scripture: An *Auseinandersetzung* with Susannah Ticciati," *JTI* 10, no. 1 (2016): 103–16; and Susannah Ticciati, "Response to Walter Moberly's 'Theological Thinking and the Reading of Scripture,'" *JTI* 10, no. 1 (2016): 117–23. See also Jan Lambrecht, *"Eh bien! Moi je vous dis." Le discours-programme de Jésus (Mt 5–7; Lc 6,20–49)*, Lectio Divina 125 (Paris: Les Éditions du Cerf, 1986), 71.

The contexts of our lives: our loves, our neighbors

Augustine proposed that any interpretation that does not lead to the greater love of God and neighbor is not a proper interpretation.[19] So we might measure an interpretation by its fruitfulness—that is, by its ability to bear good fruit in the lives of those who seek to shape their lives around that interpretation. Is a certain interpretation of a beatitude "conducive to virtue" (to borrow Ellen Charry's term)?[20] We might judge that some interpretations are especially *generative*—that is, they might stimulate someone's imagination, or awaken joy, or sting someone toward repentance, or generate new insights.[21] This shifts attention away from the content of the texts alone, and toward the relationship between the text's content and the reader's contexts.

One interpretation might be "better" (more fruitful) in one context for one set of readers, while a different interpretation would be better for another set of readers with different problems and questions. "What might incite me to love might not be what would incite you to love," observes Susannah Ticciati.[22]

This means that a final guardrail is reading in the company of others. I think this is absolutely essential. If "meaning" is produced in the interaction between text and reader, then I must read with others so that the text is not held hostage to my own whims—my selfishness, my wounds, even my joys. Who challenges my reading? Who shows me that I'm too trapped inside my own horizon to see otherwise?

For me, past interpreters have been great company—enlivening, passionate, and sometimes completely surprising. They've challenged me to

19. Augustine: "Whoever, therefore, thinks that he understands the divine Scriptures or any part of them so that it does not build the double love of God and of our neighbor does not understand it at all. Whoever finds a lesson there useful to the building of charity [love], even though he has not said what the author may be shown to have intended in that place, has not been deceived, nor is he lying in any way" (Augustine, *On Christian Doctrine*, trans. D. W. Robertson Jr. [New York: Macmillan, 1958], 1.36.40). Augustine went on to say that failing to discern correctly the author's intention while nonetheless giving an interpretation that builds up love is like arriving at the right place but by the wrong path (Augustine, *On Christian Teaching*, 1.36.41).

20. Charry, *By the Renewing*, 19; see 18–29 for the "salutarity principle."

21. I'm borrowing the language of generativity from Ben Quash and the Visual Commentary on Scripture project (https://thevcs.org).

22. Susannah Ticciati, in personal email correspondence. Hart offers 1 Cor 14:33b–5 as an example of a difficult text whose original context guides how we interpret it, but precisely in the sense that the original text guides us to interpret it differently for our own particular contexts, since what might cause offense and bring shame to the gospel is not the same now as it was then (Hart, "Imagination," 330–33).

examine my own assumptions and biases, to consider and reconsider how I relate to the Beatitudes and indeed to God, to see things I would never have otherwise noticed.[23]

Premodern comfort with multiplicity

All this assumes, of course, that texts like the Beatitudes have more than one meaning, or more than one function. This was intuitively true for premodern interpreters, who assumed that every text contained multiple meanings. They often offered several interpretations of the same beatitude, even interpretations that stood in some tension with each other. "This can be explained in three ways" might be the most common refrain in Thomas Aquinas's thirteenth-century commentary on the Gospel of Matthew.

They seemed to find this multiplicity, these tensions, generative rather than troublesome, a signal of the inexhaustible riches of Scripture and its ability to speak anew into new situations. The gospel writers themselves shared this ancient comfort with multilayered meaning; they likely would have been confounded at the modern desire to find one single meaning in their texts.[24]

This premodern tendency lingers today especially among preachers (not surprisingly, it's less common in modern academic scholarship). In the early eighteenth century, preacher Matthew Henry's influential commentary presented multiple valid meanings for each beatitude.[25] Evangelist Billy Graham named five types of mourning, three kinds of mercy, three varieties of purity, and six types of peacemaking that are all blessed.[26] The variety of nonexclusive interpretations of each beatitude will be an ongoing theme of this book.

My approach is similar to that of Ian Boxall (in his *Matthew through the Centuries*). Boxall explains that he mostly allowed "different readings of the

23. John Thompson's *Reading the Bible with the Dead* (Grand Rapids: Eerdmans, 2007); and Bob Ekblad's *Reading the Bible with the Damned* (Louisville: Westminster John Knox, 2005) are two good places to start thinking about reading in the company of others, especially others who are unlike us.

24. Perhaps, as Dale Allison suggests, "this sort of nonexclusive interpretation often corresponds to how a text was intended to be heard and was heard from the beginning" (Allison, "The History," 10).

25. Matthew Henry, *An Exposition of the Old and New Testament*, vol. 5, *Matthew to John* (New York: Revell, n.d. [1708–1710?]).

26. Billy Graham, *The Secret of Happiness: Jesus' Teaching on Happiness as Expressed in the Beatitudes* (Garden City, NY: Doubleday, 1955).

same text to sit side by side, without adjudicating between them, much in the manner of medieval commentaries where 'authorities' from the past are juxtaposed as alternative or even complementary readings." However, he also says that, from time to time, "I have been more forthright in identifying 'better' or 'worse' readings, or suggesting how unfamiliar readings might be especially illuminative."[27] As committed as I am to the joys of multiple readings, I occasionally stake a claim about a path that seems especially illuminative, or one that leads instead into the dark.

Nuts and bolts: read me first

When I give reading assignments to students, I often provide them with a document called "READ ME FIRST," with instructions that help orient them to what they're about to read. Consider these next few paragraphs my "READ ME FIRST" document.

A great scholar once claimed that "a history of the interpretation of the Sermon on the Mount throughout the past two millennia would virtually amount to an introduction to the entire development of Christian theology and ethics."[28] Luckily I'm only doing the Beatitudes, not the entire Sermon. Still, I'm well aware that this isn't a comprehensive history of the Beatitudes.

This is *a* reception history, not *the* reception history of the Beatitudes. It's necessarily selective. It's limited by my own social context, including the languages I speak and read. In a way, this book is *my* interpretation of the Beatitudes. I've chosen which interpretations to include, and in what order. No doubt I've been limited by my own leanings, but I've tried to do justice to the primary strands and to some interesting outliers. I've sought voices of both women and men from East and West and the global South. I've done my best to unearth everyday-life resources like letters and short stories alongside treatises and sermons.

In the following pages, I'll explore a variety of voices, some mainstream, others less so, with the hopes that every reader might encounter and be just a little astonished by someone they wouldn't otherwise have read, whether that person be Origen, Billy Graham, or Dhuoda of Septimania. Some readers might be a little skeptical about Origen (or about "the tradition" in general);

---

27. Ian Boxall, *Matthew through the Centuries*, Wiley Blackwell Bible Commentaries (Malden, MA: Wiley Blackwell, 2019), 9.

28. Jaroslav Pelikan, *The Melody of Theology* (Cambridge: Harvard University Press, 1988), 229.

others might assume they have nothing to learn from evangelist Billy Graham. Some of you probably haven't heard of Dhuoda (I hadn't). I've found riches in all of them, and I invite my readers to do the same. Other people, from other times and places, have found insights in the Beatitudes that I can't—not because they were more clever than me (although many of them undoubtedly were) but because they lived through events I never experienced and loved people I never knew.

I adopt relatively standard terms for the various eras of church history. The patristic era refers to the writings of the so-called church fathers and mothers (roughly, the second through the fifth centuries). From there, I use the terms medieval (roughly, the sixth through the fifteenth centuries), Reformation (roughly, the sixteenth and seventeenth centuries), Enlightenment or modern (the eighteenth through the twentieth centuries), and contemporary (the late twentieth and early twenty-first centuries).[29]

For the most part, I've chosen not to alter quotations of my sources, allowing them to speak in the cadence of their own time and place even when they (or their translators) use non-gender-inclusive language for humanity or for God. Unless otherwise indicated, quotations from Scripture are from the NRSV.

—

"The verse itself," writes Dale Allison, "from one point of view, is only a station on the way, and so its full meaning can only be pondered by retracing the paths that led to it and by uncovering the paths that have gone out from it."[30] It's time to uncover some of those paths.

---

29. On the difficulties of Byzantine historiography, see Averil Cameron, *Byzantine Matters* (Princeton: Princeton University Press, 2014).

30. Allison, *Studies in Matthew*, 61.

1

Meet the Beatitudes

Some Basic Questions

In this chapter, I want to consider six "big-picture" questions. These questions will lay the foundation for all the chapters to come. They are questions that recur throughout the interpretive history. Some may seem obvious (like question #5) but have surprisingly complex answers. Some have had a relatively uniform answer for a long time and then a new answer at an identifiable point in history (like question #1). All of them are essential for understanding the interpretation of each individual beatitude.

    1. Are Matthew's and Luke's Beatitudes the same, or are they different?
    2. Who are the Beatitudes for?
    3. (How) are they countercultural?
    4. Are they commands or descriptions?
    5. How many are there?
    6. When are they for?

Are Matthew's and Luke's Beatitudes the same, or different?

Matthew and Luke, the two "evangelists" who recorded the Beatitudes, did so with their own distinctive styles. To line up their two versions in the chart below, I've followed Matthew's order and reordered Luke's.

MATTHEW 5:1–12	LUKE 6:20–26 [REORDERED]
Blessed are the poor in spirit, for theirs is the kingdom of heaven.	Blessed are you who are poor, for yours is the kingdom of God (v. 20).

But woe to you who are rich, for you have received your consolation (v. 24).

Blessed are those who mourn, for they will be comforted.

Blessed are you who weep now, for you will laugh (v. 21b).

Woe to you who are laughing now, for you will mourn and weep (v. 25b).

Blessed are the meek, for they will inherit the earth.

Blessed are those who hunger and thirst for righteousness, for they will be filled.

Blessed are you who are hungry now, for you will be filled (v. 21a).

Woe to you who are full now, for you will be hungry (v. 25a).

Blessed are the merciful, for they will receive mercy.

Blessed are the pure in heart, for they will see God.

Blessed are the peacemakers, for they will be called children of God.

Blessed are those who are persecuted for righteousness' sake, for theirs is the kingdom of heaven.

Blessed are you when people revile you and persecute you and utter all kinds of evil against you falsely on my account. Rejoice and be glad, for your reward is great in heaven, for in the same way they persecuted the prophets who were before you.

Blessed are you when people hate you, and when they exclude you, revile you, and defame you on account of the Son of Man. Rejoice in that day and leap for joy, for surely your reward is great in heaven; for that is what their ancestors did to the prophets (vv. 22–23).

Woe to you when all speak well of you, for that is what their ancestors did to the false prophets (v. 26).

Matthew and Luke: the first interpreters of Jesus's Beatitudes

Some of the differences are immediately obvious: Matthew has more blessings; Luke has fewer. Luke has matching woes; Matthew does not.[1] Even the beatitudes that appear in both versions have minor variations.

What the chart doesn't show is where the Beatitudes occur in the narrative flow of each gospel. If you have a Bible nearby, you might open it up and take a look. In Matthew's account, Jesus goes up onto a mountain—an echo of Moses going up on Mt. Sinai to receive the Ten Commandments (Matt 5:1–2, Exod 34:4). In Luke, Jesus first goes up on a mountain to choose twelve of his disciples to be apostles; when he comes down from the mountain (like Moses in Exod 34:29), a great crowd presses around him hoping for healing and deliverance, and he "healed all of them" (Luke 6:19).[2] Then Jesus delivers the Beatitudes and their matching woes. In both accounts, two audiences are present: the disciples and the crowds (the crowd's presence is explicit in Luke 6:20; it's more ambiguous in Matt 5:1–2 but seems assumed in Matt 7:28–29).

If we back up into Matthew 1–4 and Luke 1–5, we see more differences in the unfolding story of Jesus's birth and ministry. These stories are very similar in the two accounts, but the differences are not trivial either: the weeping of Rachel (Matt 2:18) is still in our ears when we hear the blessing on those who mourn (Matt 5:4), just as Mary's Magnificat (Luke 2:46–55) sings in the background of the blessing on the poor and the woe to the rich (Luke 6:20, 24). The two evangelists have declared the speaker of the Beatitudes to be the Messiah, the son of David, the son of Abraham (Matt 1:1), God with us (Matt 1:23), the Son of the Most High and inheritor of the throne of David (Luke 1:32), and the Messiah and Lord (Luke 2:11, 26). By the time Jesus speaks the Beatitudes, his identity is clear—perhaps not yet to the disciples and the crowds participating in the story, but certainly to us, and to the readers and hearers of the two gospel accounts.

If we continued reading after the Beatitudes, we'd find echoes of the Beatitudes in various places along the way, and sometimes even an illustration of them. I'll highlight many of these connections in the chapters that

---

1. K. C. Hanson suggests that Luke's woes and Matthew 23 are parallels; see K. C. Hanson, "How Honorable! How Shameful! A Cultural Analysis of Matthew's Makarisms and Reproaches," *Semeia* 68 (1994): 103.

2. Several scholars point out that Moses also descended from the mountain to speak to the people in Exod 34:29, e.g., Frederick W. Danker, *Jesus and the New Age: A Commentary on St. Luke's Gospel*, rev. ed. (Philadelphia: Fortress, 1988), 136; and Justo L. González, *Luke*, Belief: A Theological Commentary on the Bible (Louisville: Westminster John Knox, 2010), 91.

follow.[3] If we read all the way to the end of the two gospels, we might wonder how the narrative of Jesus's crucifixion and resurrection illuminates the Beatitudes; we might return to read them with new eyes as the declarations of one who would die and be raised. What do the Beatitudes look like in the light of the resurrection?

For this point, I take my cue from New Testament scholar Richard Hays, who writes, "We interpret Scripture rightly only when we read it in light of the resurrection, and we begin to comprehend the resurrection only when we see it as the climax of the scriptural story of God's gracious deliverance of Israel."[4] What might these insights mean when we apply them to the Beatitudes? They might lead us to see the Beatitudes as an element of God's gracious deliverance of Israel. They should also remind us that the story of the Beatitudes is "not a story about human wisdom" but "a story about the power of the God who gives life to the dead and calls into existence the things that do not exist."[5] This means seeing the Beatitudes as arrows pointing toward what my mentor Allen Verhey always called "God's good future," when all the tears will be wiped away.

The contexts of the Beatitudes matter, including the end of the story. The evangelists have incorporated the Beatitudes with care into the larger narratives of their gospels. They've also made some modifications of their own to the Beatitudes themselves. Of course, it's possible that Jesus spoke both versions on two different occasions, and the two evangelists faithfully recorded the two versions separately. Interpreters throughout history suggest this possibility; this is especially true of preachers, who have experience of preaching similar sermons on more than one occasion! A few people have even proposed that Jesus delivered variants on the Beatitudes several times throughout his three-year preaching career, as preachers often do.

It's more common to assume that there was one original version of the Beatitudes preached by Jesus. If this is true, then why are the two versions in Matthew and Luke different? Either (a) they were remembered and passed down to Matthew and Luke separately, in slightly different oral and/or written forms; or (b) Matthew and/or Luke made modifications to the original, to emphasize their respective theological aims. I tend toward option (b), mainly

---

3. For a list of the links between the Sermon and other texts in Matthew's gospel, see W. D. Davies and Dale C. Allison Jr., "Reflections on the Sermon on the Mount," *Scottish Journal of Theology* 44, no. 3 (1991): 299–302.

4. Richard B. Hays, "Reading Scripture in Light of the Resurrection," in *The Art of Reading Scripture*, ed. Ellen F. Davis and Richard B. Hays (Grand Rapids: Eerdmans, 2010), 216.

5. Hays, "Reading Scripture," 232.

because I see Matthew and Luke as careful curators of their material, rather than as mere transcribers. Having once been a preacher myself, I wouldn't dismiss the earlier option either—that Jesus could have preached slightly different versions of the Beatitudes multiple times throughout his career. Clearly the gospels don't record, exhaustively, everything he said and did (John 21:25).

Another way to explain the differences in the versions is to suggest that Matthew and Luke have tailored the Beatitudes for their respective audiences. This is plausible, but the difficulty is that we know so little about the gospel audiences. Scholars speculate that Luke addressed a largely gentile audience in Asia Minor, whereas Matthew's was mostly or exclusively Jewish, perhaps in Antioch, Syria. Some scholars have argued that Luke's attention to the poor throughout his gospel springs from the low socioeconomic status of Christians in his local churches; others suggest that it derives from the growing wealth of the early Christian churches and Luke's attempt to unsettle their material comfort and call them back to the radical roots of the gospel. This shows just how difficult it can be to pin down the precise social contexts of each evangelist.

So it's obvious that the Beatitudes are not exactly the same in Matthew and in Luke. But the more important question is whether they are *fundamentally* the same. That is, are they expressing the same essential message, or not? Here opinion splits along chronological lines. Premodern interpreters uniformly assume that the two versions of the Beatitudes preserved in Matthew and Luke contain essentially the same teaching, whereas from the Enlightenment onward, modern scholars often assume the opposite.

The unity of Scripture

Augustine (354–430), in his *Harmony of the Gospels*, explored three possibilities for why Matthew and Luke recorded different versions of the Sermon on the Mount: (1) The Sermon was preached once, but the disciples remembered or reported it with some minor differences; (2) Jesus gave the Matthean version first on the mount and then descended to the "level place" (Luke 6:17) and gave the Lukan version; or (3) Jesus went up on the mountain and, after choosing the twelve disciples, he descended to a level spot on the slope of the mountain where the multitudes could sit and there delivered the one Sermon recorded with small variations by both evangelists.[6] Option #3 proved popular, but Augustine showed little interest in choosing one solution over the

---

6. Augustine, *The Harmony of the Gospels* 2.19.44–47 (NPNF² 6:124–26).

other. What mattered to him was the harmony of the two teachings. The two Sermons (and thus the two versions of the Beatitudes) offered a unified and harmonious witness.

Premodern interpreters like Augustine also had a favorite when it came to the two versions. They lavished far more attention on Matthew's Beatitudes.[7] Of the earliest patristic interpreters, it seems that only Tertullian and Ambrose of Milan gave sustained attention to Luke's version (Tertullian did so in order to refute Marcion of Sinope, who used Luke for his own anti-Jewish purposes; Ambrose was one of the few ancient Christians who wrote a commentary on Luke). For the most part, this preference simply reflected the popularity of Matthew as a Gospel in the early church. Every now and then, commentators used the differences between the two accounts to elevate Matthew's version over Luke's.

For example, an incomplete and anonymous fifth-century commentary on Matthew (ca. 425–430?) argued that Jesus first spoke the partial Lukan Beatitudes to "ordinary people" on the plain, but then ascended onto the mountain, which represents "the pinnacle of the church," to address the more complete Matthean Beatitudes to "the perfect and the rulers of the people," i.e., the apostles.[8] Several hundred years later, Bernard of Clairvaux wrote a parable in which Christ and a monk carrying eight bundles (representing the eight Matthean Beatitudes) encounter a trader carrying four bundles (representing the Lukan Beatitudes). The four Lukan Beatitudes are treated rather scornfully as an inferior teaching given to "the multitudes," in comparison to "the delights and riches" of the Matthean Beatitudes, which are available only to those in the cloistered monastery.[9]

A milder version of this view appears in a handful of nineteenth-century commentaries, one of which described Matthew's Beatitudes as "esoteric,"

---

7. Warren S. Kissinger, *The Sermon on the Mount: A History of Interpretation and Bibliography* (Metuchen, NJ: Scarecrow, 1975).

8. *Incomplete Commentary on Matthew [Opus Imperfectum]*, ed. Thomas C. Oden, trans. James A. Kellerman, Ancient Christian Texts 1 (Downers Grove, IL: IVP Academic, 2010), 84. The *Opus Imperfectum* is difficult to date and although it was for a time ascribed to Chrysostom, the author is unknown; see Fredric W. Schlatter, "The Author of the *Opus Imperfectum in Matthaeum*," *Vigiliae Christianae* 40, no. 4 (1988): 364–75.

9. Bernard of Clairvaux, *The Parables and the Sentences*, ed. Maureen M. O'Brien, trans. Michael Casey and Francis R. Swietek, Cistercian Fathers 55 (Kalamazoo, MI: Cistercian Publications, 2000), 99. So also the Venerable Bede, who wrote that the four Lukan beatitudes are four cardinal virtues, which are for Israelites in general (i.e., all people), whereas Matthew's eight are for "the more perfect" (Seán P. Kealy, *From Apostolic Times through the 19th Century*, vol. 1 of *The Interpretation of the Gospel of Luke* [Lewiston, NY: Mellen, 2005], 1:128).

meant for the disciples; and Luke's "simpler" version as "exoteric," meant for the multitudes.[10] This two-tiered understanding of the two versions of the Beatitudes was, fortunately, not embraced by many. Luke's version deserves equal treatment alongside Matthew's; the mere fact that it's shorter than Matthew's is no reason to view it as less complete or perfect.

Historical-critical challenges

The rise of historical-critical methods in the seventeenth and eighteenth centuries challenged the premodern confidence in the unity of Scripture. The first seeds of the so-called Synoptic problem were sown in this era, when scholars became increasingly interested in tracking down the literary sources of the gospels. Modern scholarly discussion of the Beatitudes came to be dominated by a hypothesis, first proposed in Germany around the year 1900, that Luke and Matthew derived the Beatitudes from a written source nicknamed Q. In 1958, Jacques Dupont devoted an entire volume of his influential three-volume work on the Beatitudes to the relationship between Q, Matthew's Sermon on the Mount, and Luke's Sermon on the Plain.[11] Also of interest to modern commentaries is the relationship between the Beatitudes and Jesus's authentic teaching; Dupont's second volume was dedicated to proving the hypothesis that the four beatitudes shared by Matthew and Luke (the poor, hungry, weeping, and those hated for the sake of the Son of Man) were authentic pronouncements of Jesus.[12]

---

10. John Peter Lange, *The Gospel according to Matthew*, vol. 16 of *A Commentary on the Holy Scriptures: Critical, Doctrinal, and Homiletical, with Special Reference to Ministers and Students*, trans. Philip Schaff, 12th ed. (New York: Charles Scribner's Sons, 1884), 99. Johannes van Oosterzee wrote that Luke preserved the Sermon "in a much less regular and perfect manner than Matthew" (Johannes Jacobus van Oosterzee, *The Gospel according to Luke: The Gospel of Universal Humanity*, trans. Philip Schaff and Charles C. Starbuck [New York: Charles Scribner & Co., 1869], 100).

11. For other source-critical analyses, see Ulrich Luz, *Matthew 1–7*, trans. James E. Crouch, Hermeneia (Minneapolis: Fortress, 2007), 185–87; Hans Dieter Betz, *The Sermon on the Mount*, Hermeneia (Minneapolis: Fortress, 1995), 109; Jacques Dupont, *Le problème littéraire—Les deux versions du Sermon sur la montagne et des béatitudes*, vol. 1 of *Les Béatitudes* (Bruges, Belgium: Abbaye de Saint-André, 1958); and H. Benedict Green, *Matthew, Poet of the Beatitudes* (Sheffield: Sheffield Academic, 2001), 270–83, among many others. Green, against the dominant view, argued that Luke's text is "secondary, a radical scaling down of Matthew's" (Green, *Matthew, Poet*, 270).

12. Jacques Dupont, *La bonne nouvelle*, vol. 2 of *Les Béatitudes* (Paris: Gabalda, 1969), 2:7.

With the rise of redaction criticism (the analysis of editorial changes made by the gospel authors to a presumed original), it became the consensus view of twentieth-century scholars that Matthew's and Luke's Beatitudes are different in meaning and function. In the most common view, Matthew spiritualized or "ethicized" Luke's more material beatitudes by adding "in spirit" to the blessing on the poor and "for righteousness" to the blessing on the hungry. The situation from previous eras has been reversed: preference is now often given to Luke as the more original of the two. New Testament scholar Mark Goodacre is one of the few to argue against this consensus view, proposing that evidence points to Luke's knowledge of Matthew's Beatitudes. For Goodacre (and others), Luke has taken Matthew's more spiritual beatitudes and pointed them in a more material direction.[13]

Now, both suggestions are plausible. One can make a case that Matthew added "in spirit" to the first beatitude, just as one can make a case that Luke eliminated it. Neither of these judgments should be allowed to determine the meaning of the Beatitudes, because they are only good guesses, impossible to verify with complete confidence one way or the other. Equally hard to prove are reconstructions of a possible "original" text (the authentic words of Jesus, as different from the recorded words in Matthew and in Luke).

This debate within modern scholarship hints at another divergence that begins to happen around the same time: a visible and widening gap between ecclesial (church-based) and Western academic interpretation. Ecclesial writings such as sermons on the Beatitudes have more continuity with past patterns; they don't break nearly as sharply with traditional interpretations as modern scholarship in North America and Western Europe does. Non-Western scholarship, in general, also remains more anchored to the church and the life of faith than the Western academy.[14] Overall, there is often less

---

In Dupont's scheme, Matthew added the blessing on the meek to further explain the poor in spirit, then added the merciful, the pure in heart, and the peacemakers; the blessing on those persecuted for righteousness is a variant on those hated for Christ's sake (Dupont, *Le problème littéraire*, 1:227, 250–59, 263, 323).

13. Mark Goodacre, *The Case Against Q: Studies in Markan Priority and the Synoptic Problem* (Harrisburg, PA: Trinity Press International, 2002), 133–51. So also Adrian M. Leske, "The Beatitudes, Salt and Light in Matthew and Luke," *The SBLSP* 30 (1991), 828–29, 832, 838. Friedrich Tholuck saw the woes as an "expansion" of the original Beatitudes, in Friedrich August Tholuck, *Commentary on the Sermon on the Mount*, trans. R. Lundin Brown (Edinburgh: T&T Clark, 1869), 62.

14. E.g., Roland Boer and Fernando F. Segovia, eds., *The Future of the Biblical Past: Envisioning Biblical Studies on a Global Key* (Atlanta: Society of Biblical Literature, 2012).

of a gap between church and academy in the global south. Readers in the global south tend to be more communally oriented, less historical-critical, and more interested in studying the biblical text for the life of the church and for the everyday lives of local Christians.[15] Fairly recently, some Western biblical scholars have made concerted efforts to recover the insights of premodern exegesis, narrowing the gap; more attention is also being paid to non-Western interpretations.

—

I've charted this divergence in approaches (from the premodern to the modern) in part to prepare you for the following chapters. I've observed what people have done throughout history, to lay the foundation for what people do with the individual beatitudes. You might be wondering, though, if it matters. What's at stake in deciding whether Matthew or Luke are essentially the same, or fundamentally different? Is there a course to recommend?

In my view, the two competing tendencies (premodern and modern) can correct and complement one another, at least to a certain extent. The typical modern insistence on the genuine differences among the two versions can provide a correction to the premodern tendency to over-harmonize the two accounts. There *are* important differences between the two. Modern readers are also typically more alert to historical background, such as the Beatitudes' roots in the Old Testament and Second Temple Jewish literature, and to the eschatological setting of the Beatitudes.

At the same time, the premodern impulse toward harmony helps us to see the differences in the two accounts as a form of creative tension rather than competition. In that sense, I side with the premodern interpreters, finding an essential harmony (if not a uniform melody) in Matthew 5 and Luke 6. I'll suggest more than once in the following chapters that the differences between the two versions of the Beatitudes are generative: they're a gift that prompts exploration and deeper reflection.[16]

15. See, e.g., Rebekah Eklund, "Jesus of Nazareth," in *The State of New Testament Studies*, ed. Scot McKnight and Nijay K. Gupta (Grand Rapids: Baker Academic, 2019), 139–60.

16. In NT scholar Frederick Bruner's view, Matthew nudges the reader in "a spiritual and ethical direction," but Luke tugs the reader back to the material: "Luke's Beatitudes protect Jesus from super-spiritualization; Matthew's Beatitudes protect Jesus from cheap grace." Frederick Dale Bruner, *The Christbook, Matthew 1–12*, vol. 1 of *Matthew: A Commentary*, rev. ed. (Grand Rapids: Eerdmans, 2004), 163, 172.

Who are the Beatitudes for?

Two groups are present when Jesus speaks the Beatitudes: the crowds and his disciples (Matt 5:1 and Luke 6:19–20). Does Jesus address his blessings to one group or to both? Who are the Beatitudes for? Readers throughout history haven't always agreed. One answer is that they are for nobody—at least not for anybody today. This answer has three subsets.

a. For no one

For no one (I): Dispensationalism

Dispensationalism, which arose in the mid-nineteenth century, divides human history into clear and separate dispensations. For some dispensationalists, the Beatitudes (and the Sermon on the Mount as a whole) are intended for the kingdom age, which is still to come, and not for the age of the church, which is the present age. The 1909 *Scofield Reference Bible*, for example, explains that the kingdom of heaven named in the first and eighth beatitude is the millennial reign of Christ on earth after his return in glory. The Sermon on the Mount will be the "governing code" in this future millennial kingdom, but is not directly applicable to the church, which is living in the dispensation of grace.[17]

For no one (II): Paul v. Christ

Some nondispensationalist modern Protestant thought achieves the same result. A handful of modern New Testament scholars drive a wedge between the Sermon on the Mount and Paul's letters, as when Hans Windisch (1881–1935) wrote that the Sermon's "doctrine of salvation is pre-Christian and pre-Pauline."[18] This effectively sidelines the Beatitudes, making them irrelevant for

17. *The Scofield Study Bible*, New King James Version (New York: Oxford University Press, 2002), 1303 (comment on Matt 3:2), 1307 (comment on Matt 5:3). For the range of dispensationalist interpretations of the Sermon, see John A. Martin, "Dispensational Approaches to the Sermon on the Mount," in *Essays in Honor of J. Dwight Pentecost*, ed. Stanley D. Toussaint and Charles H. Dyer (Chicago: Moody, 1985), 35–48. As another example see Lewis Sperry Chafer, *Systematic Theology*, vols. 4 and 5 (Dallas, TX: Dallas Seminary Press, 1948), 4:169, 4:211, 4:216, 5:103.

18. Hans Windisch, *The Meaning of the Sermon on the Mount: A Contribution to the Historical Understanding of the Gospels and to the Problem of their True Exegesis* (Philadelphia: Westminster, 1951), 130.

the church. (And, not incidentally, it risks being a mild form of anti-Judaism, for when it relegates the Sermon on the Mount to a "pre-Christian" era, it means a Jewish one.)

Neither of these first two approaches are adequate. They both misread the function of the Sermon. In both gospel accounts, Jesus's Beatitudes are clearly not intended for some other age, whether a past one or a future millennial age. They are for their hearers, now.

For no one (III): interim ethic

This third approach emerges at the turn of the twentieth century, largely in the writing of German Protestant scholars Johannes Weiss (1863–1914) and Albert Schweitzer (1875–1965). For Schweitzer, the Beatitudes were the inward qualities necessary for participation in the coming kingdom. However, because Jesus believed the present age was soon coming to an end, the Beatitudes (and the Sermon as a whole) were an interim ethic, intended for the short span of time before the eschaton's arrival.[19] As Clarence Bauman wrote, "Weiss and Schweitzer . . . convinced a generation of scholars that the Sermon on the Mount was irrelevant for modern civilization, an interim ethic that tore the hearer loose from all his natural moorings to prepare him for an imminent otherworldly Kingdom."[20] This view enjoyed a brief period of popularity.

Like the two approaches above, this one is also inadequate, but for a different reason. It rests on an assumption that Jesus was wrong about the entire purpose of his teaching and ministry—in fact, that nothing he said or taught was meant to endure for more than a year or two. This goes against the grain of the evangelists' narratives, or more accurately, tries to read beneath those narratives to unearth the history they obscure. I do not find this a very fruitful approach to the gospels.

This approach also assumes that the Beatitudes could not outlive this interim time period; that is, it assumes that by their very nature they are so impractical and short-term that they couldn't apply to a longer stretch of history once Jesus turned out to be wrong about the eschaton's arrival. This is easy to disprove simply through observation. The Beatitudes have endured.

19. Albert Schweitzer, *The Kingdom of God and Primitive Christianity*, trans. L. A. Garrard (New York: Seabury, 1968), 96.

20. Clarence Bauman, *The Sermon on the Mount: The Modern Quest for Its Meaning* (Macon, GA: Mercer University Press, 1985), 211. Martin Dibelius rejected Schweitzer's view that the precepts of the Sermon are an interim ethic but still concluded, "the Sermon on the Mount is not an ideal but an *eschatological stimulus* intended to make men well acquainted with the pure will of God" (Dibelius, *The Sermon on the Mount* [New York: Charles Scribner's Sons, 1940], 135).

b. For everybody

This view is the opposite. Like the first view, it also emerges in the modern era; it's exceedingly rare prior to the eighteenth century but common after that. Hans Dieter Betz, one of the most prominent twentieth-century commentators on the Sermon on the Mount, treats the Sermon not as a specifically religious text but as "a piece of world literature."[21] For him, it's "a call to be human beings in an uncompromising way," a view that aligns with his conviction that Jesus does not speak the Beatitudes with any special authority: "Every competent Jewish teacher would presumably understand these principles."[22]

A flurry of recent books has adopted another kind of universal stance by comparing the Beatitudes to themes and writings in other religions. For example, Elizabeth West (and others) compares them to Buddhist teachings.[23] As Albert Randall summarizes, "while the world's great religions differ in their beliefs, they affirm the same basic spiritual virtues found in the Beatitudes."[24]

This view has more to commend it. The presence of the crowds (in Matt 5:1 and Luke 6:17–19) suggests that the Beatitudes were delivered to, or at least heard by, a wide audience and not only Jesus's disciples. It also captures the universality of Jesus's good news, to be brought (eventually) to all the nations (Matt 28:19). Its weakness is that it fails to account for the way the Sermon as a whole appears to assume a specific community, with its own particular commitments (adherence to "the law and the prophets") and practices (prayer, fasting, almsgiving, forgiveness). And the Beatitudes are peppered with lan-

---

21. Betz, *Sermon on the Mount*, 1. Others propose that the Beatitudes are a religious text, but with values not particular to Christianity: "Christianity, Islam, Hinduism and Buddhism all affirm that the poor in spirit are blessed because they belong to the eternal world that transcends the empirical world of suffering and death," writes Albert B. Randall in *Strangers on the Shore: The Beatitudes in World Religions* (New York: Lang, 2006), 63.

22. Betz, *Sermon on the Mount*, 61, 94.

23. Elizabeth West, "Comparing Buddhism's Noble Eightfold Path and Jesus' Beatitudes," in *Global Perspectives on the Bible*, ed. Mark Roncace and Joseph Weaver (Boston: Pearson, 2014), 221–23.

24. Randall, *Strangers on the Shore*, 55. Randall's book concludes with brief spiritual biographies of eighteen religious leaders who exemplify the Beatitudes drawn from Judaism, Christianity, Zoroastrianism, Buddhism, Taoism, Islam, Hinduism, Sikhism, and Bahá'í (145–66). See also Roncace and Weaver, *Global Perspectives on the Bible*, chapter 26; Leo D. Lefebure, *The Buddha and the Christ: Explorations in Buddhist and Christian Dialogue* (Maryknoll, NY: Orbis Books, 1993, 1997), chapter 2; and Monika K. Hellwig, "The Blessedness of the Meek, the Merciful, and the Peacemakers," in *New Perspectives on the Beatitudes*, ed. Francis A. Eigo (Villanova, PA: Villanova University Press, 1995), 207–9.

guage anchored in a particular tradition (kingdom of heaven, sons of God, righteousness, the prophets). Even the word "comfort" in the second beatitude isn't generic but has a long biblical history behind it (Ps 23:4, 119:82; Eccl 4:1; Isa 22:4, 40:1).

The comparative approach helpfully illustrates the frequent view that the Beatitudes contain the deepest, truest form of human wisdom (more on that below). Surely other religions also access this wisdom (how much or how little of that wisdom and truth being a matter of long-standing debate within the Christian traditions). On the other hand, suggesting that the Beatitudes merely mirror truths expressed elsewhere can flatten out the differences between (say) Buddhist and Christian teachings. The Beatitudes are not general but particular truths, drawn from the well of Judaism and shaped by a specific person (Jesus of Nazareth) and by the people who came to believe that God had raised this crucified person from the dead and exalted him to God's right hand.

c. For all Christians

Almost all interpreters until the Enlightenment era took this approach. It notices that, while crowds are present for the Sermon, Jesus directly looks at and addresses his disciples (Matt 5:1–2, Luke 6:20). Interpreters who take this approach tend to view the crowds as potential disciples. Jesus speaks the Beatitudes both to those who already follow him, and (as an invitation) to those who don't yet.

For Baptist Billy Graham (1918–2018), for example, the Beatitudes are "a formula for personal happiness that applied to anyone, no matter what his race, geography, age or circumstance!"[25] But for Graham, this is not because they're general, universal principles, but because he shared Augustine's conviction that the heart is restless until it rests in God.[26] Graham, like Augustine, believed that God calls *all* people to the kingdom to lead lives of abundance—lives represented by the Beatitudes. Augustine (and Graham) represents the majority view throughout history when he described the Sermon on the Mount as "the perfect pattern of the Christian life" (*De Serm. Dom.* 1.1.1).[27] Protestant Reformers agreed and emphasized that the Beati-

---

25. Billy Graham, *The Secret of Happiness: Jesus' Teaching on Happiness as Expressed in the Beatitudes* (Garden City, NY: Doubleday, 1955), v.

26. Graham, *The Secret of Happiness*, 2, 10.

27. Augustine, *The Lord's Sermon on the Mount*, trans. John J. Jepson, ACW 5 (Mahwah, NJ: Paulist, 1948), 11.

tudes were only possible for those who had put off the "old Adam," been reborn, and chosen to follow Christ.[28]

Some modern scholars agree, and they arrive at this view by examining the original social setting of the gospel writers. Indian New Testament scholar Vanlalchhawna Khiangte sees the Beatitudes as consolations and exhortations directed to Matthew's suffering community.[29] Mary Rose D'Angelo, a Catholic, feminist New Testament scholar, concludes that the Beatitudes would have functioned to remind Matthew's first hearers "of the identity they acquired through baptism, the identity of belonging to, being members of, God's reign."[30] This approach resonates with the view that the Beatitudes are not primarily for individuals but presuppose a community whose new way of life is made possible by the life, death, and resurrection of Jesus. As American scholar Glen Stassen wrote, the Beatitudes "speak to disciples who already are being made participants in the presence of the Holy Spirit through Jesus Christ."[31] German Catholic theologian Rudolf Schnackenburg (1914–2002) took this insight even further. For him, being a disciple or follower of Jesus is the *consequence* of listening to the Sermon, not the prerequisite.[32]

28. Martin Luther, *The Sermon on the Mount*, vol. 21 of *Luther's Works*, ed. Jaroslav Pelikan (St. Louis: Concordia, 1956), 15; see also Susan E. Schreiner, "Martin Luther," in *The Sermon on the Mount through the Centuries: From the Early Church to John Paul II*, ed. Jeffrey P. Greenman, Timothy Larsen, and Stephen R. Spencer (Grand Rapids: Brazos, 2007), 111. So also D. Martyn Lloyd-Jones, *Studies in the Sermon on the Mount*, vol. 1 (Grand Rapids: Eerdmans, 1960), 117 ("Only a new man can live this new life"); and John Calvin, *A Harmony of the Gospels Matthew, Mark and Luke*, vol. 1, ed. David W. Torrance and Thomas F. Torrance, trans. A. W. Morrison (Grand Rapids: Eerdmans, 1972), 5.2, p. 169. Joachim Jeremias took the Sermon as early Christian catechesis in his *The Sermon on the Mount* (Minneapolis: Fortress, 1963), 31.

29. Vanlalchhawna Khiangte, *Matthean Beatitudes in Socio-Historical Context: Their Implications for Contemporary Christian Discipleship* (New Delhi: Christian World Imprints, 2016), 240–44, 252.

30. Mary R. D'Angelo, "'Blessed the One Who Reads and Those Who Hear': The Beatitudes in Their Biblical Contexts," in Eigo, *New Perspectives*, 46. So also Michael H. Crosby, "The Beatitudes: General Perspectives," in Eigo, *New Perspectives*, 1, 30; and Timothy D. Howell, *The Matthean Beatitudes in Their Jewish Origins: A Literary and Speech Act Analysis* (New York: Lang, 2011), 6–8, 119.

31. Glen Stassen, "The Beatitudes as Eschatological Peacemaking Virtues," in *Character Ethics and the New Testament: Moral Dimensions of Scripture*, ed. Robert L. Brawley (Louisville: Westminster John Knox, 2007), 246. See also Stanley Hauerwas, "Living the Proclaimed Reign of God," *Int* 47, no. 2 (April 1993): 157; Craig Blomberg, "The Most Often Abused Verses in the Sermon on the Mount: And How to Treat Them Right," *Southwestern Journal of Theology* 46, no. 3 (Summer 2004): 3; Davies and Allison, "Reflections," 302–3.

32. Rudolf Schnackenburg, *Die Bergpredigt: Utopische Vision oder Handlungsanweisung?*, ed. Rudolf Schnackenburg (Düsseldorf: Patmos, 1982), 61.

This view, it seems to me, is the most fruitful. It rightly notices the specific, particular nature of the Sermon, and the prominence of the disciples as its hearers. But in its conviction that the crowds also receive the Beatitudes as potential followers of Jesus, it retains a more universal aspect. I'll revisit the question of how non-Christians have often modeled the Beatitudes in the individual chapters.

d. For the orders of ministry

This approach narrows the audience even further. For these interpreters, the crowds represent everyday Christians, whereas the disciples represent the ordained clergy and those in monastic orders. This view arose in the medieval era, when some Western Christians began to distinguish between precepts (commands given to all Christians) and counsels (perfection demanded only of those in ordained orders). To which category did the Beatitudes belong? Opinion was split.

It seems that the Benedictine monk Rupert of Deutz (ca. 1100) was the first—or at least the most influential—to propose that they belonged to the counsels of perfection. He drew on a sharp division between two groups of Christians: "salvation by grace is for the laity and secular clergy; salvation through the works of the Sermon on the Mount was for the zealous monks."[33] While Rupert was undoubtedly influential, other medieval figures were more nuanced.

We may take Thomas Aquinas's (1225–1274) views on the first beatitude as an example. Like many of his predecessors (he cited the late fourth-century theologian Jerome), Aquinas understood "the poor in spirit" (Matt 5:3) as both a material and spiritual condition. Unlike his forebears, Aquinas distinguished between an inner disposition toward wealth and actual poverty; the first, he wrote, "is necessary for salvation," whereas the second "belongs to evangelical perfection."[34] The beatitude could thus be fulfilled by a layperson (through detachment toward wealth) or more perfectly by a monastic (through vowed

33. Benedict Viviano, "The Sermon on the Mount in Recent Study," *Biblica* 78, no. 2 (1997): 257; see also Luz, *Matthew 1–7*, 178; and Brigitta Stoll, *De Virtute in Virtutem: zur Auslegungs- und Wirkungsgeschichte der Bergpredigt in Kommentaren, Predigten und hagiographischer Literatur von der Merowingerzeit bis um 1200*, BGBE 30 (Tübingen: Mohr Siebeck, 1988), 50–51.

34. *Contra Impugnantes Dei Cultum et Religionem* 6.3.318–29, quoted in Christopher A. Franks, *He Became Poor: The Poverty of Christ and Aquinas's Economic Teachings* (Grand Rapids: Eerdmans, 2009), 114.

poverty). Aquinas scholar Anton ten Klooster concludes, contrary to a common perception, that "Aquinas believes that the life of the beatitudes is not for the exceptionally gifted Christian, but for all the Christian faithful."[35]

A similar example may be seen in the writings of the French Jesuit Cornelius à Lapide (1597–1637), who initially assigned the Beatitudes to the evangelical counsels (that is, to chastity, poverty, and obedience), but also went on to explain that one may keep the Beatitudes by way of either counsels or precepts. For example, one may have poverty of spirit by forsaking all riches, which is "a degree of counsel" (the way taken by the clergy and those in vowed religious orders), or by preferring to be poor rather than acquiring riches by injustice, which is "a degree of precept" (a way of life followed by all Christians).[36]

Other monastic writers, both before and after Rupert, applied the Beatitudes to the Christian life in general. Bernardino of Siena (1380–1444), despite preaching on the Beatitudes to his fellow Franciscans, seems to have assumed that the Beatitudes could or should function "at every level of the Christian community, ordained and lay."[37] In the East, the Archbishop of Bulgaria, Theophylact of Ochrid, wrote in the late eleventh century that Christ taught the Beatitudes both to the disciples and the multitudes.[38]

Finally, Dhuoda of Septimania (d. 843?) represents one of the most important medieval figures who applied the Beatitudes to the lives of all Christians. Dhuoda, a noble laywoman from the south of France, wrote a handbook for the moral development of her fifteen-year-old son William. Taking a page from Augustine's playbook, she loosely organized it around the seven gifts of the Spirit and the eight beatitudes (more on that in the next chapter).[39] Dhuoda viewed the two lists not as pairs (as Augustine did) but

---

35. Anton ten Klooster, *Thomas Aquinas on the Beatitudes: Reading Matthew, Disputing Grace and Virtue, Preaching Happiness* (Leuven: Peeters, 2018), 185.

36. Cornelius à Lapide, *The Holy Gospel According to Saint Matthew*, vol. 1 of *The Great Commentary of Cornelius à Lapide*, trans. Thomas W. Mossman, rev. Michael J. Miller (Fitzwilliam, NH: Loreto, 2008), xc, 201–2.

37. Carolyn Muessig, "Preaching the Beatitudes in the Late Middle Ages: Some Mendicant Examples," *Studies in Christian Ethics* 22, no. 2 (2009): 144.

38. Theophylact of Ochrid, *The Explanation by Blessed Theophylact of the Holy Gospel According to St. Matthew*, vol. 1 of *Blessed Theophylact's Explanation of the New Testament*, trans. Christopher Stade (House Springs, MO: Chrysostom Press, 1994), 44. Theophylact often followed the lead of Chrysostom, who saw the Sermon as the charter of the Christian life.

39. Marie Anne Mayeski, "The Beatitudes and the Moral Life of the Christian: Practical Theology and Biblical Exegesis in Dhuoda of Septimania," *Mystics Quarterly* 18, no. 1 (March 1992): 8; see Dhuoda, *Handbook for her Warrior Son*, ed. and trans. Marcelle Thiébaux (Cambridge: Cambridge University Press, 1998), 4.8. See also Stoll, *De Virtute*, 154.

"as an extended sequence," a set of fifteen steps that her son must ascend.[40] The spiritual gifts were first because they were "formative of a personal and interior spirituality." The Beatitudes then followed, which Dhuoda narrated as an essential part of her son's "assumption of adult responsibility for the creation of the Kingdom of God within the social and political realities of [his] place in the world."[41]

I've dwelt on this point at some length because it's a common perception today that medieval teaching and perhaps even contemporary Catholic teaching relegate the Beatitudes to the monastic or ordained life. Yet the historical record is more complex than this. And today the Catholic Catechism adopts Augustine's view by declaring, "[The Beatitudes] express the vocation of the faithful associated with the glory of [Jesus Christ's] Passion and Resurrection; they shed light on the actions and attitudes characteristic of the Christian life."[42] To be sure, I believe that it's a misstep to view the Beatitudes as restricted, even in some partial way, to a special subset of Christians. But overall, the Catholic and Orthodox traditions, alongside the Protestant, have mostly seen the Beatitudes as addressed to all Christians.

Are the Beatitudes countercultural, or the highest form of human wisdom?

In the late fourth century, John Chrysostom (ca. 349–407) declared that all the things Christ blesses are "so contrary to the accustomed ways of men." They are "the very things which all others avoid."[43] At the same time, Chrysostom sought to show that the Beatitudes (and the Sermon as a whole) were the highest form of human teaching, equal to or surpassing classical philosophy. His challenge, then, was to demonstrate that these contrary and upside-down virtues were in fact the true pinnacle of the philosophical virtues, when understood rightly.

This tension has endured. For interpreters across the span of history, the Beatitudes are paradoxes. (The word "paradox" is used over and over again.) They turn the world's standards upside down (another extraordinarily common claim). They are uncomfortable, countercultural, surprising. One writer

---

40. Mayeski, "The Beatitudes and the Moral Life," 10.
41. Mayeski, "The Beatitudes and the Moral Life," 10–11.
42. *Catechism of the Catholic Church*, Section 3, Article 2.I.1717.
43. Chrysostom, *Homilies on the Gospel of Saint Matthew* 15.7 (*NPNF*¹ 10:95).

marveled that they are "a theory of happiness so hostile to the senses."[44] Another writer proposed that they are "even threatening to physical survival."[45]

At the same time, Christians insist repeatedly that they contain deep truths that the world cannot see; they are in fact the path to *true* happiness or flourishing, in contradistinction to the world's self-destructive plunge into pleasure and material goods. For German Lutheran Dietrich Bonhoeffer (1906–1945), this culture clash was especially sharp; in his view, the Beatitudes were implacably opposed to his dominant culture's values—namely, the German national church under Nazi rule.[46] Several decades later, American novelist Kurt Vonnegut (1922–2007) pointed out, caustically, that Christians often ask for the Ten Commandments to be posted in public places, but never the Beatitudes. He pointed out the absurdity: "'Blessed are the merciful' in a courtroom? 'Blessed are the peacemakers' in the Pentagon? Give me a break!"[47] For Vonnegut as for Bonhoeffer, the Beatitudes clash irreconcilably with the dominant culture.

So the view that the Beatitudes are paradoxes, or countercultural values, is deeply embedded throughout history; it's a view that captures something right and true about the Beatitudes and their function. Yet when one presses a little further, one begins to find a little more complexity. *Which* culture are the Beatitudes meant to counter?

Counter to which culture? Anti-Judaism

For some interpreters throughout history, the Beatitudes run counter to the Old Testament—that is, to Jewish teachings. Moses gave law; Jesus gave grace. The evangelist Matthew himself created a link between Moses and Jesus, and between the law and the gospel (Exod 34:4; Matt 5:1–2, 17–48). But what kind of link is it—a continuity or a contrast? Interpreters frequently refer to the Torah as the old law and to Jesus's teaching as the new law, but their views on the relationship between the two range from seamless continuity to complete replacement (despite the cautionary note of Matt 5:17).

Some interpreters sharpen Matthew's contrast between Moses and Jesus

44. Henry Bolo, *The Beatitudes: The Poor in Spirit, the Meek and Humble*, trans. Madame Cecilia (London: Kegan Paul, Trench, Trübner & Co., 1906), 12.

45. Andrej Kodjak, *A Structural Analysis of the Sermon on the Mount* (Berlin: Mouton de Gruyter, 1986), 43.

46. Dietrich Bonhoeffer, *The Cost of Discipleship* (New York: Simon & Schuster, 1995), 108.

47. Kurt Vonnegut, *A Man without a Country*, ed. Daniel Simon (New York: Seven Stories Press, 2005), 98.

with colorful, imaginative accounts of the two mountains: Sinai, on which Moses gave the law, and the unnamed mount on which Jesus gave the Beatitudes. Mount Sinai is described in the grimmest possible terms (lightning, dreadful thunder, fearful darkness) while the gospel account is embellished with cheerful details (sunshine, flowers blooming, birds singing). Jesus's woes on the scribes and Pharisees (Matt 23:27–28) are frequently invoked to claim that Jesus's Beatitudes focus on the heart, whereas the Pharisees focused only on external actions. To be sure, Jesus *does* have sharp critiques for the Pharisees in Matthew's Gospel. But later writers often merge the first-century Pharisees with *all* Jews, or with the writer's contemporaneous Jewish people, in ways that have had dangerous lingering effects on Christian attitudes toward Judaism. (Jesus's critique of the Pharisees also appears in anti-Catholic rhetoric, as an indictment of the supposed Catholic focus on external actions.)

Martin Luther's anti-Jewish writings, for example, are well known. When Luther wrote that the teachings of the Sermon on the Mount were directed "against the world's way of thinking," he took special, irritable aim at "the Jews," "the Turks," and "the whole papacy." He described the Sermon as "irksome and unbearable" for Jews, to whom he ascribed the belief that "If a man is successful here on earth, he is blessed and well off."[48] (Luther noted that the book of Job opposed this theory but didn't seem to notice that Job was a Jewish text.) In the eighteenth century, American Calvinist Jonathan Edwards (1703–1758) claimed that the happiness the Jews expected the Messiah to bring was "temporal and carnal" rather than spiritual, adding, "The Jews were dreadfully in the dark at that day about spiritual things."[49]

A particularly virulent variant of this view emerged in Germany in the early to mid-nineteenth-century.[50] For example, German bishop Johannes

---

48. Luther, *Sermon on the Mount*, 11, 12, 17.

49. Jonathan Edwards, *Sermons and Discourses 1730–1733*, vol. 17 of *The Works of Jonathan Edwards*, ed. Mark Valeri (New Haven, CT: Yale University Press, 1999), 60. See also Lloyd-Jones (*Studies*, 64), who takes the Beatitudes as repudiations of Jewish materialistic and militaristic messianic hopes.

50. As early as the first half of the ninth century, a text known as the *Saxon Gospel* reinterpreted the gospels in Germanic terms and referred to the Jews as "sneaky people": *The Heliand: The Saxon Gospel*, trans. G. Ronald Murphy (Oxford: Oxford University Press, 1992), 43. On the "germanization" of the gospel in the *Heliand*, see G. Ronald Murphy, *The Saxon Savior: The Germanic Transformation of the Gospel in the Ninth-Century Heliand* (Oxford: Oxford University Press, 1989), 3–8. For broader explorations of German anti-Semitism and anti-Judaism in the early twentieth century, see Susannah Heschel, *The Aryan Jesus: Christian Theologians and the Bible in Nazi Germany* (Princeton: Princeton University Press, 2008); and Robert Morgan, "Susannah Heschel's Aryan Grundmann," *JSNT* 32, no. 4 (2010): 431–94.

Müller (1864–1949) wrote that "one must Germanize the Sermon to remove its Jewishness."[51] For Müller, as Clarence Bauman wrote, separating the "kernel" of Christ's teaching from its "husk" meant removing "the offensive Jewish-ness of Jesus . . . as the foreign element contaminating the purity of the Ger-man *Geist* and threatening the superiority of the Aryan self-consciousness."[52] Müller's book was so popular that it ran to eight editions. Adolf Hitler owned a copy.[53] Lest we think this view died out after the Holocaust, we find German Lutheran Joachim Jeremias writing (less caustically) in 1963 that the Sermon on the Mount was "the decisive break with Jewish piety."[54]

Some resisted this trend. In 1957, American evangelical Carl Henry (1913– 2003) (who was seeking to rebut dispensationalism rather than anti-Semitism per se) insisted on the continuity between the old and new covenants: "The ethic of Eden and the ethic of Sinai and the ethic of the Mount of Beatitudes . . . stand in essential unity and continuity."[55] And much recent modern scholarship has sought to correct this anti-Jewish trend by showing how thoroughly the Beati-tudes are rooted in Jewish teaching.[56] But one function of the history of inter-pretation is to chart past missteps and sins as well as past insights, and this is an especially important one to remember, to lament, and to seek to avoid.

Counter to which culture? A feminist critique

American philosopher Dallas Willard (1935–2013) told the story of a woman whose son ("a strong, intelligent man") left the church because he was told that

---

51. Bauman, *Sermon on the Mount*, 129, summarizing Johannes Müller, *Die Bergpredigt: ver-deutscht und vergegenwärtigt*, 8th ed. (München: C. H. Beck'sche Verlagsbuchhandlung, 1929), 12: "Wir müssen uns die Reden Jesu verdeutschen, denn sie sind auf jüdischem Boden gewachsen und an Juden gerichtet, an ein Boden besonderer Rasse und Geschichte."

52. Bauman, *Sermon on the Mount*, 137. Karl Bornhäuser, a professor at Marburg, wrote in 1923 that the Beatitudes were all direct contrasts against the Pharisaic scribes and their teaching, in his book *Die Bergpredigt: Versuch einer zeitgenössischen Auslegung* (Gütersloh: Bertelsmann, 1923), 18–37.

53. A copy of the eighth edition inscribed on the front fly-leaf in 1932 to Adolf Hitler by Rosel Heink-Beuthold is housed in the Third Reich Collection of the Library of Congress. Hitler's library contained three of Müller's books; see Philipp Gassert and Daniel S. Mattern, *The Hitler Library: A Bibliography* (Westport, CT: Greenwood Press, 2001), 208–9.

54. Jeremias, *Sermon on the Mount*, 5.

55. Carl F. H. Henry, *Christian Personal Ethics* (Grand Rapids: Eerdmans, 1957), 290, 315.

56. See, e.g., Craig S. Keener, *A Commentary on the Gospel of Matthew* (Grand Rapids: Eerd-mans, 1999), 164–72.

the Beatitudes describe the ideal Christian. The son protested, "I can never be like that."[57] The Beatitudes were too feminine for him. This illustrates a problem: Do the Beatitudes run counter to stereotypically masculine, or stereotypically feminine, culture? Willard showed that they've sometimes been viewed as espousing virtues that are too feminine for comfort. Because of this, interpreters have gone to great lengths to insist that they are for the masculine, too! Some feminists have shied away from the Beatitudes for the way that they seem to reinscribe stereotypical feminine values and thus chart a path away from empowerment for women.[58] Others, however, find resources in the Beatitudes for resistance to—or even a radical overturning of—patriarchal norms. For Christin Lore Weber, "Each Beatitude is an act of faith in the radical potential of our world to be made whole." Jesus was born into a patriarchal world, and he was put to death for trying to help this world "see a different vision."[59]

In some cases, a beatitude does seem to run counter to a stereotypically masculine or patriarchal way of being in the world—I'll explore this possibility in detail in the chapter on the meek. But Willard and Weber illustrate, in their own way, the more general principle that one's own social location shapes how one responds to the Beatitudes.

For example, Capuchin friar Michael Crosby (1940–2017) named his own reality ("able-bodied, educated, white, straight, male, North American, Roman Catholic cleric") before he began his commentary on the Beatitudes, and he acknowledged the possibility of "unconscious bias that comes from my position of privilege. Others not so empowered and privileged might consider the Beatitudes quite differently."[60] My own position mostly overlaps with Crosby, except that I am female and Protestant. Like Crosby, I've tried to be aware of my own privilege and biases, in part through seeking out voices unlike my

---

57. Dallas Willard, *The Divine Conspiracy: Rediscovering Our Hidden Life in God* (New York: HarperSanFrancisco, 1998), 99.

58. See Rebekah Eklund, "Blessed Are the Failures: Leaning into the Beatitudes," in *Theologies of Failure*, ed. Roberto Sirvent and Duncan B. Reyburn (Eugene, OR: Cascade, 2019), 141–50.

59. Christin Lore Weber, *Blessings: A WomanChrist Reflection on the Beatitudes* (San Francisco: Harper & Row, 1989), 3, 195. Rosemary Dowsett argues that it takes "great strength of character" to make the Beatitudes our own, but admits that "in many cultures these characteristics may be seen as more womanly than manly"; Rosemary M. Dowsett, "Matthew," in *The IVP Women's Bible Commentary*, ed. Catherine Clark Kroeger and Mary J. Evans (Downers Grove, IL: InterVarsity Press, 2002), 525.

60. Michael H. Crosby, *Spirituality of the Beatitudes: Matthew's Vision for the Church in an Unjust World*, rev. ed. (Maryknoll, NY: Orbis Books, 2005), ix.

own, and in part through attending as much as I can to the social contexts of the Christians whose writings I explore throughout this book.

Are the Beatitudes demands or descriptions?
Reversals or rewards?

When I first began studying the Beatitudes, I read them through a lens that I picked up from reading a lot of twentieth-century commentaries. This lens proposes that the Beatitudes are either descriptions or commands. Do they describe undesirable conditions that God promises to reverse, or virtuous qualities that God promises to reward? Are they the entrance requirements of the kingdom, or eschatological blessings of the age to come?[61]

This dichotomy is rooted in part in a disagreement over the genre of a beatitude. Do the Beatitudes emerge from the Jewish wisdom tradition or the Jewish apocalyptic tradition? If they derive from the wisdom tradition (Proverbs, Ecclesiastes, etc.), then they are likely to be prescriptive: to be about wisdom, flourishing, virtues, and the like. If they are rooted in the apocalyptic tradition (the book of Daniel, e.g.), then they are descriptive: they are about the dramatic in-breaking of God to bring about the reversal of all the things that cause people to suffer. But, as Jonathan Pennington points out, the wisdom and apocalyptic traditions were not cleanly compartmentalized in the Second Temple era but had become "inextricably interwoven."[62] Why couldn't the same be true of the Beatitudes as well?

A beatitude is neither merely a statement nor a command. It is a value judgment, one implied by the word that begins each beatitude: the Greek *makarios*. For the word *makarios*, most English translations choose "blessed." A handful choose "happy," which helps to highlight the paradoxical nature of the Beatitudes: happy are those who weep? Others try to capture the spirit of *makarios* with phrases like "Flourishing are," or "Congratulations to," or "How blissful are."[63] English writer Elizabeth Rundle Charles (1828–1896) de-

---

61. Robert Guelich, "The Matthean Beatitudes: 'Entrance Requirements' or Eschatological Blessing?" *JBL* 95 (1976): 415–34. According to Mark Allan Powell, Hans Windisch was the first to call them "entrance requirements for the kingdom of heaven," in his book *Der Sinn der Bergpredigt*; see Powell, "Matthew's Beatitudes: Reversals and Rewards of the Kingdom," *CBQ* 58 (1996): 470.

62. Jonathan T. Pennington, *The Sermon on the Mount and Human Flourishing: A Theological Commentary* (Grand Rapids: Baker Academic, 2017), 63.

63. For "blessed": Tyndale, Rheims (1582); KJV, RSV (1952); NRSV (1989); Geneva

scribed *makarios* as "a heart in harmony with itself, at rest, content, satisfied, full of all the music of which human hearts are capable, from the soft murmurs of content to the thunder of the many waters of ecstatic rapture: all that is involved in all the words expressive of human bliss, reaching up to Divine creative joy."[64]

Now, to say that the peacemakers are those who flourish is an observation, not a demand that one become a peacemaker. On the other hand, it implies that becoming a peacemaker is a good idea if one wants to flourish. Who wouldn't want, as Charles put it, "a heart in harmony with itself"? As Pennington puts it, then, the Beatitudes are "an *invitation to flourishing*."[65]

The dichotomy between demand and description, between reversal and reward, turns out to be too rigid.[66] As New Testament scholar Dale Allison wonders, why can't the Beatitudes be both command and declaration at the same time, "or one or the other depending upon a hearer's immediate circumstances?"[67] The announcement that the hungry and the merciful are the happy

---

(1560); Wycliffe (1388); NIV, NAB (1970); NJB (1985). For "happy": CEB, JB, *The Message*, GNT, Rotherham's Emphasized Bible. The NLT makes God the subject: "God blesses those who." Jonathan Pennington opts for "Flourishing are" (Pennington, *Sermon on the Mount*, xv, 42–67). Other options are "Congratulations to" (Jesus Seminar's Scholars' Version); "Fortunate" (Christian Community Bible 1988); "Good fortune now to" (John Nolland, *The Gospel of Matthew*, The New International Greek Testament Commentary [Grand Rapids: Eerdmans; Bletchley: The Paternoster Press, 2005], 193); the Australian idiom "Good on yer" or the Welsh *Gwyn eu byd* (lit. "White is their world," i.e., "those for whom everything is good") (both cited in R. T. France, *The Gospel of Matthew*, NICNT [Grand Rapids: Eerdmans, 2007], 161); "Good for them!" (John H. Yoder, *The Original Revolution: Essays on Christian Pacifism* [Scottdale, PA: Herald Press, 2003], 40); "are God's people" (Cotton Patch Gospel); "Honorable" or "Worthy of honor" (Michael Joseph Brown, "Matthew," in *True to Our Native Land: An African American New Testament Commentary*, ed. Brian K. Blount [Minneapolis: Fortress, 2007], 91; Crosby, *Spirituality*, 11); "Hail to those" ("μακάριος, ία, ιον," BDAG, 611); and "How blissful are" (David Bentley Hart, *The New Testament: A Translation* [New Haven, CT: Yale University Press, 2017], 7). Iván Pertiné paraphrases it "How great that" or "What's happening to you is so good" in his *The Good Sense of Jesus: A Commentary on the Beatitudes* (Charlotte, NC: TAN Books, 2018), 39.

64. Elizabeth Rundle Charles, *The Beatitudes: Thoughts for All Saints' Day* (London: Society for Promoting Christian Knowledge; New York: Young & Co., 1889), 17.

65. Pennington, *Sermon on the Mount*, 159, italics original; see also 51, 144.

66. I owe this insight in part to Pennington, *Sermon on the Mount*, 49, 62, 63. Likewise Karl Barth and Warren Carter propose that the Beatitudes contain elements of both declaration and implicit exhortation—Karl Barth, *CD* II/2.38.2, in *Church Dogmatics*, ed. G. W. Bromiley and T. F. Torrance, trans. G. W. Bromiley (Peabody, MA: Hendrickson, 1958, 2004), 694; Warren Carter, *Matthew and the Margins: A Socio-Political and Religious Reading* (Sheffield: Sheffield Academic, 2000), 130.

67. Dale C. Allison Jr., "The History of the Interpretation of Matthew: Lessons Learned,"

and fortunate ones might function for me as a message of hope, a declaration of God's favor, a command, or a warning, depending on whether I am hungry or full, merciful or merciless.

Implicit exhortations

The earliest interpreters of the Beatitudes typically understood them as implicit exhortations—or more accurately, as invitations into a Christ-patterned life. Perhaps the first example of this view occurs in the Didache (ca. 95–100), one of the earliest noncanonical Christian writings. The blessing on the meek is the only beatitude to appear in the Didache, in imperative form: "And be meek, since the meek will inherit the earth" (3:7). Of course, as recorded in Matthew and Luke, the Beatitudes aren't in the imperative: Jesus said, "Blessed *are* the meek," not "*Be* meek." On the other hand, for these early readers the implication was clear: if one wants to be blessed, or happy, then one will strive to be meek. (One clear exception is the blessing on the persecuted; Christ did not command his followers to *be* persecuted, but rather indicated that they *will* be, whether they like it or not.)[68] The exhortations implicit in the Beatitudes become explicit later in Matthew's Gospel. As New Testament scholar Nathan Eubank observes, "most of the Beatitudes correspond to ethical demands made subsequently in the narrative."[69]

It's rare to find an interpreter prior to the eighteenth century who did *not* understand the Beatitudes as exhortations or implicit commands. This doesn't mean that they were viewed as "requirements," or as burdensome: they were rather the path to true happiness and flourishing laid down by God, much as Israel saw the law as a gift that was sweeter than honey (Ps 19:7–10).

To be sure, Protestants and Catholics part ways over whether the Beatitudes are "merits," and over what the word "reward" means in Matt 5:12 and Luke 6:23.[70] Reformers like William Tyndale insisted that the rewards are free

---

In die Skriflig 49, no. 1 (2015): 9. Crosby makes a similar observation in Crosby, *Spirituality*, ix. See also Eklund, "Blessed Are the Failures," 141–50.

68. Dale C. Allison Jr., *The Sermon on the Mount: Inspiring the Moral Imagination* (New York: Crossroad, 1999), 44.

69. Nathan Eubank, *Wages of Cross-Bearing and Debt of Sin: The Economy of Heaven in Matthew's Gospel* (Berlin: de Gruyter, 2013), 75.

70. Luther addressed the "rewards" in Scripture (e.g., Matt 5:12) by describing them as consolation and recompense for the faithful, not means by which Christians earn eternal life (Luther, *Sermon on the Mount*, 292–93).

gifts and promises offered by grace and received by faith, whereas Catholics like Jesuit Cornelius à Lapide fired back that "contrary to the modern heretics" (like Tyndale!), the reward indicates "the merit of good works."[71]

Still, premodern interpreters typically viewed the Beatitudes not primarily as a method for earning one's way into heaven but rather as invitations into a way of life that ultimately leads to true well-being. Catholic theologian and Dominican Gerald Vann wrote of the Beatitudes, "even here and now you will be happy with the happiness of those of whom is the kingdom of heaven, for you will have been born again into the more abundant life, and the life will ceaselessly grow within you, until at the end you are fully alive at last, and can fully and finally enter into the joy, the complete, unshadowed beatitude, of the eternal day."[72] That's a reasonable summary of much patristic and medieval thinking about the Beatitudes.

God's priorities: the great reversal

Modern scholars, on the other hand, tend to view the Beatitudes as descriptions of oppression that God promises to reverse. There's also a tendency to trace only three or four beatitudes back to Jesus: the poor, those who weep, the hungry, and (sometimes) those who are hated for Jesus's sake. For Ulrich Luz (b. 1938), for example, Jesus's original three beatitudes (the poor, weeping, and hungry) flow from "apocalyptic hope for a total reversal of conditions."[73]

Read this way, the Beatitudes are part of the gospel themes of reversal (the last shall be first) and radical inclusion (Jesus welcoming tax collectors and

---

71. William Tyndale, *The Work of William Tyndale*, ed. G. E. Duffield (Philadelphia: Fortress, 1965), 189; Cornelius à Lapide, *The Holy Gospel According to Saint Matthew*, 229.

72. Gerald Vann, *The Divine Pity: A Study in the Social Implications of the Beatitudes* (New York: Sheed and Ward, 1946), 25.

73. Luz went on to say that Matthew "*moved the sense of the Beatitudes in the direction of parenesis*" (Luz, *Matthew 1–7*, 190, italics original). See also Dupont: "La perspective de Luc est sociale, celle de Matthieu morale" (Dupont, *Le problème littéraire*, 1:322) and Segundo Galilea, *The Beatitudes: To Evangelize as Jesus Did*, trans. Robert R. Barr (Maryknoll, NY: Orbis Books, 1984), 10, 38. So also Julius Wellhausen: "For Luke, the blessed do not come into the kingdom of God because of what they are and do, but because of what they lack and suffer"; whereas in Matthew people become worthy of the kingdom through inner qualities ("Bei Lc kommen die Seliggepriesenen in das Reich Gottes nicht wegen dessen, was sie sind und tun, sondern wegen dessen, was sie entbehren und leiden"); Julius Wellhausen, *Das Evangelium Matthaei: Übersetzt und Erklärt* (Berlin: Georg Reimer, 1904), 15.

sinners).[74] Contemporary Lutheran preacher Nadia Bolz-Weber paraphrases: "Blessed are the unemployed, the unimpressive, the underrepresented." So also evangelical Philip Yancey: "Happy are the bankrupt and the homeless."[75] The Beatitudes, like the gospel, are good news for the poor, and woeful news to the mighty, whom God will topple from their thrones.

This approach rightly identifies—and keeps at the center—God's heart for the poor, which permeates all of Scripture. It fits well with other themes elsewhere in Matthew and Luke, especially the radical reversals promised in the kingdom of God (Luke 1:46–55; Matt 20:16, 21:31). Because of the preference it gives to Luke's Beatitudes, it corrects the tendency of the premodern tradition to read Luke through Matthew's lens—or to neglect Luke altogether. Conversely, this approach tends to struggle to incorporate Matthew's unique beatitudes (especially the merciful, pure in heart, and peacemakers).

Viewed this way, the Beatitudes function as an implicit invitation not to *become* poor or hungry, but to join with God in the work of that great reversal. As René Coste writes, as a revelation of God's heart for the poor, sinners, and distressed, the Beatitudes place on the church the obligation for the Beatitudes to be realized.[76]

Descriptions of Jesus

One of the few trends that appears with utterly reliable consistency throughout history is the view that Jesus perfectly fulfills and models the Beatitudes. In other words, everyone agrees that the Beatitudes are descriptive in just this sense: they describe Jesus of Nazareth. He, and only he, perfectly embodies them. Writers from the third through the twenty-first centuries describe the Beatitudes as a biography or portrait of Jesus. This is as true for women writers as for men, for mystics as for scholastics, for Orthodox as for Pentecostals. It may be the one element of the Beatitudes' reception history where unity reigns.

74. Günther Bornkamm, *Jesus of Nazareth*, trans. Irene McLuskey, Fraser McLuskey, and James M. Robinson (New York: Harper & Row, 1960), 78–79.

75. Nadia Bolz-Weber, "Blessed Are the Unemployed, Unimpressive, and Underrepresented," YouTube video, https://www.youtube.com/watch?v=ctcjNCrGyT8; Philip Yancey, "General Schwarzkopf Meets the Beatitudes," *Christianity Today* 35, no. 7 (June 24, 1991): 72.

76. "Jusqu'à la fin de l'histoire, l'Eglise aura à œuvrer pour que l'avènement des Béatitudes se réalise pour les pauvres du monde." René Coste, *Le grand secret des béatitudes: une théologie et une spiritualité pour aujourd'hui* (Paris: Editions S.O.S., 1985), 47.

One repeated emphasis appears within this unanimous consensus. It seems to surface most prominently during the Reformation era (sixteenth and seventeenth centuries) and again in the twentieth century. For a handful of writers, it is the cross in particular that exemplifies the Beatitudes.

Geneva Reformer John Calvin, for example, described the Beatitudes as Christ's "school of the cross."[77] A similar sentiment occurs in the writing of Jacques Lefèvre d'Étaples (AKA Jacobus Faber Stapulensis, ca. 1455–1536), a French humanist theologian whose thought is typically described as a precursor to French Protestantism.[78] And for German Lutheran pastor Dietrich Bonhoeffer (1906–1945), there is only one place on earth where one can find the community that the Beatitudes describe, "and that is where the poorest, meekest, and most sorely tried of all men is to be found—on the cross at Golgotha."[79] Because disciples of Jesus should expect to look like their master, the Beatitudes are also, secondarily, a description of the disciples, precisely because they have taken up their crosses and followed Jesus.[80]

In a ninth-century Benedictine monastery, a monk named Rabanus Maurus (780–856) illustrated the same principle, but in visual form. His treatise *De laudibus sanctae crucis* ("In Praise of the Holy Cross") contains several illuminated prose poems; one of them displays the eight beatitudes in the shape of a cross. The first two beatitudes form the bottom half of the cross's vertical beam; the next four are the horizontal crossbar; and the final two comprise the top half of the vertical beam.[81] Maurus depicted the Beatitudes quite literally as the way of the cross.

A similar illustration occurs in 1665, in a pamphlet composed by an author known only as E. M.[82] The frontispiece to the pamphlet is an illustration of

77. John Calvin, *Sermons on the Beatitudes: Five Sermons from the Gospel Harmony, Delivered in Geneva in 1560* (Carlisle, PA: Banner of Truth Trust, 2006), 19.

78. Jacques d'Étaples Lefèvre, *Jacques Lefèvre d'Étaples et ses Disciples: Epistres et Evangiles pour le cinquante et deux dimenches de l'an*, ed. Guy Bedouelle and Franco Giacone (Leiden: Brill, 1976), 66B, 372.

79. Bonhoeffer, *Cost of Discipleship*, 114. Likewise for Bruno von Segni (1045–1123), Christ alone can fulfill all the Beatitudes (Stoll, *De Virtute*, 192). For another kind of christological interpretation, see George Hunsinger, *The Beatitudes* (Mahwah, NJ: Paulist, 2015).

80. Bonhoeffer, *Cost of Discipleship*, 105. So also David P. Scaer, *The Sermon on the Mount: The Church's First Statement of the Gospel* (St. Louis, MO: Concordia, 2000), 116; Graham, *Secret of Happiness*, 4; Joseph Ratzinger (Pope Benedict XVI), *Jesus of Nazareth: From the Baptism in the Jordan to the Transfiguration*, trans. Adrian J. Walker (New York: Doubleday, 2007), 71.

81. Rabanus Maurus, *De laudibus sanctae crucis* (PL 107:822); see also Stoll, *De Virtute*, 140, 156. A digitized copy is available via the website of the Bibliothèque Nationale de France at https://gallica.bnf.fr/ark:/12148/btv1b8490076p/f46.image.r=.langEN.

82. E. M., *Ashrea: Or, the Grove of the Beatitudes, Represented in Emblemes* (London: Printed

Christ on the cross, with the first seven beatitudes written on banners that stream from his mouth, head, fingertips, and sides. The eighth (the persecuted) is a long banner that forms a horizontal bar running through his pierced feet on either side of the cross. The author used a popular memorization aid known as the *Ars Memorativa* (the Art of Memory) to associate each beatitude with an aspect of Christ's body on the cross: for example, "poor in spirit" refers to Christ's naked body; and "the merciful" refers to his wounded side.

One of E. M.'s memory tricks draws on one of Christ's seven last words from the cross: "hunger and thirst" is paired with Christ's mouth saying, "I thirst." In the modern era, a few authors pair *each* of the seven last words from the cross with one of the first seven beatitudes. (The eighth beatitude is left out of the seven-part scheme because the eighth correlates not to any particular last word but to the crucifixion itself, the ultimate symbol of Jesus's persecution and rejection.) I've found three writers who take this approach (I'm sure there are more!). Interestingly, none of them offers the same pairings.[83]

F. W. Isaacs, in the closing days of the nineteenth century, lined up the last words and the Beatitudes using the traditional order of the seven last words matched to the Matthean order of the first seven beatitudes. Isaacs took each last word to be an interpretation of a beatitude: "JESUS, on the Cross, interprets the second Beatitude by the second Word."[84]

In the twentieth century, Fulton Sheen and George Barrett followed the traditional order of the seven last words, but they each varied the order of the Beatitudes in a different way, in their (sometimes creative) efforts to find correspondences between them.[85] Only two of their pairs overlap. Some of the pairings are admittedly strained. Others generate interesting reflections, such as Barrett's connections from "Father, forgive" to the peacemakers (with reference both to Vietnam and racial unrest—Barrett was writing in 1970),

---

for W. P. at Grayes-Inn Gate in Holborne, 1665); Reprint: English Emblem Books 18 (Yorkshire, England: Scolar Press, 1970). The authorship is uncertain; the author is named only as E. M. and is attributed to Edward Manning ("an obscure pamphleteer") or Edward Mico (ca. 1628–1678), an English Jesuit; see John Horden, "Note," in *Ashrea*, n.p.

83. For more see Rebekah Eklund, "Matthew, the Cross, and the Cruciform Life," in *Cruciform Scripture: Cross, Participation, and Mission*, ed. Nijay K. Gupta, Andy Johnson, Christopher W. Skinner, and Drew J. Strait (Grand Rapids: Eerdmans, 2021), 3–21.

84. F. W. Isaacs, *The Beatitudes: As Learned by the Cross: Thoughts on the Seven Last Words of Our Lord* (Oxford; London: Mowbray & Co., 1896), 20.

85. Fulton J. Sheen, *The Cross and the Beatitudes* (Garden City, NY: Garden City Books, 1937, 1952); George W. Barrett, *Christ's Keys to Happiness* (New York: The World Publishing Company, 1970).

and from "My God, my God, why have you forsaken me?" to the mourners (with reference to Vietnam and to the death of Martin Luther King Jr.).[86]

The two-stanza solution

I suggested a little earlier in this chapter that the typical modern approach— understanding the Beatitudes as descriptions of neediness that God promises to reverse—struggles to incorporate Matthew's unique beatitudes. It's time to take a closer look at Matthew's Beatitudes, to see why this is so.

Matthew was a master craftsman of words, and this is certainly true in his arrangement of the Beatitudes. One can see his eight beatitudes as two stanzas of four beatitudes each: stanza one is Matt 5:3–6, and stanza two is 5:7–10. (The ninth beatitude in Matt 5:11–12 doesn't fit neatly in this scheme; instead, it functions as a bridge between the Beatitudes proper and the "salt and light" sayings that follow.) Both stanzas contain exactly thirty-six words, and the first stanza names groups that all begin with the letter *p*: *ptōchoi* (the poor in spirit), *penthountes* (those who mourn), *praeis* (the meek), and *peinōntes* (those who hunger).[87] Additionally, the last line of each stanza (the fourth beatitude in verse 6, and the eighth beatitude in verse 10) repeats the word "righteousness" and contains an additional alliteration, since in Greek the word for "righteousness" (*dikaiosynē*, forms of which appear in verses 6 and 10), and the verbs for "thirst" (*dipsōntes*, in verse 6) and "persecute" (*dediōgmenoi*, in verse 10) all begin with the letter *d*.[88]

If we return to the describe/demand dichotomy, the first stanza looks more descriptive, whereas the second stanza looks more prescriptive. In fact, interpreters throughout history have suggested something very similar to this. Martin Luther saw the Beatitudes through the lens of the two great commandments: to love God and to love the neighbor (Matt 22:36–40). When Luther summed up the Beatitudes, he wrote that a Christian relates to them both

---

86. Barrett, *Christ's Keys*, 22, 39. See also Sam Wells's sermon "Dwelling in the Comma," which describes the first half of each beatitude as a description of the cross, and the second half of each beatitude as a description of the resurrection, in Samuel Wells, *Learning to Dream Again: Rediscovering the Heart of God* (Grand Rapids: Eerdmans, 2013), 135–41.

87. Powell, "Matthew's Beatitudes," 462. See also Christine Michaelis, "Die Π-Alliteration der Subjektsworte der ersten 4 Seligpreisungen in Mt. 5:3–6 und ihre Bedeutung für den Aufbau der Seligpreisungen bei Mt., Lk. und in Q," *Novum Testamentum* 10, no. 2–3 (Apr–Jul 1968): 148–61.

88. Green, *Matthew, Poet*, 39. Green also pointed to a "special link" between the first beatitude (poor in spirit, *hoi ptōchoi tō pneumati*) and the sixth (pure in heart, *hoi katharoi tē kardia*) because of their analogous grammar and rhythmic kinship.

"in his own person" (which for Luther indicated his relation to God) and "in relation to others" (which meant, of course, his relation to the neighbor). In sum, "in his own person he is poor, troubled, miserable, needy, and hungry" but "in relation to others he is a useful, kind, merciful, and peaceable man."[89] Luther didn't use the exact language of the Beatitudes. But the first four clearly relate to the first stanza (the first four beatitudes), and the second four terms correspond to the second stanza (the last four beatitudes).

John Calvin (1509–1564) made the same move, even more explicitly. For Calvin the first four beatitudes are inward-looking, whereas the second four are outward-looking; they are "calls for action in favor of others."[90] This two-part division mirrors his understanding (inherited from a long-standing Christian tradition) that the first "tablet" of the Ten Commandments (i.e., the first five commandments) relates to the love of God, and the second "tablet" (the second five commandments) relates to love of the neighbor. The first four beatitudes (the first stanza) are like the first tablet of the Ten Commandments; the second stanza is like the second tablet.[91] Reformed theologian Thomas Torrance (1871–1959) extended Calvin's insight, and explained what he saw as the relationship between the two stanzas: "The blessings [one] receives in the first set [one] turns round in the second to confer on others."[92] So also Margaret Aymer in the twenty-first century, who puts the Beatitudes into conversation with the Accra Confession ("Covenanting for Justice in the Economy and the Earth") adopted in 2004 by the World Alliance of Reformed Churches. Aymer

89. Luther, *Sermon on the Mount*, 45.

90. Chad Quaintance, "The Blessed Life: Theological Interpretation and Use of the Beatitudes by Augustine, Calvin and Barth" (PhD diss., Union Theological Seminary and Presbyterian School of Christian Education, 2003), 162, ProQuest 3087209; Calvin, *Harmony of the Gospels*, 171–72.

91. Calvin, *Sermons on the Beatitudes*, 133, 247–49. Calvin, like so many of his predecessors, understood the two great commandments as a summary of the ten commandments (see Allison, "The History," 6). This line of thought continues in both Protestant and Catholic thought; see, e.g., A.-M. Carré, *Quand arrive le bonheur: Les Béatitudes*, 2nd ed. (Paris: Les Éditions du Cerf, 1974), 129.

92. Thomas Torrance, *The Beatitudes and the Decalogue* (London: Skeffington & Son, 1921), 37–38; see also Powell, "Matthew's Beatitudes," 477–79. For minor variations on this theme, see Lange, *Gospel According to Matthew*, 101; Michael Gourgues, "Sur l'articulation des béatitudes matthéenes (Mt 5.3–12): une proposition," *NTS* 44, no. 3 (1998): 340–56; and David Wenham, "The Rock on Which to Build: Some Mainly Pauline Observations about the Sermon on the Mount," in *Built Upon the Rock: Studies in the Gospel of Matthew*, ed. Daniel M. Gurtner and John Nolland (Grand Rapids: Eerdmans, 2008), 199–200. See also the chart of the "interrelationships" of the Beatitudes in Kodjak, *Structural Analysis*, 68.

takes the first four beatitudes as describing the poor and the vulnerable, and the second four as a call to action against injustice.[93]

This two-stanza division of Matthew's beatitudes into the needy and the faithful endures into modern exegesis, sometimes with modifications.[94] David Wenham points out that Matthew's eighth beatitude (Matt 5:10–12) seems to have "loyalties in both groups."[95] Karl Barth capitalized on the same observation by dividing the Beatitudes into *three* groups: the sufferers (the poor in spirit/poor, meek, hungry, and mourners/weepers); the doers (the merciful, pure in heart, and peacemakers); and the persecuted and reviled, who are both active doers because they confess the kingdom of God, and passive sufferers because this confession brings hatred down on them (*CD* IV/2.64.3).[96]

How many beatitudes are there?

You might be wondering why this question needs asking. Isn't it obvious how many there are? Well, people haven't always agreed. Interpreters have counted

93. Margaret Aymer, "The Beatitudes and the Accra Confession," in Roncace and Weaver, *Global Perspectives on the Bible*, 223–24.

94. E.g., Green, *Matthew, Poet*, 208, 255. For François Genuyt, the first three beatitudes of the first stanza are necessary for the pursuit of the fourth: one cannot truly hunger for justice without emptying oneself of the desire for possessions (the poor in spirit), undergoing the test of suffering (the mourners), or rejecting the will to power (the meek). Hunger for justice (the last beatitude of the first stanza) gives rise to the first three beatitudes of the second stanza (merciful, pure in heart, peacemaking), since these are the activities that flow from justice and that inevitably result in the final beatitude (persecution). See François Genuyt, "Les Béatitudes selon saint Matthieu (Mt 5,3–12)," *Lumière et vie* 47 (1997): 25. George Hunsinger divides Matthew's beatitudes into two groups: the first four describe "the needy" and the next four "the faithful" (Hunsinger, *The Beatitudes*, 1–3, 59–60). Mark Allan Powell concurs, but concedes that it's not a watertight system, since some people might fall into both categories (Powell, "Matthew's Beatitudes," 476). J. Alexander Findlay described most of them as pairs, with the first naming a virtue of the soul in relation to God, and the second the expression of that virtue in social relations, while the third (the meek) and the last (the persecuted) are summary statements of the preceding; see Findlay, *The Realism of Jesus: A Paraphrase and Exposition of the Sermon on the Mount* (New York: Doran, 1924?), 56.

95. David Wenham, "How Do the Beatitudes Work? Some Observations on the Structure of the Beatitudes in Matthew," in *The Earliest Perceptions of Jesus in Context: Essays in Honor of John Nolland*, ed. Aaron W. White, Craig A. Evans, and David Wenham (London: Bloomsbury T&T Clark, 2018), 207.

96. Karl Barth, *Church Dogmatics*, ed. G. W. Bromiley and T. F. Torrance, trans. G. W. Bromiley (Peabody, MA: Hendrickson, 1958, 2004), 189–91. Frederick Bruner follows the same scheme in Bruner, *Matthew*, 155, describing the first four as the need beatitudes and the next three as the help beatitudes.

four, seven, eight, nine, and even ten beatitudes. Numbering the Beatitudes has had a surprising influence over interpretation, and knowing who chose which numbers will help us navigate the next two thousand years of the beatitudes' history.

Nine

Nine is the easiest number to arrive at, simply by counting how many times Matthew used the word *blessed*. The main question is whether the ninth beatitude should count as a separate beatitude or an addendum to the eighth. A few modern scholars propose that there are nine beatitudes. For these scholars, Matthew's ninth beatitude (Matt 5:11) is not merely an expansion of the eighth (Matt 5:10) but is an additional beatitude in its own right.[97]

A handful of ancient writers, perhaps following this literary trend, also placed the count at nine. Hippolytus of Rome (170–235) contended that Psalm 1 and Matthew 5:1–12 both contain nine beatitudes.[98] Dale Allison names Epiphanius of Salamis (ca. 310–403) and Severianus (d. 452) as two other ancient writers who read the beatitude as three triads (and who could not resist finding ways to link the Beatitudes to the threeness of the Trinity).[99]

Ten

The most unusual count is certainly the number ten. New Testament scholar Hans Dieter Betz considered 5:10, 5:11, *and* 5:12 as three separate beatitudes, bringing the count to ten.[100] Betz has had almost no followers in his numbering system but he did have one predecessor.

---

97. E. Stanley Jones proposed a kind of Hegelian synthesis in the three triads: the third of each group of three synthesizes the previous two; in *The Christ of the Mount: A Working Philosophy of Life* (New York: Abingdon, 1931), 53, 60–61, 67, 74, 79. Scot McKnight suggests three triads: "three on humility of the poor (the poor in spirit, the mourners, the meek); three on those who pursue justice (those who hunger and thirst for justice, the merciful, the pure in heart); three on those who create peace (peacemakers, the persecuted, the insulted)" (McKnight, *The Sermon on the Mount*, The Story of God Bible Commentary [Grand Rapids: Zondervan, 2013], 38); see also Pennington, *Sermon on the Mount*, 118.

98. Harold Smith, *Ante-Nicene Exegesis of the Gospels* (London: SPCK, 1925), 1:182.

99. Allison, *Studies in Matthew*, 174–75n3.

100. Green, *Matthew, Poet*, 26n43.

In the fourth century, Ephrem the Syrian arrived at the same number but via a different route: the Diatessaron (Tatian's second-century harmony of the four gospels). Ephrem used Matthew's nine beatitudes (counting 5:10 and 5:11–12 as two beatitudes), plus the third Lukan blessing on those who weep (Luke 6:21b), since the Eastern Diatessaron tradition included the blessings on both weepers and mourners as two separate beatitudes.[101] For Ephrem (unlike for Betz), the number ten resounded with theological significance: "Blessed are you, O church, with ten blessings that our Lord gave; a perfect mystery. For every number depends on ten. Therefore ten blessings perfected you."[102] Why ten? Well, to begin with, there were Ten Commandments—and a number of other tens throughout Scripture that Ephrem named.[103] Ephrem's approach is a glimpse into how premodern writers often used the symbolic value of numbers to count and then interpret the Beatitudes.

Eight

It's probably most common today to say that there are eight beatitudes. This count treats Matt 5:11–12 as an intensification and application of the eighth (due to the shift from third to second person), rather than its own separate beatitude. It was very common for premodern writers to number the beatitudes this way.

Gregory of Nyssa (ca. 335–395), one of the Beatitudes' most influential interpreters, counted eight beatitudes. Like other patristic writers, he saw eight as a mystical number because of its connection to the rite of circumcision (which occurs on the eighth day after birth) and to the resurrection (which occurs on an eighth day, i.e., seven days plus one, since the resurrection happened on the first day of the week).[104] (This also explains why some baptisteries are

---

101. Martin Hogan, *The Sermon on the Mount in St. Ephrem's Commentary on the Diatessaron* (Bern: Lang, 1999), 28–41; Tjitze Baarda, "The Beatitudes of 'The Mourning' and 'The Weeping': Matthew 5:4 and Luke 6:21b," in *Studies in the Early Text of the Gospels and Acts*, ed. David G. K. Taylor (Atlanta: Society of Biblical Literature, 1999), 173–76, 184, 191.

102. Ephrem, *Hymns on the Nativity* 25.10; quoted in Hogan, *Sermon on the Mount*, 28. Philo of Alexandria also connects the number ten to perfection and to the "divine mysteries" in Q. *Gen.* 4.10; see Betz, *Sermon on the Mount*, 105n83.

103. On the significance of the number ten, see John W. Welch, "Counting to Ten," *JBMS* 12, no. 2 (2003): 40–57; and John W. Welch, *The Sermon on the Mount in the Light of the Temple* (Surrey, England: Ashgate, 2009), 46.

104. Gregory of Nyssa, *Gregory of Nyssa's Treatise on the Inscriptions of the Psalms: Introduction, Translation, and Notes*, trans. Ronald E. Heine (Oxford: Clarendon Press, 1995), 2.5.53.

octagons; and why some of these octagonal baptisteries are inscribed with the Beatitudes.)

In the early days of the church, certainly prior to Gregory, the eighth day or "the Octave" had become shorthand for the eschaton or the new creation. How they arrived at this idea is a bit complicated. In Genesis, creation begins on "the first day" (Gen 1:5), which both Jews and Christians understood as the first day of the week. Jesus's resurrection also technically takes place on the first day of the week (Matt 28:1, Mark 16:2, Luke 24:1, John 20:1). But for Christians like Gregory, Jesus's resurrection actually took place on an *eighth* day—that is, a *second* first day of the week (seven plus one), as a reprise of the first day of creation.[105] The day of his resurrection signaled that God was remaking creation and inaugurating his new creation. Associating the Beatitudes with the eighth day inescapably ties them to the eschaton—the new age. All the promises ("for they shall see God," etc.) are then seen through the lens of God's new creation.

Four

Of course, if one counts Luke's beatitudes, there are four. This is also the modern way of arriving at the number four, if one assumes that Jesus only spoke four of the beatitudes (the blessings on the poor, the weeping, the hungry, and the hated), and that Matthew's other four or five are later additions. The other way to arrive at the number four is an ancient one, and it uses the formula $4 \times 2 = 8$.

According to Ambrose of Milan (339–397), Luke recorded four beatitudes "in honour of the four cardinal virtues." Like his contemporary Gregory, he saw eight as a number of mystical significance. Matthew chose to record eight beatitudes, said Ambrose, because of the phrase "for the octave" found at the head of many psalms, since the octave "denotes the completion and fulfillment of our hopes" (*Comm. Luke* 5.49).[106] For Ambrose the four and the eight are

---

See also Casimir McCambley, "On the Sixth Psalm, Concerning the Octave by Saint Gregory of Nyssa," *GOTR* 32, no. 1 (1987): 39–50. Philo of Alexandria "associates the number eight with equality and justice" (*Q. Gen.* 1.75, 3.49; quoted in Betz, *Sermon on the Mount,* 105n83).

105. Possible Jewish precedent in Enoch 91:12–13. See also *Epistle of Barnabas* 15.6–9; Justin Martyr, *Dialogue with Trypho* 24.1, 41.4, 138.1; Cyprian, *Epistles* 64.4.3; Augustine, *City of God* 22.30.5.

106. Ambrose of Milan, *Commentary of Saint Ambrose on the Gospel According to Saint Luke,* trans. Íde M. Ní Riain (Dublin: Halcyon, 2001), 133. Ambrose claimed that the phrase "for the octave" occurs at the head of "many psalms," but in the existing versions of the LXX and the Vulgate, it occurs at the beginning of only two psalms: Psalm 6 and Psalm 11.

harmoniously interrelated, since eight is simply two sets of four. The number four is primary because Matthew's eight are contained in Luke's four. Ambrose matched each Lukan beatitude (and its Matthean parallel) with a cardinal virtue and then with one of the unique Matthean beatitudes, which he saw as corollaries. For example, the hungry (Luke 6:21a/Matt 5:6) represent the virtue of justice, and if one is just, one is also merciful (Matt 5:7).

Seven (or, 7 + 1 = 8)

The number seven is the surprise. There appears to be no straightforward way of counting the beatitudes and arriving at the number seven. But that's what Augustine of Hippo (354–430) did—and his counting method proves enormously influential.

Augustine, like Ambrose and Gregory before him, counted the beatitudes using the formula "seven plus one." He also noted (as Ambrose did too) that both the first and eighth beatitude contain the same promised reward: "for theirs is the kingdom of heaven" (*De Serm. Dom.* 1.3.10).[107] His innovation was to use this detail to conclude that the eighth beatitude therefore circles around and returns to the first, meaning that the true number of the beatitudes is seven.[108] The eighth is a recapitulation and perfection of the first, just as the resurrection on the eighth day is a recapitulation of the first day and the dawn of the new creation. Like Gregory, then, he achieved the same result—the Beatitudes as a sign of the arriving eschaton—but with a different number.[109]

---

107. Ambrose, *Comm. Luke* 5.61, in *Gospel According to Saint Luke*, 137; Augustine, *The Lord's Sermon*, 18. Long before Augustine, Polycarp (69–155) merged the blessings on the poor and the persecuted into one beatitude ("Blessed are the poor, and those that are persecuted for righteousness' sake, for theirs is the kingdom of God") and placed it into a series of other scriptural quotations (1 Peter 3:9; Matt 7:1; Luke 6:36; Matt 7:2/Luke 6:38) but he never made anything else of this combination (Polycarp, *Epistle to the Philippians* 2.3 [ANF 1:33]).

108. Augustine, ever the attentive and detailed exegete, also treated Matt 5:11–12 as separate from the other beatitudes because of the shift from third person to second person.

109. For the more on the connection between the Beatitudes and the "eighth day" or the eschaton, see Rebekah Eklund, "Octaves and Septenaries," *Studia Patristica* (forthcoming, 2021). Some modern scholars count seven beatitudes in less theological fashion, by considering the eighth blessing on the persecuted as an appendix or a bridge to the salt and light sayings. A few point out that Jesus gives seven "woes" against the scribes and Pharisees later in Matthew (chapter 23); see Tholuck, *Commentary on the Sermon*, 63.

With this knowledge in hand, you'll now understand why we'll encounter the numbers eight and seven over and over again in later exegesis of the Beatitudes, especially in medieval writing.

Some of these numbering systems may strike you as fanciful. But they reveal the early Christians' abiding belief that every word of Scripture, every jot and tittle, was a word of life for God's people—therefore the number of the Beatitudes was not incidental but had riches of meaning to unearth.

When are they for?

The numbers themselves, and their symbolic meanings, point the way to our last big-picture question (for now). When do the promised rewards of the Beatitudes come to fruition? When do the merciful receive mercy; when are the mourners comforted?

On this point, scholastic medievalist Thomas Aquinas and twentieth-century New Testament scholar Hans Dieter Betz are in agreement. Aquinas wrote that the rewards of the Beatitudes can be had "perfectly and completely" only in heaven, but can be had "as a beginning and imperfectly" here in this life.[110] (Aquinas was following a path already laid by Augustine, who wrote first that all the rewards of the Beatitudes "can be realized even in this life, as we believe the Apostles realized them," but he also qualified himself, adding that "no words can express that complete transformation into the likeness of angels which is promised for the afterlife" [*De Serm. Dom.* 1.4.12].[111]) Betz agreed: the rewards are for a future that is both eschatological and this-worldly.[112] On this score, the history of interpretation has achieved a surprising consensus. German Protestant scholar Johannes Weiss (1863–1914) is one of the very few who saw *all* the promises of the Beatitudes as wholly future, with no present sense at all.[113]

110. Thomas Aquinas, *Commentary on the Gospel of Matthew, Chapters 1–12*, ed. The Aquinas Institute, trans. Jeremy Holmes and Beth Mortensen, Biblical Commentaries 33 (Lander, WY: The Aquinas Institute for the Study of Sacred Doctrine, 2013), C.5 L.2.413. See also ten Klooster, *Thomas Aquinas on the Beatitudes*, 92.

111. Augustine, *The Lord's Sermon*, 21. Augustine later qualified his remarks to say that the perfection enjoyed in this life is not equal to that in the next life (Augustine, *Lord's Sermon*, 180n22; see also ten Klooster, *Thomas Aquinas on the Beatitudes*, 91).

112. Betz, *Sermon on the Mount*, 93. This is a view shared widely across history and appears in Protestant, Catholic, and Orthodox thought.

113. Johannes Weiss, *Jesus' Proclamation of the Kingdom of God*, ed. and trans. Richard Hyde Hiers and David Larrimore Holland (Philadelphia: Fortress, 1971), 9–10, 12, 71n26, 73–74.

Conversely, Swiss Reformed theologian Karl Barth (1886–1968) is one of the few who described the kingdom as wholly present. (Apart from Barth, there are relatively few interpreters, and none prior to the modern age, who understood the promises of the Beatitudes as only for the present life.)[114] For Barth, this is because the kingdom has not merely dawned but has definitively arrived in the person of Jesus. Barth thus read all the promises of the Beatitudes in the present tense (despite their grammatical future): "Because they hope in what is promised to them by this declaration, they already have it" (*CD* II/2.38.2).[115] Barth insisted that the promises of the Beatitudes are "not merely a promise and proclamation, but the present (if hidden) impartation of full salvation, total life and perfect joy." As God speaks at creation and brings the world into being, Jesus's words are *effectual*; "[Jesus] makes actual what He declares to be true" (*CD* IV/2.64.3).[116]

Even for Barth, however, although the rewards of the Beatitudes are already genuinely present in this life, they are also indicative of the life to come.[117] As Barth's contemporary Bonhoeffer wrote: "There shall the poor be seen in the halls of joy. With his own hand God wipes away the tears from the eyes of those who had mourned upon earth. He feeds the hungry at the Banquet. There stand the scarred bodies of the martyrs, now glorified and clothed in the white robes of eternal righteousness instead of the rags of sin and repentance."[118]

114. See, e.g., David P. Scaer, who takes "the kingdom of the heavens" (Matt 5:3, 10) as a synonym for "the salvation which God is accomplishing in Jesus . . . in his death for sinners and its proclamation," in *The Sermon on the Mount: The Church's First Statement of the Gospel* (St. Louis, MO: Concordia, 2000), 81.

115. Barth, *Church Dogmatics*, 689; see also Henry Churchill King, "The Fundamental Conditions of Happiness, as Revealed in Jesus' Beatitudes," *The Biblical World* 23, no. 3 (March 1904): 180–87.

116. Barth, *Church Dogmatics*, 192.

117. Barth later did refer to the receiving of mercy at "the judgment," citing Matt 5:7 (*CD* II/2.38.2, in *Church Dogmatics*, 692); and he mentioned mercy and the ceasing of hunger and thirst as occurring in the glory of eternal life (Quaintance, "The Blessed Life," 212).

118. Bonhoeffer, *Cost of Discipleship*, 114. The Beatitudes are eschatological because "It is precisely in the eschaton that the ultimate human flourishing will occur, as this can only come about when God restores his reign of justice, peace, and rest" (Pennington, *Sermon on the Mount*, 63).

2

The Tangled Skein of Our Lives

A Whirlwind Tour through History

It's time to take a quick tour through two thousand years of history. I'll start with the two key trajectories (laid down in the fourth and fifth centuries) that influenced beatitude interpretation for the next thousand years. Then I'll explore how those two trajectories took on their own character in the medieval era, especially in art and in liturgy. Finally, I'll summarize the twentieth-century tendencies to apply the Beatitudes to personal spirituality and to social justice. I'll conclude the chapter with one final big-picture question that I've saved for last: what's the role of grace in the Beatitudes?

Early trajectories: steps and septenaries

In the fourth and fifth centuries, three theologians laid down two tracks that profoundly influenced readers for the next thousand years. After them, Christians not only read the Beatitudes; they read Ambrose of Milan, Gregory of Nyssa, and Augustine of Hippo reading the Beatitudes. While Gregory was more influential in the East, Augustine's influence dominated the West.[1] As a convenient shorthand, I'm calling their two tracks the steps and the septenaries. Together, Ambrose and Gregory set the "steps" trajectory, and Augustine launched the "septenaries."

---

1. John Chrysostom also helped lay down this track. It's unclear if Latin writers were influenced by Gregory and/or Chrysostom directly (given that few of them read in Greek), or if they arrived independently at this theme. For centuries, Western (Latin) and Eastern (Greek) thought developed in partial independence from one another, separated by language; but there was also frequent contact and negotiation between the two. See Averil Cameron, *Byzantine Matters* (Princeton: Princeton University Press, 2014), 16–17, 20–21, 105–6.

Steps of ascent

The first trajectory emerges from a detail that ancient readers took very seriously: the order of the text. They assumed that the Beatitudes were put in a certain order for a reason. They didn't always agree on *how* the order mattered—or even what the order was, since some manuscripts switched the second and third beatitudes (verses 4 and 5). Many patristic and medieval interpreters had access to the Western manuscript tradition (followed also by the Latin Vulgate), which presents "blessed are the meek" as the second beatitude and "blessed are those who mourn" as the third.[2] English versions today almost unanimously follow the manuscript tradition in which the mourners are blessed before the meek.[3]

Whatever the order was, ancient interpreters often used beatitudes to interpret other beatitudes—one beatitude singing to another, one flowing out of another or leading to the next, another circling back to illuminate an earlier one. This is, incidentally, a theme beautifully captured by Vladimir Martynov's musical setting of the Beatitudes, with its repeated central melody, itself built up from small, constantly repeated motives (a motive is a short melodic-rhythmic block that forms the basic building block of a larger melody or theme).[4]

John Chrysostom (ca. 349–407), the golden-mouthed preacher of Constantinople, lived and wrote at the same time as Gregory and Ambrose. He proposed that the Beatitudes form a sort of "golden chain," with each "former precept making way for the following one."[5] Ambrose and Gregory extended this insight upward: for them, the Beatitudes were not a chain but a set of

---

2. D 33 b f q vg sy^c bo^ms. Writers who followed this manuscript tradition include Gregory of Nyssa, Ambrose, Augustine, Hilary, Jerome, and Leo the Great.

3. With the exception of the Jerusalem Bible, which follows the Vulgate order. Some commentators, especially if they could read in both Greek and Latin, were aware of the difference. The Catholic humanist Erasmus of Rotterdam followed the order of the Vulgate (meek first, then mourners) in his paraphrase of Matthew, but from 1516 his edition of the NT adopted the order of the older Greek texts (mourners first, then meek).

4. My colleague and music historian Remi Chiu explained Martynov's piece to me, and provided the definition of the motive. Chiu explains that the repeated melody "functions as the constant backbone of the piece, adorned with changing countermelodies" (Chiu, in email correspondence).

5. Chrysostom: "in each instance, by the former precept making way for the following one, He hath woven a sort of golden chain for us. Thus, first, he that is 'humble,' will surely also 'mourn' for his own sins: he that so 'mourns,' will be both 'meek,' and 'righteous'" (Chrysostom, *Homilies on the Gospel of Saint Matthew* 15.9 [*NPNF*¹ 10:96]).

steps, or a ladder. The Beatitudes were sequential and ascending steps toward the kingdom of God—that is, toward union with God (Ambrose, *Comm. Luke* 5.52, 5.60; Gregory, *Beati.* Sermon 1, 2, 5).[6]

For Gregory, the Beatitudes were a ladder of virtue that facilitated the soul's ascent toward God. The Beatitudes were thus virtues to be sought out and practiced, beginning with the first: poverty of spirit was the virtue of humility, which combatted the vice of pride—the root of all sin. Once one became humble, this disposed one toward meekness, or the virtue of kindness, which helped one to resist the vice of envy, and so on. As one ascends the ladder of the Beatitudes, living more fully into them, one becomes more like God, as the image of God is progressively cleansed and restored.[7]

Gregory was not the first to associate the Beatitudes with the virtues. The earliest extant discussion of the Beatitudes as a whole occurs in the early third century in the *Stromata* of Clement of Alexandria, who borrowed concepts from Plato to describe Christ's Beatitudes as teaching that trains and disciplines the soul.[8] But Gregory and Ambrose appear to be the first to imagine the Beatitudes as a set of steps ascending toward God. Today, Gregory's interpretation of the Beatitudes continues to shape Orthodox thought.[9]

The view that the Beatitudes were ascending steps of virtue leading toward union with God dominated interpretation from the fifth through the sixteenth centuries. To be sure, not all interpreters followed this path; in the decades immediately following Gregory and Ambrose, neither Jerome (347–420) nor Chromatius of Aquileia (d. ca. 406) discussed the order of the Beatitudes or the virtues in their analysis of Jesus's blessings. But it becomes increasingly difficult to find an interpreter who doesn't follow the path laid down by Am-

6. Ambrose of Milan, *Commentary of Saint Ambrose on the Gospel According to Saint Luke*, trans. Íde M. Ní Riain (Dublin: Halcyon, 2001), 134, 137. Gregory of Nyssa, *The Lord's Prayer; The Beatitudes*, trans. Hilda C. Graef, ACW 18 (Mahwah, NJ: Paulist, 1954), 85, 97, 130.

7. Gregory of Nyssa, *The Lord's Prayer*, 89, 131, 148. For more, see Rebekah Eklund, "Blessed Are the Image-Bearers: Gregory of Nyssa and the Beatitudes," *AThR* 99, no. 4 (Fall 2017): 729–40.

8. Clement of Alexandria, *Stromata* 4.6 (*ANF* 2:413–14). Clement also discussed the Beatitudes in relation to doing all things for the sake of Christ in times of persecution; see Judith L. Kovacs, "Clement of Alexandria and Gregory of Nyssa on the Beatitudes," in *Gregory of Nyssa: Homilies on the Beatitudes*, ed. Hubertus R. Drobner and Albert Viciano (Leiden: Brill, 2000), 314.

9. Vigen Guroian, "Liturgy and the Lost Eschatological Vision of Christian Ethics," *Annual of the Society of Christian Ethics* 20 (2000): 227, 236; Mother Alexandra, "Blessed Are the Persecuted," *Diakonia* 22, no. 2 (1989): 81–84; Liviu Barbu, "The 'Poor in Spirit' and Our Life in Christ: An Eastern Orthodox Perspective on Christian Discipleship," *Studies in Christian Ethics* 22, no. 3 (2009): 263.

brose and Gregory. A good example is found in the medieval poet Dante, who conceived of the Beatitudes quite literally as an ascent toward God in *Purgatorio*, pairing each beatitude with one of seven terraces on the way to the top of Mount Purgatory. (He gets the steps from Ambrose and Gregory, and the number seven from Augustine.) Each time a penitent soul completes a stage of purgation and prepares to leave one of the terraces, an angel blesses the soul with the beatitude associated with that terrace, and the soul advances closer to God and God's realm.[10]

One might suppose that this approach died out after the close of the medieval era, but it continues to surface in unexpected places across the theological spectrum. Of course, it continues to guide Catholic understanding of the Beatitudes, but John Wesley (1703–1791), one of the founders of the Methodist Church, also adopted this understanding of the Beatitudes in his sermons.[11] English Nonconformist Thomas Watson (ca. 1620–1686) took a page from Gregory's book when he described the Beatitudes as "eight steps leading to true blessedness" and compared them to Jacob's ladder.[12] The widely influential Reformed theologian John Peter Lange (1802–1884) described them as "an ascending line, in which the new life is traced from stage to stage."[13] Evangelical preacher Charles Haddon Spurgeon (1834–1892) referred to the Beatitudes as a "celestial ascent" and a "ladder of light" culminating in "the beatific vision . . . the eternal ecstasy."[14] Baptist Clarence Jordan

10. Like many of his predecessors, Dante also paired each beatitude with a vice: e.g., the soul receives the blessing on the poor in spirit after the purgation of pride. But Dante, unlike many others, did not keep the beatitudes in their canonical order, giving them instead in this order: first, fifth, seventh, third, fourth (used twice), sixth; see V. S. Benfell III, "'Blessed Are They That Hunger after Justice': From Vice to Beatitude in Dante's Purgatorio," in *Seven Deadly Sins: From Communities to Individuals*, ed. Richard Newhauser (Leiden: Brill, 2007), 194–95.

11. John Wesley, *The Nature of the Kingdom: Wesley's Messages on the Sermon on the Mount*, ed. Clare George Weakley Jr. (Minneapolis: Bethany House Publishers, 1979), 49.

12. Thomas Watson, *The Beatitudes: An Exposition of Matthew 5:1–10* (Carlisle, PA: Banner of Truth Trust, 2014), 55. Watson obviously read widely among the patristic writers; he cited Chrysostom, Jerome, Theophylact, and many others.

13. John Peter Lange, *The Gospel According to Matthew*, vol. 16 of *A Commentary on the Holy Scriptures*, trans. Philip Schaff, 12th ed. (New York: Charles Scribner's Sons, 1884), 101. Gerald Heard "decodes" the Beatitudes using Gregory's key, and Gerald Vann describes them as sequential steps toward union with the Creator. Gerald Heard, *The Code of the Beatitudes: An Interpretation of the Beatitudes* (Eugene, OR: Wipf & Stock, 1941, 2008); and Gerald Vann, *The Divine Pity: A Study in the Social Implications of the Beatitudes* (New York: Sheed and Ward, 1946), 26.

14. Timothy Larsen, "Charles Haddon Spurgeon," in *The Sermon on the Mount through the Centuries: From the Early Church to John Paul II*, ed. Jeffrey P. Greenman, Timothy Larsen, and

(1912–1969) described them as "steps into the kingdom" that are a detailed description of "the new birth" of John 3:3.[15] This approach even pops up in a modern commentary from time to time: Robert Guelich wrote that three of Matthew's beatitudes (5:7–9) "form an ascending scale in their promises and consequently their order. . . . Each expression of the eschatological blessing is an extension of the former."[16]

Septenaries: Augustine's sevens

Augustine took a different tack. Initially, he followed his predecessors by interpreting the Beatitudes as a series of steps undertaken by the soul (*De Serm. Dom.* 1.3.10).[17] His innovation springs from the number seven. Recall from the last chapter that he considered seven to be the true number of the beatitudes, since the eighth is a recapitulation of the first. From there, he proceeded to match the seven beatitudes to two other lists of sevens: the seven petitions of the Lord's Prayer, and the seven gifts of the Spirit as named in the Old Latin text of Isa 11:2: wisdom, understanding, counsel, fortitude, knowledge, godliness, and fear of the Lord. Augustine made one key change;

Stephen R. Spencer (Grand Rapids: Brazos, 2007), 195n45–46. Spurgeon also followed Augustine in counting only seven beatitudes (Larsen, "Charles Haddon Spurgeon," 194–95). Larsen wonders if the medieval tradition was mediated to Spurgeon "through seventeenth-century English Protestants" (ibid., 199). J. C. Carlile's biography of Spurgeon claims a close resemblance between Spurgeon's thought and the fourteenth-century Dominican mystic Johannes Tauler (J. C. Carlile, *C. H. Spurgeon* [Westwood, NJ: Barbour and Co., 1987], 271). See also influential Baptist preacher and writer Frank Boreham, who titled his book on the Beatitudes *The Heavenly Octave* (Grand Rapids: Baker Books, 1936, 1968).

15. Clarence Jordan, *Sermon on the Mount*, rev. ed. (Valley Forge, PA: Judson, 1952), 19. Similarly John Wick Bowman saw them as sequential steps in moral progression, in "Travelling the Christian Way—The Beatitudes," *RevExp* 54, no. 3 (1957): 377–78, 385.

16. E.g., Robert Guelich, "The Matthean Beatitudes: 'Entrance Requirements' or Eschatological Blessing?" *JBL* 95 (1976): 422–23; and J. Alexander Findlay, *The Realism of Jesus: A Paraphrase and Exposition of the Sermon on the Mount* (New York: Doran, 1924?), 56.

17. Augustine, *The Lord's Sermon on the Mount*, trans. John J. Jepson, ACW 5 (Mahwah, NJ: Paulist, 1948), 17. In *On Christian Teaching*, Augustine used the gifts and Beatitudes, in sequential order, as the necessary stages for a student of the divine Scriptures to learn to read and understand them properly—Augustine, *On Christian Teaching* 2.7.9–11, trans. R. P. H. Green, Oxford World's Classics (Oxford: Oxford University Press, 1997), 33–35. Ulrich Duchrow argues that one can divide the *Confessions* into seven stages and map them onto the seven beatitudes; see his "Der Aufbau von Augustinus Schriften Confessiones und De Trinitate," *ZTK* 62, no. 3 (1965): 338–63.

he inverted the order of the spiritual gifts, so that his list *begins* with fear of the Lord and ends with wisdom. (To justify this move, he appealed to Eccl 1:16: "the fear of the Lord is the *beginning* of wisdom" [*De Serm. Dom.* 1.4.11–12, 2.11.38].[18])

LORD'S PRAYER PETITION	GIFT OF THE SPIRIT	BEATITUDE
Hallowed be your name	Fear of the Lord	Poor in spirit
Your kingdom come	Godliness	Meek
Your will be done	Knowledge	Mourn
Give us our daily bread	Fortitude	Hunger and thirst
Forgive us our debts	Counsel	Merciful
Lead us not into temptation	Understanding	Pure in heart
Deliver us from evil	Wisdom	Peacemakers

Only small clues suggest why Augustine put these three texts together. The notion that Isa 11:2 named the seven gifts of the Spirit was relatively well-established in the Christian tradition by the time of Augustine.[19] But nobody prior to Augustine had paired the Beatitudes with these seven gifts (or, as explicitly as he does, with the petitions of the Lord's Prayer). It's a natural enough connection, given his conviction that the Christian life is made possible by the gifts of the Holy Spirit.[20]

Augustine's chart is the first septenary: the famous "sets of sevens" that proliferate during the medieval era.[21] His initial three sets of seven (beatitudes,

18. See Augustine, *The Lord's Sermon*, 19, 20, 125–26, emphasis added.

19. See Karl Schlütz, *Isaias 11, 2 (die sieben Gaben des Hl. Geistes) in den ersten vier christlichen Jahrhunderten* (Münster: Aschendorff, 1932).

20. Another bread crumb on Augustine's trail is a connection made by Chrysostom between the seventh spiritual gift (the fear of God) and the Beatitudes. While preaching on the Beatitudes, Chrysostom declared that the divine laws pronounce a blessing on "the man who has gotten hold of virtue," and that in all that is required of us, "the fear of God should be the foundation" (Chrysostom, *Twenty-One Homilies on the Statues* 18.10 [*NPNF¹* 9:462]). Another predecessor, Irenaeus of Lyon (ca. 130–202), connected the fear of God to the metaphor of the ladder (used by Ambrose and Gregory to describe the Beatitudes) when he wrote that the Holy Spirit is "a ladder whereby we ascend to God" and that the first rung of the ladder is fear of the Lord (Sir. 1:16) (Irenaeus, *Against Heresies* 3.24.1 [*ANF* 1:458]).

21. Paschasius Radbertus (785–865) followed Augustine's (and Hugh's) scheme except that he reversed the order of the Lord's Prayer petitions, matching the poor in spirit and the gift

gifts, petitions) expanded when later theologians like Hugh of St. Victor (ca. 1096–1141) added seven virtues that represented (or flowed from) each beatitude, seven vices overcome by those virtues, and the seven fruits of the Spirit (even though there are nine fruits listed in Gal 5:11–12).[22] The easy availability of other sets of seven in Scripture and Christian tradition increased the size of the septenaries even more. Bernardino of Siena used the Beatitudes, sacraments, virtues, gifts of the Spirit, and fruits of the Spirit.[23] Hugh of Amiens (ca. 1085–1164) may hold the record for the most septenaries, including the usual sets and then adding (in various writings) the seven sacraments, the seven seals of Revelation, the seven clerical orders, and the seven days of creation.[24]

The association of each beatitude with a particular virtue does not originate with Augustine, but it emerged from the seeds of his septenary, and it was the dominant view of Western medieval writers. Of course, another set of seven virtues already existed in theological thought—the so-called three-

---

of fear with the final petition for deliverance from evil; see Servais Pinckaers, *The Sources of Christian Ethics* (Edinburgh: T&T Clark, 2001), 156; Ryan P. Freeburn, *Hugh of Amiens and the Twelfth-Century Renaissance* (Surrey, England: Ashgate, 2011), 196. Later theologians followed either Augustine (inverting the spiritual gifts but retaining the petitions in scriptural order) or Radbertus (inverting the order of both the spiritual gifts and the petitions). Anselm of Canterbury (1033/4–1109) followed Radbertus (Anselm, *Homiliae et Exhortationes* [PL 158:595–97]), and so did the influential *Glossa Ordinaria*, which included an abbreviation of Radbertus's commentary on Matthew; on the *Glossa* see Brigitta Stoll, *De Virtute in Virtutem: zur Auslegungs- und Wirkungsgeschichte der Bergpredigt in Kommentaren, Predigten und hagiographischer Literatur von der Merowingerzeit bis um 1200*, BGBE 30 (Tübingen: Mohr Siebeck, 1988), 198.

22. Hugh of St. Victor, in his *De quinque septenis seu septenariis*; see Freeburn, *Hugh of Amiens*, 198. For an exploration of the relationship between the gifts, virtues, Beatitudes, and fruits in medieval thought, see D. O. Lottin, "Les dons du Saint-Esprit chez les théologiens depuis P. Lombard jusqu'à S. Thomas d'Aquin," *RTAM* 1 (January 1929): 41–61.

23. Carolyn Muessig, "Preaching the Beatitudes in the Late Middle Ages: Some Mendicant Examples," *Studies in Christian Ethics* 22, no. 2 (2009): 143. In the modern era, Gerald Vann follows the septenary tradition by pairing each beatitude with a gift of the Spirit and a sacrament, in Vann, *Divine Pity*.

24. Freeburn, *Hugh of Amiens*, 114. By the fourteenth century, the seven penitential psalms were also being used as prayers against the vices (e.g., Ps 6 against anger), and medieval writers understood the seven penitential psalms (much like the Beatitudes!) as "seven steps on the ladder of repentance"; Bruce K. Waltke, James M. Houston, and Erika Moore, *The Psalms as Christian Lament: A Historical Commentary* (Grand Rapids: Eerdmans, 2014), 15, 17. But (so far) I can find no evidence that the seven penitential psalms themselves were ever paired with the Beatitudes. In 1228, Gregory IX's papal bull canonizing Francis of Assisi described him as one who had uprooted the vices and make his heart an altar for God by following the path of the "sevenfold grace of the Spirit" and with "the help of the eight beatitudes of the Gospel" as well as "the fifteen steps of the virtues mystically represented in the psalter (gradual psalms)" (Muessig, "Preaching the Beatitudes," 137).

plus-four, or the three theological virtues (faith, hope, love) plus the four cardinal virtues of classical philosophy (prudence, fortitude, temperance, justice). Bonaventure, for one, paired the seven gifts of the Spirit with the three-plus-four rather than the beatitude-virtues.[25] But as far as I am aware, these early writers did not match the three-plus-four directly to the Beatitudes. Instead, the Beatitudes had their own virtues.

This can be seen in medieval art, which frequently personifies the virtues as seven women. Sometimes they're the three-plus-four, but just as often they represent the beatitude-virtues.

Personified virtues

If you've seen a statue or a picture of Lady Justice, blindfolded and holding a sword in one hand and scales in the other, then you're already familiar with the persistent tendency to personify virtues as women. Once the Beatitudes came to be viewed as virtues, they, too, made their way into texts and visual art as sets of seven or eight women. As writings on the virtues and vices proliferated, some visual art retained the number seven (or eight) but used a set of virtues that overlap only partially with the beatitude-virtues.[26]

Sometimes, though, the personifications are unmistakably the beatitude-virtues. For example, they appear as eight "Dames" in the fourteenth-century poem "Patience" penned by the Gawain-poet: Dames Poverty, Pity, Penance, Meekness, Mercy, Purity, Peace, and Patience.[27] The poet revealed his dependence upon Augustine by linking the virtues of poverty and patience, which are the virtues of the first and eighth beatitudes, respectively.[28] Even the cir-

25. Bonaventure, *The Breviloquium*, vol. 2 of *The Works of Bonaventure*, trans. José de Vinck (Paterson, NJ: St. Anthony Guild Press, 1963), 5.5, 6.3.3. The Church of the Beatitudes (built in 1938 for a Franciscan order of nuns), is eight-sided, representing the eight beatitudes, but the three-plus-four virtues are depicted in symbols in the mosaic floor around the altar (http://www.seetheholyland.net/mount-of-beatitudes/).

26. Colum Hourihane's thorough index of the virtues and vices in medieval Christian art lists no less than 109 virtues, in Hourihane, ed., *Virtue and Vice: The Personifications in the Index of Christian Art* (Princeton University Press, 2000). See also Adolf Katzenellenbogen, *Allegories of the Virtues and Vices in Medieval Art: From Early Christian Times to the Thirteenth Century* (Toronto: University of Toronto Press, 1989).

27. Gawain-Poet, "Patience," in *Complete Works: Patience, Cleanness, Pearl, Saint Erkenwald, Sir Gawain and the Green Knight*, trans. Marie Borroff (New York: Norton, 2011), Prologue lines 31–33.

28. Jay Schleusener, "'Patience,' Lines 35–40," *Modern Philology* 67, no. 1 (August 1969): 66.

cular nature of the poem—the last line echoing the first—reflects Augustine's view that the eighth beatitude recapitulates the first.[29]

In one of the oldest copies of the *Speculum Virginum* (Mirror for Virgins), a twelfth-century treatise written at a Cistercian abbey for women monastics, a complex illumination depicts four cardinal virtues as women perched atop flowering shrubs. Leaning against the trunk of each shrub is a pair of women, two per tree, representing the eight beatitudes.[30] A magnificent full-page illumination in the twelfth-century Floreffe Bible depicts seven beatitudes as female busts enclosed in medallions and arranged around three women representing the three theological virtues (faith, hope, and love).[31] In a late thirteenth-century illumination called the Virtue Garden, the women are the gardeners and the beatitude-virtues are the trees: seven women, representing the petitions of the Lord's Prayer, pour streams of water representing the gifts of the Spirit onto the roots of seven trees that represent the Beatitudes and their associated virtues.[32]

Augustine's influence

Augustine's interpretation of the Beatitudes exerted a powerful pull on subsequent centuries, especially in Western thought.[33] Benedictine abbot Ælfric of

29. Miriam Grove Munson, "Humility, Charity, and the Beatitudes in Patience and The Scale of Perfection," *14th Century English Mystics Newsletter* 4, no. 3 (Sept 1978): 22.

30. The *Speculum Virginum* is in the collection of the Walters Art Museum, Ms. W72; the illumination can be found on fol. 12r. Image available to view in the World Digital Library at https://www.wdl.org/en/item/13014/view/1/29/. For a description see Katzenellenbogen, *Allegories of the Virtues*, 69.

31. The Floreffe Bible is housed in the British Library, Add MS 17738; the illumination can be found on fol. 3v. Image available from the British Library at http://www.bl.uk/manuscripts /Viewer.aspx?ref=add_ms_17738_f003v.

32. The Virtue Garden is found in *La Somme le Roi et Le Miroir de l'âme*, by Laurent of Orleans, Bibliothèque Mazarine, Paris, MS 870, fol. 61v. Image available from the Bibliothèque Mazarine at mazarinum.bibliotheque-mazarine.fr/idviewer/3053/128. Ellen Kosmer, "Gardens of Virtue in the Middle Ages," *Journal of the Warburg and Courtauld Institutes* (1978): 303. An eleventh-century casket known as the Beatitudes Casket, now in the Museo Arqueológico in Madrid, illustrates seven beatitudes (the fourth beatitude is, mysteriously, missing) not as women but as an angel paired with a haloed male figure (Julie A. Harris, "The Beatitudes Casket in Madrid's Museo Arqueológico: Its Iconography in Context," *ZKunstG* 53, no. 1 [1990]: 135). Julie Harris suggests that the angel is either the messenger delivering the beatitude to the saint, or a personified form of the beatitude itself (ibid., 139).

33. In another sermon (Sermon 53A), Augustine preached at length on the Beatitudes with-

Eynsham (ca. 950–1010) is representative when he reported in his sermon on the Beatitudes that "he presents Augustine's teaching."[34] Another example is in Thomas Aquinas's *Catena aurea*, a florilegium (an anthology of Latin and Greek writers commenting on Scripture) compiled at the request of Pope Urban IV in 1264; eighty-nine complete manuscripts of the *Catena* for Matthew are in existence today, testifying to its extraordinary reach.[35] The section on the Beatitudes (Matt 5:1–12) cites ten authors in all, with Augustine the clear winner at twenty-six quoted excerpts; in second and third place are Chrysostom (fifteen excerpts) and Pseudo-Chrysostom (fourteen).[36]

Aquinas himself, the towering intellect of the medieval era in the West, both followed Augustine and expanded on his thought. Like his patristic predecessors, Aquinas connected the Beatitudes to the virtues. For him, virtue "removes one from evil, works and makes one to do what is good, and disposes one to what is best."[37] In relation to the Beatitudes, virtue removes one from the evil of greed (blessed are the poor), disturbance [Lat. *inquietudinis*] (blessed are the merciful), and harmful pleasure (blessed are the clean of heart).[38]

Although Augustine's influence began to wane after the Reformation, it did not die out completely in Protestant writing; Martin Luther consulted Au-

---

out ever mentioning Isaiah or the gifts of the Spirit. He did pair one beatitude with a line from the Lord's Prayer, but it is a *different* match than the one made in his commentary; he quoted "Your will be done on earth as it is in heaven" (Matt 6:10) in relation to the blessing on those who hunger and thirst for justice, rather than the blessing on those who mourn. Augustine, Sermon 53A.9, in Augustine, *Essential Sermons*, ed. Boniface Ramsey, trans. Edmund Hill, The Works of Saint Augustine: A Translation for the 21st Century (Hyde Park, NY: New City Press, 2007), 80–81.

34. Derek A. Olsen, *Reading Matthew with Monks: Liturgical Interpretation in Anglo-Saxon England* (Collegeville, MN: Liturgical Press, 2015), 167.

35. Jean-Pierre Torrell, *The Person and His Work*, vol. 1 of *Saint Thomas Aquinas*, trans. Robert Royal (Washington, DC: Catholic University of America Press, 1996), 137, 139.

36. Thomas Aquinas, *St. Matthew*, vol. 1 of *Catena Aurea: A Commentary on the Four Gospels Collected out of the Works of the Fathers*, trans. John Henry Newman (London: The Saint Austin Press, 1999), 145–60. If Chrysostom was the genuine author of the *Opus Imperfectum*, Aquinas would have cited Chrysostom more than any other author, at twenty-nine excerpts. The other authors quoted are Jerome (10x), Ambrose (8x), Hilary of Poitiers (7x), Remigius (4x), Rabanus Maurus (2x), Gregory of Nyssa (2x), and Anselm of Laon's *Glossa Ordinaria* (10x).

37. Thomas Aquinas, *Commentary on the Gospel of Matthew, Chapters 1–12*, ed. The Aquinas Institute, trans. Jeremy Holmes and Beth Mortensen, Biblical Commentaries 33 (Lander, WY: The Aquinas Institute for the Study of Sacred Doctrine, 2013), C.5 L.2.414.

38. Aquinas, *Commentary on Matthew*, C.5 L.2.414.

gustine's commentary on the Sermon on the Mount when he began preaching on the text, and generally approved of it.[39]

Beatitudes in liturgy

Placing the Beatitudes into worship is another way of interpreting them. Catholic and Orthodox liturgies both include the Beatitudes, but in different places. Orthodox liturgy includes the Beatitudes in two places. They appear in the Lesser Entrance (the procession of the Gospels into the sanctuary), which symbolizes the worshippers' entrance into heaven and eschatological glory. They also appear in the Byzantine rite of burial, where they are read immediately following a lament over the fall of Adam and Eve after their creation in God's image.[40] Both liturgical settings resonate with Gregory of Nyssa's view that embodying the virtue of the Beatitudes participates in the restoration of the image of God that was damaged in the fall.

By the early medieval period, Catholic liturgy associated the Beatitudes with the saints and martyrs. The Beatitudes first appeared in Western lectionaries as early as the ninth century in relation to the feast days for several different martyrs.[41] Catholic and Anglican lectionaries still use Matt 5:3–12 as the gospel lesson for All Saints' Day. Thus Western medieval (and modern) Christians often heard the Beatitudes interpreted in relation to the lives of the saints.[42] These All Saints' sermons frequently explored the lives of the saints as exemplars of the Beatitudes.[43]

---

39. Jaroslav Pelikan, *Divine Rhetoric: The Sermon on the Mount as Message and as Model in Augustine, Chrysostom, and Luther* (Crestwood, NY: St. Vladimir's Seminary Press, 2001), 128. Of course, Luther departed from Augustine's exegesis in significant ways, but he often consciously interacted with and even adopted Augustine's insights. For deeper analysis, see Stephen J. Chester, *Reading Paul with the Reformers: Reconciling Old and New Perspectives* (Grand Rapids: Eerdmans, 2017), 95–103.

40. Guroian, "Liturgy," 227, 236–37.

41. All Saints' was established by the second half of the tenth century. See the lists in Olsen, *Reading Matthew with Monks*, 171n156–157.

42. Stoll, *De Virtute*, 27; Olsen, *Reading Matthew with Monks*, 171. For descriptions of several texts that use the Beatitudes to describe the life and virtues of a saint, see Stoll, *De Virtute*, 165–77.

43. The trend may be seen in art as well. Two manuscript illustrations, dating from the tenth century, personify the Beatitudes as unnamed, haloed male saints (the Canon Tables of the Sacramentary of St. Maximin of Trier and the Dedication Pages of the Codex Aureus in the Escorial)—see Harris, "The Beatitudes Casket," 135.

As part of this trend, it became increasingly common to identify exemplars for the virtue of each beatitude, drawn both from Scripture and from contemporary life. Medieval Irish commentaries often linked the eight beatitudes to eight patriarchs (Job, Isaac, Jacob, Samuel, Abraham, Lot, Solomon, David).[44] Dante named three exemplars for the virtues of each beatitude, always beginning with Mary (mother of Jesus), then naming a Christian saint, then a pagan. Some of Dante's associations seem straightforward, such as meekness with St. Stephen, who prayed for those stoning him to death (*Purg.* 15.106–14), whereas others are a surprise, like Dante's presentation of Emperor Trajan as an exemplar of humility or the "poor in spirit" (*Purg.* 10.73–96).[45]

Another Western medieval tradition connected each beatitude not to individual saints but to a particular group or category of saints, a list of which likely derived first from a sermon attributed to the Venerable Bede (ca. 672–736), an English Benedictine monk. The list eventually made its way into the All Saints' Day Litany of Saints.[46] The lists varied; no firm standard was established for which beatitude indicated which group. For example, preachers identified the pure in heart variously as female saints, confessors, prophets, and martyrs.[47] The famous Ghent altarpiece in St. Bavo Cathedral in Belgium draws on this tradition by personifying the Beatitudes as groups of apostles (the poor in spirit), prophets (the mourners), pilgrims and hermits (the meek), Old Testament patriarchs (those who hunger and thirst), just judges and knights (the merciful), virgins or female martyrs and saints (the pure in heart), confessors (the peacemakers), and martyrs (the persecuted), all of whom approach the heavenly throne to worship the Lamb in a scene derived from Revelation 7.[48] Thomas Aquinas likewise

44. Stoll, *De Virtute*, 181.

45. Dante drew on a tradition that Gregory the Great's prayers resulted in Trajan's salvation (Dante Alighieri, *Purgatorio*, trans. Jean Hollander and Robert Hollander [New York: Anchor Books, 2003], 224, note to *Purgatorio* 10.73–93).

46. "Aligning the *beati* [blessed] in heaven with the beatitudes was a known procedure in medieval preaching, which probably was begun by Peter Comestor" (Anton ten Klooster, *Thomas Aquinas on the Beatitudes: Reading Matthew, Disputing Grace and Virtue, Preaching Happiness* [Leuven: Peeters, 2018], 220). Many thanks to Anton ten Klooster for pointing out to me the overlap with the Litany of the Saints.

47. For Pseudo-Bede's sermon, see Louis Jacques Bataillon, "Béatitudes et types de sainteté," *Revue Mabillon* 7 (1996): 79–80. For a thorough chart of identifications, see ibid., 93.

48. See Rebekah Eklund, "The Blessed," Visual Commentary on Scripture, http://thevcs.org/blessed. Luca Signorelli's frescoes in the Orvieto cathedral display a similar set of saints: apostles, prophets, martyrs, church fathers, patriarchs, and virgins; see Sara Nair James, "Penance and Redemption: The Role of the Roman Liturgy in Luca Signorelli's Frescoes at Orvieto," *Artibus et Historiae* 22, no. 44 (2001): 121–22, 126–28.

matched the Beatitudes to similar groups of saints in two All Saints' sermons, but only two of his identifications are the same as those in the Ghent altarpiece.[49]

The tendency to identify exemplars—and to link the Beatitudes to the lives of the saints—endures in the present day, as reflected in the *Catholic Catechism*, which declares that the Beatitudes "have begun in the lives of the Virgin Mary and all the saints."[50] In visual form, the south rose window in the Cathedral of St. Paul, designed by Charles Connick (1875–1945), depicts eight saints of the Americas, mostly from the seventeenth and eighteenth centuries, as personifications of the Beatitudes.

Personal spirituality and social justice

With the Reformation things got more complicated. But by and large, Reformation interpreters were still in transition; at least in relation to the Beatitudes, they rarely jettisoned wholesale the insights of earlier eras. It was the Enlightenment that created the first truly momentous shift in how the Beatitudes are viewed. I've already traced the rise of historical-critical methods in the previous chapter. Most gospel commentaries today are likely to concentrate their energies on the relationship between the two versions of the Beatitudes in Matthew and Luke (redaction criticism), their respective oral and written sources (source or form criticism), their roots in Old Testament texts, and their setting within Second Temple Judaism and first-century Greco-Roman culture.

Eastern Orthodox interpretation has remained far more immune to these Enlightenment trends. Likewise, while Catholic biblical interpreters today are influenced by historical-critical methods, they, too, remain indebted to past traditions.

Protestant interpretations in the West tend to diverge into two main strands: a personal spirituality stream and a social justice stream. (This mirrors at least in part the two divergent furrows ploughed by the fundamentalist-modernist split at the turn of the twentieth century.)

At the extreme end of the first strand—the personal spirituality stream—is American megachurch pastor Robert Schuller's description of the Beatitudes as "Be-Happy Attitudes." Schuller drew from Norman Vincent Peale's popular positive thinking movement to narrate the Beatitudes as positive attitudes (the blessing on the mourners is paraphrased, "I'm really hurting—but I'm going

---

49. See chart in ten Klooster, *Thomas Aquinas on the Beatitudes*, 220.
50. *Catechism of the Catholic Church*, Part Three, Article 2.I.1717.

to bounce back!").[51] Schuller's book is peppered throughout with cheery clichés ("Passionate persistence without impertinence produces progress!"[52]). At the same time, it still includes typical, long-standing interpretations, such as viewing meekness as the ability not to fly into a rage but to remain calm and self-possessed when provoked.[53]

A more moderate version of this strand is a series of late twentieth-century books that compare the Beatitudes to twelve-step programs such as Alcoholics Anonymous. Read charitably, this is a particularly modern twist on Gregory of Nyssa's understanding of the Beatitudes as ascending steps. Many of these books blend the therapeutic with more traditional exegesis.[54] Some are written by practicing psychotherapists or psychologists. Erik Kolbell, a minister and a psychotherapist, blends insights from his therapy practice with insights from a wide variety of Christian writers, including Dag Hammarskjöld, Dorothy Day, William Sloane Coffin Jr., and Gregory Thaumaturgus.[55] Psychologist and spiritual director J. Marshall Jenkins acknowledges that reading the Beatitudes as "pathways through emotional pain" is only one small facet of the many-faceted diamond that is the Beatitudes, but he also gently insists that "Jesus cut that facet."[56]

These books have their potential pitfalls. Peale's positive thinking is antithetical to the spirit of the Beatitudes, which means that Schuller's book—despite the vestiges of traditional Reformed interpretation—has largely emp-

---

51. Robert Schuller, *The Be (Happy) Attitudes: Eight Positive Attitudes* (World Books, 1985, 1996), vi, 29.

52. Schuller, *Be (Happy)*, 65.

53. Schuller, *Be (Happy)*, 59. Perhaps Schuller was indebted to his Reformed/Calvinist heritage. See also Dorothy Kelley Patterson's *BeAttitudes for Women: Wisdom from Heaven for Life on Earth* (Nashville, TN: Broadman & Holman, 2000), whose interpretations are completely traditional and peppered with quotations by women from throughout Christian history: Mahalia Jackson, Susanna Wesley, Charlotte von Kirschbaum, Francis de Sales, St. Gertrude the Great, St. Teresa of Avila, Simone Weil, St. Catherine of Genoa, Fanny Crosby, Meschthild of Magdeburg, Rebecca Grant, Elizabeth Seton, Kandela Groves, Amy Carmichael, Venerable Thecla Merlo, Katherine von Bora, Madame Jeanne Guyon.

54. E.g., Richard Wilson, *Journey of the Beatitudes* (Center City, MN: Hazelden, 1986), who compares the Beatitudes to AA but also draws from the Beatitudes' background in the prophet Isaiah. See also The Celebrate Recovery program, available as a series of books/participant guides: John Baker, *Celebrate Recovery Updated Participant's Guide Set, Volumes 1–4: A Recovery Program Based on Eight Principles from the Beatitudes*, rev. ed. (Grand Rapids: Zondervan, 2016).

55. Erik Kolbell, *What Jesus Meant: The Beatitudes and a Meaningful Life* (Louisville: Westminster John Knox, 2003).

56. J. Marshall Jenkins, *Blessed at the Broken Places: Reclaiming Faith and Purpose with the Beatitudes* (Nashville, TN: Skylight Paths, 2016), xv.

tied the Beatitudes into meaningless platitudes. But other books on the less extreme end of this tendency have much to commend them for the way they connect the Beatitudes deeply to the struggles of everyday life. The best among them, like Jenkins's *Blessed at the Broken Places*, carefully avoid the trap of the self-help genre.[57] They might be thought of as representing the "contemplative" strand of the Christian tradition, the one that focuses inward on the spirit and the inner life. The next strand turns outward; it could be thought of as the "active" approach to the Christian life.

Interpreters in the second strand focus on the Beatitudes as a call for just action in the world. Chilean theologian Segundo Galilea (1928–2010) viewed the Beatitudes through the lens of God's special care for the poor; the Beatitudes are a sign of the kingdom, "a solid hope of liberation for the poor and the oppressed."[58] The 2018 volume *Blessed Are the Refugees* pairs each beatitude with the story of a child refugee receiving services at Baltimore's Esperanza Center.[59] Lazare S. Rukundwa and Andries G. Van Aarde use postcolonial theory to interpret Matthew's first four beatitudes as Jesus's "religious, political, social and economic reforms" in light of Roman colonial rule.[60] And New Testament scholar Margaret Aymer compares the Beatitudes to the Accra Confession adopted in 2004 by the World Alliance of Reformed Churches (longer title: "Covenanting for Justice in the Economy and the Earth").[61] For Aymer, the first four beatitudes represent the poor and the vulnerable; the second four represent the confession's call to stand against injustice.

Of course, not all twentieth-century books fit neatly into one strand or the other. American Reformed theologian George Hunsinger's "Christ-centered interpretation" describes the Beatitudes both as "exemplified by Jesus" and also as "fraught with consequences for today." His book offers (for example) a spirituality of meekness in conversation with Brother Lawrence, Thérèse

---

57. Jenkins, *Blessed at the Broken Places*, 160–64.

58. Segundo Galilea, *The Beatitudes: To Evangelize as Jesus Did*, trans. Robert R. Barr (Maryknoll, NY: Orbis Books, 1984), 15.

59. Scott Rose et al., with Leo J. O'Donovan, *Blessed Are the Refugees: Beatitudes of Immigrant Children* (Maryknoll, NY: Orbis Books, 2018).

60. Lazare S. Rukundwa and Andries G. Van Aarde, "Revisiting Justice in the First Four Beatitudes in Matthew (5:3–6) and the Story of the Canaanite Woman (Mt 15:21–28): A Postcolonial Reading," *HvTSt* 61, no. 3 (2005): 927.

61. Margaret Aymer, "The Beatitudes and the Accra Confession," in *Global Perspectives on the Bible*, ed. Mark Roncace and Joseph Weaver (Boston: Pearson, 2014), 223–24.

of Lisieux, and Dorothy Day, alongside reflections on the climate crisis and restorative justice.[62]

Both strands capture something true about the Beatitudes. Internal transformation is inextricably linked to outward actions. Bodies and souls can't be compartmentalized. Faith becomes active in love (Gal 5:6b). As Jenkins observes, when "we recognize a right relationship to God through Christ as the truth that sets us free, we are willing to suffer and die for this truth."[63] The Beatitudes are both spiritual and political. They address the inner life and the outer; they include both attitudes and actions. Apart from one another, neither of the two strands is sufficient.

What's the role of grace?

I've saved one last big-picture question until now. What's the role of grace in the Beatitudes? What's the role of divine agency (God's action) versus human agency (our actions)? This is one of the most persistently recurring questions in the Beatitudes' history.

The natural outpouring of the Spirit's grace in one's life

Reformed theologian and revivalist preacher Jonathan Edwards (1703–1758) captured the tension between divine and human agency in a sermon on the pure of heart: "Though it be God's work to purify the heart, yet the actual, or rather the active, procuring of it is your act."[64] (One might think of the similarly paradoxical claim in Phil 2:12–13.)

Long before Edwards, Augustine's impulse to link the Beatitudes to the gifts of the Holy Spirit and to the petitions of the Lord's Prayer tied them closely to prayer and to God's grace. This had a profound influence on medieval writers, who often speculated on the relationship among the three sets of seven. As the septenaries increased in size and complexity, medieval writers did not always agree on the exact order or relationship among the gifts, virtues, petitions, and Beatitudes. The gifts, however, al-

---

62. George Hunsinger, *The Beatitudes* (Mahwah, NJ: Paulist, 2015), xi.

63. Jenkins, *Blessed at the Broken Places*, 139.

64. Jonathan Edwards, *Sermons and Discourses 1730–1733*, vol. 17 of *The Works of Jonathan Edwards*, ed. Mark Valeri (New Haven, CT: Yale University Press, 1999), 85, citing James 4:8.

most always preceded the Beatitudes; the empowerment of the Spirit enabled the Beatitudes.

For example, one of the most influential early medieval theologians was Paschasius Radbertus (785–865), a ninth-century abbot. He wrote that one first asked for the gifts of the Holy Spirit by praying the petitions of the Lord's Prayer and then, with the help of the Spirit, fulfilled the Beatitudes.[65] For Radbertus, the virtues of the Beatitudes are not primarily human virtues but rather "virtues fulfilled in us"; the power and grace of God creates in a person the "prerequisites" for the performance of the beatitude-virtues.[66] For Bernardino of Siena the Beatitudes themselves are not commands; instead, they describe a person who has been healed by the sacraments, enabled to do good works by the virtues and the gifts of the Spirit, and kept from growing weary by the fruits of the Spirit; only then do the Beatitudes follow.[67]

For Thomas Aquinas, the Beatitudes are the actions that result from a transformed life. In this he adopted the medieval ideal that "the outward action is what shows the inner disposition."[68] The gifts of the Spirit result in virtues, which are interior qualities or ways of being, while the Beatitudes are the actions that result from those qualities or interior states.[69]

In Aquinas's understanding, the theological virtues (faith, hope, and love) are always infused by God as a gift, but the other virtues (patience, fortitude, and so on) can be either acquired (which means that a person gradually acquires them through repeated practice) or infused (given by God's grace along with the theological virtues). For Aquinas, the Beatitudes refer to acts stemming from the *infused* virtues.[70] That is to say, they arise from the grace of the Spirit—from divine agency.[71] This conclusion sprang in part from Aquinas's sustained attention to Augustine's link between the Beatitudes and the gifts of the Spirit. The gifts of the Spirit are "the basis for the actions of the beati-

---

65. Freeburn, *Hugh of Amiens*, 196.

66. Stoll, *De Virtute*, 186. The same order (petitions, gifts, Beatitudes) appears in the writing of Hugh of Amiens (Freeburn, *Hugh of Amiens*, 167–68) and Zacharias Chrysopolitanus (d. ca. 1155) (Stoll, *De Virtute*, 197).

67. Muessig, "Preaching the Beatitudes," 143.

68. Muessig, "Preaching the Beatitudes," 138.

69. Muessig, "Preaching the Beatitudes," 139–40; see Thomas Aquinas, *Summa Theologica*, trans. Fathers of the English Dominican Province (Westminster, MD: Christian Classics, 1948), Ia–IIae, q.69, art.1.

70. ten Klooster, *Thomas Aquinas on the Beatitudes*, 101.

71. ten Klooster, *Thomas Aquinas on the Beatitudes*, vii, 67.

tudes."[72] Prompted by the Spirit, the Beatitudes are not burdensome but result in delight, which is the fruit of the Spirit streaming forth from the action of the Beatitudes.[73]

Perhaps the best illustration of the standard relationship between the Beatitudes, prayer, and the spiritual gifts is a visual one. Earlier in the chapter, I mentioned an illumination known as the Virtue Garden. At least fifteen copies of the thirteenth-century moral treatise *Somme le roi*, written or compiled by the Dominican Frère Laurent in 1279 for King Philippe III of France, contain a variation of an illumination known as the Virtue Garden. Seven trees in the garden represent the seven beatitudes and their associated virtues; for example, "those who mourn" corresponds to the virtue of patience.[74] Seven women pour streams of water onto the roots of the trees; the women represent the seven petitions of the Lord's Prayer, and the water symbolizes the gifts of the Spirit. That is, the garden depicts a petition producing a spiritual gift, which in turn "waters" the virtue of each beatitude. For example, praying "Deliver us from evil" produces the gift of wisdom, which nurtures poverty of spirit (Matt 5:3), or the virtue of humility. An eighth, taller tree in the garden represents Christ, "under whom the virtues grow." In this way, the Virtue Garden points to the necessity of God's grace and Christ's help in attaining the Beatitudes.[75]

In his sermons on the Lord's Prayer, Thomas Aquinas took the priority of grace one step further. In his order, the gifts of the Spirit are first, *then* the petitions, and then the Beatitudes: a person doesn't even have the will to pray to the Father until God gives her the grace to desire the good.[76] Grace comes first.

This emphasis on the priority of grace—of gift before demand—continues to appear in the modern era. Puritan preacher Robert Harris (1581–1658), like Jonathan Edwards, claimed the necessity of both divine help and human effort for achieving the Beatitudes. He exhorted his listeners to strive for the

---

72. Thomas Aquinas, *Summa Theologica*, Ia-IIae, q. 68–70; see ten Klooster, *Thomas Aquinas on the Beatitudes*, 146. See also Vann, *Divine Pity*, 18.

73. ten Klooster, *Thomas Aquinas on the Beatitudes*, 149.

74. Kosmer, "Gardens of Virtue," 304.

75. For the image, see thevcs.org/blessed. See also E. M., *Ashrea: Or, the Grove of the Beatitudes, Represented in Emblemes* (London: Printed for W. P. at Grayes-Inn Gate in Holborne, 1665); reprint: English Emblem Books 18 (Yorkshire, England: Scolar Press, 1970). The author of *Ashrea* told his readers that the word *ashrea* means in Hebrew "a wood or grove" and is "derived from Ashar, which signifies 'to Beatifie or make blessed'" (a4r–v), and he invites his readers into "the grove of Beatitudes," where each beatitude is represented by a different tree.

76. ten Klooster, *Thomas Aquinas on the Beatitudes*, 234.

Beatitudes but always with the help of prayer and God's grace.[77] Contemporary scholar Dale Allison arrives at a similar conclusion through a narrative analysis of Matthew's Gospel. He notes that the crowds who hear the Beatitudes are "those who have already been healed by Jesus"; and he uses this detail to argue, "So grace comes before task, succor before demand, healing before imperative. The first act of the Messiah is not the imposition of his commandments but the giving of himself. . . . The Beatitudes, then, depict the future as a gift."[78]

Orthodox writers tend to connect the Beatitudes to grace through the theme of *theōsis* or divinization, drawing on Gregory of Nyssa and other ancient theologians. Vigen Guroian writes that the Beatitudes "are traits of character gained humanly by ascetical striving, but they are also blessings conferred mystically by the Holy Spirit in the sacrament of communion on the journey to God in his kingdom."[79] Human goodness can only be achieved through the transformation of the human person into the holiness of God, as a human being makes his way "to the healing of the wound inflicted upon his likeness to God."[80]

All these approaches assume that the Beatitudes are achievable—in fact, that they are the natural outpouring of the Spirit's grace in one's life. There is one main exception to this long rule.

An impossible ideal

The "Lutheran" view of the Sermon on the Mount is usually described in this way: the high demands of the Sermon on the Mount are meant to lay bare the believer's need of God and thus drive her toward God's grace. This follows Martin Luther's conviction that nobody is capable of fulfilling even an iota of God's commandments on their own power.[81]

---

77. Robert Harris, *The Way to True Happiness: Delivered in Twenty-Four Sermons upon the Beatitudes*, ed. Don Kistler (Morgan, PA: Soli Deo Gloria, 1998), 79.

78. Dale C. Allison Jr., *Studies in Matthew: Interpretation Past and Present* (Grand Rapids: Baker Academic, 2005), 198. See also Dale C. Allison Jr., *The Sermon on the Mount: Inspiring the Moral Imagination* (New York: Crossroad, 1999), 9; and Timothy D. Howell, *The Matthean Beatitudes in Their Jewish Origins: A Literary and Speech Act Analysis* (New York: Lang, 2011), 119.

79. Guroian, "Liturgy," 227.

80. Guroian, "Liturgy," 235, quoting Paul Evdokimov, *Woman and the Salvation of the World* (Crestwood, NY: St. Vladimir's Seminary Press, 1994), 191–92.

81. Martin Luther, *The Sermon on the Mount*, vol. 21 of *Luther's Works*, ed. Jaroslav Pelikan (St. Louis: Concordia, 1956), 72.

Luther himself, however, adopted the traditional view that God's grace enables the Beatitudes. He described all the Beatitudes as "fruits of faith, which the Holy Spirit Himself must create in the heart."[82] Furthermore, Luther assumed that the Beatitudes are the characteristic mark of all Christians. For Luther, the Beatitudes are primarily inner attitudes, but they also flow into certain actions, such as the merciful (of the fifth beatitude) forgiving the sinful and doing good to those in need of help.[83] Therefore, the view that the Beatitudes are "an impossible ideal" is associated with later Lutheran writers but does not appear to be the view of Luther himself.[84]

Although Karl Barth usually followed in Calvin's footsteps, and not in Luther's, his understanding of the Beatitudes occupied an interesting middle ground between Augustine and the "Lutheran" view. Barth's emphasis on God's grace and prior action was so strong that he essentially reversed the blessings and the promises: one is merciful because one *has* received God's mercy; one is able to be a peacemaker because one *has* received the blessing of divine adoption.[85] In this way, he came closest to Aquinas's understanding of the absolute priority of grace.

Yes, said Barth, there are demands made in the Sermon on the Mount, but they are demands made of "the new creature"—the human being reborn and remade by God. The good works of the transformed human being flow from thankfulness toward God, but even that is a work of divine grace. "For the demand addressed to the new creature [in the Sermon] is the gift in itself and as such" (*CD* II/2.38.2).[86] For Barth, we're *not* capable of "actualizing" the

---

82. Luther, *Sermon on the Mount*, 15; see also 26.

83. Luther, *Sermon on the Mount*, 30. Luther also seems to assume that a Christian is capable of keeping all the demands of the Sermon by drawing on the distinction between a Christian-as-Christian and a Christian-in-relation, or the Christian as a secular person subject to the laws and customs of the state and the family—see, e.g., Luther, *Sermon on the Mount*, 109–13.

84. Also pointed out by Lisa Sowle Cahill, "The Ethical Implications of the Sermon on the Mount," *Int* 41, no. 2 (April 1987): 146. See also Lisa Sowle Cahill, "Nonresistance, Defense, Violence, and the Kingdom," *Int* 38, no. 4 (October 1984): 380–97. Jeremias ascribes the theory of the "impossible ideal" (German *Unerfüllbarkeitstheorie*) to "Lutheran orthodoxy" (Joachim Jeremias, *The Sermon on the Mount* [Minneapolis: Fortress, 1963], 6).

85. Chad Quaintance, "The Blessed Life: Theological Interpretation and Use of the Beatitudes by Augustine, Calvin and Barth" (PhD diss., Union Theological Seminary and Presbyterian School of Christian Education, 2003), 234, ProQuest 3087209.

86. Karl Barth, *Church Dogmatics*, ed. G. W. Bromiley and T. F. Torrance, trans. G. W. Bromiley (Peabody, MA: Hendrickson, 1958, 2004), 695.

Beatitudes. Or, we're only capable of actualizing them "as the Word of Jesus." Barth continued:

> We must be pleased to allow our very different life to be illuminated by Jesus. This is the point of these imperatives. They demand of us that we be pleased to accept the supremely wonderful and unexpected interpretation of the dark text of our lives by the grace of God which has appeared in Jesus. You wretched ones are truly blessed! . . . How does this come about? It comes about by . . . the Word which contradicts your life, and in so doing catches it and holds it and saves it, interpreting it according to the purpose of its Creator. It comes about by the light which, from the fact that I am in your midst, falls from above upon the tangled skein of your life. (*CD* II/2, 38.2)[87]

—

It's now time to turn to the individual beatitudes, and discover what stories they have to tell as they fall on the tangled skeins of lives past and present.

---

87. Barth, *Church Dogmatics*, 689–90. "Sie fordern von uns, daß wir uns die allerdings höchst wunderliche, höchst unerwartete Auslegung jenes dunklen Textes (unseres eigenen Lebens!) durch die in Jesus auf den Plan getretene Gnade Gottes gefallen lassen: Ihr die Unseligen Selige! . . . Wieso das Alles? Durch das eurem Leben entgegengesetzte und gerade so euer Leben auffangende, haltende, rettende, euer Leben im Sinn seines Schöpfers auslegende Wort, das ich euch sage—durch das Licht, das damit, daß ich in eurer Mitte bin, senkrecht von oben in dieses euer Leben hineinfällt!" (*CD* II/2 38.2), *Die Lehre von Gott*, vol. II/2 of *Die Kirchliche Dogmatik* (Zürich: Evangelischer Verlag A. G. Zollikon, 1942), 770.

3

Drained of All Other Waters

The Poor in Spirit and the Poor

Blessed are the poor in spirit, for theirs is the kingdom of heaven (Matt 5:3).

Blessed are you who are poor, for yours is the kingdom of God. . . . But woe to you who are rich, for you have received your consolation (Luke 6:20, 24).

Before Mother Alexandra was an abbess, she was a princess. Born in 1909, she was the youngest daughter of the king and queen of Romania. As a child during World War I, she visited soldiers in hospitals and prayed with them on trains. She moved to Austria after marrying an archduke (as one does, when one is a princess); she later converted their castle into a Red Cross hospital. When she returned to Romania, she established another hospital, "to serve soldiers, villagers, and anyone in need of medical attention." In 1947, she was exiled from Romania, along with her family; she returned only once, in 1990, shortly after Communism fell and one year before she died. In her late fifties, she took vows as an Orthodox nun, and went on to establish the first English-speaking Orthodox monastery for women in the United States. When she died in 1991, the following verse was inscribed on her gravestone at her request: "We do not live to ourselves, and we do not die to ourselves. If we live, we live to the Lord, and if we die, we die to the Lord; so then, whether we live or whether we die, we are the Lord's" (Rom 14:7–8).[1]

---

1. The information in this paragraph is taken from The Orthodox Monastery of the Transfiguration, "Mother Alexandra," accessed February 10, 2020, http://www.orthodoxmonastery ellwoodcity.org/about/foundress.

The life of Mother Alexandra illuminates multiple sides of the many-sided prism that is the first beatitude. When she was born, she was not one of the poor but one of the rich (*Woe to the rich!*). Later, she became poor (of a certain kind), first living in exile and eventually renouncing all her earthly possessions to enter a monastery. Her generosity and humility illustrate two facets of the beatitude that became important in its history.

She also wrote about the Beatitudes, on at least one occasion. This first beatitude, said Mother Alexandra, "has the key to the entrance of the kingdom of heaven."[2] But what kind of key is it? For some, it opens a door to a path that leads upward to God. For others, it unlocks the next three beatitudes, by revealing that the poor (in spirit) are the same as the meek, hungry, and mourning.

—

Each beatitude has a story, and this one tells two intertwined stories: one about humility, and one about poverty. Because one of these stories is material and the other spiritual, it might initially appear that we can create a neat division of labor between Matthew's version and Luke's, assigning the spiritual to Matthew ("poor in spirit") and the material to Luke ("the poor"). But the history of interpretation is not that clean-cut. As we will see, "poor in spirit" is not simply a reference to a spiritual state; nor is "poor" only a reference to material deprivation.

Matthew's "poor in spirit" and Luke's "poor" have prompted readers over time to wrestle with both the material and spiritual aspects of this beatitude. Prior to the Enlightenment, interpreters almost unanimously saw the two versions of the beatitude as expressing the same fundamental idea (but didn't always agree on what that idea was). Most of them argued that Matthew expressed Jesus's teaching more fully or more clearly. Conversely, modern interpreters frequently accuse Matthew of "spiritualizing" Luke's concrete, material blessing. That is, Jesus blesses the materially poor, as recorded in Luke 6:20, but Matthew adds "in spirit," giving the blessing a new, spiritual meaning. A few others (most prominently New Testament scholar Mark Goodacre), argue instead that Luke has "concretized" the original blessing on the poor in spirit, in accord with his repeated emphasis on God's good news for the poor and the coming reversal of the rich and powerful (Luke 1:46–55; 4:16–19).[3]

---

2. Mother Alexandra, "Blessed Are the Persecuted," *Diakonia* 22, no. 2 (1989): 81–82.

3. Mark Goodacre, *The Case Against Q: Studies in Markan Priority and the Synoptic Problem* (Harrisburg, PA: Trinity Press International, 2002), 133–51.

This split between premodern and modern interpreters is one good example of the chronological aspect of this first beatitude's history. Views about the harmony or difference between Matthew and Luke changed over time, with earlier interpreters choosing harmony and later interpreters often choosing difference. Still, it's not easy to chart a tidy chronological trajectory for this first beatitude. For example, it's not accurate to conclude that premodern interpreters uniformly emphasized a spiritual interpretation, whereas modern interpreters always give a material meaning. Material and spiritual strands interweave in sometimes surprising ways throughout history—just as they interweave in Scripture itself.

I'll begin with one of the most prominent interpretations, and one that remains common today: poverty of spirit as humility, or humble dependence on God. Next, I'll turn to modern-day explorations of the term "poor in spirit," and then to the early church's insistence on the serious dangers of wealth, which incorporates Luke's woe to the rich. Finally, I'll show how interpreters throughout history largely agree over the promised reward of the kingdom of heaven, which they typically agree arrives in part now and in full in the next life or at the dawning of the new age.

Humility

With this first beatitude, Jesus blesses humility: this is the strand that dominates premodern interpretation of the first beatitude and exercises the greatest influence over the history of interpretation for hundreds of years.

The poor in spirit are the broken-hearted (Ps 51:17)—not the humbled or the humiliated—but those who voluntarily humble themselves before God.[4] This interpretation, of course, puts all its weight on Matthew's version and its reference to spiritual poverty. Leo the Great (Pope Leo I, ca. 400–461) expressed a common view when he claimed that Matthew added "in spirit" to the blessing on the poor to make it clear that Jesus intended to speak of humility and not material poverty.[5] Indeed, this interpretation was applied equally to Matthew's blessing on the poor in spirit and Luke's blessing on the poor.[6]

---

4. Gregory of Nyssa, *The Lord's Prayer; The Beatitudes*, trans. Hilda C. Graef, ACW 18 (Mahwah, NJ: Paulist, 1954), 90–91; Chrysostom, *Homilies on the Gospel of Saint Matthew* 15.2 (*NPNF¹* 10:92).

5. Leo the Great, *Sermons* 95.2 (*NPNF²* 12:203).

6. Theophylact: the poor in Luke 6:20 are "either those who are humble or those who live without greed for money" (Theophylact of Ochrid, *The Explanation by Blessed Theophylact of the*

The association of poverty of spirit with humility was firmly established by at least the third century. It permeates the writings of both Eastern Greek fathers and Western Latin fathers.[7] Gregory of Nyssa (ca. 335–395) and Augustine of Hippo (354–430), two of the church's most influential interpreters, understood the beatitude in this way. This approach dominated interpretation throughout the medieval era and remains prominent today in Catholic, Protestant, and Orthodox thought.

It's hard to overestimate the importance of humility (and thus of this first beatitude) in premodern Christian thought. In ancient Greco-Roman philosophical thought, humility was typically seen as a weakness, not a virtue.[8] Christian writers pushed hard against this assumption. Augustine characterized the Christian life as a whole as one of humility, and he traced humility's key role back to the fall itself: "So because man had fallen through pride, [Wisdom] applied humility to his cure."[9] Seen through this lens, it makes perfect sense that the blessing on the poor in spirit (that is, on the humble) is the first beatitude, because the virtue of humility combats the vice of pride, which is the root of all sin.

Humility vs. pride

The association of humility with poverty of spirit taps into two "big-picture" approaches to the Beatitudes (see chapter 1): the significance of the Beatitudes' order, and the view that the Beatitudes are virtues. The same large group of premodern writers who viewed poverty of spirit as humility likewise understood it as the remedy for pride, and thus the first step on the path toward God.[10] In

---

Holy Gospel According to St. Luke, vol. 3 of *Blessed Theophylact's Explanation of the New Testament*, trans. Christopher Stade [House Springs, MO: Chrysostom Press, 1997]), 67.

7. E.g., Tertullian, *Of Patience* 11 (*ANF* 3:714). It also appears in Hilary of Poitiers (ca. 315–367), Gregory of Nyssa (ca. 335–394), Chrysostom (ca. 347–407), Chromatius of Aquileia (d. ca. 406), Cyril of Alexandria (d. 444), Augustine (354–430), the author of the *Opus Imperfectum* (ca. 425–430), and the eleventh-century Byzantine Theophylact of Ochrid. See also the list in Jacques Dupont, *Les évangélistes*, vol. 3 of *Les Béatitudes* (Paris: Gabalda, 1973), 399–411.

8. In his *Nicomachean Ethics*, Aristotle described greatness of soul (*megalopsychia*) as the virtuous mean between vanity (*chaunotētos*) and smallness of soul or humility (*mikropsychia*) (*Eth. nic.* IV.3.35, 37). The term "small-souled man" appears in the LCL translation, 225, 227.

9. Augustine, *De Doctrina Christiana* [*On Christian Doctrine*] 1.14.13, quoted in Susannah Ticciati, *A New Apophaticism: Augustine and the Redemption of Signs* (Leiden: Brill, 2015), 192.

10. Examples include Chrysostom, *Homilies on the Gospel of Saint Matthew* 15.3 (*NPNF*[1] 10:92); Cyril of Alexandria, Homily 27, in *Commentary on the Gospel of St. Luke*, trans. R. Payne

the late eleventh century, Theophylact of Ochrid echoed Augustine: "Since Adam fell through pride, Christ raises us up by humility."[11] The medieval septenaries (see chapter 2) usually associated the first beatitude with the virtue of humility and opposed it to the vice of pride.[12] It is the "queen of the virtues" for medieval thinkers not because it happens to be first in the Beatitudes—rather, for them it was first in the Beatitudes because it was the first virtue that laid the foundation for all the others.[13] Remember Mother Alexandra's claim that the first beatitude is the key that opens the entrance to the kingdom of God.

Some of these writers maintained a slender connection to the beatitude's material aspect by identifying pride as one of the particular perils of wealth. Tertullian colorfully described the "incentives of the rich" as "their pride, their pomp [*gloriam*], their love of the world, and their contempt of God."[14] In a sermon on the first beatitude, Augustine urged the rich not to be proud, for "nothing so easily generates pride as riches."[15] And Leo the Great assumed that the poor can acquire humility more easily than the rich.[16] While links to the material are often loosened or lost in this strand of interpretation, many others retain a connection.

Smith (Long Island, NY: Studion, 1983), 129; Gregory of Nyssa, *The Lord's Prayer*, 90–91; *Incomplete Commentary on Matthew [Opus Imperfectum]*, ed. Thomas C. Oden, trans. James A. Kellerman, Ancient Christian Texts 1 (Downers Grove, IL: IVP Academic, 2010), 85; Erasmus of Rotterdam, *Paraphrase on Matthew*, vol. 45 of *Collected Works of Erasmus*, trans. Dean Simpson (Toronto: University of Toronto Press, 2008), 84.

11. Theophylact of Ochrid, *The Explanation by Blessed Theophylact of the Holy Gospel According to St. Matthew*, vol. 1 of *Blessed Theophylact's Explanation of the New Testament*, trans. Christopher Stade (House Springs, MO: Chrysostom Press, 1994), 44.

12. Septenaries often followed the order of vices in Gregory the Great's *Morals on Job*, which began with pride. A few others, however, followed the order given by John Cassian, who placed gluttony first. A Latin poem from the Carolingian era contrasts a man who is poor in spirit with a man "given over to food" (V. S. Benfell III, "'Blessed are They That Hunger after Justice': From Vice to Beatitude in Dante's Purgatorio," in *Seven Deadly Sins: From Communities to Individuals*, ed. Richard Newhauser [Leiden: Brill, 2007], 188).

13. For humility as a personified virtue, see Colum Hourihane, ed., *Virtue and Vice: The Personifications in the Index of Christian Art* (Princeton: Princeton University Press, 2000), 230–39. Hildegard of Bingen's play *Ordo Virtutum* (*The Play of the Virtues*) depicts Humility (*Humilitas*) as the "queen" of the virtues (Scene 2, line 68 and line 72).

14. Tertullian, *Against Marcion* 4.15 (*ANF* 3:368).

15. Augustine, Sermon 53A.3–5, in Augustine, *Essential Sermons*, ed. Boniface Ramsey, trans. Edmund Hill, The Works of Saint Augustine: A Translation for the 21st Century (Hyde Park, NY: New City Press, 2007), 77–78. Augustine described poverty of spirit as the beginning of the Christian journey in *Confessions* 7.18.24, 20.26–21.27.

16. Leo the Great, *Sermons* 95.2 (*NPNF²* 12:203).

Trust and dependence on God (Isa 66:2)

Why did the ancient writers see "poor in spirit" and read "humble"? They found a precedent in some scriptural texts that linked a lowly spirit to humility. Some exegetes pointed to Prov 29:23, which contrasts lowliness of spirit with pride.[17] In rabbinic thought, *Abot.* 5:22 compares "a haughty mind and a proud spirit" to "a humble mind and a lowly spirit."[18]

But for the majority of interpreters in this strand of thought, one text from Isaiah appears over and over again as a warrant for viewing poverty of spirit as humility: God's declaration, "But this is the one to whom I will look, to the humble [Hebrew: *ʿāniy*] and contrite in spirit, who trembles at my word" (Isa 66:2). The Latin Vulgate translation, read by so many Western thinkers, strengthens the connection even further between the spiritually poor, the humble, and those who submit to God's word: "But to whom shall I have respect, but to him that is poor and little [Latin: *pauperculum*], and of a contrite spirit, and that trembles at my words?" When the unknown author of the fifth-century commentary *Opus Imperfectum* described humility as the ability to ask for God's help, he captured the predominant view, shared by Jerome (ca. 347–420), Chrysostom (ca. 349–407), Cyril of Alexandria (ca. 376–444), and so many others.[19]

Augustine's influential exegesis contributed to the widespread popularity of this view. Recall from chapter 2 that Augustine matched each beatitude to a gift of the Spirit (from Isa 11:2) and to a petition of the Lord's Prayer. In this case, he associated the poor in spirit with the fear of the Lord (the first gift of the Spirit) and with the petition "Hallowed be your name." The poor in spirit are those who fear the Lord with proper reverence, and who therefore

17. An illustrated version of the Beatitudes produced in 1868 links Prov 29:23 to the first beatitude: *The Beatitudes, Or the Blessings Promised by Our Lord in His Sermon on the Mount: Six Illustrations* (London: Thomas Nelson & Sons, 1868), n. p.

18. Quoted in Beryl Cohon, *Jacob's Well: Some Jewish Sources and Parallels to the Sermon on the Mount* (New York: Bookman Associates, 1956), 21. Samuel Lachs notes what he calls the "great confusion" in the MT between "*ani*" (poor) and "*anav*" (humble), an overlap that may have carried over into Greek renderings of the terms (Samuel Tobias Lachs, *A Rabbinic Commentary of the New Testament: The Gospels of Matthew, Mark, and Luke* [Hoboken, NJ: Ktav, 1987], 71).

19. *Incomplete Commentary on Matthew*, 85. Chrysostom, *Homilies on the Gospel of Saint Matthew* 15.2 (*NPNF* 10:92); Cyril of Alexandria, Frag. 27, Homilia 27: Lk 6,20, in Joseph Reuss, ed., *Lukas-Kommentare aus der griechischen Kirche* (Berlin: Akademie-Verlag, 1984), 65; Jerome, *Comm. Isa.* 6.34, in *Commentary on Isaiah; St. Jerome's Translation of Origen's Homilies 1–9 on Isaiah*, trans. Thomas P. Scheck, ACW 68 (Mahwah, NJ: The Newman Press, 2015), 320; Jerome cited Isa 14:28–30.

pray for God's name to be revered or hallowed. After Augustine, the link between poverty of spirit and fear of the Lord became firmly established in the exegetical stream. Centuries later, Thomas Aquinas concurred: "through fear a person reveres God and submits to him [and] is less inclined to delight in things apart from God."[20]

The view that poverty of spirit is dependence upon God remained prominent among Reformation-era interpreters and continues to be common in the twentieth and twenty-first centuries. This is one area in which Catholic and Reformer are in close agreement. Catholic humanist Erasmus of Rotterdam (1466–1536) described the person who embodies the first beatitude as someone "who claims nothing for himself, who yields to everyone, who is dissatisfied with himself... the spirit that distrusts itself and trusts God, that distrusts human supports and depends on heaven."[21] Likewise, Reformers John Calvin (1509–1564) and Huldrych Zwingli (1484–1531) both described poverty of spirit as humility.[22]

A generation later, Puritan preacher Robert Harris (1581–1658) wrote that spiritual poverty, or awareness of one's own "extreme need" of God, is the necessary first step toward the happiness of the Beatitudes: "Thus God undoes a man before He saves him, mars him before He makes him, takes him all to pieces and then joins him together forever." A person must empty herself before there is room for God.[23] In the words of twentieth-century evangelist Sherwood Wirt, poverty of spirit or self-emptying is the necessary condition for God's powerful action: "[God] cannot fill our cups with the Water of Life until they have been drained of all other waters."[24] Indeed, it's not uncommon

---

20. Thomas Aquinas, *Summa Theologica: Complete English Edition in Five Volumes*, trans. Fathers of the English Dominican Province (Westminster, MD: Christian Classics, 1948), IIa IIae q.19 a.12 ad.2, cited in Anton ten Klooster, *Thomas Aquinas on the Beatitudes: Reading Matthew, Disputing Grace and Virtue, Preaching Happiness* (Leuven: Peeters, 2018), 187. See also Ælfric, Homily I, 36, lines 181–83, quoted in Derek A. Olsen, *Reading Matthew with Monks: Liturgical Interpretation in Anglo-Saxon England* (Collegeville, MN: Liturgical Press, 2015), 167–68; and Hendrik Niclaes, *The first exhortation of H. N. to his children, and to the Family of Love: Likewise H. N. upon the Beatitudes, and the Seven Deadly Sins* (London: For Giles Calvert, 1656), 181–82.

21. Erasmus, *Paraphrase on Matthew*, 85.

22. John Calvin, *A Harmony of the Gospels Matthew, Mark and Luke*, vol. 1, ed. David W. Torrance and Thomas F. Torrance, trans. A. W. Morrison (Grand Rapids: Eerdmans, 1972), 1.169–70; for Zwingli, see Ulrich Luz, *Matthew 1–7*, trans. James E. Crouch, Hermeneia (Minneapolis: Fortress: 2007), 192n71.

23. Robert Harris, *The Way to True Happiness: Delivered in Twenty-Four Sermons upon the Beatitudes*, ed. Don Kistler (Morgan, PA: Soli Deo Gloria, 1998), 28–29, 32.

24. Sherwood E. Wirt, *Magnificent Promise: A Fresh View of the Beatitudes from the Cross* (Chicago: Moody Press, 1964), 3.

for exegetes from every century to connect poverty of spirit to the example of Christ's *kenōsis* or self-emptying in Phil 2:5–11.[25]

Another text often paired with the beatitude is Jesus's parable of the tax collector and the Pharisee (Luke 18:9–14). The tax collector's prayer "Lord, have mercy on me, a sinner!" is frequently taken to represent poverty of spirit. The idea that poverty of spirit is humble dependence on God and awareness of one's need of God, after the manner of the tax collector, persists into the modern day, in interpreters as varied as German New Testament scholar Günther Bornkamm (1905–1990), American evangelist Billy Graham (1918–2018), and Peruvian theologian Gustavo Gutiérrez (b. 1928).[26]

A popular nineteenth-century story for children illustrates the principle. Authors Susan Bogert Warner (1819–1885) and Anna Bartlett Warner (1827–1915) were American authors and sisters. Susan (under the pseudonym Elizabeth Wetherell) wrote the first American book that sold one million copies (*The Wide, Wide World*, in 1852), and Anna wrote part of the song "Jesus loves me, this I know."[27] In their story "The French Cap," a teacher arrives at a girls' boarding school with the express purpose of teaching the young students the

---

25. E.g., Cyril of Alexandria, Frag. 27, Homilia 27: Lk 6,20, in Reuss, ed., *Lukas-Kommentare*, 65; Gregory of Nyssa, *The Lord's Prayer*, 90–91; Cabasilas, *The Life in Christ*, trans. Carmino J. deCatanzaro (Crestwood, NY: St. Vladimir's Seminary Press, 1974), 6.11a (see pp. 176–78); Jeremiah Burroughs, *The Saints' Happiness* (Edinburgh: James Nichol, 1867; Soli Deo Gloria, 1988, 1992), 21; E. Stanley Jones, *The Christ of the Mount: A Working Philosophy of Life* (New York: Abingdon, 1931), 54–60; George Hunsinger, *The Beatitudes* (Mahwah, NJ: Paulist, 2015), 5; Liviu Barbu, "The 'Poor in Spirit' and Our Life in Christ: An Eastern Orthodox Perspective on Christian Discipleship," *Studies in Christian Ethics* 22, no. 3 (2009): 268–71; Michael H. Crosby, *Spirituality of the Beatitudes: Matthew's Vision for the Church in an Unjust World*, rev. ed. (Maryknoll, NY: Orbis Books, 2005), 44–45; Charles Gore, *The Sermon on the Mount: A Practical Exposition* (London: John Murray, 1907), 24. Perhaps most famously, Johann Baptist Metz devoted his entire (albeit little) book on *Poverty of Spirit* to the theme of *kenōsis* (Metz, *Poverty of Spirit*, trans. John Drury [Glen Rock, NJ: Newman Press, 1968]).

26. Günther Bornkamm, *Jesus of Nazareth*, trans. Irene McLuskey, Fraser McLuskey, and James M. Robinson (New York: Harper & Row, 1960), 76; Billy Graham, *The Secret of Happiness: Jesus' Teaching on Happiness as Expressed in the Beatitudes* (Garden City, NY: Doubleday, 1955), 14–15. Liberation theologian Gustavo Gutiérrez views the poor in spirit as "spiritual childhood," or a state of dependence on and openness to the will of God, but he also insists that spiritual childhood includes radical solidarity with the poor (Gutiérrez, *The God of Life*, trans. Matthew J. O'Connell [Maryknoll, NY: Orbis Books, 1991, 1998], 121–22). Liviu Barbu notes that contemporary Eastern Orthodox traditions often understand poverty of spirit as a humble attitude that recognizes "our total dependence on God" (Barbu, "The 'Poor in Spirit,'" 267–68).

27. Judith C. Reveal, "Warner, Susan Bogert and Anna Bartlett Warner," in *Women in World History: A Biographical Encyclopedia*, https://www.encyclopedia.com/women/encyclopedias -almanacs-transcripts-and-maps/warner-susan-bogert-and-anna-bartlett-warner.

meaning of the blessing on the poor in spirit. The teacher recites the parable of the tax collector and the Pharisee from Luke 18:9–14 (alongside 2 Chr 7:14; Ps 34:18; Isa 57:15, 61:1; Rev 3:17).

Two little girls named Annie are present for this lesson. When a prank goes terribly wrong, the two Annies suffer serious burns and are forced to convalesce together. One Annie (the Pharisee) is rich and proud and thinks she is a very good person; the other Annie (the tax collector) is poor and humble and knows that she is not good ("I am not good at all . . . but I trust in Jesus").[28] Although the story focuses on humble dependence on God's mercy, it retains a material element to the beatitude by linking the first Annie's pride with her material riches and the second Annie's humility with her actual poverty. A few years later, Lily Watson's short story about the beatitude (in her volume *A Garden of Girls*) makes the same connection: the poor, lower-class girl is humble; the rich girl is self-sufficient and arrogant.[29]

They're not alone in this connection. Many (but certainly not all) of the writers who describe poverty of spirit as humility also propose that material poverty disposes one toward spiritual poverty. This anticipates the Christian emphasis on the spiritual dangers of wealth (more on that below). For Flemish Jesuit Cornelius à Lapide (1567–1637) as for English Reformer William Tyndale, poverty of spirit is linked to material poverty in part because lack of possessions enables (or requires) a person to hope entirely in God.[30] The rich are more likely to be rich in goods *and* in spirit, because their wealth enables them to be self-sufficient; the poor are more likely to be poor in spirit because they depend on God and others. This relationship allows Luke's blessing on the poor to resurface rather than remain buried under the purely spiritual interpretation of humility alone. The connection between humility and material need also anticipates a much more modern interpretation, which mines the caves of Qumran for assistance in understanding the phrase "poor in spirit."

28. Susan Warner and Anna Bartlett Warner, *The Golden Ladder; Stories Illustrative of the Eight Beatitudes* (London: Frederick Warne, 1887), 37.

29. Lily Watson, *A Garden of Girls: Stories Illustrating the Beatitudes* (London: Religious Tract Society, 1893), 14–21.

30. Cornelius à Lapide, *The Holy Gospel According to Saint Matthew*, vol. 1 of *The Great Commentary of Cornelius à Lapide*, trans. Thomas W. Mossman, rev. Michael J. Miller (Fitzwilliam, NH: Loreto, 2008), 203; William Tyndale, *The Work of William Tyndale*, ed. G. E. Duffield (Philadelphia: Fortress, 1965), 195. So also Martin Luther, *The Sermon on the Mount*, vol. 21 of *Luther's Works*, ed. Jaroslav Pelikan (St. Louis: Concordia, 1956), 13; and Calvin, *Harmony of the Gospels* 5.3, pp. 169–70.

Crushed in spirit: the oppressed

It's not immediately obvious what Matthew means by "poor in spirit," since it's a phrase that occurs neither elsewhere in the New Testament nor in the Septuagint (the Greek Old Testament, or the LXX). Some modern scholars see parallels in the expressions "a crushed spirit" or "a humbled spirit" in the psalms (Ps 34:18/33:19 LXX; Ps 51:17/50:19 LXX), in Isa 66:2, and in at least one Qumran text (1QM XIV, 7).[31] For those who draw on these parallels, the poor in spirit are the Old Testament's *ănāwîm*, or "the dispossessed and abandoned ones in Israel on whose behalf the prophets speak (Isa 11:4; 29:19; 32:7; 61:1; Amos 2:7; 8:4; Zeph 2:3)."[32] From this starting point, interpretations then diverge in two directions.

The despondent

First, the "poor in spirit" understood as *ănāwîm* could mean those poor in spiritual resources: those who are "on the verge of giving up" or who have lost hope,[33] who are "fainthearted" or "despondent,"[34] who are "stripped even of their spirit,"[35] who are "at the end of [their] rope."[36] They are "the destitute, [the] abject in spirit,"[37] "the spiritual zeros—the spiritually bankrupt, deprived and deficient,"[38] or "those who are oppressed by the rich and powerful" (Pss 9:12; 35:10; Isa 49:13).[39]

31. E.g., Hans Dieter Betz, *The Sermon on the Mount*, Hermeneia (Minneapolis: Fortress, 1995), 111–12. For a list of the Qumran texts, see Betz, *Sermon on the Mount*, 116n178; and see Simon Légasse's analysis in Légasse, "Les pauvres en esprit et les 'volontaires' de Qumran," *NTS* 8 (1962): 336–45.

32. Mark Allan Powell, "Matthew's Beatitudes: Reversals and Rewards of the Kingdom," *CBQ* 58 (1996): 463.

33. Powell, "Matthew's Beatitudes," 463–64.

34. E. Best, "Matthew 5:3," *NTS* 6 (1960/61): 255–58.

35. William Domeris, "'Blessed are you . . .' (Matthew 5:1–12)," *Journal of Theology for South Africa* 73 (1990): 71.

36. *The Message* translation.

37. David Bentley Hart, *The New Testament: A Translation* (New Haven, CT: Yale University Press, 2017), 7; see also Timothy D. Howell, *The Matthean Beatitudes in Their Jewish Origins: A Literary and Speech Act Analysis* (New York: Lang, 2011), 181.

38. Dallas Willard, *The Divine Conspiracy: Rediscovering Our Hidden Life in God* (New York: HarperSanFrancisco, 1998), 100.

39. Michael Joseph Brown, "Matthew," in *True to Our Native Land: An African American New Testament Commentary*, ed. Brian K. Blount (Minneapolis: Fortress, 2007), 91.

This view often combines elements of material and spiritual poverty, but understands spiritual poverty not as humility but as desperation. Vittorio Macchioro, for example, followed Tertullian by preferring the translation "blessed are the beggars," which points the beatitude both to material poverty and to (as Macchioro wrote) "the spiritual annihilation" experienced by a person reduced to begging.[40] Why does Jesus declare the beggars blessed? Both poverty and its accompanying poverty of spirit are states of oppression that God promises to overturn.

This is, by and large, a view that emerged in the twentieth century and remains popular in scholarly discourse today. Art historian John Harvey suggests the prodigal son in Rembrandt's famous painting as a visual representative of this view. The prodigal son represents the poor in spirit because he is "bent down, humbled, afflicted, and miserable."[41] Yet the prodigal son's act of kneeling at the feet of his father points to the second possibility: the ʿănāwîm as the reverent poor.

The righteous poor

For many modern scholars, the link between poverty and piety was forged in the Old Testament and other Jewish texts that use "the poor" to refer synonymously to "the just" or to Israelites who remain faithful to the law (as in Isa 29:19, 57:18; Ps 34:15–19; Pss. Sol. 10:7).[42] The tendency to use the poor as a synonym for the righteous appears also in Qumran writings (e.g., 1QH^{a}VI, 14–15 and 4Q521 2 II, 5–6).[43] When the Qumran community referred to itself as "the poor," this designation typically referred to their sense of themselves as a faithful remnant community alongside their "corporate submission to the will of God."[44]

---

40. Vittorio Macchioro, "The Meaning of the First Beatitude," *JR* 12, no. 1 (1932): 48. Macchioro approved of Tertullian's translation "*beati mendici*." Similarly, Schlatter: "Jesus spricht von der inwendigen Not der Darbenden, aber eben der Darbenden, derer, die im Ringen um die Lebensmittel auch in ihrem inwendigen Leben verarmen und leiden" (Adolf Schlatter, *Der Evangelist Matthäus: Seine Sprache, sein Ziel, seine Selbständigkeit* [Stuttgart: Calwer Verlag, 1959], 133).

41. John Harvey, *The Bible as Visual Culture* (Sheffield: Sheffield Phoenix, 2013), 136–37.

42. Émile Puech, "4Q525 et les pericopes des Beatitudes en Ben Sira et Matthieu," *RB* 98, no. 1 (1991): 103; Lachs, *A Rabbinic Commentary*, 71; Bornkamm, *Jesus of Nazareth*, 202n23.

43. Puech, "4Q525," 103–4. David Flusser argues that Matt 5:3–5 (or the source for these verses) likely "originated in the Dead Sea Sect or in some milieu close to it" (Flusser, "Blessed are the Poor in Spirit . . . ," *IEJ* 10, no. 1 [1960]: 1–13).

44. H. Benedict Green, *Matthew, Poet of the Beatitudes* (Sheffield: Sheffield Academic, 2001),

The theme of the poor as those who humbly depend on God is already found in other Jewish texts. Jewish writings from the Old Testament and the Second Temple period describe the "poor" variously as the materially poor; as the abused, mistreated, and humbled; and as those who put all their help in God and who await the reign of the Messiah (e.g., Ps 72:2–4; Pss. Sol. 5:13, 18:3).[45] In the Old Testament, the crushed in spirit are those who await God's deliverance (Ps 34:19, Isa 57:15).[46]

This second view of the *'ănāwîm* creates a potential bridge between Matt 5:3 and Luke 6:20, since it suggests that the terms "poor" and "poor in spirit" could have had much the same connotation within the thought world of first-century Judaism.[47] The two versions of the beatitude are then approximately equivalent because they reflect the relationship between poverty and dependence upon God that Scripture often assumes. Contemporary scholar Paul John Isaak, for example, placing the beatitude in his African context, writes that destitution "can and does lead to a deep dependence upon God (Luke 6:20)."[48]

Even in Luke's Gospel, which modern scholars often see as more focused on material poverty, "the poor" is not merely an economic category but has spiritual overtones (Luke 1:46–53; 14:25–33).[49] Mary's song of reversal places the poor and hungry in parallel with "those who fear [God]"; their opposites

183. Green, however, didn't think this is what Matthew had in mind. Zeph 3:11–13 also describes the "poor" ("*ana*") as the remnant of Israel and contrasts them with the proud and haughty. For an exploration of the spiritual and religious dimensions of poverty language in OT, Second Temple Judaism, and NT, see David J. Armitage, *Theologies of Poverty in the World of the New Testament*, WUNT, 2/423 (Tübingen: Mohr Siebeck, 2016), 45–47, 159–75, 216–18, 248.

45. M.-J. Lagrange, *Évangile selon Saint Luc*, 2nd ed. (Paris: Gabalda, 1921), 187.

46. Adrian M. Leske, "The Beatitudes, Salt and Light in Matthew and Luke," *The SBLSP* 30 (1991): 826.

47. Jack R. Lundbom, *Jesus' Sermon on the Mount: Mandating a Better Righteousness* (Minneapolis: Fortress, 2015), 96; Jacques Dupont, *Le problème littéraire—Les deux versions du Sermon sur la montagne et des béatitudes*, vol. 1 of *Les Béatitudes* (Bruges, Belgium: Abbaye de Saint-André, 1958), 217, 250; Craig S. Keener, *A Commentary on the Gospel of Matthew* (Grand Rapids: Eerdmans, 1999), 168–69; Frederick W. Danker, *Jesus and the New Age: A Commentary on St. Luke's Gospel*, rev. ed. (Philadelphia: Fortress, 1988), 139; Brian Wintle, "Matthew," in *South Asia Bible Commentary*, ed. Brian Wintle (Rajasthan, India: Open Door Publications; Grand Rapids: Zondervan; Cumbria, UK: Langham Partnership, 2015), 1230.

48. Paul John Isaak, "Luke," in *Africa Bible Commentary*, ed. Tokunboh Adeyemo, 2nd ed. (Nairobi, Kenya: WordAlive; Grand Rapids: Zondervan, 2010), 1144.

49. W. D. Davies and Dale C. Allison Jr., *A Critical and Exegetical Commentary on the Gospel According to Saint Matthew*, ICC 1 (London: T&T Clark, 1988), 1:444; Herman Hendrickx, *Ministry in Galilee (Luke 3:1–6:49)*, vol. 2A of *The Third Gospel for the Third World* (Collegeville, MN: Liturgical Press, 1997), 289.

are the powerful and the proud, who do not. Likewise the rich in Luke are not only materially wealthy, but they are also the proud and self-sufficient (and sometimes the unjust): absorbed in the pleasures of wealth, they have no desire for God.[50] Other obvious examples are the rich fool who stores up treasures for himself but fails to be "rich toward God" (Luke 12:16–21) and the wealthy ruler who will not follow Jesus because he cannot renounce his riches (Luke 18:18–25). The tax collector Zacchaeus, on the other hand, represents a wealthy man who does respond to Jesus's call, by promising to give half of his possessions to the poor and pay back fourfold those whom he had defrauded in his duties as a tax collector (highlighting again the Lukan connection between wealth and injustice) (Luke 19:1–10). Their clearest counterpart is the poor widow who puts two small coins into the temple treasury, giving to God out of her poverty (Luke 21:21).[51]

Resistance to blessing all poor

Many patristic writers resonate with this second strand; for them, Jesus is declaring blessed the reverent poor, that is, the poor who put their trust in God. But unlike the modern writers just discussed, who tend to see "the poor" and "the reverent poor" as the same category, these ancient writers did not. Instead, they resisted the idea that Jesus blesses *all* the poor because they insisted that not all of the poor are virtuous.

Since they typically understood the Beatitudes as virtues, this excluded for them the idea that Jesus could be blessing a nonvirtuous state. Instead, they distinguished between the ungodly poor and the faithful poor. Origen was willing to concede the possibility that "the Word knows some poverty altogether counted blessed and some riches altogether blameable," but he concluded tartly, "not even any casual speaker would have praised the poor indiscriminately, many of them being of very worthless character."[52] This view

---

50. Lagrange, *Évangile selon Saint Luc*, 191. See also Luke Timothy Johnson, *The Gospel of Luke*, SP 3 (Collegeville, MN: Liturgical Press, 1991), 108; Clarence Jordan, *Sermon on the Mount*, rev. ed. (Valley Forge, PA: Judson, 1952), 21.

51. This text functions as both praise of the widow's trust in God, and an indictment of the scribes, since immediately before Jesus's observation about the widow he condemns the scribes as the ones who "devour widows' houses" (Luke 20:47).

52. Origen, *Against Celsus* 6.16 (ANF 4:581). As another example, the author of the Pseudo-Clementine Homilies also distinguished between the sinful or ungodly poor and the faithful poor, in *Pseudo-Clementine Homilies* 15.10 (ANF 8:311).

occasionally appears today in both Catholic and Protestant exegesis. Joseph Ratzinger writes vividly that "the heart of those who have nothing can be hardened, poisoned, evil—interiorly full of greed for material things, forgetful of God, covetous of external possessions."[53] Preacher Lloyd-Jones wrote, more mildly, "Poverty does not guarantee spirituality."[54]

The North African church father Tertullian (ca. 155–240) was an outlier among his peers. According to Tertullian, Jesus blesses those who live in actual material poverty. The ancient scholar arrived at this conclusion because of his interest in demonstrating the unity of the Old and New Testaments. In the Latin Vulgate, Luke 6:20 reads, *Beati pauperes* ("Blessed are the poor"), but Tertullian gave the phrase as *Beati mendici*—"Blessed are the needy," or "Blessed are the beggars."[55]

In order to refute Marcion's argument that the Creator God of Israel was a vengeful Old Testament God and not the loving Father of Jesus Christ, Tertullian wrote that in this beatitude Christ displays the attributes of the Creator, "who ever in language of the same sort loved, consoled, protected and avenged the beggar, and the poor, and the humble, and the widow, and the orphan."[56] In other words, Tertullian noticed that the Old Testament frequently portrays God as the defender of the poor, and extended that insight into his reading of the beatitude. In this way, Tertullian was the forerunner of later exegetes like liberation theologians, who read the Beatitudes through the lens of God's preferential option for the poor, as well as some radical Reformers, who argued that Jesus blessed the literal poor and who used the beatitude to advocate for communal ownership of goods.[57]

---

53. Joseph Ratzinger (Pope Benedict XVI), *Jesus of Nazareth: From the Baptism in the Jordan to the Transfiguration*, trans. Adrian J. Walker (New York: Doubleday, 2007), 77.

54. D. Martyn Lloyd-Jones, *Studies in the Sermon on the Mount*, vol. 1 (Grand Rapids: Eerdmans, 1960), 43. John MacEvilly wrote more sharply that many poor may be robbers and liars (MacEvilly, *An Exposition of the Gospels* [Dublin: W. B. Kelly; London: Simpkin, Marshall & Co., 1876], 76).

55. Tertullian, *Against Marcion* 4.14 (ANF 3:365).

56. Cites several examples including Psalm 82:3–4 (Tertullian, *Against Marcion* 4.14 [ANF 3:365]). Arthur Carr quoted Psalm 72:12–13 to suggest that in the messianic kingdom, "it is especially characteristic of the King that he cares for the poor" (Arthur Carr, *The Gospel according to St. Luke* [London: Rivingtons, 1875], 77).

57. So Peter Walpot (Moravian minister and bishop of the Hutterite community, d. 1578), in Walpot, *The Great Article Book: On Peace and Joint Property* 12:181, quoted in Beth Kreitzer, ed., *Luke*, Reformation Commentary on Scripture, New Testament 3 (Downers Grove, IL: IVP Academic, 2015), 135–36.

Blessed are those who help the poor

Liberation theologians typically agree with Tertullian that Jesus's blessing is for the materially poor, but they vigorously disagree with those who see any link (or lack thereof) between the poor and virtue; for them, the problem is not the moral status of the poor but that the state of poverty itself is ungodly.

Mexican theologian Elsa Tamez (b. 1950) is a good representative of this view. She reads the Beatitudes through the lens of the biblical condemnation of the rich (Jas 5:1–6) and God's identification with the poor (e.g., Prov 14:31, 17:5). Tamez warns against the danger of spiritualizing biblical passages about the poor by extolling the advantages of poverty. "We must always keep in mind, therefore, that poverty is an unworthy state that must be changed. I repeat: poverty is not a virtue but an evil that reflects the socioeconomic conditions of inequality in which people live."

She echoes Tertullian when she writes, "Poverty is a challenge to God the Creator; because of the insufferable conditions under which the poor live, God is obliged to fight at their side." The beatitude is descriptive, not prescriptive; it promises a reversal to the suffering. The poor are blessed not because their poverty is desirable but "because the reign of God is at hand and because the eschatological promise of justice is drawing ever nearer to fulfillment and, with it, the end of poverty."[58]

Some modern interpreters take this line of thought a step further. Like Tamez, Capuchin-Franciscan priest Michael Crosby described material poverty as ungodly. Unlike Tamez, he interpreted the Matthean "poor in spirit" as recognition of an inner poverty that leads to submitting to God's leading and doing good to those in need.[59] For him, the two versions of the beatitude taken together suggest a reversal that might come about through human action; by doing good to those in need, the poor in spirit might help relieve the material deprivation of the poor. Likewise for Reformed Protestant theologian George Hunsinger, the beatitude presses those who are poor in spirit but not in material goods toward "responsible action" to address global poverty.[60] As African theologian Paul John Isaak writes, "We are responsible for formulating concrete ethics and principles and policies that will ensure blessedness for the poor today."[61]

---

58. Elsa Tamez, *Bible of the Oppressed* (Maryknoll, NY: Orbis Books, 1982), 73–74. So also Hendrickx, *Third Gospel*, 276–77.

59. Crosby, *Spirituality*, 40–41, 45, 49.

60. Hunsinger, *Beatitudes*, 11.

61. Isaak, "Luke," 1242. See also Segundo Galilea, *The Beatitudes: To Evangelize as Jesus Did*,

Similarly, for Chinese theologian Wu Leichuan (1869–1944), the beatitude points to "a society of economic equality, where all work hard and receive what they need, without disparity between the rich and the poor." He placed the Lukan blessing on the poor alongside Matt 6:33 ("Seek first the kingdom . . . and all that you need will be added to you"). Jesus's teaching encourages not only help for the poor but the building of "a new society with economic justice for all."[62] God favors those in material poverty and promises to relieve their suffering. Blessed are those who help the poor—because that's what God does.[63]

The identification of poverty as an evil, as a sign of a fallen world, provides a helpful counterbalance to the earlier concerns about the moral status of the poor, which too often have shaded into Christian contempt for the poor. The mild observation "poverty does not guarantee spirituality" can all too easily drift into a belief that "poverty hinders holiness." One need think only of the saying "Cleanliness is next to godliness"—or read any number of disapproving upper-class indictments of the squalor or laziness of the poor—to see how an apparently innocuous belief has had harmful applications.[64]

Woe to the rich! The dangers of wealth

On the other hand, if poverty is a certain kind of evil, riches aren't an unmitigated good either. Instead, wealth is viewed with deep suspicion by Scripture

---

trans. Robert R. Barr (Maryknoll, NY: Orbis Books, 1984), 20; and Danker, *Jesus and the New Age*, 140–41. Bernard Häring proposes as an extension of the beatitude: "Blessed are they who serve the poor and work to eliminate the conditions that oppress them" (Häring, *The Blessed Beatitudes: Salt and Light* [Liguori, MO: Liguori, 1999], 16).

62. John Y. H. Yieh, "Reading the Sermon on the Mount in China: A Hermeneutical Inquiry into Its History of Reception," in *Reading Scriptures in China*, ed. Chlöe Starr (London: T&T Clark, 2008), 147.

63. One of George Frederic Handel's anthems is titled "Blessed Are They That Considereth the Poor" (HWV 268, "The Foundling Hospital Anthem").

64. Jerry Falwell: "Why have Americans been able to do more to help people in need around the world than any other country in history? It's because of free enterprise, freedom, ingenuity, entrepreneurism and wealth. A poor person never gave anyone a job. A poor person never gave anybody charity, not of any real volume. It's just common sense to me." Joe Helm, "Jerry Falwell Jr. Can't Imagine Trump 'Doing Anything That's Not Good for the Country,'" *Washington Post* (January 1, 2019), https://www.washingtonpost.com/lifestyle/magazine/jerry-falwell-jr-cant-imagine-trump-doing-anything-thats-not-good-for-the-country/2018/12/21/6affc4c4-f19e-11e8-80d0-f7e1948d55f4_story.html.

(Mic 6:12; Matt 6:24, 19:23; 1 Tim 6:10–11) and by early Christians alike. For premodern writers, poverty may not guarantee spirituality, but riches certainly do not. In fact, early Christian writers had a lively sense of the spiritual perils of wealth, which shaped their exegesis of the first beatitude.

Luke's version of the beatitude and its corresponding woe provided special ammunition for this perspective. Depending on when James was written, it might be considered the earliest "inner-canonical" exegesis of Luke's beatitude. Benedict Green saw Jas 2:5 as an allusion to the beatitude, since in that text "the poor in the world" are "heirs of the kingdom that [God] has promised to those who love him."[65] In any case, it contains interesting echoes of the first beatitude:

> Jas 2:5: "Has not God chosen the poor [*ptōchos*] in the world to be rich [*plousios*] in faith and to be heirs of the kingdom [*basileia*] that he has promised to those who love him?"

> Luke 6:20: "Blessed are you who are poor [*ptōchos*], for yours is the kingdom [*basileia*] of God." / Matt 5:3: "Blessed are the poor [*ptōchos*] in spirit, for theirs is the kingdom [*basileia*] of heaven."

> Jas 5:1: "Come now, you rich [*plousios*] people, weep [*klaiō*] and wail for the miseries that are coming to you."

> Luke 6:24a, 25c: "But woe to you who are rich [*plousios*] . . . for you will mourn and weep [*klaiō*]."

Like many Christians after him, James associates "the poor in the world" with those who are "rich in faith." And he also has some harsh words for the rich that echo Luke's woe. Tertullian follows in James's footsteps.

It's no surprise that Tertullian, who viewed the first beatitude through the lens of God's special care for the poor, also pointed to the potential dangers of wealth. Tertullian conceded that the rich are capable of doing works of justice and charity, but argued that there are "serious faults [*vitia*] which accompany riches."[66] In his discussion of whether Christians should flee in times of persecution, Tertullian quoted Christ's blessing on the poor (Luke 6:20) to argue that Christians should be willing to give up their wealth (and even their lives)

---

65. Green, *Matthew, Poet*, 269–70.
66. Tertullian, *Against Marcion* 4.15 (ANF 3:368).

rather than buy their way out of persecution. "For who will serve mammon [wealth] more than the man whom mammon has ransomed?"[67]

Ambrose of Milan (ca. 339–397) issued an even fiercer condemnation of the rich in "On Naboth," a sermon based on the story of King Ahab and Queen Jezebel, who arrange for the poor man Naboth to be falsely accused and stoned to death so that they might acquire his vineyard (1 Kgs 21). "The story of Naboth," said Ambrose, "is old in time but daily in practice. For who of the rich does not daily covet the goods of others? Who of the wealthy does not strive to drive off the poor man from his little acre and turn out the needy from the boundaries of his ancestral fields?" (*De Nabuthae* 1.1).[68] To those who might object that people are poor through their own fault or because God has cursed them, Ambrose quoted Luke's version of the beatitude (Luke 6:20) (*De Nabuthae* 8.40).[69]

For Ambrose's Eastern contemporary Gregory of Nyssa (ca. 335–395), the blessing on the poor in spirit encourages the pursuit of "the spiritual wealth" of the virtues and necessarily involves the rejection of material wealth. Because earthly riches are a burden and hinder the ascent of the soul to God, one must shake them off in order to begin to ascend toward God on the "ladder" of the Beatitudes: "Gold is a heavy thing . . . but virtue is light and bears souls upwards."[70]

For these thinkers, wealth itself hinders one's wholehearted pursuit of God, a view that explains why Jesus blesses the poor. It also accords with the later medieval emphasis on voluntary poverty—if wealth enslaves, then poverty could be a means of freedom. Jesus, after all, promises the inheritance of the kingdom to the poor, and warns that it will be difficult for a rich man to enter into that same kingdom (Matt 19:23).

Voluntary poverty

Meditation on the spiritual dangers of wealth and the blessedness of the poor led naturally into the view that the first beatitude was commending the volun-

67. Tertullian, *De Fuga* 1.12 (*ANF* 4:123).

68. Ambrose of Milan, *De Nabuthae* [*On Naboth*]: *A Commentary, with an Introduction and Translation*, trans. Martin R. P. McGuire (Washington, DC: Catholic University of America Press, 1927), 47.

69. Ambrose, *De Nabuthae*, 73.

70. Gregory of Nyssa, *The Lord's Prayer*, 89, 95. See also Clement, *Who Is the Rich Man* 17 (*ANF* 2:595).

tary renunciation of worldly goods. Alongside the beatitude, the early church fathers and mothers cited Jesus's uncompromising teachings on renouncing worldly goods in order to serve God: "Go, sell your possessions, and give the money to the poor" (Matt 19:21); "Do not store up for yourselves treasures on earth" (Matt 6:19); and "You cannot serve God and wealth" (Matt 6:24).[71] They also had the example of Christ himself, who—though being rich—became poor for the sake of salvation (2 Cor 8:9).

This all led to an understanding that Christ was declaring blessed those who had voluntarily chosen poverty for his sake, an interpretation that appears as early as the writings of Clement of Alexandria (ca. 150–215), Ephrem the Syrian (ca. 306–373), and Jerome (ca. 347–420).[72] As the monk Cassian wrote, recording the teaching of Egyptian hermit Abba Isaac, poverty and poverty of spirit (humility) intertwine when one is dependent continually both on the generosity of others and on God's help.[73]

This interpretation thus preserves a material component to the beatitude. But it also sometimes tries to balance the material aspect with an acknowledgement that involuntary poverty is not a good or desirable state in and of itself. For example, early Jesuit Juan Maldonado (1533–1583) accepted Tertullian's judgment that the first beatitude referred to the materially poor or "the beggars" (Maldonado could read Greek, and he pointed out that the Greek word *ptōchos* in Matt 5:3 and Luke 6:20 means material destitution). But Maldonado also insisted that Christ added "in spirit" to show that "compulsory poverty is not a blessing, but a misery"; instead, Christ is only blessing those who undertake poverty voluntarily in order to give to the poor and then follow "the poor and naked Christ." Maldonado made Christ's saying about wealth and the kingdom even more stringent, claiming, "it is *impossible* [rather than merely difficult] for a rich man to enter the kingdom of heaven."[74]

---

71. Matt 19:21 is cited in Basil of Caesarea, *Shorter Rules* 205 (PG 31:1217C–D). Matt 6:19–20 and Matt 6:24 are cited by Clare of Assisi in "First Letter to Blessed Agnes of Prague," in *Francis and Clare: The Complete Works*, trans. Regis Armstrong and Ignatius C. Brady (New York: Paulist, 1982), 192–93.

72. Clement of Alexandria, *Stromata* 4.6 (*ANF* 2:415); Ephrem the Syrian, *St. Ephrem's Commentary on Tatian's Diatessaron*, trans. Carmel McCarthy (Oxford: Oxford University Press, 1993), 6.1b, see also 6.5; and Jerome, *Commentary on Matthew*, trans. Thomas P. Scheck, FC 117 (Washington, DC: Catholic University of America, 2008), 75.

73. Cassian, "The Conference of Cassian," in *Western Asceticism*, ed. Owen Chadwick, Library of Christian Classics Ichthus Edition (Philadelphia: Westminster, 1958), Conf. 10.11 (p. 243).

74. Juan Maldonado, *S. Matthew's Gospel, Chapters I to XIV*, vol. 1 of *A Commentary on the*

Maldonado's identity as a member of the Society of Jesus (the Jesuit order) highlights an important element of this interpretation. It was, not surprisingly, an especially prominent interpretation in monastic communities, both for those who owned communal property (the monastic orders) and those who renounced ownership altogether and begged to support themselves (the mendicant orders).[75] To be sure, it wasn't the *only* interpretation among monastics or mendicants.

Francis of Assisi (ca. 1181–1226), for example, declared that those who practice "much abstinence and many mortifications of their bodies" but are quick to anger are not poor in spirit. Instead, "a person who is truly poor in spirit hates himself (cf. Luke 14:26) and loves those who strike him on the cheek (cf. Mt. 5:39)."[76] But it was far more common for monastic writers to interpret Jesus's blessing on the poor (and/or poor in spirit) as reference to those who had renounced all their worldly goods for Christ's sake, just as they themselves had. It's also an interpretation that goes relatively quiet in post-Reformation and modern Protestant scholarship, likely because of Protestant resistance to monastic vows, which included voluntary poverty.[77]

Holy Gospels, trans. and ed. George J. Davie (London, UK: John Hodges, 1888), 132, emphasis added.

75. Basil of Caesarea, *The Long Rules* 20, in Saint Basil, *Ascetical Works*, trans. M. Monica Wagner, FC 9 (New York: Fathers of the Church, 1950), 277; Bernard of Clairvaux, "First Sermon for the Feast of All Saints. On the Eight Beatitudes," *St. Bernard's Sermons for the Seasons and Principal Festivals of the Year*, vol. 3 (Westminster, MD: Carroll, 1950), 338–40; Clare, "First Letter to Blessed Agnes," 190–94; Carolyn Muessig, "Preaching the Beatitudes in the Late Middle Ages: Some Mendicant Examples," *Studies in Christian Ethics* 22, no. 2 (2009): 138; Hildegard of Bingen, Homily 57 and Homily 58, *Homilies on the Gospels*, trans. Beverly Mayne Kienzle (Collegeville, MN: Liturgical Press, 2011), 201; Cornelius à Lapide, *The Holy Gospel According to Saint Matthew*, 197. Jacques Bénigne Bossuet wrote that all Christians are under the obligation to practice poverty of spirit as detachment from earthly goods, but that "the humble Religious must be further" and rejoice in their renunciation of all earthly goods (Bossuet, *The Sermon on the Mount*, trans. F. M. Capes [London: Longmans, Green: 1900], 6–7). Meister Eckhart (mis)quoted Matt 5:3 as "Blessed are the poor" and connected it to Luke 14:33 ("So therefore, none of you can become my disciple if you do not give up all your possessions") (Eckhart von Hochheim, *Meister Eckhart: Teacher and Preacher*, ed. Bernard McGinn [Mahwah, NJ: Paulist, 1986], 220).

76. Francis of Assisi, "Admonition 14," in *Francis and Clare: The Complete Works*, trans. Regis Armstrong and Ignatius C. Brady (New York: Paulist, 1982), 32.

77. E.g., Edward Stillingfleet wrote in 1673 that false teachers turned the beatitude into a blessing on those who "vow poverty, and leave the world" (Stillingfleet, *A sermon preached November 5, 1673, at St. Margarets Westminst by Edward Stillingfleet*, 2nd ed. [London: Robert White, for Henry Mortlock, 1674], 25). Not all post-Reformation writers rejected the theme of voluntary poverty. While Puritan preacher Increase Mather declared that involuntary poverty is a misery and "an evil to be deprecated," he praised those who renounce wealth for the sake of

The voluntary element means that this interpretation had a spiritual aspect to it alongside the material. Throughout the medieval era, it was common to interpret the blessing on the poor in spirit as a reference *both* to humility and to voluntary poverty.[78] This was a move already made by Jerome (ca. 347–420), whom Thomas Aquinas (1225–1274) cited as support when he explained that "poor in spirit" applies to both humility and material poverty.[79]

Unlike Jerome, Aquinas also distinguished between an inner disposition toward wealth (renunciation) and actual poverty (abandonment); the first "is necessary for salvation" whereas the second "belongs to evangelical perfection."[80] That is, every Christian is required to be poor in spirit inwardly by being humble, generous, and detached toward whatever wealth they may have, whereas those who have taken religious vows must be poor in spirit through the outward action of abandoning their worldly goods.

In other words, as Christopher Franks explains, "Voluntary poverty displays a material pattern of life that actualizes the direction in which poverty of spirit points."[81] Carolyn Muessig points out that this was typical of medieval thinkers, for whom "the outward action is what shows the inner disposition of the person."[82] A modern writer, perhaps not incidentally another monastic, picked up this theme by describing poverty of spirit as a humble confidence in God and an inner renunciation that remains "illusory and vacuous" without expressing itself in actual, voluntary material poverty.[83]

Even for those who do not share this particular writer's view that the beatitude commends voluntary (or vowed) poverty, it serves as a pointed reminder

---

Christ, as in Heb 11:26 (Mather, *Sermons Wherein Those Eight Characters of the Blessed Commonly Called the Beatitudes Are Opened and Applied in Fifteen Discourses* [Boston: B. Green, for Daniel Henchman, 1718], Sermon 1).

78. Brigitta Stoll, *De Virtute in Virtutem: zur Auslegungs- und Wirkungsgeschichte der Bergpredigt in Kommentaren, Predigten und hagiographischer Literatur von der Merowingerzeit bis um 1200* (Tübingen: Mohr Siebeck, 1988), 202.

79. Jerome, *Commentary on Matthew*, 75. Thomas Aquinas, *Commentary on the Gospel of Matthew, Chapters 1–12*, trans. Jeremy Holmes and Beth Mortensen, ed. The Aquinas Institute, Biblical Commentaries 33 (Lander, WY: The Aquinas Institute for the Study of Sacred Doctrine, 2013), C.5 L.2.415, 416. See also Thomas Aquinas, *Summa Theologica*, IIa IIae q.19 a.12; and Gregory of Palamas, *Homilies* 15.5 (PG 151:396A).

80. Christopher A. Franks, *He Became Poor: The Poverty of Christ and Aquinas's Economic Teachings* (Grand Rapids: Eerdmans, 2009), 114.

81. Franks, *He Became Poor*, 114.

82. Muessig, "Preaching the Beatitudes," 139. Similarly, Ælfric argued that even the materially rich can be spiritually poor, but that those "most worthy of emulation" are the materially *and* spiritually poor, including monks (Olsen, *Reading Matthew with Monks*, 168).

83. Galilea, *The Beatitudes*, 34–36, quotation on 36.

to those who view the beatitude through an entirely spiritual lens. Humility or humble trust in God may turn out to be illusory for those who simultaneously cling to riches.

Poverty as inevitable rather than voluntary

For some post-Reformation Protestants, the poverty declared blessed by Jesus was not voluntarily chosen but was an inevitable outcome of choosing to follow Jesus. This reverses the relationship proposed earlier between the *'ănāwîm* and the reverent—the poor are not pious because they are poor; they are poor because they are pious. A hint of this view appears in Martin Luther's companion Philip Melanchthon (1497–1560), who wrote that the Beatitudes "[begin] with poverty because it is the commonest misery of the pious."[84]

This approach comes to full flower in the work of German theologian Dietrich Bonhoeffer (1906–1945), who saw the poverty of the first beatitude as a result of responding to Christ's call. In Bonhoeffer's words, the disciples "are the 'poor' *tout court* (Luke 6.20)," because they have renounced everything to respond to Christ's call and to follow him. To be sure, he agreed with his monastic forebears that the poverty in view here is a renunciation and not a natural state. But the call of Christ, the way of discipleship, is prior for Bonhoeffer, and it includes *every* true follower of Christ. Once one chooses to follow, one will inevitably (and not simply out of choice) end up renouncing everything in order to do so.

For Bonhoeffer, there is no material difference between Matthew's "poor in spirit" and Luke's "poor," because both describe those who respond to "the call and promise of Jesus."[85] Bonhoeffer adopted Luther's view that Jesus did not forbid ownership of property per se, which meant that Christ was not *commanding* all of his disciples to give up everything. But like his ancient predecessors he also warned, "Worldly possessions tend to turn the hearts of the disciples away from Jesus."[86]

Centuries before Bonhoeffer, Nonconformist minister Matthew Henry (1662–1714) proposed the same interpretation of the beatitude.[87] Both Henry

---

84. Melanchthon, *Annotations on the Gospel of Matthew* 14:567–68, quoted in Kreitzer, ed., *Luke*, 135.

85. Dietrich Bonhoeffer, *The Cost of Discipleship* (New York: Simon & Schuster, 1995), 106–7. So also Hendrickx, *Third Gospel*, 271–72.

86. Bonhoeffer, *Cost of Discipleship*, 174.

87. Matthew Henry, *Matthew to John*, vol. 5 of *An Exposition of the Old and New Testament* (New York: Revell, n.d. [1708–1710?]), comment on Luke 6:20, section I.1.

and Bonhoeffer experienced tension with an established, national church—Bonhoeffer with the National German Church during the Nazi regime, and Henry with the Church of England during a time when "Nonconformist" Protestants were clashing with the established church. Both authors could look to the gospels to see that Jesus's disciples were the poor and the hungry, since they had left behind fathers and fishing nets and toll collectors' tables to follow a man who had no place to lay his head. But they could also look to the situation of their own fellow Christians, in Bonhoeffer's case to those who dared to oppose the Nazi regime and break with the national church—driven underground, refugees from their homes, imprisoned, and even executed, as Bonhoeffer himself was. "[D]iscipleship with a deviant like Jesus is costly," as contemporary New Testament scholar Herman Hendrickx says of the first disciples.[88]

Most of the interpretations encountered so far have retained a material aspect to the two versions of the first beatitude. But for other writers—many more others—the issue is not wealth itself, but one's attitude toward it.

Detachment

Despite Ambrose's strident condemnation of the wealthy, he exhorted the rich not to renounce wealth entirely but to use it rightly, which for him meant giving generously and not desiring riches too much. Similarly, and even more optimistically regarding the right use of wealth, Clement of Alexandria wrote that riches that benefit our neighbors are not to be thrown away, but must be used for good. In order for riches to be used rightly, the rich person must be virtuous and good, renouncing the passions of the soul, especially the desire for wealth.[89]

For Clement, the person who is poor in spirit is the one who holds possessions lightly "as the gifts of God; and ministers from them to the God who gives them for the salvation of men; and knows that he possesses them more for the sake of the brethren than his own; and is . . . not the slave of the things he possesses; and does not carry them about in his soul, nor bind and circumscribe his life within them," and who "is able with cheerful mind to bear

88. Hendrickx, *Third Gospel*, 276.

89. Ambrose, *Gospel according to Saint Luke*, 5.53, 5.64, 5.69. Similarly Peter Chrysologus (406–450): almsgiving "raises the heart of a man into heaven," while greed "buries it in the earth" (Chrysologus, "Sermon 22 on Luke 12:34," in *Selected Sermons*, trans. George E. Ganss, FC 17 [Washington, DC: Catholic University of America Press, 1953], 67).

their removal equally with abundance." While Clement knew that riches have the potential to fetter a person "in the toils of the world," he believed that greed provides the chains, not the riches themselves.[90] The view that poverty of spirit indicates detachment toward wealth persists into the Reformation era in the writing of Genevan Reformer John Calvin (1509–1564), English Reformer William Tyndale (ca. 1494–1536), and Spanish Jesuit Luis de la Puente (1554–1624). It appears in modern writers as varied as American author Hannah Adams (1755–1831), German Lutheran and Christian socialist Christoph Blumhardt (1842–1919), and Anglican Charles Gore (1853–1932).[91]

For this group of thinkers, Abraham was a ready biblical example of a notably wealthy man who was nonetheless an exemplar of faith.[92] Abraham is an interesting example because of his appearance in the parable of the rich man and Lazarus (Luke 16:19–31); Abraham is the one who tells the rich man to "remember that during your lifetime you received your good things, and Lazarus in like manner evil things; but now he is comforted [*parakaleō*] here, and you are in agony" (Luke 16:25). This echoes the woe to the rich in Luke 6:24 ("for you have received your consolation [*paraklēsis*]"), leading many to see the parable as a commentary on the first beatitude and its corresponding woe.[93]

90. Clement, *Who Is the Rich Man* 16 (*ANF* 2:595). Others who interpret the first beatitude as detachment regarding riches include Dionysius bar Salibi, Basil of Caesarea, Apaphrat, Sévère of Antioch, Chromatius, Augustine, Leo the Great, Symeon the New Theologian, and Ælfric (for examples see Dupont, *Les évangélistes*, 3:411–18, and Olsen, *Reading Matthew with Monks*, 168).

91. Calvin, *Harmony of the Gospels*, 174; Tyndale, *The Work*, 194; William H. Russell, "The Eight Beatitudes in the School Program," *The Catholic Educational Review* 26 (1928): 198; Gerald Vann, *The Divine Pity: A Study in the Social Implications of the Beatitudes* (New York: Sheed and Ward, 1946), 27; MacEvilly, *Exposition*, 76; Lloyd-Jones, *Studies*, 44; Gore, *Sermon on the Mount*, 24; Hannah Adams, *Letters on the Gospels* (Cambridge, MA: Hillard & Metcalf, 1824), 45. For Blumhardt see Clarence Bauman, *The Sermon on the Mount: The Modern Quest for Its Meaning* (Macon, GA: Mercer University Press, 1985), 286. For Puente, see C. W. Barraud, *Meditations on the Mysteries of Our Holy Faith* (New York: Benziger, 1916), 226.

92. An observation made (for example) by Augustine (cited by John Calvin), Ælfric (who also named Jacob and David in this category), Thomas Aquinas, and Cornelius à Lapide; see Calvin, *Harmony of the Gospels*, 174; Franks, *He Became Poor*, 130; Olsen, *Reading Matthew with Monks*, 168; Cornelius à Lapide, *The Holy Gospel According to Saint Matthew*, 202. Johannes Jacobus van Oosterzee added Chuza and his wife Joanna (Luke 8:2–3) and "the family of Bethany" (Luke 10:38–42) as other examples of the righteous rich (van Oosterzee, *The Gospel According to Luke: The Gospel of Universal Humanity*, trans. Philip Schaff and Charles C. Starbuck [New York: Charles Scribner & Co., 1869], 102).

93. Cyril of Alexandria cited the parable in relation to Luke's woe on the rich; Cyril of Alexandria, Frag. 30, Homilia 29, in Joseph Reuss, ed., *Lukas-Kommentare*, 68. See also Henry, *Matthew to John*, comment on Luke 6:24, section II.1.

Through this lens, then, the blessing on the poor in spirit applies to any person—no matter their social station—who adopts a certain attitude toward wealth. Likewise the woe to the rich is construed as a warning to "those for whom [riches] was their only desire."[94] The emphasis on compassionate motives and renunciation anticipates discussions of the blessing on the pure of heart; the highlighting of generosity foreshadows the blessing on the merciful. Indeed, these other two beatitudes are often mentioned in relation to the first, demonstrating the close connections between them.

One might object that these interpreters have stretched the text beyond its plain sense. After all, Jesus said, "Woe to the rich," not "Woe to the greedy." It's tempting to view this as a reading that arises from discomfort with the "literal" sense of the beatitude, especially Luke's version. More charitably, one can also see these readers using Scripture to interpret Scripture, whether it be the parable of the rich man and Lazarus, Jesus's warning that nobody can serve God and wealth (Matt 6:24), or the parable of the rich fool who built bigger barns rather than give his surplus to the needy (Luke 12:13–21). This interpretation does risk blunting the force of Luke 6:20, and allowing comfortably wealthy readers to dodge the uncomfortable force of this beatitude; the prosperity gospel is an obvious example. The idol of security is another.[95] But it does not say something flatly false either. At its best, it has provoked a fascinating and fruitful discussion for centuries in the church over the right use of wealth and the Christian's obligation toward the poor.

Inheriting the kingdom

The two versions of the Beatitudes vary in their first halves but align in the second: both the poor and the poor in spirit have, or get, the kingdom of heaven (or the kingdom of God). (While some modern scholars have proposed that these are different concepts, I take them as synonyms.) It's the only beatitude in Luke and one of only two beatitudes in Matthew whose promised reward is in the present tense rather than the future ("theirs *is* the kingdom"). This could indicate fulfillment in this life—the kingdom is already theirs. Many readers of the gospels point out that the kingdom arrives in the person of Jesus.

94. Ephrem, *St. Ephrem's Commentary*, 109.

95. John Dear: "The first Beatitude confronts . . . the idolatry of money, possessions, privilege, and power" (*Beatitudes of Peace: Meditations on the Beatitudes, Peacemaking and the Spiritual Life* [New London, CT: Twenty-Third Publications, 2016], 34).

In that sense, "the Kingdom of God is the very person of Jesus, his teaching and his miracles."[96] In this first meaning of the kingdom, the poor (in spirit) are already in the kingdom of God because they already live under God's reign.[97] This is the "now" of the kingdom.

But there's another sense in which the kingdom of God is a future reality. Jesus's story and his proclamation of the kingdom does not end in the present, for Matthew and Luke. Both evangelists look toward the coming of the Son of Man "at the renewal of all things" (Matt 19:28)—that is, the return of Christ to judge the living and the dead. This kingdom has dawned but not risen. We catch glimpses of it but not its full glory. This is the "not yet" of the kingdom. In this second sense, the promise "theirs *is* the kingdom" is a proleptic present, in which the future is presented as already occurring; in other words, the future inheritance of the eschatological kingdom is so secure that it's already theirs. Most commentators see the possession of the kingdom of God through a "now and not yet" lens, as a matter of partial fulfillment now and completion in the next age: "both grace here, and glory hereafter."[98]

If the kingdom belongs to the poor, then what of the rich? Luke's corresponding woe makes explicit what Matthew leaves unsaid. Both evangelists record Jesus's warning that it will be difficult for the rich to enter the kingdom (Matt 19:23, Luke 18:24). When paired with Luke's parable of the rich man and Lazarus, the implication seems clear: because the rich have received material comfort in this life, they should not expect divine comfort in the next (Luke 16:19–31).

Conclusion

The history of this beatitude reveals a long, lively conversation about the relationship between humility and material poverty. This beatitude has generated a confusing proliferation of meanings, from the purely spiritual (humility) to the purely material (the poor and oppressed), with a range of options in between. Some of these interpretations appear to be in direct conflict with

---

96. Clifard Sunil Ranjar, *Be Merciful Like the Father: Exegesis and Theology of the Sermon on the Plain (Luke 6,17–49)* (Rome: Pontifical Biblical Institute, 2017), 134.

97. So Michael H. Crosby, "The Beatitudes: General Perspectives," in *New Perspectives on the Beatitudes*, ed. Francis A. Eigo (Villanova, PA: Villanova University Press, 1995), 37.

98. Richard Watson, *Exposition of the Gospels of St. Matthew and St. Mark* (London: John Mason, 1833), 68. John Farrer used a very similar phrase in his *Sermons on the Mission and Character of Christ, and on the Beatitudes* (Oxford: Oxford University Press, 1804), 252.

one another—can Jesus be declaring blessed *both* the humiliated and the voluntarily humble? Both the actual poor and the generous rich?

This range of meanings originates at least in part from the two versions recorded in Matthew and Luke. Should we allow one of the two evangelists to "control" the meaning of the beatitude? Some writers suggest (as I've hinted throughout this chapter) that Matthew and Luke can be held in creative tension with one another. Perhaps they can even exert a corrective function on each other, as can the respective voices in the history of interpretation, on one side urging us not to sentimentalize poverty, and on the other reminding us not to demean the poor either.[99]

Karl Barth, for example, wrote that Luke's beatitude doesn't allow us to soften Scripture's stark contrast between economic wealth and poverty, while Matthew's version "guards us against another form of softening, i.e., the limitation of the concepts [of the poor, hungry, and weeping] to a purely economic sense." As an example, Barth appealed to the gospel portrayals of the tax collectors, who were not economically poor, but were still poor in spirit (Matt 9:9–13/Luke 5:27–32; Matt 21:31–32; Luke 15:1–7) (*CD* IV/2.64.3).[100]

Furthermore, the tension between the two versions of the beatitude is a tension in Matthew's Gospel itself. Peruvian theologian Gustavo Gutiérrez points out that, in Matthew, "The proclamation of the kingdom begins with the promise made to the poor in spirit [Matt 5:3] and ends with the gift of the kingdom to those who come to the aid of the materially poor [Matt 25:31–46]." Gutiérrez finds "a fruitful relation" between the Beatitudes in the two gospels. Luke's Beatitudes "emphasize the gratuitous character of the love shown by the God who has a preferential love for the materially poor," while Matthew's "complement those in Luke by bringing out the ethical demands made of the followers of Jesus, demands that flow from the loving initiative taken by God."[101] Gutiérrez's view of spiritual poverty as spiritual childhood encompasses both humble dependence on God ("openness to the gift of God's love") and "a pref-

---

99. For the corrective function of the canon, see Richard B. Hays, "The Palpable Word as Ground of *Koinōnia*," in *Christianity and the Soul of the University: Faith as a Foundation for Intellectual Community*, ed. Douglas V. Henry and Michael D. Beaty (Grand Rapids: Baker Academic, 2006), 31, 32.

100. Karl Barth, *Church Dogmatics*, trans. G. W. Bromiley, ed. G. W. Bromiley and T. F. Torrance (Peabody, MA: Hendrickson, 1958, 2004), 169. See also Frederick Bruner, who insists on the importance of holding Matthew's and Luke's versions in balance, in Frederick Dale Bruner, *The Christbook, Matthew 1–12*, vol. 1 of *Matthew: A Commentary*, rev. ed. (Grand Rapids: Eerdmans, 2004), 159–60.

101. Gutiérrez, *God of Life*, 132.

erential solidarity with the poor and oppressed" that leads to efforts to eliminate the injustices and imbalances that cause the misery of the poor.[102]

This brief tour of history might also remind us that this beatitude *means* (that is, *functions*) differently in different social settings. Anthony Meredith, for example, suggests that Clement of Alexandria (ca. 150–215) and Gregory of Nyssa (ca. 335–395) interpreted the beatitude differently in relation to their respective social contexts. Clement lived in the second century, when wealthy converts were still not numerous and Christians still faced persecution. When Gregory wrote two hundred years later, persecution had ceased, it was more common to be Christian and rich, and "the need to offer a more radical calling was being increasingly felt."[103] Bonhoeffer wrote during a time in which obeying God rather than the earthly government put one at risk of losing one's livelihood and possessions, creating a direct link between humble submission to God and material poverty.

This is not to say that the social context of these writers *determined* their exegesis, but that it influenced their applications. No doubt I hear the beatitude differently, and may be moved to some corresponding action differently, from a fourth-century woman in a wealthy Egyptian Christian household, or from a young Syrian Christian refugee living today in a tent. So also with Luke's "woe to the rich!" which issues a warning and a challenge to me in a way that it does not to those living in material want.

One final example. When contemporary American artist Laura James painted a series of small panels illustrating the Beatitudes, she depicted the "poor in spirit" in a scene of a slave ship transporting African slaves to the American South: two white men prepare to throw a dead black man overboard while another grieving slave huddles nearby.[104] This is the kind of image that refuses to allow the beatitude to become too pleasant or too easy, especially for affluent Western Christians. Instead, it stops us in our tracks, making us wonder anew who are the poor and the poor in spirit today, and whether we might be among them, or not.

---

102. Gutiérrez, *God of Life*, 121–22.

103. Anthony Meredith, "Gregory of Nyssa, *De Beatitudinibus*, Oratio I: 'Blessed are the Poor in Spirit, For Theirs Is the Kingdom of Heaven' (Mt 5,3)," in *Gregory of Nyssa: Homilies on the Beatitudes*, ed. Hubertus R. Drobner and Albert Viciano (Leiden: Brill, 2000), 108.

104. See Rebekah Eklund, "The Blessed," Visual Commentary on Scripture, http://thevcs. org/blessed. See also Carole Weatherford's children's book that illustrates the first beatitude with Africans in chains on a slave ship in the Middle Passage (Carole Boston Weatherford, *The Beatitudes: From Slavery to Civil Rights*, Eerdmans Books for Young Readers, ill. Tim Ladwig [Grand Rapids: Eerdmans, 2010], n.p.).

4

By Trials Furrowed

Those Who Mourn and Weep

Blessed are those who mourn, for they will be comforted (Matt 5:4).

Blessed are you who weep now, for you will laugh. . . . Woe to you who are laughing now, for you will mourn and weep (Luke 6:21b, 25b).

A spoiled young woman named Sylvia is the main character in Lily Watson's late-nineteenth-century short story about the second beatitude. When Sylvia's beloved mother falls dangerously ill and is sent away to a warmer climate, she is filled with remorse for her selfish ways. While grieving, she happens to read a poem on the second beatitude, which reassures her that "Life, by trials furrowed, bears / The fruit of loving deeds."[1] Sylvia is confused; she had thought that Jesus's blessing was only for people who mourn for their sins.[2] But then she devotes herself to the idea that "this great trial of her mother's illness was to bring forth the fruit of tender actions" toward her siblings, whom she had always neglected.[3] She learns that the blessing of comfort is for her, too, once her own grief had broken open her heart and made her see beyond herself.

Sylvia represents a turning point in this beatitude's history. For a long time—almost 1,400 years—most Christian writings supposed, like Sylvia did,

---

1. The poem is by William H. Burleigh; it was published as Wm. H. Burleigh, "Blessed Are They That Mourn," *The Signs of the Times* 8, no. 10 (March 9, 1882): 109. Quoted in Lily Watson, *A Garden of Girls: Stories Illustrating the Beatitudes* (London: Religious Tract Society, 1893), 37.

2. Watson, *Garden of Girls*, 41.

3. Watson, *Garden of Girls*, 41. Similarly, John Browne wrote, "'they shall be comforted' when they give up the false gods of material and selfish thinking and embrace the opportunity to render service to others" (Browne, *The Great Sermon* [Boston, MA: Stratford, 1935], 21).

that the mourners of the beatitude were mourning for their sins. *That's* what was blessed—not any other kind of grief. But Watson wrote her tale at the end of the nineteenth century, when Christians had started to suppose that other kinds of mourning—in fact, *lots* of other kinds of grief—were included in the beatitude. So the story of this beatitude is about what kind of tears are included in the blessing, and why.

—

I'll set the stage by comparing briefly the two different versions recorded in Matthew and Luke and their shared background in Isaiah 61 and Isaiah 65. Then, I'll consider the dominant interpretation of mourning as repentance and sorrow over sin, asking first why this interpretation took root so early and endured for so long, and next whether this interpretation might fail either to be "correct" or "salutary" (more on those designations below). I turn next to the transition that occurs in the Reformation era, when the dominant interpretation was occasionally rejected but mostly supplemented; this section includes a brief exploration of some of the primary additions in meaning. Finally, I summarize the possible meanings of comfort and laughter—and suggest that they indicate the same promised reversal or reward.

Weeping, mourning, and the prophet Isaiah

As with the first beatitude, there are two different versions to contend with. Matthew's version blesses the mourners (*pentheō*) and promises comfort (*parakaleō*); Luke's blesses those who weep (*klaiō*), with a promise of future laughter and a corresponding warning to those who now laugh. Are the weepers who will laugh and the mourners who will be comforted the same? In this case, unlike with the first beatitude, the differences seem less sharp, since "mourning" and "weeping" are, on the face of it, synonyms. Interestingly enough, at least one ancient source—Tatian's Diatessaron—understood them as two distinct beatitudes, since it included both in its harmony of the four gospels. (By comparison, it drops Luke's blessing on the "poor" and includes only Matthew's blessing on the poor in spirit.)[4] But Tatian is an outlier; most

---

4. Martin Hogan, *The Sermon on the Mount in St. Ephrem's Commentary on the Diatessaron* (Bern: Lang, 1999), 28–41; Tjitze Baarda, "The Beatitudes of 'The Mourning' and 'The Weeping':

interpreters (even those who read the Diatessaron!) consider the two versions to be largely the same.

Readers throughout history have noticed that Matthew's version alludes to the Greek text of Isa 61:2, where the same words for mourning (*pentheō*) and comfort (*parakaleō*) appear in the prophet's declaration of God's comfort to all who mourn in Zion. A mourner has appeared earlier in Matthew's Gospel, refusing to be comforted—Rachel, weeping for her children (i.e., Israel) who have gone into exile (Matt 2:18, citing Jer 31:15). This further strengthens the connection between Matthew's beatitude and Isaiah's promise of restoration after the exile.[5]

Yet Luke's version also connects to the theme of God's rescue of God's people who suffer in exile. Isaiah 65:13–16 contains a set of reversals similar to Luke's, a correspondence noted by Tertullian. In Isaiah 65, those who "shall wail for anguish of spirit" are the ones who have turned away from the LORD toward evil ways (Isa 65:11–14), while God's servants "shall sing for gladness of heart." Perhaps, like the wealthy revelers of Amos 4 or the fattened shepherds of Ezekiel 34, those who laugh now in Luke 6:25 have bought their pleasure at the expense of the poor and needy: they laugh because others weep.

Tertullian also connected Luke's version of the beatitude to Psalm 126, a psalm that celebrates the restoration of Zion: "Then our mouth was filled with laughter, and our tongue with shouts of joy. . . . May those who sow in tears reap with shouts of joy. Those who go out weeping, bearing the seed for sowing, shall come home with shouts of joy, carrying their sheaves" (Ps 126:2, 5–6).[6] This psalm reduces the apparent distance between the Matthean promise of comfort and the Lukan promise of laughter; both signify the joy of the restored. When Christian commentators interpreted Israel's return to the land as eschatological restoration, their equation of the promised land with heaven

---

Matthew 5:4 and Luke 6:21b," in *Studies in the Early Text of the Gospels and Acts*, ed. David G. K. Taylor (Atlanta: Society of Biblical Literature, 1999), 173–76, 184, 191.

5. See Rebekah Eklund, *Jesus Wept: The Significance of Jesus' Laments in the New Testament*, LNTS (London: T&T Clark, 2015), 20, 144–51. The evangelists and many early Christians favored the Septuagint (the Greek text of the Old Testament) over the Hebrew text.

6. Tertullian, *Against Marcion* 4.14 (*ANF* 3:366). For laughter used largely in a pejorative sense in the Bible ("Contrairement à la 'joie', le 'rire' a généralement dans la Bible un sense péjoratif"), see Jacques Dupont, *Le problème littéraire—Les deux versions du Sermon sur la montagne et des béatitudes*, vol. 1 of *Les Béatitudes* (Bruges, Belgium: Abbaye de Saint-André, 1958), 269.

(or the new creation) led them to understand mourning as a form of sorrow over our long sojourn here away from home. Before we arrive at this interpretation, however, we need to take a long detour through another way that the text was often received.

Penitence: the sorrow of repentance

No other beatitude has such a singular tradition of interpretation for so long— or such a clear change at a particular moment in time. Until the Reformation, Christian interpreters in both East and West viewed mourning almost exclusively as sorrow for sin.

This view arose very early. It appeared at least by the end of the second century, in Clement of Alexandria's *Stromata*, composed ca. 192–202. Clement described the mourners of the beatitude as "they who have repented of their former evil life."[7] In fact, it's difficult to find writers in the first thirteen centuries of the church's life who interpreted the beatitude otherwise: as we have already seen, Tertullian (ca. 155–240) was one, since he oriented the beatitude around Old Testament texts about Israel's exilic anguish and God's promise of restoration. Cyril of Alexandria (b. ca. 376) was another (proving that the Alexandrians did not always see eye to eye).[8] Yet the predominant view was that mourning is sorrow over sins (one's own sins and/or the sins of others). It was found in the East as in the West; it took more or less equal root in later Orthodox and Catholic thought and continues to be the dominant interpretation today in both those traditions.

To modern readers, who may be accustomed to a different set of meanings (more on that below), this may be a surprising uniformity. What factors led so many early interpreters to interpret mourning and weeping as penitence, and not as (say) grief over loss?

---

7. Clement of Alexandria, *Stromata* 4.6 (*ANF* 2:416). It appears also in the writings of Cyprian, Ephrem the Syrian, Hilary of Poitiers, Basil of Caesarea, Ambrose of Milan, Gregory of Nyssa, Chrysostom, Chromatius of Aquileia, Jerome, and Augustine, among many others.

8. Cyril of Alexandria interpreted Luke 6:21 as referring to those "who shun a life of merriment and vanity, and carnal pleasures" (Cyril of Alexandria, Homily 27, *Commentary on the Gospel of St. Luke*, trans. R. Payne Smith [Long Island, NY: Studion, 1983], 130). Both Tertullian and Cyril were commenting on Luke's version of the beatitude.

Why?

Many interpreters appealed to a distinction made by the apostle Paul: "For godly grief produces a repentance that leads to salvation and brings no regret, but worldly grief produces death" (2 Cor 7:10).[9] Elsewhere in the same letter, Paul worried that he might have to mourn (*pentheō*) over those who had previously sinned but had not yet repented (2 Cor 12:21). Although it was less common for premodern authors to cite James, the book of James also associates mourning and weeping indirectly with penitence for sin. James contains an interesting echo of the beatitude (using both Matthew's mourning and Luke's weeping) and the Lukan woe: "Cleanse your hands, you sinners, and purify your hearts, you double-minded. Lament and mourn and weep. Let your laughter be turned into mourning and your joy into dejection. Humble yourselves before the Lord, and he will exalt you" (Jas 4:8b–10).

Additionally, Stoic philosophy influenced both Second Temple Jewish writers and early Christian thought. Christian writers often resisted or modified Stoic principles, but they certainly interacted with them. Stoics generally viewed death as natural—and what was natural was to be embraced, not resisted. Stoic philosophers also valued control over or even erasure of the passions, which may help explain why patristic writers breathing this Stoic air typically did *not* view grief over loss as a godly type of mourning.

For example, Jerome invoked a Stoic principle when he wrote that the mourning of Matt 5:5 is not for "those who have died in accordance with the common law of nature."[10] Augustine wrote that sorrow over the "loss of dear ones" is an emotion that will be dismissed once people turn to God and learn to love what is eternal, and in his *Confessions* he famously wrestled with whether he should weep for the death of his mother.[11] It might not be a co-

---

9. Among those who cite this verse are Basil of Caesarea (*Shorter Rules* 31 [PG 31:1104B]); Chrysostom (*Homilies on the Gospel of Saint Matthew* 15.4 [*NPNF*¹ 10:93]); and Gregory of Palamas (*Ad Xenam de passionibus* [PG 150:1073D; 1076A]).

10. Jerome, *Commentary on Matthew*, trans. Thomas P. Scheck, FC 117 (Washington, DC: Catholic University of America, 2008), 75–76. See also Chromatius of Aquileia, *Sermons and Tractates on Matthew*, trans. Thomas P. Scheck, ACW 75 (New York: The Newman Press, 2018), 17.3.1. So also Hilary of Poitiers, *Commentary on Matthew*, trans. D. H. Williams, FC 125 (Washington, DC: Catholic University of America, 2012), 4.4; Leo the Great, *Sermons* 95.4 (*NPNF*² 12:203–4); Cabasilas, *The Life in Christ* 6.11b, trans. Carmino J. deCatanzaro (Crestwood, NY: St. Vladimir's Seminary Press, 1974), 178–80. For Stoic views on death, see C. Kavin Rowe, *One True Life: The Stoics and Early Christians as Rival Traditions* (New Haven, CT: Yale University Press, 2016), 15–21, 68–71. For Stoic views on the emotions, see Rowe, *One True Life*, 30–36, 54–59.

11. Augustine, *The Lord's Sermon on the Mount* 1.2.5, trans. John J. Jepson, ACW 5 (Mahwah,

incidence that Tertullian, one of the fathers who most resisted the merger of Christian thought with "worldly" (Greco-Roman) philosophy, did *not* interpret the beatitude as penitence.

A final potential factor was the apparent decline of the lament as a prayer and the rise of penitential prayer in postexilic Israel and in Second Temple Judaism. Lament is a type of prayer in the midst of suffering that often includes elements of complaint or protest; it's the most common form of prayer in the Psalter (see, e.g., Pss 13, 22, 69, and 88). Penitential prayer, on the other hand, is a type of prayer that usually excludes protest and focuses on crying out to God for forgiveness. Whereas lament was a dominant form of prayer in early Israel, penitential prayer rose to prominence after the exile, displacing (at least in part) the lament.[12] The extent of this displacement is widely disputed; it's not always easy to distinguish neatly between penitence and lament, or repentance and protest (see, e.g., Isa 63:7–64:11, or the book of Job).[13] Yet some Second Temple texts do appear to display this shift. For example, the dominance of the penitential prayer is especially evident in the Dead Sea Scrolls.[14] In the

---

NJ: Paulist, 1948), 14; Augustine, *Confessions*, trans. Henry Chadwick (Oxford: Oxford University Press, 1991), 9.12.29–34.

12. Claus Westermann argued that postexilic prayer in Israel shifted away from lament and toward penitential prayer (Westermann, *Praise and Lament in the Psalms*, trans. Keith R. Crim and Richard N. Soulen [Atlanta: John Knox, 1965, 1981], 195–212); see also Samuel E. Balentine, "'I Was Ready to Be Sought Out by Those Who Did Not Ask,'" in *The Origins of Penitential Prayer in Second Temple Judaism*, vol. 1 of *Seeking the Favor of God*, ed. Mark J. Boda, Daniel K. Falk, and Rodney A. Werline (Atlanta: Society of Biblical Literature, 2006), 4–8. Lambert argues that repentance begins to be naturalized in the late Second Temple era (e.g., in the Prayer of Manasseh) but is not institutionalized in Judaism until the rabbinic era (David A. Lambert, *How Repentance Became Biblical: Judaism, Christianity, and the Interpretation of Scripture* [Oxford: Oxford University Press, 2016], 170–74). See also Richard J. Bautch, *Developments in Genre between Post-Exilic Penitential Prayers and the Psalms of Communal Lament* (Leiden: Brill, 2003); and Rodney Alan Werline, *Penitential Prayer in Second Temple Judaism: The Development of a Religious Institution* (Atlanta: Scholars Press, 1998).

13. For Isaiah, see Richard J. Bautch, "Lament Regained in Trito-Isaiah's Penitential Prayer," in Boda, Falk and Werline, *The Origins of Penitential Prayer*, 83–99; and Elizabeth Boase, "Blurring the Boundaries: The Rhetoric of Lament and Penitence in Isaiah 63:7-64:11," in *Spiritual Complaint: The Theology and Practice of Lament*, ed. Miriam J. Bier and Tim Bulkeley (Eugene, OR: Pickwick, 2013), 71–87. For Job, see Samuel E. Balentine, afterword in Boda, Falk and Werline, *The Origins of Penitential Prayer*, 203. For arguments that penitential prayer never completely displaced lament, see Donald P. Moffat, "The Profit and Loss of Lament: Rethinking Aspects of the Relationship between Lament and Penitential Prayer," in Bier and Bulkeley, *Spiritual Complaint*, 88–101; and Lena-Sofia Tiemeyer, "The Doubtful Gain of Penitence: The Fine Line between Lament and Penitential Prayer," in Bier and Bulkeley, *Spiritual Complaint*, 102–24.

14. In the Dead Sea Scrolls, "[t]he lament for Jerusalem, in and of itself, seems to have dimin-

Thanksgiving Psalms (*Hôdayôt*), the author laments primarily over his own guilt and over the guilt and sinfulness of humanity (e.g., 1QHᵃ XII, 28–37). The Qumran psalmist laments over the evil inclination that is in humanity (1QHᵃ XIX, 19–27), but does not protest or argue with God.[15] In general, then, it seems to be the case that first-century Jewish thinkers (such as the evangelists) and the earliest Christians inherited from Judaism a tendency to focus on the importance of repentance and penitential prayer.

Is it "wrong"?

Dale Allison is not alone among modern interpreters when he writes that the traditional interpretation "is likely wrong."[16] He bases this conclusion on the observation that the beatitude echoes Isa 61:2, in which mourning is equated with Israel's grief in exile. I proposed in my introduction that original context can help provide "guard rails" for potential new meanings, or can pose a challenge to interpretations that seem to directly violate a feature of the text's original context. Does this text's original context, in Luke or in Matthew, challenge the meaning of penitence?

The context of the exile suggests a wide variety of griefs (the potential loss of the covenant with God, foreign domination, starvation, loss of land and home, death). We've already seen above that the catastrophe of the exile itself moved at least some Jewish texts in a penitential direction.[17] Some Old Testament texts associated the catastrophe of the exile with Israel's idolatry, injustice, and disobedience (e.g., Lam 1:5, 8, 18). In Isaiah, Israel's comfort is announced after she has paid the penalty for her sins (Isa 40:2). So the provisional answer is no: the text's original context does not immediately rule out this meaning, since

---

ished in the post-exilic period, and to have been absorbed into penitential prayer" (Adele Berlin, "Qumran Laments and the Study of Qumran Literature," in *Liturgical Perspectives: Prayer and Poetry in Light of the Dead Sea Scrolls*, ed. Esther G. Chazon, Ruth Clements, and Avital Pinnick [Leiden; Boston: Brill, 2003], 11).

15. As Michael Moore writes, "*Hodayot*, as a general rule, never challenges the deity's motives . . ." Michael S. Moore, "The Laments in Jeremiah and 1QH: Mapping the Metaphorical Trajectories," in *Uprooting and Planting: Essays on Jeremiah for Leslie Allen*, ed. John Goldingay (New York: T&T Clark, 2007), 249.

16. Dale C. Allison Jr., *The Sermon on the Mount: Inspiring the Moral Imagination* (New York: Crossroad, 1999), 47.

17. So H. Benedict Green, *Matthew, Poet of the Beatitudes* (Sheffield: Sheffield Academic, 2001), 221–22.

even the context of the exile mixes repentance with other forms of nonpenitential sorrow. But neither does the original context rule out other meanings.

The words for "weeping" and "mourning" in the two versions of the beatitude likewise provide little definitive help, since both are used in penitential and nonpenitential contexts. The Septuagint frequently uses Matthew's word for "mourning" (*pentheō*) to indicate grief in the face of death (Gen 23:2; 37:34, 35; 50:3; 2 Sam 14:2; 19:1; 1 Chr 7:22; 2 Chr 35:24; 1 Esdr 8:72); its only occurrences in the psalms refer to mourning over death (Pss 34:14, 77:63). In postexilic literature (Ezra and Nehemiah) and in the prophets (Hosea, Amos, Isaiah, Jeremiah), mourning is strongly associated with grief at God's judgment and its accompanying afflictions, including the destruction of Jerusalem and the exile. In the LXX, Luke's word for "weeping" (*klaiō*) indicates a variety of griefs, including death and calamity; it occasionally occurs in conjunction with fasting while seeking God's will (Judg 20:26; 2 Sam 12:22). *Klaiō* is also used in penitential contexts, in concert with humbling oneself before God, in 2 Kgs 22:19; 2 Chr 34:27; Ezra 10:1; Joel 1:5, 2:17; and Isa 22:4.

In Matthew's Gospel, the only other use of *pentheō* occurs in Jesus's statement that "The wedding guests cannot mourn as long as the bridegroom is with them" and uses fasting as a parallel act ("The days will come when the bridegroom is taken away from them, and then they will fast") (Matt 9:15). The parallelism between fasting and mourning could indicate that mourning is repentance in this case, since both acts can be penitential, but this seems unlikely since it would be strange of Matthew to claim that the disciples cannot repent while Jesus is still with them.

Luke's Gospel uses *klaiō* for a variety of griefs: sorrow at death (7:13; perhaps 7:32; 8:52); the penitent act of the sinful woman who bathes Jesus's feet with her tears (7:38); Jesus's prophetic mourning over the coming fall of Jerusalem (19:41), as well as Jesus's instructions to the women of Jerusalem not to weep for him but for themselves and their children (22:62); and Peter's regretful grief over his betrayal of Jesus (22:62).

All this suggests that both terms *may* mean penitence, but also bear within them the capacity to mean something other than penitence. Still, this does not determine meaning. Nor, even, does authorial intention. We may conjecture what type(s) of mourning Matthew and Luke had in mind based on their narratives and presumed social settings, but I've already made a case that the meaning of a biblical text cannot be restricted to its original sense, even if we could determine precisely what that was. While Allison suggests that the tradition misses the mark in relation to the beatitude's original setting in relation to Isaiah 61, he also writes elsewhere that "Exegetical history in its entirety rather confronts us with an ongoing, evolving divine disclosure."[18] That is, "new readers inevitably make for new readings, and . . . multiple meanings need not always be contradictory meanings."[19]

Rather than suggest that the tradition is wrong, I want to argue instead that it's simply too narrow, that it homed in on one aspect of mourning at the expense of too many other possibilities—indeed, other fruitful and faithful possibilities.

Is it "salutary"?

In that sense, I wonder if a more promising question is not whether the majority tradition is wrong but whether it is salutary. I'm drawing the language of salutarity from theologian Ellen Charry, who describes the "salutarity principle" as an examination of a doctrine for its pastoral function, or for its function to foster Christian virtue in those who seek to live by that doctrine.[20] Another way to ask the same question is to consider Augustine's principle of interpreting Scripture by the double love command. Does understanding mourning as penitence lead to greater love of God and greater love of neighbor?

Yet another approach is to consider whether the interpretation is beneficial (in the Pauline sense of 1 Cor 6:12, 10:23), or whether it is fruitful (Col 1:10)—that is, does the interpretation cause the bearing of good fruit in those who seek to shape their lives by that interpretation? Margaret Mitchell, a scholar who studies early Christian thought, advocates for "a carefully calibrated balance among three cardinal virtues of ancient textual interpretation: a close examination (with *akribeia*, 'precision,' 'keen attention') of what the text says in whole and part, an awareness of the benefit for present readers (*ôpheleia*), and *epieikeia* or clemency, which seeks to keep the two in balance."[21]

18. Dale C. Allison Jr., *Studies in Matthew: Interpretation Past and Present* (Grand Rapids: Baker Academic, 2005), 63.

19. Allison, *Studies in Matthew*, 63.

20. Ellen T. Charry, *By the Renewing of Your Minds: The Pastoral Function of Christian Doctrine* (Oxford: Oxford University Press, 1997), 18, 28–29; see also Jonathan T. Pennington, *The Sermon on the Mount and Human Flourishing: A Theological Commentary* (Grand Rapids: Baker Academic, 2017), 14–16.

21. Margaret M. Mitchell, *Paul, the Corinthians and the Birth of Christian Hermeneutics* (Cambridge: Cambridge University Press, 2010), 108; see also 3, 12.

Seen through these lenses, I suggest that viewing mourning as penitence could certainly pass these tests, but viewing it *only* as penitence fails to pass. Why? First, this narrow view doesn't account for the beatitude's background in Old Testament texts where mourning and weeping have broad and multiple resonances. As New Testament scholar Scot McKnight observes, "Exile for the mourner [meant] grief, faithfulness, suffering, and hope."[22]

Second, it doesn't account for the clear scriptural witness that God comforts the brokenhearted, not only the repentant. Nor does it attend to the biblical principle that Christians may grieve (with hope) over death (1 Thess 4:13). Even Jesus wept at the grave of Lazarus.

Reformation transition: additions

Additional meanings of mourning began to proliferate beginning in the sixteenth century. We've examined the dominant traditional interpretation but have not yet encountered the shift, the turning point in the plot, which first occurs—perhaps unsurprisingly—during the Reformation. The two most prominent magisterial Reformers prove to be an exception to a long rule; neither Martin Luther nor John Calvin understood the mourning of the beatitude to be for sins at all. Instead, they both took mourning as a natural state of human existence arising from the trials of everyday life.[23] It is difficult to say precisely what motivated this change. There is some important, if rare, precedence in the tradition. Thomas Aquinas, with his characteristic multiplicity, declared three kinds of mourning blessed: repentance, or grief over "the continual conflict between our flesh and our spirit"; "the grief caused by sojourning in this life with all its wretchedness"; and dying to the world by abandoning its joys for the sake of Christ (as in Gal 6:14).[24]

22. Scot McKnight, *The Sermon on the Mount*, The Story of God Bible Commentary (Grand Rapids: Zondervan, 2013), 40.

23. Martin Luther, *The Sermon on the Mount*, vol. 21 of *Luther's Works*, ed. Jaroslav Pelikan (St. Louis: Concordia, 1956), 17–22; John Calvin, *Sermons on the Beatitudes: Five Sermons from the Gospel Harmony, Delivered in Geneva in 1560* (Carlisle, PA: Banner of Truth Trust, 2006), 28–29. In one letter, Luther quoted the beatitude to the evangelical bishop of Naumburg, who had written to Luther in discouragement over the burdens of his episcopal office (Martin Luther, *Luther: Letters of Spiritual Counsel*, LCC 18, trans. Theodore G. Tappert [Philadelphia: Westminster, 1955], 167–68).

24. This translation of the second kind of mourning appears in Servais Pinckaers, *The*

Certainly the Reformers' rejection of penance as a sacrament reoriented repentance around a different set of practices, but the Reformers and their inheritors still had a lively sense of the need for some form of confession and penitence, an emphasis that appears with special prominence in the writings of the post-Reformation Puritans. Jeremiah Burroughs interpreted mourning *entirely* as penitence (no additions to the list for him!) but may have had the sacrament of penance in mind when he explained, "There is nothing more evangelical than faith and repentance; mourning for sin in this way that I have spoken it is no legal thing, it is not a work of the law . . . but it is a work of the Spirit of God."[25]

Luther may have also had his religious and political context in mind when he wrote that mourning arises in Christians who look at the world and see "wickedness, arrogance, contempt, and blasphemy of God and His Word, so much sorrow and sadness. . . . Therefore simply begin to be a Christian, and you will soon find out what it means to mourn and be sorrowful." Yet Luther was also worried about an *over*-emphasis on mourning: "Those who mourn this way are entitled to have fun . . . so that they do not completely collapse for

---

Pursuit of God's Happiness—God's Way: Living the Beatitudes, trans. Mary Thomas Noble (New York: Society of St. Paul, 1998), 76; for the three kinds see Thomas Aquinas, *Commentary on the Gospel of Matthew, Chapters 1–12*, ed. The Aquinas Institute, trans. Jeremy Holmes and Beth Mortensen, Biblical Commentaries 33 (Lander, WY: The Aquinas Institute for the Study of Sacred Doctrine, 2013), C.5 L.2.422; and Thomas Aquinas, *The Three Greatest Prayers: Commentaries on the Lord's Prayer, the Hail Mary, and the Apostles' Creed* (Manchester, NH: Sophia Institute Press, 1990), 134–35.

25. Jeremiah Burroughs, *The Saints' Happiness* (Edinburgh: James Nichol, 1867; Soli Deo Gloria, 1988, 1992), 50. Edward Stillingfleet (1673, London) preached that false teachers turned the beatitude into a blessing on those who confess their sins to a priest and receive the sacrament of penance (Edward Stillingfleet, *A sermon preached November 5, 1673, at St. Margarets Westminst by Edward Stillingfleet*, 2nd ed. [London: Robert White, for Henry Mortlock, 1674], 25). Puritan and Nonconformist preachers appear to have been especially drawn to the notion of mourning as repentance—e.g., Burroughs, *Saints' Happiness*, 37, 50; Puritan preacher Robert Harris (*The Way to True Happiness: Delivered in Twenty-Four Sermons upon the Beatitudes*, ed. Don Kistler [Morgan, PA: Soli Deo Gloria, 1998], 57, 58, 63); Puritan Nonconformist Thomas Watson (*The Beatitudes: An Exposition of Matthew 5:1–10* [Carlisle, PA: Banner of Truth Trust, 2014], 55–58, 63). John Wesley saw mourning as sorrow over the lack of sanctification in one's life (John Wesley, *The Nature of the Kingdom: Wesley's Messages on the Sermon on the Mount*, ed. Clare George Weakley Jr. [Minneapolis: Bethany House Publishers, 1979], 58–60). In 1690, Protestant John Norris insisted that mourning means repentance but not the "rigid measures" of the religious orders of the Roman Catholic Church, which he saw as too extreme (John Norris, *Christian Blessedness: Or Discourses upon the Beatitudes*, vol. 1 of *Practical Discourses Upon the Beatitudes*, 5th ed. [London: S. Manship, 1707], 33–34).

sorrow." Christ's beatitude does not commend continual mourning (perhaps Luther thought of his monastic past; there were plenty of monastic writings that *did* commend perpetual mourning); instead, Christ issues a warning against those who try to escape all mourning and have nothing but fun.[26]

Calvin also expressed concern about the problem of "prolonged compunction for one's sins," which he saw as unhelpful (see *Inst.* III.4.3).[27] Calvin rejected the idea that "repentance consists chiefly of fasting and weeping" in part because he argued that those two actions are meant for special times of calamity, not for everyday confession of sins (*Inst.* III.3.17). This, of course, effectively uncouples mourning from repentance.

Whatever pushed these two Reformers away from mourning as repentance, they were charting an almost entirely unprecedented path in their complete dissociation of mourning from penitence. Indeed, relatively few followed in their footsteps until the modern era, when their view became much more prevalent, but for different reasons: modern historical-critical commentators often view the mourners as a subset of the poor and hungry. The mourners are seen as "the afflicted" (as in the Jerusalem Bible translation)—those "for whom the world holds no consolation" and "those for whom brutal death is a constant companion."[28]

It's far more common to find interpreters in the wake of the Reformation until today retaining penitence while adding to the list of blessed types of mourning. Billy Graham, for example, described five kinds of mourning implied by the beatitude: the mourning of inadequacy (unworthiness and helplessness before a holy God, as Isa 6:5); of repentance; of love (compassion and distress over the misfortune of others); of "soul travail" ("the continual flow of prayer which rises out of the Christian heart for a world unborn spiritually"); and of bereavement (which is blessed generally because God promises comfort to all who suffer in this "vale of tears").[29]

---

26. Luther, *Sermon on the Mount*, 20, 21, 22. In the late nineteenth century, Catholic bishop Jean François Anne Thomas Landriot also rebuked the "misanthropic authors" and certain mystical writers who commended only sadness and tears, arguing instead that joy is the heart of the Christian life (Landriot, *Les Béatitudes évangéliques*, 2 vols. [Paris: Palmé, 1866–67], 2:7, 2:156).

27. Chad Quaintance, "The Blessed Life: Theological Interpretation and Use of the Beatitudes by Augustine, Calvin and Barth" (PhD diss., Union Theological Seminary and Presbyterian School of Christian Education, 2003), 145n40, ProQuest 3087209. It's possible that Calvin was following the lead of Thomas Aquinas on this score; see Laura M. Lysen, "Vicious Sorrow: The Roots of a 'Spiritual' Sin in the *Summa Theologiae*," *Studies in Christian Ethics* 30, no. 3 (2017): 329–47.

28. Günther Bornkamm, *Jesus of Nazareth*, trans. Irene McLuskey, Fraser McLuskey, and James M. Robinson (New York: Harper & Row, 1960), 76; William Domeris, "'Blessed are you . . .' (Matthew 5:1–12)," *Journal of Theology for South Africa* 73 (1990): 71.

29. Billy Graham, *The Secret of Happiness: Jesus' Teaching on Happiness as Expressed in the*

This is a capacious list, encompassing a wide variety of griefs. It's a good representative list, because it includes many of the varieties of mourning that one sees added to such lists over time. This widening of meaning is certainly not exclusive to Protestants, either. Graham could have taken notes from the Spanish Jesuit Luis de la Puente (1554–1624), who also named five blessed causes for sorrow: sins, proneness to sin, the triumph of evil, the disappointments of life, and the weariness of exile.[30] Shortly after de la Puente, the author of the 1665 treatise *Ashrea* described mourning as "tears of remorse, compunction, compassion, commiseration, and devotion."[31]

But has this newer tradition done justice to the beatitude? If I faulted the pre-Reformation tradition for being too narrow, has this post-Reformation tradition become too wide? One might protest that if mourning can mean "anything that breaks the heart" (so Dallas Willard), then it has become too vague to be meaningful.[32] But Willard knew that Scripture elsewhere promises comfort precisely to those who have had their hearts broken: "The LORD is near to the brokenhearted" (Ps 34:18). As Thomas Beckett wrote, the mourners belong to the kingdom not *because* they mourn, but because sorrow evokes Christ's compassion.[33] To be sure, as Gustavo Gutiérrez cautions, weeping in Luke is not a momentary or passing pain: "This suffering is profound."[34] What kinds of profound suffering, then, might be included within the blessing of this beatitude?

Beatitudes (Garden City, NY: Doubleday, 1955), 18–28. Increase Mather named four types of mourning, including for sin (Increase Mather, *Sermons Wherein Those Eight Characters of the Blessed Commonly Called the Beatitudes Are Opened and Applied in Fifteen Discourses* [Boston: B. Green, for Daniel Henchman, 1718], Sermon 3). John Norris named five: zeal for God's honor, mourning for sin, grief for "the Miseries of Human Life" and its "Multitude of Evils," weeping with those who weep, and weeping over the relative uncertainty of one's salvation (Norris, *Christian Blessedness*, 35–42).

30. C. W. Barraud, *Meditations on the Mysteries of Our Holy Faith, Together with a Treatise in Mental Prayer* (New York: Benziger, 1916), 230. Likewise Jacques Bénigne Bossuet wrote that God consoles all those who mourn (Rev 2:14), whether for troubles or for sin (although mourning for sin is best, since "Sin is the only evil that can be cured by deploring it") (Bossuet, *The Sermon on the Mount*, trans. F. M. Capes [Longmans, Green: 1900], 14).

31. E. M., *Ashrea: Or, the Grove of the Beatitudes, Represented in Emblemes* (London: Printed for W. P. at Grayes-Inn Gate in Holborne, 1665; Reprint: English Emblem Books 18; Yorkshire, England: Scolar Press, 1970), 28.

32. Dallas Willard, *The Divine Conspiracy: Rediscovering Our Hidden Life in God* (New York: HarperSanFrancisco, 1998), 116–17. See also Hans Dieter Betz, *The Sermon on the Mount*, Hermeneia (Minneapolis: Fortress, 1995), 123; Mark Allan Powell, "Matthew's Beatitudes: Reversals and Rewards of the Kingdom," *CBQ* 58 (1996): 465.

33. Thomas A. Beckett, *The Sermon on the Mount* (London: H. R. Allenson, 1909), 12.

34. For Gutiérrez, the profound suffering expressed by Luke's verb *klaiein* (to weep) "springs

Let's explore a few specific examples of other kinds of mourning identified in the interpretive tradition, to test them for their generative power, for their capacity to nudge the reader toward a flourishing life, and for their warrant elsewhere in Scripture. The first kind also arose during the Reformation era, and was deeply informed by that turbulent context.

Divisions in the church

In approximately 1522, around the same time that Martin Luther was excommunicated, Catholic humanist Erasmus of Rotterdam paraphrased the second beatitude as a blessing on "those who mourn because of their love for the gospel, who are even torn from their loved ones, who see the people they hold most dear beaten and slaughtered on account of gospel righteousness, who, spurning the pleasures of this world, pass their lives in tears, in vigils, and fastings."[35]

Erasmus's paraphrase is a prescient description of the turmoil that had already started within the church and would only intensify in the years to come. A few decades later (ca. 1580), the Jesuit Juan Maldonado also linked mourning to the grief of those being persecuted for the kingdom of heaven (citing John 16:33; Rom 5:3–4; 2 Tim 3:12). Maldonado wrote that this is certainly the meaning of the beatitude and its corresponding woe in Luke, "where Christ opposes those who laugh to those who mourn—as oppressors to oppressed; conquerors to conquered."[36]

Several post-Reformation Protestants who faced internal divisions and splits within their own Christian communions viewed the mourning of the beatitude as grief over the fracturing of the church and over the trauma of Christians persecuted by their own brethren. Jeremiah Burroughs, for example, wrote that the mourners are those "who take to heart the afflictions of the church," and he made a case that it is important to mourn not only for sins but also for the afflictions and divisions of the church.[37] Surely this type of

---

from permanent marginalization" (Gustavo Gutiérrez, "Option for the Poor," in *Mysterium Liberationis: Fundamental Concepts of Liberation Theology*, ed. Ignacio Ellacuría and John Sobrino [Maryknoll, NY: Orbis Books, 1993], 242).

35. Erasmus of Rotterdam, *Paraphrase on Matthew*, vol. 45 of *Collected Works of Erasmus*, trans. Dean Simpson (Toronto: University of Toronto Press, 2008), 87.

36. Juan Maldonado, *S. Matthew's Gospel, Chapters I to XIV*, vol. 1 of *A Commentary on the Holy Gospels*, trans. and ed. George J. Davie (London, UK: John Hodges, 1888), 1:134.

37. Burroughs, *The Saints' Happiness*, 49, 60–74. Ca. 1730, B. Edwards Wells commended

mourning remains relevant today, within individual congregations fractured by conflict and in relation to the ongoing deep divisions among the various Christian communions worldwide. It encircles the fault lines within the church not only with the appropriate anguish but with the hope of God's promised comfort to those who suffer the pain of Christian brothers and sisters rent from one another.

One need not look far to find examples of mourning over a broken communion—the wounds within the Anglican Communion and fractures in the Methodist Church being only two of the most recent ones. Reaching further back, we might still mourn over the historic divisions between Orthodox, Catholic, and Protestant, and grieve that Christians of these churches are not welcome to break bread at the Lord's Table together. As I write this, I mourn over wounds in the church I have always called home (the Evangelical Covenant Church), for the ways a church that has always managed to live with tensions now seems unable to do so. It's the kind of mourning that might move one to action—say, in ecumenical conversations and friendships, or in peacemaking efforts among estranged brothers and sisters. It's the kind of mourning that also brings one to the throne of grace to plead for help from the one who makes whole.

Structural sin and injustice

One possible weakness of viewing mourning as penitence is that it focuses undue attention on individual sins and personal repentance. Several modern interpreters correct this focus by widening the scope of penitence to include repenting for one's involvement in structures of sin and injustice as well. Two commentators from an African context, for example, suggest that mourning is for both personal and structural sin. Hannah Kinoti describes the mourners in part as "those who count themselves party to the common guilt" and who "play the prophetic role to prick the conscience of their society." Paul John Isaak describes mourning for a wide variety of human actions, including global warming and ethnic cleansing, all of which "must make us weep with a deep grief."[38]

mourning "for the distressed state of the church" (Wells, *A Paraphrase with Annotations on the New Testament*, vol. 1 [London, 1730?], 45).

38. Hannah W. Kinoti, "Matthew 5:1–12. An African Perspective," in *Return to Babel: Global Perspectives on the Bible*, ed. Priscilla Pope-Levison and John R. Levison (Louisville: Westminster John Knox, 1999), 129; Paul John Isaak, "Luke," in *Africa Bible Commentary*, ed. Tokunboh Adeyemo, 2nd ed. (Nairobi, Kenya: WordAlive; Grand Rapids: Zondervan, 2010), 1144.

In an American context, author Sherwood Wirt and artist Laura James connect the mourning of the beatitude to the deep injustices of African slavery, lynching, and Jim Crow laws.[39] Anti-war activist John Dear paraphrases the beatitude, "Blessed are the billions who mourn their loved ones lost to starvation, injustice, relievable disease, and war—from Hiroshima and Vietnam to El Salvador and Iraq."[40] Dear describes grief as a spiritual practice that opens us to the anguish of those around the world affected by war, violence, and poverty. "Only then will our hearts be broken," he writes, "and the God of peace will console us."[41]

In the Cathedral of St. Paul in Minnesota, the south rose windows, designed by Charles Connick, depict eight saints of the Americas as personifications of the Beatitudes. Those who mourn are represented by St. Peter Claver, a Catalan Jesuit who ministered to slaves in Colombia for forty years and is today the patron saint of slaves and ministry to African Americans. In all these examples, the addition of structural injustice to the list of what counts as mourning can provide a helpful counterbalance to a potentially exclusive focus on personal sins, and can focus attention on lament for all "the death-dealing forces that undermine health in our lives and world."[42]

This kind of mourning points to both human and divine agency. It encourages human action to strive against the things that cause suffering, while still invoking the power of God to bring justice. If God is the kind of God who opposes and ultimately destroys all the "death-dealing forces" in our world, then mourning over those forces leads us to align ourselves with God in order to oppose them.

39. Sherwood E. Wirt, *Magnificent Promise: A Fresh View of the Beatitudes from the Cross* (Chicago: Moody Press, 1964), 21; for Laura James's "Sermon for our Ancestors," see Rebekah Eklund, "The Blessed," Visual Commentary on Scripture, http://thevcs.org/blessed.

40. John Dear, "The Beatitudes of Peace," *National Catholic Reporter* (Nov 21, 2006), https://www.ncronline.org/blogs/road-peace/beatitudes-peace.

41. John Dear, *Beatitudes of Peace: Meditations on the Beatitudes, Peacemaking and the Spiritual Life* (New London, CT: Twenty-Third Publications, 2016), 51.

42. Michael H. Crosby, *Spirituality of the Beatitudes: Matthew's Vision for the Church in an Unjust World*, rev. ed. (Maryknoll, NY: Orbis Books, 2005), quotation 59, see also 60, 80. For another example see Soong-Chan Rah, *Prophetic Lament: A Call for Justice in Troubled Times* (Downers Grove, IL: IVP Books, 2015).

Weeping with those who weep

Lily Watson's character Sylvia has already illustrated this form of weeping. Sylvia's grief teaches her to weep with her siblings, who are also grieving their mother's illness. We've also seen this kind of weeping earlier in the chapter in Graham and de la Puente. One of Graham's types of blessed mourning was "the mourning of love," or compassion for others. De la Puente likewise wrote that "all sorrow is sanctifying, except that which despairs; for it softens and humbles the heart, teaches sympathy for others and prepares the way for grace."[43] In this way, mourning becomes a form of bearing one another's burdens (Gal 6:2), or a way to offer a foretaste of the promised comfort by consoling "those who are in any affliction with the consolation with which we ourselves are consoled by God" (2 Cor 1:4). Both texts appear often in modern exegesis of this beatitude.

This is a fitting addition to the list. It resonates with several deeply scriptural principles, including weeping with those who weep, loving the neighbor, and bearing one another's burden. It captures something of the incarnation (*God with us*) in its commitment to draw near to all those who mourn, to enter into their grief with them.

Loss

It's common today to see the mourning of the beatitude as grief over loss and death. Luke's Gospel lends support to this interpretation. He included two scenes that we might think of as narrative enactments of the principle that those who weep now will laugh, both of which involve weeping over death. In the first, Jesus sees a widow whose only son has just died. He tells her, "Do not weep," and then raises her son back to life (Luke 7:11–17). In the second, the twelve-year-old daughter of a synagogue leader named Jairus dies. Once again, Jesus tells the mourners, "Do not weep," and raises the girl back to life (Luke 8:40–56).[44]

Patristic and medieval interpreters frequently argued that grief over death is *not* included in the beatitude, because it's simply a natural human reaction

---

43. Graham, *Secret of Happiness*, 23–24; for de la Puente see Barraud, *Meditations on the Mysteries*, 230.

44. For an exploration of these cases, see Sung Min Hong, *Those Who Weep Shall Laugh: Reversal of Weeping in the Gospel of Luke* (Eugene, OR: Pickwick, 2018), 66–80, 90–101.

to loss. For them, Jesus only blesses the countercultural, not the natural. A few, however, pressed gently against this principle, including two premodern thinkers who went against the grain of their eras. They were from Milan and Siena, respectively, and they both lost people they loved.

In the late fourth century, Ambrose of Milan (339–397) reoriented grief and death around the hope of the resurrection, not as a cause for triumph but as a matter of longing. Recall from chapter 1 that Ambrose linked the four Lukan Beatitudes to the four cardinal virtues. He connected weeping to the virtue of prudence, since "prudence weeps for this transitory world, and sighs for what is eternal" (*Comm. Luke* 5.68).[45] In other words, weeping is not merely sorrow over sin, but is a form of longing for the eternal, including the future resurrection of the dead. The same theme appears in Ambrose's second funeral oration for his brother Satyrus, when he defended his own weeping as yearning for the ultimate triumph of God over death: "What I am doing is not contrary to Scripture, namely, that I should grieve more patiently, but long more ardently."[46]

A millennium later, Bernardino of Siena (1380–1444) explicitly broke with the long tradition of connecting mourning to penitence by including a lamentation for his friend Vincent's death in a sermon on the beatitude. Like Ambrose, Bernardino was aware of and rejected the Stoic condemnation of sorrow: "sometimes we can and ought to mourn and be afflicted."[47] Modern thinkers typically agree with this rejection of Stoic principles: "God that was made flesh remembers that we are but flesh, and does not require of us to be insensible."[48]

45. Ambrose of Milan, *Commentary of Saint Ambrose on the Gospel According to Saint Luke*, trans. Íde M. Ní Riain (Dublin: Halcyon, 2001), 138–39.

46. Ambrose of Milan, "On His Brother Satyrus," in Gregory Nazianzen and Ambrose, *Funeral Orations*, ed. Martin R. P. McGuire, FC 22 (New York: Fathers of the Church, 1953), 214.

47. Carolyn Muessig, "Preaching the Beatitudes in the Late Middle Ages: Some Mendicant Examples," *Studies in Christian Ethics* 22, no. 2 (2009): 146, 148, quotation from 148. Bernardino followed the example of Bernard of Clairvaux, who likewise inserted a lamentation for the death of his brother Gerard into his commentary on *Song of Songs* (Muessig, "Preaching the Beatitudes," 146). Puritan preacher Jeremiah Burroughs cited Chrysostom to support his point that mourning over the death of a friend or child is blessed, but does not cite a source (Burroughs, *Saints' Happiness*, 37). For both Burroughs and Chrysostom, mourning is still primarily penitence for sin. In a 1672 funeral sermon, a preacher identified only as "Mr. Newton" invoked the beatitude as evidence against the Stoics that "it is not unlawful nor unfit sometimes to express our grief in tears" (Theodosia Alleine, *The life & death of Mr. Joseph Alleine*... [London: for Nevil Simmon, at the Princes-Arms in St. Pauls Church-yard, 1672], 6).

48. So Richard Allestree in 1684, in *Forty sermons whereof twenty one are now first publish'd, the greatest part preach'd before the King and on solemn occasions* (Oxford; London: R. Scott, G. Wells, T. Sawbridge, R. Bentley, 1684), 81.

These two theologians appealed to elements of Scripture, such as Jesus weeping at the grave of Lazarus, to make their case. On the one hand, both writers accepted the traditional Christian view that death is the gate to eternal life. Simultaneously, they remembered that Christian tradition views sin and death as the two great enemies of God whose power is broken on the cross and whose tyranny will finally be undone at Christ's second coming. Death is the last enemy to be destroyed by God (1 Cor 15:26). In that sense, death is *not* natural (contra Stoicism) and mourning over death flows into mourning over the state of a world broken by the fall—or to borrow Ambrose's language, into longing more ardently for the kingdom to come and death to be no more.[49]

Eschatological mourning: grief over the fallen world

By connecting death and the corresponding hope of resurrection with the eschaton, Ambrose and Bernardino pointed the way to the final "addition" to the list that I would like to consider. We likewise find its origins not in the modern era but in the fourth century. Gregory of Nyssa described mourning as godly repentance, but also as "something deeper." For Gregory, this deeper mourning was weeping over the fall—the rebellion of Adam and Eve that estranged God and humanity, and shattered the original harmony of creation. Mourning is the profound sorrow that results from recognizing the loss of the true good (the image of God) in human nature.[50] For Gregory, the more we recognize our tragic separation from the goodness and beauty in whose likeness we were fashioned, the more sorrow we should feel, since we realize that we are now distanced from our source of joy.[51] One must awaken, or become sensible, to the truth of this condition, and this awakening provokes grief and longing.[52] Like Ambrose, then, Gregory links mourning to a much wider narrative spanning all of Scripture, anchored in the fall and straining forward to God's new age.

Augustine, deliberately or incidentally, unveiled a similar logic when he paired the blessing on the mourners with the petition "Your will be done" from the Lord's Prayer. Placing the two lines in conversation with one another presses

49. Ambrose of Milan, "On His Brother Satyrus," 214.

50. Gregory of Nyssa, *The Lord's Prayer; The Beatitudes*, trans. Hilda C. Graef, ACW 18 (Mahwah, NJ: Paulist, 1954), 107–8.

51. Gregory of Nyssa, *The Lord's Prayer*, 112.

52. Françoise Vinel, "Grégoire de Nysse, *De Beatitudinibus*, Oratio III: 'Bienheureux les affligés, parce qu'ils seront consolés,' (Mt 5,5)," in *Gregory of Nyssa: Homilies on the Beatitudes*, ed. Hubertus R. Drobner and Albert Viciano (Leiden: Brill, 2000), 142–43.

the reader to consider the relationship between the two. As Aquinas observed, the mourners weep because God's will is *not* yet done, because eternal life is delayed and we are not yet "restored to the dignity of the first man [Adam]."[53]

Although penitence remains the dominant view, this minor key of mourning as eschatological longing does appear occasionally but persistently through the premodern eras. Indeed, according to Birgitta Stoll, medieval Irish commentaries usually included three blessed reasons for mourning: one's own sins, the sins of neighbors, and cries of longing for heaven.[54]

In a way, modern interpretations that focus on the backdrop of Isaiah 61 bring us full circle to this older emphasis, since through that lens the righteous mourn because "[u]ntil the eschatological reversal takes place, it is not possible to be content with the status quo."[55] Clarence Jordan, similarly, insisted that the mourners are those who are deeply grieved "that things are as they are" and are therefore moved to action.[56] In Dietrich Bonhoeffer's words, the mourners refuse "to be in tune with the world"; they "mourn for the world, for its guilt, its fate and its fortune."[57] Bonhoeffer's biographer Eberhard Bethge suggested that the intensified violence against Jews in the late 1930s led Bonhoeffer to tell his students that one could only rejoice in Christ if one also wept with the Jewish community in their suffering: "Only he who cries out for the Jews may sing Gregorian chants."[58] The mourners are those who *see* the suffering of the world, and enter into it, lifting it up to God in lament.

Discontentment with the status quo (in the words of Davies and Allison), or deep grief over the way things are (in the words of Clarence Jordan), is not very far removed from the painful conviction that God's will is not yet done.

53. Thomas Aquinas, *The Three Greatest Prayers: Commentaries on the Lord's Prayer, the Hail Mary, and the Apostles' Creed* (Manchester, NH: Sophia Institute Press, 1990), 134–35. In Aquinas's commentary on Matthew, he wrote that sorrow for our present sojourn in a place of misery is also blessed (Aquinas, *Commentary on Matthew*, C.5 L.2.422, 424).

54. Brigitta Stoll, *De Virtute in Virtutem: zur Auslegungs- und Wirkungsgeschichte der Bergpredigt in Kommentaren, Predigten und hagiographischer Literatur von der Merowingerzeit bis um 1200* (Tübingen: Mohr Siebeck, 1988), 177–78.

55. W. D. Davies and Dale C. Allison Jr., *A Critical and Exegetical Commentary on the Gospel According to Saint Matthew*, ICC 1 (London: T&T Clark, 1988), 1:448.

56. Clarence Jordan, *Sermon on the Mount*, rev. ed. (Valley Forge, PA: Judson, 1952), 24.

57. Dietrich Bonhoeffer, *The Cost of Discipleship* (New York: Simon & Schuster, 1995), 108.

58. Quoted in Eberhard Bethge, *Dietrich Bonhoeffer: A Biography*, rev. and ed. Victoria J. Barnett (Minneapolis: Fortress, 2000), 607. Paul Louis Metzger uses this as an example of the mourners in his *Beatitudes, Not Platitudes: Jesus' Invitation to the Good Life* (Eugene, OR: Cascade, 2018), 29.

The mourners are those who pray for God's kingdom to come because they feel the agony of its (even partial) absence.

Some modern commentators follow the same path when they connect the mourning of the beatitude to the yearning of all creation for the day of redemption (Rom 8:22). "The sound of mourning," writes Thomas Long, "is the whole creation 'groaning in labor pains' (Romans 8:22) and the faithful shouting defiantly, 'Where, O death, is your victory?' (1 Cor. 15:55)."[59] Segundo Galilea echoed Ambrose: mourning is "ardent, painful longing for the kingdom" and its full arrival.[60]

I will give Nicholas Wolterstorff the last word on this theme, for his meditation on this beatitude elegantly captures its ethos when he laments for the death of his son Eric: "The mourners are those who have caught a glimpse of God's new day, who ache with all their being for that day's coming, and who break out into tears when confronted with its absence. . . . They are the ones who realize that in God's realm of peace there is neither death nor tears and who ache whenever they see someone crying tears over death. The mourners are aching visionaries."[61]

They will be comforted / They will laugh

Comfort and laughter: joy

Comfort might seem too weak a word to bear the weight it is meant to bear here. But, wrote Elizabeth Rundle Charles, "when we drink deep enough into this quiet word we find it indeed all we want."[62]

Still, perhaps the slightly less familiar word *consolation* is better, as when Simeon yearns for "the consolation of Israel" (Luke 2:25). For Simeon, the con-

---

59. Thomas Long, "The Christian Funeral and the Blessedness of Mourning," *The Yale ISM Review* 4, no. 2 (Fall 2018), online at http://ismreview.yale.edu/article/the-christian-funeral-and-the-blessedness-of-mourning/). See also Carl G. Vaught, *The Sermon on the Mount: A Theological Investigation* (Waco, TX: Baylor University Press, 2001), 19; Karl Kertelge, "'Selig die Trauernden . . .' (Mt 5,4)," *IKaZ* 20, no. 5 (1991): 391. Kertelge links the mourning (*Trauern*) of the beatitude to lament (*Klage*) over suffering, especially that of the unredeemed creation (Rom 8:19–23) and the "incompleteness" (*Unvollendetheit*) of the salvation already obtained by faith (Kertelge, "Selig," 391).

60. Segundo Galilea, *The Beatitudes: To Evangelize as Jesus Did*, trans. Robert R. Barr (Maryknoll, NY: Orbis Books, 1984), 45.

61. Nicholas Wolterstorff, *Lament for a Son* (Grand Rapids: Eerdmans, 1987), 85–86.

62. Elizabeth Rundle Charles, *The Beatitudes: Thoughts for All Saints' Day* (London: Society for Promoting Christian Knowledge; New York: Young & Co., 1889), 49.

solation of Israel was "God's intervention to deliver Israel from its enemies and so to usher in the epoch of peace under the peaceful, just dominion of God."[63] Jewish scholar C. G. Montefiore defined the biblical notion of consolation as "solace": "to make whole or sound, to repair . . . an injured spirit, a broken faith."[64] The comforted, the consoled, are "not merely solaced" but "strengthened, fortified, defended, deepened, enlarged, elevated."[65] Comfort in the biblical sense is not a pat on the shoulder or a band-aid on a scraped knee, but is apocalyptic: it is the remaking of the old age into a new age where there are no more tears.[66]

Similarly, laughter doesn't mean chuckling at a good joke. It is an upwelling and outpouring of deep joy in those who once had no reason to laugh, much less to smile. One of the psalms that celebrates the Israelites' return from exile and the rebuilding of Jerusalem declares, "May those who sow in tears reap with shouts of joy. Those who go out weeping, bearing the seed for sowing, shall come home with shouts of joy, carrying their sheaves" (Ps 126:5–6).

Unlike the disagreement over what counts as mourning, understandings of what constitute comfort (and laughter) are relatively straightforward in the historical record. The primary question is the recurring one of time: when do the mourners receive their comfort? When will those who weep begin to laugh? The answer is typical: both in this life and the next. The comfort received in this life, for ancient and modern interpreters alike, is but a foretaste of the heavenly consolation to come.

Comfort now

The Holy Spirit is, of course, the Comforter—the Paraclete (Greek *Paraklētos*), which leads many writers to describe the comfort of this life as the presence and help of the Holy Spirit.[67] Because the word *Paraklētos* can also mean advo-

---

63. Joel B. Green, *The Gospel of Luke*, NICNT (Grand Rapids: Eerdmans, 1997), 145.

64. C. G. Montefiore, *Ancient Jewish and Greek Encouragement and Consolation* (Bridgeport, CT: Hartmore House, 1971), 1.

65. John Burr, *The Crown of Character: A Study of the Beatitudes of Our Lord* (James Clarke & Co., 1932), 44.

66. Michael Figura: "Eine Theologie des Trostes bewegt sich innerhalb der Gnadenlehre, der Soteriologie, der Pneumatologie und der Eschatologie" ("A theology of comfort moves within the doctrine of grace, soteriology, pneumatology, and eschatology") Michael Figura, "Der Heilige Geist als Tröster," *IKaZ* 20, no. 5 (1991): 396.

67. The word *paraklētos* is closely related to the word *paraklēsis* (encouragement, consolation, exhortation) and to the verb form (*parakaleō*) used by Matthew in his beatitude (comfort, console, urge, encourage, exhort).

cate or helper, some exegetes describe the promised consolation as the Spirit's accompaniment and help as we journey through this vale of tears.[68] As Bernard of Clairvaux wrote, "the loving-kind Lord sometimes refreshes the soul during her earthly pilgrimage."[69] Gene Davenport wrote more vividly that comfort is "the strength to endure the ravages of the Darkness without bitterness or despair."[70] Others point to the Spirit's role as providing assurance of the forgiveness of sins or the joy of salvation.[71]

For some, the Spirit's consolation spills over into the imperative to comfort one another in their suffering. Interpreters sometimes appeal to the apostle Paul: "the God of all consolation . . . consoles us in our affliction, so that we may be able to console those who are in any affliction with the consolation with which we ourselves are consoled by God" (2 Cor 1:4–5). For writers like Sherwood Wirt, this means not only spiritual or emotional support for those who suffer, but also providing comfort to mourners through concrete acts of mercy, and material assistance to the poor and all those who suffer (through organizations like World Vision, for example).[72]

Comfort in the next life

Consolations in this life, however, whether spiritual or material, are only the firstfruits of the joy to come. The "great consolation" in the world to come is the wedding supper of the Lamb, God's great banquet of overflowing abundance. Interpreters both ancient and modern find a description of God's promised

68. I'm grateful to John Donahue for pointing out this aspect of comfort to me. See John Donahue, "'Blessed are the Mourners': Lamentation and the Path to Justice" (paper presented at the Second Annual Marquette Scripture Conference: Biblical Ethics in the Twenty-First Century: In Memory of Rev. Yiu Sing Lúcás Chan, SJ, Marquette, MI, April 9, 2016).

69. Bernard of Clairvaux, "First Sermon for the Feast of All Saints. On the Eight Beatitudes," in St. Bernard's Sermons for the Seasons and Principal Festivals of the Year, vol. 3 (Westminster, MD: Carroll, 1950), 343.

70. Gene Davenport, Into the Darkness: Discipleship in the Sermon on the Mount (Eugene, OR: Wipf & Stock, 1988, 2003), 61.

71. Aquinas, Commentary on Matthew, C.5 L.2.423; Thomas Watson, The Beatitudes: An Exposition of Matthew 5:1–10 (Carlisle, PA: Banner of Truth Trust, 2014), 93; D. Martyn Lloyd-Jones, Studies in the Sermon on the Mount, vol. 1 (Grand Rapids: Eerdmans, 1960), 60–61; Kyriaki Karidoyanes FitzGerald and Thomas FitzGerald, Happy in the Lord: The Beatitudes for Everyday: Perspectives from Orthodox Spirituality (Brookline, MA: Holy Cross Orthodox Press, 2000), 50.

72. Wirt, Magnificent Promise, 28–29.

comfort in the words of a Christian visionary: a man named John who recorded a series of visions he experienced on the island of Patmos. Two texts are quoted over and over again. I will let them have the last word.

The first describes a great multitude from every nation standing before the throne of the Lamb, "who have come out of the great ordeal." They are now protected by the Lamb so that:

> They will hunger no more, and thirst no more;
>> the sun will not strike them,
>> nor any scorching heat;
> for the Lamb at the center of the throne will be their shepherd,
>> and he will guide them to springs of the water of life,
> and God will wipe away every tear from their eyes.   (Rev 7:9, 14–17)

The second text occurs after God's last adversaries, Satan and Death, have been destroyed. The old age has passed away, and the new creation arrives, the new Jerusalem descending from heaven, indicating the merging of God's dwelling place with the earthly realm. And the seer hears a loud voice from the heavenly throne declaring:

> See, the home of God is among mortals.
> He will dwell with them;
> they will be his peoples,
> and God himself will be with them;
> he will wipe every tear from their eyes.
> Death will be no more;
> mourning and crying and pain will be no more,
> for the first things have passed away.   (Rev 21:1–4)

5

Yield Your Ground

The Meek

Blessed are the meek, for they will inherit the earth (Matt 5:5).

Frederick Douglass was born a slave, in Tuckahoe, Maryland. Twenty years later, in 1838, he escaped. An eloquent orator, he became one of the country's most persuasive abolitionists. He met, and influenced, five American presidents. He stood in a long line of prophets, including Jeremiah and Jesus of Nazareth, when he fiercely denounced the hypocrisy of white American Christians. To do so, he used the Sermon on the Mount: "They strain at a gnat, and swallow a camel" (Matt 23:24). In Douglass's stinging rebuke, they would never admit into their fellowship a man who stole sheep but embraced those who steal men.[1]

A student in my Forgiveness and Reconciliation course once wrote me an essay describing some of his experiences as a young black man growing up in America. I'll call him Shawn. He talks about the racist comments people have made to him and about him, and how that's hurt him. He writes about being followed by security guards when he goes into stores. He tells me he's afraid of being shot by the police someday, just for being black. He writes about how angry he gets and how easy it would be to fight back. But he also talks about the real strength that it takes not to. He talks about Martin Luther King Jr.'s way of fighting evil with love as his model.[2]

---

1. Frederick Douglass, *Narrative of the Life of Frederick Douglass, an American Slave* (New York: Barnes & Noble Classics, 2003), 103.

2. Martin Luther King Jr., "Loving Your Enemies" (sermon delivered at Dexter Avenue Baptist Church, Montgomery, Alabama, November 1957 [MLKEC, INP, Martin Luther King, Jr. Estate Collection, In Private Hands, ET-1; Atl-5A & 5B]), https://kinginstitute.stan ford.edu/king-papers/documents/loving-your-enemies-sermon-delivered-dexter-avenue -baptist-church.

Frederick Douglass and Shawn might not be the kind of people who come to mind when you hear the word *meek*. We usually think of a meek person as someone who's passive or timid, someone who doesn't stand up for herself. Aren't the meek "the shy ones, the intimidated, the mild, the unassertive"?[3] A. M. Hunter complained, "For the modern man ... no Beatitude is more perplexing than this one. In it Jesus seems to be promising the meek the mastery of the world, when in fact everybody knows that the weak—and the meek—go to the wall."[4] (An old proverb declares, "The weakest go to the wall.")

Yet this understanding of meekness appears to be relatively recent. Hunter made that claim to his contemporaries in 1976. The view that meekness is weakness seems to have emerged in full force only in the eighteenth century. A visual clue hinting at the later emergence of this view appears in French painter Eustache Le Sueur's depiction in 1650 of the meek as a woman (likely a personified virtue) stroking a lamb who nuzzles her hand.[5] One of the earliest examples in written form occurs in 1764, when Samuel Collett paraphrased Matt 5:5 as a blessing on the inoffensive and harmless, the gentle and mild.[6] (Perhaps he was indebted to Charles Wesley's 1742 hymn "Gentle Jesus, meek and mild.")[7]

---

3. Dallas Willard, *The Divine Conspiracy: Rediscovering Our Hidden Life in God* (New York: HarperSanFrancisco, 1998), 117.

4. Archibald M. Hunter, *A Pattern for Life: An Exposition of the Sermon on the Mount*, rev. ed. (Philadelphia: Westminster, 1965), 37. Hunter goes on to propose that the word means "the gentleness and humility that go with strength in the greatest" (Hunter, *Pattern for Life*, 37).

5. Eustache Le Sueur, *Meekness*, 1650, oil on panel, Charles H. and Mary F. S. Worcester Collection, Art Institute of Chicago, https://www.artic.edu/artworks/47159/meekness. Le Sueur painted all eight beatitudes but only two survive. The other surviving painting depicts justice as a woman holding a flaming sword and a set of scales.

6. Samuel Collett, *A Paraphrase of the Fifth, Sixth, and Seventh Chapters of Matthew, with Proper Soliloquies at Every Period* (London: J. Williams, 1764), 12–13. Similarly for Isaac Allen, meekness is quiet submission to the trials of life, whether injuries from men or chastisements from God (Isaac Allen, *Reflection on Portions of the Sermon on the Mount. Intended Principally for Soldiers* [London: SPCK, 1848], 11). So also John Cennick, who in 1753 described a meek person as tender-hearted and contrite, "a bruised or broken-hearted soul" (Cennick, *The Beatitudes, Being the Substance of a Discourse Delivered in Dublin, Dec. the 21st, 1753*, 2nd ed. [London: M. Lewis, 1756], 13). Ca. 1730, B. Edward Wells wrote that the meek are those "of a gentle and quiet Temper" who are not apt to give offense and who patiently bear offenses from others (Wells, *A Paraphrase with Annotations on the New Testament*, vol. 1 [London, 1730?], 45). Wells's use of the word "offense" (giving or taking offense) may help to explain Collett's use of the word "inoffensive."

7. Judith Lechman points out that our understanding of meekness shaped—and is shaped by—nineteenth-century depictions of "a bland and docile Christ" (Judith C. Lechman, *The Spirituality of Gentleness: Growing toward Christian Wholeness* [New York: Harper & Row, 1987], 1).

To be sure, not all late eighteenth-century interpreters shared this view. In 1738, Arthur St. George described meekness as "just abhorrence of strife and contention" and the refusal to take revenge.[8] In the 1740s and 1750s, John Wesley's sermons on the Beatitudes took a page straight from Aristotle's book by describing meekness as the "midline" between two extremes: neither apathy nor uncontrolled emotion; neither insensibility nor unregulated anger, hatred, or fear.[9] Wesley's view gives us a glimpse into the interpretation that dominated prior to the eighteenth century. And, as late as 1845, the abolitionist William Lloyd Garrison could still use the word meek to describe, with great admiration, the powerful prophet Frederick Douglass.[10]

It's possible that English readers like Collett and Hunter were hampered by a translation difficulty. The Greek word *praÿs* has no good single equivalent in English. The earliest English translation used "mild" (Wycliffe Bible, 1388). "Meek" made its first appearance in William Tyndale's translation (1530–1534). Modern translations, following Tyndale and the KJV, usually use "meek," but a few opt for "gentle" or (less commonly) "humble" or "lowly." But for an English speaker today, gentleness is not usually the same trait as meekness or lowliness.

In the previous chapter, I suggested that Reformation and modern interpreters helpfully supplemented the dominant interpretation of the second beatitude (mourning only as penitence) by adding other forms of mourning such as grief over loss and longing for God's justice.

In this chapter, I will seek to persuade you of the reverse: that the tradition prior to the modern era has rich resources that somewhere along the way we largely, or least partially, lost.

In this case, ancient readers had wisdom worth recovering about the function and associations of the word *praÿs*. The past reveals something very different from the modern view that meekness is timidity. For many of our predecessors, meekness was a form of power, not of weakness. It referred not to those who never get angry but to those who never lose their temper. The meek are not the weak but the self-controlled, not those who shrink back but those who willingly choose to yield. We might paraphrase the beatitude, "Blessed are those who yield"—to others and to God.

8. Arthur St. George, *The Blessings of Christian Philosophy; Being a Treatise on the Beatitudes* (London: W. Innys & R. Manby, 1738), 93.

9. John Wesley, *The Nature of the Kingdom: Wesley's Messages on the Sermon on the Mount*, ed. Clare George Weakley Jr. (Minneapolis: Bethany House Publishers, 1979), 64–65.

10. William Lloyd Garrison, preface to *Narrative of the Life of Frederick Douglass, an American Slave*, by Frederick Douglass (New York: Barnes & Noble Classics, 2003), 5.

The second part of this beatitude's story is about its second half—about what kind of earth the meek inherit, and why. Two views emerge; they are in tension, but are often held together: the practical possession of the things of this world, and the glorious inheritance of the new earth of the eschatological age.

Jesus as meek

Praÿs is a rare word in the New Testament. It occurs only once outside of Matthew's Gospel, in reference to "the lasting beauty of a gentle [*praÿs*] and quiet spirit" rather than outer displays of wealth and social status (1 Pet 3:4). Matthew used it three times, once in the beatitude and twice in reference to Jesus. In Matt 11:29, Jesus describes himself as "gentle [*praÿs*] and humble in heart." More allusively, the word appears in the Zechariah passage quoted at the triumphal entry to explain why Jesus will enter Jerusalem seated on a donkey: "your king is coming to you, humble [*praÿs*], and mounted on a donkey" (Matt 21:5). (These examples show that the NRSV has chosen three different words to render the Greek *praÿs*: meek [Matt 5:5], gentle [Matt 11:29], and humble [Matt 21:5].)

Whatever meekness meant to Matthew, then, it must be a quality displayed by Jesus. Some understand it as humility, since Matt 11:29 pairs gentleness (or meekness) with a humble heart. This observation leads some readers to connect meekness to Christ's *kenōsis* or self-emptying as narrated in Phil 2:3–11. Karl Barth, for example, saw only Jesus as truly meek, because he willingly renounced his exalted power and divine status; only Christ has "truly fallen . . . from the height and majesty of God" to the humiliation of the cross and "the depths of hell."[11] Others point to the triumphal entry and explain meekness as the restrained power of "a king whose rule does not depend on political and military might."[12] Both these associations will resurface later in this chapter.

Finally, some writers have noted that in the same gospel in which Jesus describes himself as meek, he later overturns tables in the temple (Matt 21:12) and issues scathing denunciations of the religious leaders (Matt 23:1–36). Whatever

11. Karl Barth, *Against the Stream: Shorter Post-War Writings (1946–52)* (New York: Philosophical Library, 1954), 54.

12. Joseph Ratzinger (Pope Benedict XVI), *Jesus of Nazareth: From the Baptism in the Jordan to the Transfiguration*, trans. Adrian J. Walker (New York: Doubleday, 2007), 81. On meekness as Christ's forbearance, see also Chromatius of Aquileia, *Sermons and Tractates on Matthew*, trans. Thomas P. Scheck, ACW 75 (New York: The Newman Press, 2018), 17.4.1; Chrysostom, *Three Homilies* 4.4 (NPNF¹ 9:205–6).

the meekness of the beatitude is, then, if Jesus helps to define it (as Matthew suggests), it must not rule out decisive and even confrontational action—as Frederick Douglass modeled.

The meek as the poor in spirit

For many modern scholars, Jesus's meekness lies in his self-identification with the poor. In this view, the meek are not the gentle but the lowly; they are, in fact, the same as the poor in spirit. As Powell observes, "Most [modern] interpreters regard the meek (*praeis*) in 5:5 as an approximate synonym for the 'poor in spirit' of 5:3."[13]

This is not an entirely unprecedented view. Origen and Jerome anticipated this modern move when they viewed the poor in spirit as parallel to the meek. For these two ancient thinkers, unlike their modern historical-critical counterparts, both poverty of spirit and meekness indicated a humble trust in God. Origen aligned the two beatitudes through their respective promises "inherit the earth" and "inherit the kingdom of heaven," which he took, counterintuitively, to be the same reward (more on that below).[14] Jerome found the meek and the poor in spirit described together in Isa 61:1–3, which he understood as the background to both blessings (*Comm. Isa.* 17.13).[15]

Like Jerome, modern scholars see Isaiah 61 as the most important background to the Beatitudes as a whole, but they also usually see Psalm 37 as the key text for the third beatitude. Interpreters throughout history have noted that Matt 5:5 quotes from Ps 36:11 LXX.

13. Mark Allan Powell, "Matthew's Beatitudes: Reversals and Rewards of the Kingdom," *CBQ* 58 (1996): 466. So also John Farrer, *Sermons on the Mission and Character of Christ, and on the Beatitudes* (Oxford: Oxford University Press, 1804), 257–58. Farrer understood them in parallel in part because of the KJV of Isa 61:1 ("good tidings unto the meek"), which becomes in Luke "the gospel to the poor" (Luke 4:18 KJV) (Farrer, *Sermons on the Mission*, 257).

14. Origen, *De Principiis* 2.3.7 (*ANF* 4:245). Calvin elided the poor of Luke 6:20 with the meek who patiently persevere and trust God to care and provide for them (John Calvin, *Sermons on the Beatitudes: Five Sermons from the Gospel Harmony, Delivered in Geneva in 1560* [Carlisle, PA: Banner of Truth Trust, 2006], 36).

15. Jerome, *Commentary on Isaiah; St. Jerome's Translation of Origen's Homilies 1–9 on Isaiah*, ACW 68, trans. Thomas P. Scheck (Mahwah, NJ: The Newman Press, 2015), 785. Mackintosh Mackay described meekness as the result of the previous two beatitudes: "the meek are those who have become truly poor in spirit before God, and who are brought truly to mourn for their sins" (Mackay, *A practical exposition of the first ten verses of the fifth chapter of the Gospel by Matthew*, 2 vols. [Edinburgh: William Whyte & Co., 1840–1842], 1:199).

Matt 5:5: Blessed are the meek, for they will inherit the earth
Makarioi hoi praeis, hoti autoi klēronomēsousin tēn gēn

Ps 36:11 LXX: And the meek will inherit the earth
Hoi de praeis klēronomēsousin gēn

The modern exegetes who see poverty of spirit and meekness as synonyms appeal to what they see as the common Hebrew word (*'āniy* / *'ānāw*) underlying the word "poor" (Greek *ptōchos*) in the first beatitude and Isaiah 61 (Matt 5:3/Luke 6:20; Isa 61:1 LXX) and the word "meek" (Greek *praeis*) in the third beatitude and Psalm 37 (Matt 5:5; Ps 36:11 LXX).[16] From there, interpretations diverge in two directions, depending on whether one understands the *'ănāwîm* to be the humble or the humbled. (I've already mapped out this same divergence in detail in the chapter on the first beatitude.)

For some, the meek are those who have been humbled or humiliated.[17] Rather than being those who choose not to assert themselves, they have no power by which they might do so. Robert Brawley argues that the promise to inherit land is so prominent in Psalm 37 because the meek are the poor and oppressed who are often deprived of land or access to it.[18] Benedict Green, however, appealed to the same Hebrew background to suggest that meekness refers to "humility toward people, which can be qualified as gentle, non-assertive and non-violent."[19] This aligns him more closely with his ancient predecessors.

Psalm 37 and Greek literature

Psalm 37, then, provides the first essential background for the beatitude. To encounter the other backdrop, we turn from the world of the Old Testament

---

16. E.g., Jacques Dupont, *Le problème littéraire—Les deux versions du Sermon sur la montagne et des béatitudes*, vol. 1 of *Les Béatitudes* (Bruges, Belgium: Abbaye de Saint-André, 1958), 252; H. Benedict Green, *Matthew, Poet of the Beatitudes* (Sheffield: Sheffield Academic, 2001), 182.

17. E.g., Frederick Dale Bruner, *The Christbook, Matthew 1–12*, vol. 1 of *Matthew: A Commentary*, rev. ed. (Grand Rapids: Eerdmans, 2004), 165; Donald A. Hagner, *Matthew 1–13*, WBC 33A (Nashville: Nelson, 1993), 87; Powell, "Matthew's Beatitudes," 466.

18. Robert L. Brawley, "Evocative Allusions in Matthew: Matthew 5:5 as a Test Case," *HvTSt* 59, no. 3 (2003): 612.

19. Green, *Matthew, Poet*, 182–88, quotation 188. See also Glen Stassen, "The Beatitudes as Eschatological Peacemaking Virtues," in *Character Ethics and the New Testament: Moral Dimensions of Scripture*, ed. Robert L. Brawley (Louisville: Westminster John Knox, 2007), 249.

to a stream of thought that exerted a powerful influence on Second Temple Judaism and on early Christianity: Greco-Roman philosophy. It is here that we find the explicit connection between the word *praÿs* and the dominant premodern understanding of meekness as the ordering, restraint, and proper use of anger.

In his *Republic*, Plato (ca. 428–348 BCE) described meekness as a quality not of the powerless but the powerful. Guardians (the rulers and protectors of a society) "must be amenable [*praous*] toward their own people, but intractable against their enemies."[20] In another ancient writing it is associated with the stance that "judges should punish with more leniency than the laws prescribe."[21] It is the tyrant who is weak, not the just ruler or judge. Ignatius of Antioch (ca. 35–107) adopted this understanding when he described the meekness of a bishop as "a great power" (Ignatius, Letter to the Trallians, 3.2–3).

Meekness is sometimes also used to describe a gentle or calm person, as opposed to a short-tempered or violent person.[22] Xenophon of Athens (ca. 430–354 BCE), a Greek philosopher and historian, used the verb form of the word (*praunō*) in relation to both the calming of a spirited horse and the calming of an irritated person.[23] (In modern English, the verb *gentle* is still used to refer to the "gentling" of a wild or untrained horse.)

But the primary source for understanding meekness as restraint of anger comes from Aristotle. For Aristotle, every virtue is a mean, or a middle ground, between two extremes. As a virtue, meekness (Gk. *praotēs*, another spelling of Matt 5:5's noun) is the mean between *horgilotēs* and *aorgēsia* (Aristotle, *Nicomachean Ethics* IV.5; *Magna Moralia* I.22).[24] The first extreme, *horgilotēs*, is irascibility, angriness, bad temper, or the tendency to get angry "against everyone and on all occasions." The second extreme, *aorgēsia*, is

20. Plato, *Republic, Books 1–5*, trans. Chris Emlyn-Jones and William Preddy, LCL 216 (Cambridge, MA: Harvard University Press, 2013), Book 2, 375c. For more on *praytēs* as a leadership quality in the Hellenistic world, see Deirdre J. Good, *Jesus the Meek King* (Harrisburg, PA: Trinity Press International, 1999), 5, 42, 71, 87.

21. Friedrich Hauck and Siegfried Schulz, "πραΰς, πραΰτης," TDNT 6:646.

22. E.g., Plato, *Republic*, 2.375c; 1.354a.

23. Xenophon, *De equitandi ratione* [On the Art of Horsemanship], 9.2, 9.6, 9.10. Mary Karr's poem "Who the Meek Are Not" perfectly captures this imagery of meekness as a powerful stallion "holding that great power in check" (in Karr, *Sinner's Welcome* [New York: HarperCollins, 2006], 23).

24. Aristotle, *The Great Ethics of Aristotle*, trans. Peter L. P. Simpson (New Brunswick: Transaction Publishers, 2014), 1.22. The authorship of the *Great Ethics* (*Magna Moralia*) is debated; scholars ascribe it to Aristotle or his students, like Aristotle's son Nicomachus and/or Eudemus of Rhodes.

literally "un-anger" or "without anger"; it is also described as lack of spirit, more colorfully as a form of spineless incompetence, or as the characteristic of never being angry with anyone for any reason.[25] A meek person, then, "is angry at the right things and with the right people, and, further, as he ought, when he ought, and as long as he ought." Meek or gentle-tempered people are the opposite of hot-tempered, quick-tempered, and sulky people (in other words, people who get angry too often, too much, and for too long); they are also the opposite of people who are thought "not to feel things nor to be pained by them" (*Eth. nic.* 4.5).[26]

This influential stream of thought certainly provided the background for early Christian interpreters to understand *praÿs* as the restraint of anger. Now, one might object that Jesus likely spoke the Beatitudes in Aramaic, not in Greek, so it is irrelevant what the Greek word is. One might also worry that relying on Aristotle gives too much weight to a pagan Greek background and not enough to Matthew's Jewish background. There are a number of ways to address these concerns. First, we should remember that Judaism and Hellenistic thought were not two wholly distinct worlds in the first century. Second, since we don't have access to the original Aramaic (if indeed it was spoken in Aramaic), attempts to reconstruct an Aramaic version of the Beatitudes are tenuous at best. We are on firmer footing when we trace the beatitude back to its origins in Psalm 37—or, more precisely, to the Greek version of the Psalm (Ps 36 LXX), which does use the word *praeis*.

Premodern and modern interpreters alike recognize Psalm 36 LXX as the background to the beatitude. One key question is how much of the psalm undergirds Matthew's beatitude. Psalm 36 LXX repeats the promise of inheriting the land five times. According to the psalmist, who shall inherit the land? The inheritors are those who refrain from anger, forsake wrath, and wait patiently for the LORD (vv. 7–9); the meek (v. 11); the righteous who are generous and are blessed by the LORD (vv. 21b–22); the righteous and faithful ones (vv. 28–29); and those who wait for the LORD and keep to his way (v. 34). Espe-

---

25. For the various translations see Aristotle, *Metaphysics, Books X–XIV, Oeconomica and Magna Moralia*, trans. G. Cyril Armstrong (London: William Heinemann; Cambridge, MA: Harvard University Press, 1947), 521; Aristotle, *Great Ethics*, trans. Simpson, 29; and Hauck and Schulz, "πραΰς, πραΰτης," *TDNT* 6:645.

26. Aristotle, *Nicomachean Ethics*, trans. David Ross, rev. ed., Oxford World Classics (Oxford, 2009), 73. Repeated in very similar terms in Arius Didymus, *Epitome of Peripatetic Ethics* 139.11–15 (a summary of Aristotelian philosophy), which repeats Aristotle's claims that it is not virtuous to get angry either at everything or at nothing; rather, "mildness is the habit that is praised, whereby we get angry when and as and at what we should" (Aristotle, *Great Ethics*, 97).

cially in verses 7–9, the psalm provides further warrant for linking the meek with those who refrain from anger.

To be sure, this is a loose connection. When the word *praÿs* appears in other psalms and in prophetic literature, it usually indicates (as it does in Ps 37), the faithful and devout, those who are humble before God, the opposite of the sinners and the wicked (Pss 24:9 LXX, 33:3 LXX, 146:6 LXX, 149:4 LXX; Zeph 3:12; Isa 26:6). It refers once to Moses, in apparent reference to his close relationship with God (Num 12:3). Once, it is used of the weak and powerless (Job 36:15); and once it is applied to the coming messianic king, in the verse that appears also in Matthew's Gospel (Zech 9:9; Matt 21:5).

Aside from Psalm 37, two other texts appear relatively often in premodern exegesis of the beatitude, neither of which contain the word *praÿs* but both of which use the phrase "slow to anger." Several writers appealed to a biblical proverb to explain the beatitude: "One who is slow to anger is better than the mighty, and one whose temper is controlled than one who captures a city" (Prov 16:32). In the New Testament, Jas 1:19–21 uses not the adjective *praÿs* but the noun form, *praÿtēs* (gentleness). James contrasts gentleness with anger (*orgē*) and pairs it with the qualities of being quick to listen and slow to anger. Dhuoda of Septimania defined meekness by quoting Jas 1:19 (the meek are those who are "slow to speech and slow to anger"); the meek person is patient and is able to control their spirit and their tongue.[27]

Restraint of anger

Dhuoda had a long history of interpretation behind her. For around 1500 years, the vast majority of interpreters in East and West—Orthodox, Catholic, and Protestant—understood meekness as the moderation of anger. Ambrose of Milan, who associated the Beatitudes with the cardinal virtues, saw meekness as an example of the virtue of fortitude (courage), since "it belongs to fortitude to conquer anger" (*Comm. Luke* 5.54, 5.67, 5.68).[28]

For Thomas Aquinas, conquering anger does not mean never getting angry. Instead, the meek person never loses her temper, even when provoked.[29] Interpreters frequently invoke Aristotle's concept of the mean to

---

27. Dhuoda, *Handbook for her Warrior Son* 4.8, ed. and trans. Marcelle Thiébaux (Cambridge: Cambridge University Press, 1998), 149.

28. Ambrose of Milan, *Commentary of Saint Ambrose on the Gospel According to Saint Luke*, trans. Íde M. Ní Riain (Dublin: Halcyon, 2001), 135, 139.

29. Thomas Aquinas, *Commentary on the Gospel of Matthew, Chapters 1–12*, trans. Jeremy

argue that meekness describes a person "who is angry for the right reasons, in the right way, at the right things and for the right length of time."[30] Of course, this leaves quite a lot of room for interpretation over what counts as "right," so some interpreters try to give more concrete suggestions.

John Norris invoked the command "love your neighbor as yourself" when he proposed that one's anger should never injure the neighbor.[31] Paul John Isaak writes, similarly, that the meek person uses her power only for the benefit of others and never for their harm.[32] Cornelius à Lapide offered a practical word of advice: don't say or do *anything* while you're still angry. (He suggested that you consider reciting the letters of the alphabet to calm yourself down.)[33] Alexander Findlay counseled his listeners to make allowances "in matters of smaller moment" and to distinguish between the trivial and the important: a meek person "knows by instinct where he must fight and where he can safely yield ground."[34] Sometimes it's better to lose an argument than to hurt a friend.

Many interpreters expand meekness to include the taming not only of anger but of other unruly desires as well: impatience, envy, fear, lust, despair, vanity, vengefulness.[35] Gregory of Nyssa wrote that meekness is the habit that

---

Holmes and Beth Mortensen, ed. The Aquinas Institute, Biblical Commentaries 33 (Lander, WY: The Aquinas Institute for the Study of Sacred Doctrine, 2013), C.5 L.2.419.

30. William Barclay, *The Old Law and the New Law* (Philadelphia: Westminster, 1972), 53; see also William Barclay, *Plain People Look at the Beatitudes* (Nashville: Abingdon, 1965), 36. This is an almost direct quotation of the translation in Aristotle, *The Ethics of Aristotle: The Nicomachean Ethics*, trans. J. A. K. Thomson, revd. Hugh Tredennick (New York: Penguin Books, 1953, 1976), 160; see similar language in Jeremiah Burroughs, *The Saints' Happiness* (Edinburgh: James Nichol, 1867; Soli Deo Gloria, 1988, 1992), 70–72; and Robert Harris, *The Way to True Happiness: Delivered in Twenty-Four Sermons upon the Beatitudes*, ed. Don Kistler (Morgan, PA: Soli Deo Gloria, 1998), 93.

31. John Norris, *Christian Blessedness: Or Discourses upon the Beatitudes*, vol. 1 of *Practical Discourses Upon the Beatitudes*, 5th ed. (London: S. Manship, 1707), 50.

32. Paul John Isaak, "Luke," in *Africa Bible Commentary*, ed. Tokunboh Adeyemo, 2nd ed. (Nairobi, Kenya: WordAlive; Grand Rapids: Zondervan, 2010), 1144.

33. Cornelius à Lapide, *The Holy Gospel According to Saint Matthew*, vol. 1 of *The Great Commentary of Cornelius à Lapide*, trans. Thomas W. Mossman, rev. ed. (Fitzwilliam, NH: Loreto, 2008), 213.

34. J. Alexander Findlay, *The Realism of Jesus: A Paraphrase and Exposition of the Sermon on the Mount* (New York: Doran, 1924?), 54.

35. Cornelius à Lapide, *The Holy Gospel According to Saint Matthew*, 209; Servais Pinckaers, *The Pursuit of God's Happiness—God's Way: Living the Beatitudes*, trans. Mary Thomas Noble (New York: Society of St. Paul, 1998), 61; Henry Churchill King, "The Fundamental Conditions of Happiness, as Revealed in Jesus' Beatitudes," *The Biblical World* 23, no. 3 (March 1904): 182–83;

gives way only reluctantly to the evil impulses in human nature. He appealed to the Platonic principle that a person's "reasoning power restrains the desires like a rein."[36] Thus meekness becomes understood not only as the mean between fury and apathy, but in general as a calm equilibrium between uncontrolled emotions and the inability to care about anything at all. For early twentieth-century writer Henry Bolo, meekness is a form of detachment that delivers a person "from the twofold bondage of self-conceit and human respect" because it frees the meek person from "anxiety as regards the judgments of man."[37] (Or as physicist Richard Feynman often said, "What do *you* care what other people think?")[38]

A minority strand of interpretation about the beatitude's promise illuminates the same principle. For some, inheriting the earth means the possession of one's own body. Think of the phrase "a self-possessed person": that's the meaning in view here. This creative exegesis appears in the writing of the monk Bernard of Clairvaux (1090–1153?), who took "the earth" in Matt 5:5 as "the earth of our own body," and meekness as the virtue that allows the soul to possess and reign over her own body.[39] This is a rare interpretation; it occurs only occasionally as a supplement to other interpretations.[40] But it fits neatly with the concept of meekness as restraint of uncontrollable anger. A self-possessed person does not lose her temper.

William H. Russell, "The Eight Beatitudes in the School Program," *The Catholic Educational Review* 26 (1928): 199; Billy Graham, *The Secret of Happiness: Jesus' Teaching on Happiness as Expressed in the Beatitudes* (Garden City, NY: Doubleday, 1955), 36–37; Clement of Alexandria, *Stromata* 4.6 (ANF 2:415).

36. Gregory of Nyssa, *The Lord's Prayer; The Beatitudes*, trans. Hilda C. Graef, ACW 18 (Mahwah, NJ: Paulist, 1954), 101–3.

37. Henry Bolo, *The Beatitudes: The Poor in Spirit, the Meek and Humble*, trans. Madame Cecilia (London: Kegan Paul, Trench, Trübner & Co., 1906), 180.

38. Richard Feynman, *What Do You Care What Other People Think? Further Adventures of a Curious Character* (New York: Norton, 2018).

39. Bernard of Clairvaux, "First Sermon for the Feast of All Saints. On the Eight Beatitudes," in *St. Bernard's Sermons for the Seasons and Principal Festivals of the Year*, vol. 3 (Westminster, MD: Carroll, 1950), 341.

40. E.g., Pinckaers wrote that the earth is "obviously" the kingdom of heaven, but it is also "the peaceful possession of ourselves—the earth of our bodies and hearts" (Pinckaers, *Pursuit of God's Happiness*, 71). Lapide referred to this as the anagogical interpretation, citing Hilary and Ambrose (Cornelius à Lapide, *The Holy Gospel According to Saint Matthew*, 212). See also E. M., *Ashrea: Or, the Grove of the Beatitudes, Represented in Emblemes* (London: Printed for W. P. at Grayes-Inn Gate in Holborne, 1665; Reprint: English Emblem Books 18; Yorkshire, England: Scolar Press, 1970), A5, 21.

Do not return evil for evil

If meek people never lose their tempers, meek people likewise do not repay "evil for evil" (Rom 12:17, 1 Thess 5:15, 1 Pet 3:9). This phrase (and these biblical verses) occurs over and over again in exegesis of the beatitude.[41] In light of the exhortations not to return evil for evil, meekness becomes understood as the refusal to take revenge when wronged or to hit back when hurt. One is willing to put aside even one's rights because vengeance belongs to God.[42] Indeed, a meek person not only refrains from vengeful actions but from a vengeful spirit. For Calvin the meek are "the calm and quiet ones, who are not easily provoked by wrongs, who do not sulk over offences, but are more ready to endure everything, than pay the wicked the same back."[43] The meek "would rather forgive twenty injuries than revenge one."[44] As Bonhoeffer wrote, the meek "yield their ground."[45]

Yielding one's ground could easily be seen as weak in a culture that praises standing one's ground. But the meek yield not out of fear or lack of strength, but deliberately, for the sake of the other, for the sake of Christ. Rather than striking back when mistreated, the meek pay back good for evil; they turn the other cheek; they bless the enemy rather than curse; they love and pray for their persecutors.[46] If you need a more concrete and light-hearted example,

41. E.g., Augustine, *Serm. Dom.* 1.2.4, in *The Lord's Sermon on the Mount*, trans. John J. Jepson, ACW 5 (Mahwah, NJ: Paulist, 1948), 14; Calvin, *Sermons on the Beatitudes*, 37–38; Thomas Watson, *The Beatitudes: An Exposition of Matthew 5:1–10* (Carlisle, PA: Banner of Truth Trust, 2014), 110–14, 117.

42. D. Martyn Lloyd-Jones, *Studies in the Sermon on the Mount*, vol. 1 (Grand Rapids: Eerdmans, 1960), 70; similarly, Carl F. H. Henry, *Christian Personal Ethics* (Grand Rapids: Eerdmans, 1957), 503; and Ellen Gould White, *Thoughts from the Mount of Blessing* (Mountain View, CA: Pacific Press Publishing Association, 1900, 1928), 30.

43. John Calvin, *A Harmony of the Gospels Matthew, Mark and Luke*, vol. 1, ed. David W. Torrance and Thomas F. Torrance, trans. A. W. Morrison (Grand Rapids: Eerdmans, 1972), 170. Aquinas: Through this blessing, Christ condemns the irascible appetite, "which desires vengeance on enemies" (Thomas Aquinas, *Commentary on Matthew*, C.5 L.2.406; see also Thomas Aquinas, *The Three Greatest Prayers: Commentaries on the Lord's Prayer, the Hail Mary, and the Apostles' Creed* [Manchester, NH: Sophia Institute Press, 1990], 128). John Norris claimed that the beatitude rules out private vindication (revenge) but leaves room for some "public vindication of injuries," which he saw (against the Anabaptists) as necessary for society (Norris, *Christian Blessedness*, 64).

44. Matthew Henry, *Matthew to John*, vol. 5 of *An Exposition of the Old and New Testament* (New York: Revell, n.d. [1708–1710?]), comment on Matt 5:5; section III.

45. Dietrich Bonhoeffer, *The Cost of Discipleship* (New York: Simon & Schuster, 1995), 109.

46. Luis de la Puente, in C. W. Barraud, *Meditations on the Mysteries of Our Holy Faith, To-*

Sherwood Wirt suggested, "consider driving in traffic. If there is one place where our century needs to understand the meaning of meekness, it is behind the wheel of an automobile."[47] Wirt didn't live into the twenty-first century; if he were living today, he might have suggested social media as another context that sorely needs more meekness.

For another set of interpreters, the prohibition against revenge implied in the beatitude extends into a refusal to use any kind of violence in any context. Thomas Aquinas hinted at this broad use by contrasting meekness with war.[48] Hannah Adams contrasted meekness with the "military spirit" of those who hoped for a Messiah to subdue the Romans through violence, especially those who caused the Jewish-Roman War.[49] One modern German translation used in Catholic liturgy perfectly captures this meaning by rendering the beatitude "Blessed are those who do not employ violence" (*Selig, die keine Gewalt anwenden*).[50] Perhaps the translators followed the lead of Catholic humanist Erasmus, who paraphrased the beatitude as a declaration of blessing on "the people who do not use force against anyone, who after being harmed readily pardon the injury, who would rather lose something than fight for it, who regard harmony and tranquility of mind more valuable than a large estate, who regard quiet poverty more desirable than quarrelsome riches."[51]

This interpretation appears on the Protestant side as well, perhaps not surprisingly in the work of Anabaptist Huldrych Zwingli, who wrote that meekness "does not permit violence and injustice to be done to anyone."[52] Among modern writers, Glen Stassen turned to Psalm 37 to find the theme of nonviolence there, since the psalm aligns the meek with the peace-

gether with a Treatise in Mental Prayer (New York: Benziger, 1916), 228; Wesley, Sermon 23.3.12–13, in *Nature of the Kingdom*, 100–101.

47. Sherwood E. Wirt, *Magnificent Promise: A Fresh View of the Beatitudes from the Cross* (Chicago: Moody Press, 1964), 44.

48. Thomas Aquinas, *Commentary on Matthew*, C.5 L.2.412.

49. Hannah Adams, *Letters on the Gospels* (Cambridge, MA: Hillard & Metcalf, 1824), 47.

50. Michael H. Crosby, *Spirituality of the Beatitudes: Matthew's Vision for the Church in an Unjust World*, rev. ed. (Maryknoll, NY: Orbis Books, 2005), 82. Lohfink renders the beatitude "Blessed are those who do not use violence" (Gerhard Lohfink, "The Appeasement of the Messiah: Thoughts on Psalm 37 and the Third Beatitude," *TD* 44 [1997]: 234). René Coste refers to it as the beatitude of nonviolence in *Le grand secret des béatitudes: une théologie et une spiritualité pour aujourd'hui* (Paris: Editions S.O.S., 1985), 159.

51. Erasmus of Rotterdam, *Paraphrase on Matthew*, vol. 45 of *Collected Works of Erasmus*, trans. Dean Simpson (Toronto: University of Toronto Press, 2008), 86.

52. Ulrich Luz, *Matthew 1–7*, trans. James E. Crouch, Hermeneia (Minneapolis: Fortress: 2007), 194, citing Zwingli, *Opera* vol. 6/1: *Annotationes in Evangelium Matthaei*, 220.

able (v. 37) and contrasts them with the violent and the wicked with their drawn swords and bows (v. 14, v. 35). Stassen also appealed to Zech 9:9–10, in which a meek king banishes the tools of war and speaks peace to the nations.[53] For others, meekness rules out any action that "returns evil for evil" and never permits the use of torture, assassinations, or war crimes, but is not an absolute prohibition of the use of force—mirroring the extensive discussions about Christian approaches to war in relation to the blessing on the peacemakers (see chapter 9).[54]

Moses as meek

With these interpretations in view, we're better positioned to make sense of the fact that Moses was viewed by Jewish and Christian exegetes alike as "the man of meekness par excellence," as the book of Numbers claims: "Now the man Moses was very humble [Heb. *'ānāw*; Gk. *praÿs*], more so than anyone else on the face of the earth" (Num 12:3).[55] If meekness means being timid or intimidated, then one must wonder if Ignatius had read the Old Testament when he declared that Moses was "meek above all men" and that David was "exceeding meek."[56] After all, just as the meek Jesus overturns tables in the temple, the meek Moses becomes so angry at the sight of the Israelites worshipping a golden calf that he breaks the two tablets of the Ten Commandments, burns the calf, grinds it into powder, and forces the Israelites to drink it (Exod 32:19–20). If meekness is the *proper* display of anger, then one can only conclude that Moses was right to be angry in this situation. And, he stops short of harming any of the Israelites (vengeance belongs to God:

---

53. Stassen, "The Beatitudes as Eschatological," 250. For meekness as nonviolence, see also Green, *Matthew, Poet*, 184, 187; Crosby, *Spirituality*, 81–82; Jacques Bénigne Bossuet, *The Sermon on the Mount*, trans. F. M. Capes (Longmans, Green: 1900), 8; John Dear, *Beatitudes of Peace: Meditations on the Beatitudes, Peacemaking and the Spiritual Life* (New London, CT: Twenty-Third Publications, 2016), 53–59.

54. See discussion in A.-M. Carré, *Quand arrive le bonheur: Les Béatitudes*, 2nd ed. (Paris: Les Éditions du Cerf, 1974), 152–57. See also J. Marshall Jenkins: the meek "honor their anger and do not apologize for it, but they discipline it radically. . . . [They] commit not violence without, at least, anguish," in *Blessed at the Broken Places: Reclaiming Faith and Purpose with the Beatitudes* (Nashville, TN: Skylight Paths, 2016), 41.

55. See list in Dale C. Allison Jr., *The Sermon on the Mount: Inspiring the Moral Imagination* (New York: Crossroad, 1999), 48, including Philo, *On the Life of Moses* 1.26; Babylonian Talmud *Nedarim* 38a; Theodoret of Cyrus, *Religious History* 11.2.

56. Ignatius, *Epistle of Ignatius to the Ephesians, Longer Version* 10 (ANF 1:54).

Exod 32:35), reinforcing the view that meekness includes the refusal to enact revenge.[57]

Meek men, meek women

We might pause to notice at this point that this chapter's primary examples of meekness have all been men. The beatitude's history makes clear how uncomfortable modern male interpreters have sometimes been with this particular blessing. As Jim Forest points out, "men especially have fled from being labeled as meek. We have been made to think of meekness as a feminine quality."[58] As early as 1653, preacher Robert Harris addressed concerns that meekness makes a man "silly" or "effeminate." Harris insisted that it is not meekness but rage that "disables a man, and takes away his courage and discretion."[59] This might help explain why so many (male) interpreters insist that "Meekness is compatible with great strength."[60] Servais Pinckaers was even more direct: "In the moral realm, the expression 'a meek man' invariably conjures up a domineering wife: we decide the man lacks character. . . . Apart from the question of temperament, the valor, strength and *virility* of Christian morality are being challenged."[61]

I would like to linger momentarily over the assumption that Christian morality is "virile," in relation to the declaration that the meek are the blessed. The word *virile* is, of course, a gendered word, as is the word *effeminate*. I have argued in this chapter that meekness is indeed a certain kind of strength, not weakness. Have I thus fallen into the trap of arguing that meekness is in fact a form of virility—a masculine value, rather than a stereotypically feminine

---

57. This understanding of meekness also helps to explain why the preface to Frederick Douglass's *Narrative of the Life of Frederick Douglass* praises Douglass for his "gentleness and meekness" (Garrison, preface to *Narrative*, 5).

58. Jim Forest, *The Ladder of the Beatitudes* (Maryknoll, NY: Orbis Books, 1999), 49.

59. Harris, *Way to True Happiness*, 105; see also R. T. Kendall, *The Sermon on the Mount* (Oxford, UK: Monarch Books, 2011, 2013), 36; and Lloyd-Jones, *Studies*, 37. Carl Henry claimed that meekness today suggests "timid, effeminate, pusillanimous and spineless" (Henry, *Christian Personal Ethics*, 503).

60. Lloyd-Jones, *Studies*, 68.

61. Pinckaers, *Pursuit of God's Happiness*, 59–60, emphasis added. John Burr also used the word virile, in Burr, *The Crown of Character: A Study of the Beatitudes of Our Lord* (James Clarke & Co., 1932), 48. Sherwood Wirt offered the images of a "meek little man" who is spineless and "something less than a man" and a "meek little wife" who lets her husband get away with anything (Wirt, *Magnificent Promise*, 32–33).

one? Is it indeed problematic, as Forest suggests, to think of meekness as a feminine quality?

To be sure, both men and women are equally prone to anger. But modern American culture tends to view angry men and angry women (and mild men and mild women) through different lenses. This is not even to bring in the question of race, which adds another set of issues. Societies don't always have the same standards for what counts as "right" in relation to the expression of anger by men and women or by, say, white men and black men.

All this raises fraught questions over what meekness looks like in practice—questions that have no simple solutions. Instead, it points us again to the importance of social location and context for how we hear and live out the Beatitudes.[62] Women tend to be accustomed to yielding ground. As a woman, I may have to learn how to yield my ground without timidity, yielding in a way that doesn't reinforce harmful gender dynamics. As a white woman, I may have to learn to yield in a different way, in a way that submits myself humbly to those of a nondominant culture.

—

So far, all the interpretations considered in this chapter have construed meekness as a stance toward others—toward the neighbor, if you will. The second central strand of interpretation turns its attention toward God. The meek yield not only to others but also to God.

Submission to God (Psalm 37); tremble at my words (Isa 66:2)

Psalm 37 is a key text for this strand as well; the meek of verse 11 are viewed in parallel with those who trust in the Lord (v. 3), commit their way to the Lord and trust in him (v. 5), and wait for the Lord and keep to his way (v. 34). Another key text, which will be familiar from its even more central role in relation to the poor in spirit, is Isa 66:2: "But this is the one to whom I will look, to the humble and contrite in spirit, who trembles at my word." It's unclear exactly what led exegetes to this text, since it does not use the word *meek* (in either

62. Rebekah Eklund, "Blessed Are the Failures: Leaning into the Beatitudes," in *Theologies of Failure*, ed. Roberto Sirvent and Duncan B. Reyburn (Eugene, OR: Cascade, 2019), 141–50. For an insightful exploration of the "stand your ground" laws, see Kelly Brown Douglas, *Stand Your Ground: Black Bodies and the Justice of God* (Maryknoll, NY: Orbis Books, 2015).

the Greek or Latin versions). Perhaps the link originates in the Didache, which cites a modified form of the beatitude—"Be meek, since the meek will inherit the earth"—and then goes on to instruct its readers, "Become long-suffering [*makrothymos*] and merciful [*eleēmōn*] and harmless [*akakos*] and gentle [*hēsychios*] and good [*agathos*] and one who always trembles at the words that you have heard [Isa 66:2]" (Didache 3:7).[63]

In any case, when meekness indicates a stance toward God (rather than toward one's neighbor), it includes another kind of willingness to yield, a humble submitting to the just will of God.[64] A.-M. Carré contrasted it with being "stiff-necked" (as in Exod 32:9; Acts 7:51).[65] For some, it includes a teachable spirit when approaching the word of God—that is, a willing submission to Scripture.[66]

Depending on the writer's (or reader's) view of God, this can sound a little stern. The word *submission* has fallen on especially hard times in feminist interpretation, and for good reason. But for most of these interpreters, this willingness to yield to God was a form of trust in a good God, as opposed to a misguided confidence in one's own (limited) abilities.[67] It was a form of surrender that was sweet rather than bitter, one that yielded the good fruit of a life directed in life-giving rather than self-defeating ways.[68] Indeed, it was a form of love toward God, which spilled over into love of neighbor (since loving one's neighbor is God's will). As Hendrik Niclaes wrote, meekness means humble submission and obedience to "God and his service of Love."[69] For Karl

---

63. English translation from William Warner, *The Way of the Didache* (Lanham, MD: University Press of America, 2007), 30–31. The word "lowly" (meek) leads Ephrem the Syrian from Matt 5:5 to Isa 66:2 (Ephrem the Syrian, *St. Ephrem's Commentary on Tatian's Diatessaron* 6.1a, trans. Carmel McCarthy [Oxford: Oxford University Press, 1993], 108).

64. E.g., Augustine, Sermon 53A.7, in Augustine, *Essential Sermons*, ed. Boniface Ramsey, trans. Edmund Hill, The Works of Saint Augustine: A Translation for the 21st Century (Hyde Park, NY: New City Press, 2007), 80; and Mackay, *A practical exposition*, 198, 214.

65. Carré, *Quand arrive le bonheur*, 148.

66. Augustine, *The Lord's Sermon*, 1.3.10. Wirt cited James 1:21b to support this point (Wirt, *Magnificent Promise*, 35); see also Watson, *The Beatitudes*, 109–10.

67. Lloyd-Jones, *Studies*, 64. Judith Lechman devotes four chapters in *The Spirituality of Gentleness* to this theme (Lechman, *Spirituality of Gentleness*, 53–91).

68. Graham, *Secret of Happiness*, 34.

69. Hendrik Niclaes, *The first exhortation of H. N. to his children, and to the Family of Love: Likewise H. N. upon the Beatitudes, and the Seven Deadly Sins* (London: For Giles Calvert, 1656), 191. Herman Hendrickx writes that the meek are those "who have surrendered themselves completely to God" and God's service, in Hendrickx, *The Sermon on the Mount*, rev. ed. (London: Geoffrey Chapman, 1979, 1984), 23; so also Clarence Jordan, *Sermon on the Mount*, rev. ed. (Valley Forge, PA: Judson, 1952), 25.

Barth, it results simply in worship, since the meekness to which Jesus invites his followers is to "bend their knees in His name."[70]

They shall inherit the earth

The earth

English translations usually render the Greek word *gē* "earth," but a handful choose "land" instead (Rheims, NAB, Christian Community Bible). The Good News Translation hedges its bets by paraphrasing "the earth" as "what God has promised." But what *has* God promised to the meek? A literal earth, or a metaphorical one? The present world, or a future inheritance?

It's common to understand *all* the promised rewards of the Beatitudes (comfort, seeing God, and so on) as variations on the promise "theirs is the kingdom of heaven." This raises an obvious question in relation to the inheritance of the earth. How can the land, or the earth, be an aspect of the kingdom of God? Equating the two either pulls the kingdom of God toward a more material, this-worldly meaning, or it pulls the earth toward a more metaphorical meaning. Most interpreters, aside from a few modern historical-critical scholars, choose the latter.

This-worldly, practical

This is not to say that all past interpreters saw the inheritance of the earth as purely figurative or spiritual. Chrysostom cited Ps 37:11 to argue that the reward has both a present and future component.[71] He understood the present element (the possession of *this* earth) in largely practical terms, as the natural result of displaying meekness toward one's neighbors. As Servais Pinckaers asked, "Is there anything that favors relationships with others better than genuine meekness?"[72]

---

70. Barth, *Against the Stream*, 55.

71. Chrysostom, *Homilies on the Gospel of Saint Matthew* 15.5 (*NPNF* 10:93–94). Theophylact of Ochrid, who relied greatly on Chrysostom, also described the earth as an inheritance both in this life and as heaven, in *The Explanation by Blessed Theophylact of the Holy Gospel According to St. Matthew*, vol. 1 of *Blessed Theophylact's Explanation of the New Testament*, trans. Christopher Stade (House Springs, MO: Chrysostom Press, 1994), 45.

72. Pinckaers, *Pursuit of God's Happiness*, 72.

Martin Luther likewise adopted this practical view, but unlike Chrysostom he is one of the few who understood the promise "inherit the earth" in entirely material and present terms. For Luther, the beatitude is utterly practical advice, which manifests itself in the secure possession and retention of one's worldly goods: the one who lives meekly and patiently with his neighbors is able to keep his property "with peace and a good conscience," whereas the boisterous and blustery end up losing it.[73] Luther's practical bent is shared by numerous other interpreters. Thomas Aquinas, too, saw a practical aspect in the beatitude: "For many go to court to acquire possessions, but frequently they lose their life and all their things; but frequently the gentle have it all."[74]

Like Chrysostom and Aquinas, John Calvin found in the promised reward both a present-day meaning and a future one: in the present, the inheritance of the earth means that the meek are secure under God's protection "and even now enjoy this grace of God." The non-meek are the wolves who devour their fellow men, and are therefore friendless and insecure: "In possessing much they finally possess nothing."[75] Puritan preacher Robert Harris was likewise very practical: people who brawl get thrown off their estates, whereas the meek can live peaceably anywhere.[76] The meek person, claimed fellow Puritan Increase Mather, "often lives to a good Old Age."[77] A meek character in a short story by nineteenth-century author Lily Watson inherits the earth in a metaphorical sense because "her meek submission to her lot set her free. . . . Untroubled about self and its claims, she could enjoy the beauty and glory of the world . . . with a heart at leisure."[78]

---

73. Martin Luther, *The Sermon on the Mount*, vol. 21 of *Luther's Works*, ed. Jaroslav Pelikan (St. Louis: Concordia, 1956), 24–25.

74. Aquinas, *Commentary on the Gospel of Matthew*, C.5 L.2.420.

75. Calvin, *Harmony of the Gospels* 5.5, 171; Calvin, *Sermons on the Beatitudes*, 35.

76. Harris, *Way to True Happiness*, 85. So also Lloyd-Jones: The meek already inherit the earth in this life because a meek person is "always satisfied . . . already content" (Lloyd-Jones, *Studies*, 71).

77. Increase Mather, *Sermons Wherein Those Eight Characters of the Blessed Commonly Called the Beatitudes Are Opened and Applied in Fifteen Discourses* (Boston: B. Green, for Daniel Henchman, 1718), Sermon 6. Matthew Henry: "Meekness . . . has a real tendency to promote our health, wealth, comfort, and safety" (Henry, *Matthew to John*, comment on Matt 5:5, section III). Burroughs was also practical about the promise: the meek inherit the earth because the quarrelsome often squander their inheritances, don't enjoy what they have, and are disliked both by other people and (more or less) by God, who won't take their side (Burroughs, *Saints' Happiness*, 77–78).

78. Lily Watson, *A Garden of Girls: Stories Illustrating the Beatitudes* (London: Religious Tract Society, 1893), 56.

Apart from Luther, none of these interpreters *limited* the beatitude's promise to the practical inheritance of this-worldly goods or security. Instead, they followed the usual tendency to see a "now and not-yet" aspect to each reward. In this case, the future promise is that the meek will, on the last day, "reach the inheritance of the World"[79] or "the heavenly Canaan."[80] In other words, inheriting the earth means inheriting heaven.

From land of Israel to eschatological promise

At first glance, this interpretation seems to strain against or even directly violate the plain sense of the word *earth* or *land*. How can *earth* mean *heaven*? Contemporary scholars Lazare Rukundwa and Andries Van Aarde argue that the land in Matthew's context is literally the occupied land of Israel; inheriting the land means overthrowing the Romans and restoring the land to its rightful owners: the people of Israel, especially the peasants.[81] This rightly calls attention to one important aspect of Matthew's first-century context, one which points to the promise to inherit the land of Israel in God's covenant with Abraham. On the other hand, it may overlook another key aspect of Matthew's Gospel: his eschatological milieu.

Some Jewish texts in the late Second Temple era had already reinterpreted the promise of inheriting the land as a reference to the world to come. For example, the Jewish book of 1 Enoch, which likely originated in the first century BCE, contains the same promise as the eighth beatitude ("they shall inherit the earth"). In 1 Enoch, the promise occurs in Enoch's vision concerning the "day of tribulation" (1 Enoch 1:1), or the final judgment when God will destroy the wicked and preserve the righteous elect: "But to the elect there shall be light, joy and peace, and they shall inherit the earth" (1 Enoch 5:7). The first-century CE book of 2 Enoch contains a similar saying, which also draws from Psalm 37 but replaces "the land" with "endless life": "Now therefore, my children,

---

79. Calvin, *Harmony of the Gospels* 5.5, 171; see also Calvin, *Sermons on the Beatitudes*, 35.

80. Richard Watson, *Exposition of the Gospels of St. Matthew and St. Mark* (London: John Mason, 1833), 70. Farrer takes "the earth" as this-worldly and material, but argues that Scripture often uses the "shadows of the natural to delineate the truths of the spiritual world" and "the images of the present life to describe the realities of the life to come" (Farrer, *Sermons on the Mission*, 258–59, 267–72, quotations 273).

81. Lazare S. Rukundwa and Andries G. Van Aarde, "Revisiting Justice in the First Four Beatitudes in Matthew (5:3–6) and the Story of the Canaanite Woman (Mt 15:21–28): A Postcolonial Reading," *HvTSt* 61, no. 3 (2005): 934–36.

in patience and meekness spend the number of your days, that you inherit endless life" (2 Enoch 50:3).[82]

One of the Dead Seas Scrolls contains a commentary on Psalm 37 (in the manuscript known as 4Q171 = 4QpPs37 = 4QpPs[a]), which offers an eschatological interpretation of the psalm.[83] The commentary aligns the inheritance of the land with God's vindication of the "congregation of the chosen ones"; at the same time, God will judge "the ruthless ones of the covenant, the wicked ones of Israel, who will be cut off and will be destroyed forever" (4QpPs[a] II, 5; III, 12–13). When the righteous inherit the land, "they will take possession of the high mountain of Israel, and on his holy mountain they will delight" (4QpPs[a] III, 11).[84]

New Testament scholar Robert Brawley proposes that Matthew's beatitude alludes to two themes of the Abrahamic covenant—"inheritance of the land and the blessing of all the families of earth" (Gen 12:3, 7)—as these two themes were mediated through later Jewish traditions that explained the covenantal promise of land as an eschatological promise to inherit the whole earth.[85] Matthew himself, then, may be steeped in a Jewish mode of thinking that merged the promised land with the eschatological age. As Dennis Hamm writes, "Matthew stands at the end of a trajectory in which 'inheriting the land' has evolved from an interpretation of the takeover of Canaan to the end-time promise of the Kingdom of God."[86] Later Christian interpreters use a similar logic to extend the meaning of the land (or the earth) even further, seeing the promised land as a "Type and Pledge of [the Christian's] future Inheritance with the Saints in Light."[87]

---

82. Scholars debate whether 2 Enoch is Jewish or Christian. Christfried Böttrich makes the case for it as a first-century Jewish document in "The 'Book of the Secrets of Enoch' (2 En): Between Jewish Origin and Christian Transmission. An Overview," in *New Perspectives on 2 Enoch: No Longer Slavonic Only*, ed. Andrei A. Orlov and Gabriele Boccaccini (Leiden: Brill, 2012), 2. Enoch 50 and 51 have interesting overlaps with the Beatitudes.

83. Maurya P. Horgan, "Psalm Pesher 1 (4Q171 = 4QpPs[a] = 4QpPs37 and 45)," in *Pesharim, Other Commentaries, and Related Documents*, vol. 6B of *The Dead Sea Scrolls: Hebrew, Aramaic, and Greek Texts with English Translations*, ed. James H. Charlesworth (Louisville: Westminster John Knox; Tübingen: Mohr Siebeck, 2002), 6.

84. Horgan, "Psalm Pesher 1," 11, 15.

85. Robert L. Brawley, "Evocative Allusions," 597, 610. See also Ratzinger, *Jesus of Nazareth*, 82–83.

86. M. Dennis Hamm, *The Beatitudes in Context: What Luke and Matthew Meant* (Wilmington, DE: Michael Glazier, 1990), 92. Julius Wellhausen wrote that the promise meant Palestine in Ps 37:11 but here refers to the kingdom of heaven; see Wellhausen, *Das Evangelium Matthaei: Übersetzt und Erklärt* (Berlin: Georg Reimer, 1904), 14.

87. Norris, *Christian Blessedness*, 73; so also Bossuet, *The Sermon on the Mount*, 11; Gregory

The land of the living (earth = heaven)

Another psalm provides support for the counterintuitive view that "the earth" in Matt 5:5 refers to the heavenly realm. The phrase "the land of the living" from Psalm 27 appears repeatedly in exegesis of the beatitude. Christian exegetes reread the declaration "I believe that I shall see the goodness of the LORD in the land of the living" (Ps 27:13) as a reference to the hope of the resurrection. It was a short step from there to connect "the land [of the living]" of Ps 27:13 (or Ps 142:5) with "the land" of Matt 5:5. For example, third-century Syriac theologian Aphrahat simply replaced "inherit the earth" with "inherit the land of the living" when he cited the beatitude.[88]

In the *Apocalypse of Paul*, an imaginative third-century exploration of what Paul might have seen when he was "caught up to the third heaven" (2 Cor 12:2), an angel escorts Paul through a golden gate where only the righteous are allowed to enter. The angel tells Paul that they have entered "the land of the meek" where the souls of the righteous are kept; the angel quotes the beatitude to illustrate the point.[89] In this text, the inheritance of the earth has been merged fully with the inheritance of the heavenly realm. For the *Apocalypse of Paul*, seeing God (the promise to the pure in heart) is the same as inheriting the earth (the promise to the meek).

As we've already seen, this overlapping of all the Beatitudes' promised rewards is common. Premodern and modern scholars alike tend to see *all* the promised rewards as variations on the promise to inherit the kingdom of God. For Origen, for example, the promises "theirs is the kingdom of heaven" and "they shall inherit the earth" refer to the same reality: the secure inheritance of the faithful in the heavenly realm.[90] The order of the Beatitudes becomes significant here as well. This beatitude is either second or third in the ancient manuscripts; either way, it comes *after* the promise of the kingdom of heaven in the first beatitude. Because many premodern

---

of Nyssa, *The Lord's Prayer*, 97, 105; John of Damascus, *Exposition of the Orthodox Faith* 10.29 (*NPNF²* 9:29); and Aquinas, *Commentary on Matthew*, C.5 L.2.420, among others.

88. Aphrahat, *Demonstrations*, Catholic Theological Studies of India 3, trans. Kuriakose Valavanolickal (Kerala, India: HIRS Publications, 1999), Demonstration on Charity 2.19 (p. 47); Demonstration on the Sons of the Covenant 6.1 (p. 105); Demonstration on Humility 9.1 (p. 169). Augustine describes the earth as "the land of the living" in Ps 142:5 (Augustine, Sermon 53A.7, in Augustine, *Essential Sermons*, 80).

89. *Apocalypse of Paul* 21, in J. K. Elliott, *The Apocryphal New Testament* (Oxford: Clarendon Press, 1993), 628.

90. Origen, *De Principiis* 2.3.6–7 (*ANF* 4:274–5).

readers followed Gregory of Nyssa and Ambrose's proposal that the Beatitudes are a set of sequential steps, they also sometimes concluded that the promised rewards likewise increase sequentially. From that vantage point, it made little sense that the faithful would receive the kingdom of heaven first (in Matt 5:3) and then the material earth later (in Matt 5:4 or 5:5). Thus the order of the Beatitudes also pressed some exegetes to view the promise to inherit the earth in spiritual terms.

New creation

Some interpreters maintain a closer connection between the present earth and the eschatological dwelling place of the saints by understanding "the earth" of Matt 5:5 as the *new* earth—that is, the new heavens and the new earth, or the new creation (Rev 21:1–7). Jerome, for example, saw both possession of the kingdom of heaven (in the first beatitude) and the inheritance of the earth (in the third beatitude) as references to the promise that God will make a new heavens and a new earth, as in Isa 66:22–23 (*Comm. Isa.* 18.32).[91] Of course, the description of the new creation in Revelation 21–22 is replete with allusions to the original creation of Genesis 1–2. Dale Allison thus suggests that inheriting the earth in the beatitude might be thought of as "recovery of the dominion of what Adam and Eve lost."[92]

Aside from Jerome, few ancient interpreters capitalized on the connection with the new heavens and the new earth. Several modern exegetes, however, understand the beatitude in just this way.[93] In Barth's Good Friday sermon on the beatitude, he described the earth inherited by the meek as the created world at peace, with no more enemies, or quarrels, or evil desires, with tears wiped away and the first things having passed away (Rev 21:1, 4).[94] This is a promising line of thought, since it retains some connection to "the

---

91. Jerome, *Commentary on Isaiah*, 876. Jerome added that we can also understand the land the saints will possess as "the Holy Scriptures" (*Comm. Isa.* 18.32 in ibid., 730).

92. Allison, *Sermon on the Mount*, 48.

93. Burroughs, *Saints' Happiness*, 76; D. A. Carson, *The Sermon on the Mount: An Evangelical Exposition of Matthew 5–7* (Grand Rapids: Baker Books, 1978), 21; Collett, *A Paraphrase*, 13; Robert Henley, *Saintliness: A Course of Sermons on the Beatitudes; Preached at St. Mary's Church, Putney* (London; Oxford: Rivingtons, 1864), 32; Isaak, "Luke," 1144; Mather, *Sermons Wherein*, Sermon 6; Carl G. Vaught, *The Sermon on the Mount: A Theological Investigation* (Waco, TX: Baylor University Press, 2001), 21; White, *Thoughts from the Mount*, 31.

94. Barth, *Against the Stream*, 53–54. See also Bonhoeffer, *Cost of Discipleship*, 110.

earth" in Matt 5:5, rather than erasing the material component by construing it simply as heaven. It also retains a more strongly eschatological character to the beatitude, as seems appropriate. Benedict Green captured this connection when he described the earth promised in the beatitude as neither "wholly distinct" from the kingdom of heaven nor "fully coexistent with it; rather it is that proleptic and provisional form in which that kingdom already exists and is at work on earth in the interim period before the final eschatological reign."[95]

Resurrected body

We are now positioned to appreciate (at least in theory!) the most creative interpretation of "the earth" in premodern thought, which likewise preserves a materiality to the beatitude, and which also draws on the theme of resurrection and new creation. It does so, however, via a completely unexpected route, by seeing "the earth" as Christ's resurrected body and the resurrected bodies of all the saints.

We find here a small but significant group of early interpreters—Hilary of Poitiers (ca. 310–367), Chromatius of Aquileia (d. ca. 406), Leo the Great (ca. 400–461), and Thomas Aquinas (1225–1274). Hilary understood the inheritance of the land as "the inheritance of [the] body, which the Lord himself assumed as his dwelling. Because Christ will have dwelt in us through the gentleness [meekness] of our disposition, we also will be clothed in the glory of his bodily splendor" (cf. 1 Cor 15:40, 53).[96] Chromatius also claimed that the earth most in view in the beatitude is "the land of our body," which will be transformed into glory.[97] Leo the Great followed his two predecessors by writing that the promised earth is the very flesh of the saints, which will be transformed at the resurrection and "clothed with the glory of immortality" (1 Cor 15:53).[98] Thomas Aquinas, ever alert to the interpretations of his forebears, mused that the land could be the glorified body of Christ or the saints, or "the fiery heaven, where the blessed are."[99]

95. Green, *Matthew, Poet*, 188–89.

96. Hilary of Poitiers, *Commentary on Matthew* 4.3, trans. D. H. Williams, FC 125 (Washington, DC: Catholic University of America, 2012), 60.

97. Chromatius of Aquileia, *Sermons and Tractates on Matthew*, Tractatus 17.4.4.

98. Leo the Great, *Sermons* 95.5 (*NPNF*² 12:204).

99. Aquinas, *Commentary on Matthew*, C.5 L.2.420.

Meekness and power

Earlier, I noted that interpreters placed this beatitude in relation to two biblical texts that both contain the phrase "slow to anger" (Prov 16:32, Jas 1:19). These are, in fact, the only two biblical books that apply this trait to human beings. Elsewhere in Scripture, it's always a description of God (Exod 34:6; Num 14:18; Neh 9:17; Pss 86:15, 103:8, 145:8; Joel 2:13; Jonah 4:2; Nah 1:3). In fact, a handful of writers see God as the greatest exemplar of meekness. Robert Harris wrote that God overcame his prophet Jonah (who objected that God was far too slow to become angry) not with force but with gentleness.[100] Thomas Watson cited 2 Pet 3:9 to describe God's patience as a form of meekness.[101] And Judith Lechman points out that the psalmist describes God as meek when he writes, "thy gentleness hath made me great" (Ps 18:35b KJV).[102] (The Hebrew word for "gentleness" comes from the same root that produces the word 'ănāwîm—the "poor" or "humble.")

For Monika Hellwig, because God and Jesus are both described as meek in Scripture, meekness is a characteristic that means "restraint of power to crush, conquer, overwhelm, or subdue." This applies to human rulers and other powerful people, but it also points toward meekness as nonviolent action (rather than violent force) to address injustice.[103] Yiu Sing Lúcás Chan offers Mahatma Mohandas Gandhi as an example of the meek due to his insistence on nonviolence.[104] Meekness is not complacency; it "resolutely contend[s] for the right."[105]

Jim Forest even points to meekness as the strength to practice civil disobedience. Submitting to God—that is, obeying God rather than human beings (Acts 5:29)—gives meekness a spine. "Meek Christians," writes Forest, "do not allow themselves to be dragged along by the tide of political power or to be led by the smell of money. . . . The person who is meek toward God will have the strength not to commit or sanction evil deeds against a

---

100. Harris, *Way to True Happiness*, 86.

101. Watson, *The Beatitudes*, 119–21.

102. Lechman, *Spirituality of Gentleness*, 97.

103. Monika K. Hellwig, "The Blessedness of the Meek, the Merciful, and the Peacemakers," in *New Perspectives on the Beatitudes*, ed. Francis A. Eigo (Villanova, PA: Villanova University Press, 1995), 193–94.

104. Yiu Sing Lúcás Chan, *The Ten Commandments and the Beatitudes* (Lanham, MD: Rowman & Littlefield, 2012), 182.

105. Elizabeth Rundle Charles, *The Beatitudes: Thoughts for All Saints' Day* (London: Society for Promoting Christian Knowledge; New York: E. & J. B. Young & Co., 1889), 77.

neighbor. True meekness provides the strength to disobey, no matter what the punishment."[106]

Charles Duhigg's 2019 study of American anger isn't about the beatitude, but it does illuminate what it might mean to get angry about the right things when it describes how Cesar Chavez used moral outrage at the treatment of migrant workers to galvanize a civil rights movement for migrants.[107] In the late nineteenth century, English writer Elizabeth Rundle Charles suggested that people who have a tendency toward domination or imperial ambitions (today, one might add a tendency toward racial supremacy) are in special need of meekness.[108]

Forest, Duhigg, and Charles reveal how meekness, surprisingly, might function not as passivity but as certain forms of resistance or even direct action. For Catholic priest and activist John Dear, if we are not meek (that is, nonviolent) we will not have an earth left to inherit at all. Dear pleads, "A life of nonviolence leads to oneness with creation and her creatures. A life of violence . . . leads to an abrupt discord with creation."[109]

—

This chapter has closed, then, the same way that it began, by proposing that meekness may be understood as a certain kind of power—not only that of loving self-restraint, but of the ability to resist certain pressures (racism, materialism, violence) and to yield to others (as self-sacrifice for a person—or a planet—who is suffering). Meekness willingly yields to the other and to God, not out of weakness but as voluntary renunciation. Some of our interpreters have also shown us that this form of meekness must be accompanied by a practical wisdom that Greek speakers called *phronēsis* so that one knows the

106. Forest, *Ladder*, 50. Kathleen Chesto's examples of meekness are the Canaanite woman's challenge to Jesus, Sister Theresa Kane's public entreaty to Pope John Paul II to open all the church's ministries to women, and Martin Luther King Jr.'s speech on the steps of the Lincoln Memorial (Kathleen O. Chesto, "Get a New Beatitude," *U.S. Catholic* 68, no. 1 [January 2003]: 31–32). "The blessing of meekness," Chesto writes, "is freedom to be courageous" (ibid., 32).

107. Charles Duhigg, "The Real Roots of American Rage," *The Atlantic* (January/February 2019), https://www.theatlantic.com/magazine/archive/2019/01/charles-duhigg-american-anger/576424/.

108. Charles, *The Beatitudes*, 77.

109. John Dear, *They Will Inherit the Earth: Peace and Nonviolence in a Time of Climate Change* (Maryknoll, NY: Orbis Books, 2018), 2.

right kinds of things to be angry about, and for how long, and with how much passion—all without losing one's temper and injuring the neighbors (and the enemies) whom Christians are commanded to love. This is a timely skill. As author Jerry Bridges wrote, in these times it will take "strength, God's strength, to be truly gentle."[110]

110. Jerry Bridges, *The Practice of Godliness* (Colorado Springs, CO: NavPress 1983), 221, quoted in Lechman, *Spirituality of Gentleness*, 142.

6

Our Daily Bread

The Hungry and Thirsty (for Justice)

Blessed are those who hunger and thirst for righteousness, for they will be filled (Matt 5:6).

Blessed are you who are hungry now, for you will be filled. . . . Woe to you who are full now, for you will be hungry (Luke 6:21a, 25a).

Mary Francesca Cabrini (1850–1917) was, for a while, an elementary school teacher in Italy. When she decided to found a new religious order, the Institute of the Salesian Missionaries of the Sacred Heart, some Catholic leaders objected to the term *missionary*. They informed her that "missionaries had always been men." Cabrini stood her ground. She pointed out that if "the mission of announcing the Lord's resurrection to his apostles had been entrusted to Mary Magdalene," she saw no reason why the same mission could not now be entrusted to her and her sisters.[1]

Cabrini won the argument. In 1889, she and her sisters sailed for New York City, joining the 100,000 Italian immigrants already in the city. Over the next three decades, she founded hospitals, orphanages, and schools in New York and in several other cities, including Chicago, Denver, Seattle, Los Angeles, and New Orleans. They served Italian immigrants and all those who were "poor and rejected."[2] Cabrini's hunger for justice couldn't be confined to the United States: she established houses for her order in Nicaragua, Panama,

1. Mary Louise Sullivan, *Mother Cabrini: "Italian Immigrant of the Century"* (New York: Center for Migration Studies, 1992), 36.
2. Sullivan, *Mother Cabrini*, 128.

Argentina, France, Spain, England, and Brazil.[3] "Few women of her time," noted modern-day Missionary Sister Mary Louise Sullivan, "undertook comparable arduous and extensive travels or acted as agents of change in a male-dominated society."[4]

Several decades after her death, when Mother Frances Xavier Cabrini was named "Italian Immigrant of the Century" by the American Committee on Italian Migration (ACIM), a New York judge praised her: "Her accomplishments . . . put to shame those men whose bigotry helps raise the cry of intolerance towards the immigrant."[5] The ACIM was founded as a response to immigration legislation passed in 1952 that favored immigrants from northern and western Europe and excluded "undesirable aliens"[6]—which Italians were considered to be at the turn of the century when Cabrini arrived in the shadow of the Statue of Liberty (at whose base Mother Cabrini's likeness is now engraved). According to one report written in 1889, Italians were "hated" and "treated like animals."[7] In New Orleans in 1891, thirteen Italians were dragged from a jail and lynched in the public square.[8] These—and all others like them—were the people Mother Cabrini devoted her life to defending, loving, and serving.

The ACIM award describes her as "mother of the immigrant, servant of the poor, consoler of the sick, guardian of the orphan, teacher of the little ones, friend of the laborer."[9] Today she is the patron saint of all immigrants. In the rose windows designed by Charles Connick in the Cathedral of St. Paul, Minnesota, she is the exemplar of those who hunger and thirst for justice.

In the year 258 CE, the governor of Rome approached a young deacon of the church in Rome with a demand: turn over all the riches of the church to the Roman authorities. The deacon, whose name was Lawrence, asked for three days to gather up the church's wealth. He then proceeded to give away as much of the church's money as he could to the poor. When the third day arrived, he presented to the governor what he called the true riches of the church: he had gathered up the beggars, the crippled, the widows, and the blind. The governor was not amused, and Lawrence was sentenced to death.

---

3. Sullivan, *Mother Cabrini*, 113, 245.
4. Sullivan, *Mother Cabrini*, 113.
5. Remarks by Justice Juvenal Marchisio, quoted in Sullivan, *Mother Cabrini*, 1.
6. Sullivan, *Mother Cabrini*, 1.
7. Sullivan, *Mother Cabrini*, 72.
8. Sullivan, *Mother Cabrini*, 124.
9. Sullivan, *Mother Cabrini*, 8.

For medieval theologian Rupert of Deutz, Lawrence embodied Jesus's blessing on those who hunger and thirst.[10]

The lives of Lawrence and Cabrini resonate with both Matthew's and Luke's versions of the fourth beatitude. They both served and lived with the materially hungry. Their hunger for justice came at a cost: Cabrini died young, worn down by her travels; Lawrence was executed. Their lives also help us to see that the fourth beatitude shares many of the first beatitude's complexities. Here again we find tension and overlap between Matthew's version and Luke's, between the spiritual and the material. For one evangelist, the blessed are the hungry; for the other, they are those who hunger and thirst for righteousness—or for justice.

The Greek word *dikaiosynē* could be either. The range of meanings possible for the word *dikaiosynē* is indicated by its various translations in the New Testament: righteousness, justice, justification, and even piety (see Matt 6:1). In Matthew's Gospel, Jesus consents to baptism in order to "fulfill all righteousness" (Matt 3:15). The phrase "for righteousness" occurs in the fourth beatitude and again in the eighth, creating a certain parallel between those who hunger and thirst and those who are persecuted (Matt 5:6, 10). Later in the Sermon on the Mount, Jesus warns his listeners not to "practice their righteousness before others in order to be seen by them" and exhorts them to "strive first for the kingdom of God and his righteousness" (Matt 6:1, 33). And in one of his most challenging sayings, Jesus tells his listeners that they have no chance of entering the kingdom of heaven unless their righteousness exceeds that of the scribes and Pharisees (Matt 5:20).

In the New Testament as a whole, righteousness is often a characteristic of God. In Romans, a righteous God can "reckon" or "consider" (*logizomai*) human beings as righteous (Rom 4:3, 5, 6, 9, 11, 22) and can likewise *make* people righteous (or justify them, or in archaic language "right-wise" them) (Rom 3:26). The Latin Vulgate (the text of many Western premodern interpreters) uses *iustitia* (justice), a word which itself had a broad range of meanings associated with it. *Iustitia* could refer to a moral state or to an action. It was used as a synonym for justification (*iustificatio*); it could indicate that which is right or proper, or the moral virtue that disposes a person "to render to every man what is rightly due him."[11]

---

10. Brigitta Stoll, *De Virtute in Virtutem: zur Auslegungs- und Wirkungsgeschichte der Bergpredigt in Kommentaren, Predigten und hagiographischer Literatur von der Merowingerzeit bis um 1200* (Tübingen: Mohr Siebeck, 1988), 149.

11. Roy J. Deferrari and M. Inviolata Barry, with Ignatius McGuiness, *A Lexicon of Saint Thomas Aquinas* (Baltimore: J. D. Lucas, 1948, 1949), 617–18.

Most English translations of Matt 5:6 opt for "righteousness," whereas only a few choose "justice." The word *righteousness* is more likely to evoke themes of moral uprightness and rarely resounds outside of religious contexts except in negative ways (a self-righteous person). The term *justice* could evoke the legal system, the theme of social justice for the vulnerable, or the concepts of fairness or equity. Righteousness might suggest a more individual sphere (a person's character), whereas justice typically points toward a wider societal context. Finally, righteousness might suggest the status of a human being before God, while justice could indicate either God's vindicating action or human actions on behalf of others ("to do what God requires" is the translation of the Good News Bible and the TEV).[12]

Indeed, these respective themes reflect the emphases of much of this beatitude's interpretive history, which dwells as usual on Matthew's version rather than on Luke's. The story this beatitude tells is about human and divine agency; it's a tale of bodily and spiritual human longings, and how they intertwine. It's about God's justice and human obedience, and about the limits and possibilities of human goodness.

I'll begin with interpretations that focus on actual hunger, then turn to those that focus on spiritual hunger.

Actual hunger

Historical-critical scholar Hans Dieter Betz represents the dominant strand of the modern scholarly guild when he writes that Luke's beatitude speaks of physical hunger whereas Matthew's refers to metaphorical hunger.[13] On the one hand, this seems so straightforwardly true that it hardly seems worth mentioning. But as we've already seen in relation to the first beatitude, the biblical record itself rarely separates out physical longings from spiritual ones

---

12. Mary Rose D'Angelo worries that translating *dikaiosynē* as "righteousness" "tends to evoke the narrowly individualistic version of sin and justification that is often the focus of post-Reformation interpreters (both Protestant and Catholic), obscuring the communal concerns with God's justice and the demand for moral rightness and equity, especially economic equity for the poor, that are central to early Judaism and Christianity"; Mary R. D'Angelo, "'Blessed the One Who Reads and Those Who Hear': The Beatitudes in Their Biblical Contexts," in *New Perspectives on the Beatitudes*, ed. Francis A. Eigo (Villanova, PA: Villanova University Press, 1995), 64. See also Michael H. Crosby, *Spirituality of the Beatitudes: Matthew's Vision for the Church in an Unjust World*, rev. ed. (Maryknoll, NY: Orbis Books, 2005), 101.

13. Hans Dieter Betz, *The Sermon on the Mount*, Hermeneia (Minneapolis: Fortress, 1995), 129.

that cleanly; and in relation to interpretive history, Betz's is a minority view. Whereas many twentieth-century scholars see hunger (and mourning) as a subset of the first beatitude—such that the poor are also those who are hungry and weeping—the vast majority of interpreters throughout history saw those who hunger (in both Matthew and Luke) as a distinct category.

Spiritual but with some material aspect

This is not to say that all premodern interpreters understood the beatitude as purely spiritual. In fact, a significant number of influential exegetes included a material component, in various ways. For example, while Gregory of Nyssa thought that the beatitude primarily indicates hunger and thirst for the spiritual food of justice, he refused to rule out that it also means hunger for actual food, so long as the desire for food is only for sustenance and does not include desire for superfluous things like fancy silverware.[14] Augustine created another link with food, once again through his association of the Beatitudes with the petitions of the Lord's Prayer. In this case, he matched hungering and thirsting for righteousness with "Give us our daily bread."[15] For Augustine, the primary meaning of the petition "give us our daily bread" is spiritual, but he also conceded that one may see three meanings there simultaneously: "that which is necessary for the body," the sacrament of the Lord's Body, and the bread of the Word of God.[16]

By the medieval era, each beatitude was associated with a virtue and therefore also with the vice that it opposed. Thomas Aquinas (1225–1274), who understood this beatitude (naturally enough) as the cardinal virtue of justice, placed it in opposition to greed.[17] The poet Dante Alighieri (ca. 1265–1321) made the connection to hunger for actual food even stronger by associating the

---

14. Gregory of Nyssa, *The Lord's Prayer; The Beatitudes*, trans. Hilda C. Graef, ACW 18 (Mahwah, NJ: Paulist, 1954), 123.

15. See Augustine, *The Lord's Sermon on the Mount* 2.11.38, trans. John J. Jepson, ACW 5 (Mahwah, NJ: Paulist, 1948), 126. Elsewhere, Augustine paired this beatitude with a different petition: "Your will be done" (Sermon 53A.9, in Augustine, *Essential Sermons*, ed. Boniface Ramsey, trans. Edmund Hill, The Works of Saint Augustine: A Translation for the 21st Century [Hyde Park, NY: New City Press, 2007], 80–81).

16. Augustine, *The Lord's Sermon*, 2.7.27.

17. Thomas Aquinas, *Commentary on the Gospel of Matthew, Chapters 1–12*, ed. The Aquinas Institute, trans. Jeremy Holmes and Beth Mortensen, Biblical Commentaries 33 (Lander, WY: The Aquinas Institute for the Study of Sacred Doctrine, 2013), C.5 L.2.427.

beatitude with both greed and gluttony; he contrasted hungering and thirsting for justice with excessive hunger or thirst for material goods. He used the beatitude's two verbs (hunger and thirst) to split the beatitude into two, pairing thirst with avarice and hunger with gluttony. These two vices are resisted, respectively, by generosity (the virtue of those who thirst) and temperance (the virtue of those who hunger).[18]

These associations linger. For example, the Anglican *Book of Homilies* (1547, 1563, 1570) took Luke's "Woe to the full" as a condemnation of excessive eating and drunkenness.[19] Contemporary Catholic author Servais Pinckaers (1925–2008) wrote of the beatitude that voluntarily going hungry (i.e., fasting for a set period of time) can free one from the "excessive hold" of earthly goods and reorient one's desires toward God.[20]

Reformer John Calvin provides a bridge between the medieval and the modern eras. Like Dante and the *Book of Homilies*, he saw Luke's woe to the full as a warning "against greedy excess" or over-reliance on earthly riches.[21] Like many modern interpreters, he saw those who hunger as people who are literally hungry, describing them as essentially the same as those who mourn and are poor [in spirit]; they are all people whose afflictions cause them to "turn to God for refuge and relief."[22] Thus he also followed his premodern predecessors by understanding hunger and thirst both as material conditions and as an inner attitude oriented toward God.

Similarly, Jesuit Juan Maldonado (1534–1584) knew that most of his predecessors thought the beatitude means an ardent desire for God and God's righteousness (more on that below). Nonetheless, he parted ways with them, writing that he found it "more probable . . . that Christ spoke of actual hunger and thirst," since in his view Scripture always uses thirst but *not* hunger as a metaphor for vehement desire. Furthermore, he argued that the beatitude could not indicate merely the desire for justice because Christ's Beatitudes

18. Dante Alighieri, *Purgatorio*, trans. Jean Hollander and Robert Hollander (New York: Anchor Books, 2003), Cantos 20–24.

19. The *Book of Homilies* was mainly written by Thomas Cranmer and John Jewel. See "Homily 17: Against Gluttony and Drunkenness," quoted in Beth Kreitzer, ed., *Luke*, Reformation Commentary on Scripture, New Testament 3 (Downers Grove, IL: IVP Academic, 2015), 137.

20. Servais Pinckaers, *The Pursuit of God's Happiness—God's Way: Living the Beatitudes*, trans. Mary Thomas Noble (New York: Society of St. Paul, 1998), 94.

21. John Calvin, *Sermons on the Beatitudes: Five Sermons from the Gospel Harmony, Delivered in Geneva in 1560* (Carlisle, PA: Banner of Truth Trust, 2006), 80. People who are "drunk on prosperity . . . are as good as dead: they bury themselves in their perishable possessions and are incapable of seeing heaven above" (ibid., 79).

22. Calvin, *Sermons on the Beatitudes*, 39.

only praise virtues that the world holds in contempt. Since the longing for justice is universally shared, it does not need to be praised.[23]

Fasting: going hungry for God

Another way of linking the material with the spiritual was to see the beatitude as a blessing on those who were hungry "for the sake of righteousness"—that is, it was a blessing for those who practiced voluntary poverty, who were hungry for the sake of Christ.[24] Basil of Caesarea pointed to the hunger and thirst of the apostle Paul, who was hungry, thirsty, cold, and naked for the sake of the gospel and his apostolic vocation (2 Cor 11:27). For Basil, the one who hungers and thirsts for righteousness is the person who shows his "desire and zeal" by fasting willingly and voluntarily.[25]

This is a relatively small stream of interpretation. It never assumes the importance that voluntary poverty does in relation to the first beatitude. But it does find a way to connect physical hunger to spiritual hunger, and it does have at least one modern advocate. Contemporary scholar Benedict Green views the beatitude as a reference to fasting, in part because he sees mourning and fasting as linked acts of penitential mourning (as in Matt 9:15). Thus, for Green, the beatitude refers both to "the real physical hunger that fasting involves" and to a metaphorical hunger for fulfilling the will of God, just as Jesus hungered for both when he fasted in the wilderness prior to his testing by the devil and the launch of his public ministry (Matt 4:2, Luke 4:2; see also Ps 106:5 LXX, Amos 8:11, Isa 49:10).

In the temptation narrative in both Matthew and Luke, Jesus fasts and then proceeds to have a debate with the devil over the meaning of bread. When the tempter tells Jesus, "If you are the Son of God, command these stones to

23. Juan Maldonado, *S. Matthew's Gospel, Chapters I to XIV*, vol. 1 of *A Commentary on the Holy Gospels*, trans. and ed. George J. Davie (London, UK: John Hodges, 1888), 135. He contradicted Gregory of Nyssa, for whom hungering for justice means longing for all the virtues, since the virtues form a whole and one cannot truly have one (justice) without all the others, and since the glory of God is "the true virtue, the good that is unmixed with evil," desiring the virtues is in the end desiring God himself (Gregory of Nyssa, *The Lord's Prayer*, 125, 129).

24. Cyril of Alexandria, Homily 27 in *Commentary on the Gospel of St. Luke*, trans. R. Payne Smith (Long Island, NY: Studion, 1983), 130; Cyril of Alexandria, Frag. 80 on Luke 6:21, in *Lukas-Kommentare aus der griechischen Kirche*, ed. Joseph Reuss (Berlin: Akademie-Verlag, 1984), 259.

25. Basil of Caesarea, *Shorter Rules* 130 (PG 31:1169B–C). Theodotus also linked the beatitude to fasting, which he said makes the soul and the body "pure and light for the divine words" (Theodotus, *Excerpts* 14 [ANF 8:44–45]).

become loaves of bread," Jesus refuses and quotes Deuteronomy instead: "One does not live by bread alone, but by every word that comes from the mouth of God" (Matt 4:3–4; Luke 4:3–4; quotation of Deut 8:3).[26] The temptation narrative, then, combines the themes of actual hunger, voluntary fasting, longing to do God's will, and God's Word as sustenance.

Going hungry for God—so that you can feed others

The Gospel of Thomas contains a verse that's a close parallel to the fourth beatitude. It's often translated, "Blessed are those who are hungry, for the belly of the needy will be filled."[27] As in the canonical beatitude, the saying appears to promise a reversal of status: the hungry are declared blessed for (or because) they will be filled. Stephan Witetschek argues that the "for" in the original Coptic should be translated not as "because" but as "in order that." The saying thus reads, "Blessed are they that go hungry in order that they may fill the stomach of him who desires to be filled."[28] In other words, this version of the beatitude "is addressed to those who radically share the little they have in order to support others who may be even worse off."[29]

If this translation is correct, the version of the beatitude in the Gospel of Thomas represents an early (perhaps mid-second century) reinterpretation of the beatitude to indicate a blessing on those who deliberately go hungry in order to feed others. Witetschek calls this practice "social fasting," or "voluntary fasting in order to support others with the resources that have been saved by this self-restriction," and points to early Christian examples of it in the Shepherd of Hermas (Herm. Sim. 5.3.7), Aristides's *Apology* (*Apol.* 15.7), the *Didascalia* (5.1.3–4; 5.20.9), and the Apostolic Constitutions (Const. ap. 5.20.18).[30]

---

26. H. Benedict Green, *Matthew, Poet of the Beatitudes* (Sheffield: Sheffield Academic, 2001), 228.

27. Gos. Thom. 69.2; in J. K. Elliott, *The Apocryphal New Testament* (Oxford: Clarendon Press, 1993), 144.

28. This translation of the beatitude is Kendrick Grobel's, in his article "How Gnostic is the Gospel of Thomas?," *NTS* 8, no. 4 (1962): 373.

29. Stephan Witetschek, "Going Hungry for a Purpose: On Gos. Thom. 69.2 and a Neglected Parallel in Origen," *JSNT* 32, no. 4 (2010): 384.

30. Witetschek, "Going Hungry," 386–87. Witetschek also points to a possible parallel in Origen, *Hom. Lev.* 10.2 (ibid., 388). An interesting modern-day example is World Vision's "30-Hour Famine," an event designed to educate young people about world hunger while raising funds to feed the hungry (https://www.30hourfamine.org/).

Of course, none of these texts cites the beatitude as support for the practice. But it is a fascinating interpretation of the canonical beatitude, reading it through the lens of fasting but with an eye toward the voluntary renunciation of food in order to fill the hungry. It anticipates two streams of later interpretation: the small stream of thought, especially in monastic communities, that linked the beatitude to fasting, and the eventual emphasis on hungering for righteousness by doing concrete acts of mercy and justice—including feeding the hungry.

Longing for God—spiritual food

It's probably fair to say that the fourth beatitude becomes even more detached from its material moorings through the course of its history than the first beatitude does. The predominant interpretation—longing for God—draws its inspiration from the psalmist: "As a deer longs for flowing streams, so my soul longs for you, O God. My soul thirsts for God, for the living God" (Ps 42:1–2). And, "O God, you are my God, I seek you, my soul thirsts for you; my flesh faints for you, as in a dry and weary land where there is no water. . . . My soul is satisfied as with a rich feast" (Ps 63:1, 5). Interpreters repeatedly quote these verses to explain the meaning of Matthew's beatitude (and sometimes even Luke's).[31]

Other New Testament texts provide additional warrant for viewing hunger and thirst as metaphorical, including Jesus's quotation of Deuteronomy to the devil. John's Gospel refers to Jesus as the bread from heaven, the bread of life, and the living water (John 4:14; 6:35, 58).[32] Also in John's Gospel, Jesus tells his disciples, "My food is to do the will of him who sent me and to complete his work" (John 4:34).[33]

For many interpreters, the beatitude indicates those who hunger for God rather than for the things of this world: money, glory, luxury, pleasures. Be-

---

31. Athanasius cited both psalms in *Festal Letter* 7 (for Easter 335) (*NPNF*² 4:525).

32. Erasmus of Rotterdam, *Paraphrase on Matthew*, vol. 45 of *Collected Works of Erasmus*, trans. Dean Simpson (Toronto: University of Toronto Press, 2008), 88; Erasmus of Rotterdam, *Paraphrase on Luke 1–10*, vol. 47 of *Collected Works of Erasmus*, trans. Jane E. Phillips (Toronto: University of Toronto Press, 2016), 193–94; Ellen Gould White, *Thoughts from the Mount of Blessing* (Mountain View, CA: Pacific Press Publishing Association, 1900, 1928), 33, 35; James Buck, *A Treatise of the Beatitudes, or, Christ's Happy Men* (London: printed by B. A. and T. F. for Iohn Clark, and Wil. Cooke, 1637), 138.

33. Augustine, *The Lord's Sermon*, 1.2.6.

cause the beatitude praises those who hunger for justice, wrote Chromatius of Aquileia, it implicitly condemns those who hunger for injustice—for worldly riches, honor, and the desires of the flesh.[34] Sometimes Luke's woe to the filled is invoked: the full are the unjust, as in Amos 4:1–2.

The beatitude's implicit condemnation of the unjust suggests another theme: longing for God's vindication in the face of evil and injustice. As contemporary scholar Craig Keener writes, yearning for God above all else (cf. Zeph 2:3) "includes yearning for God's justice, for his vindication of the oppressed."[35]

Hungering for God's justice because the hungry need justice

For Rupert of Deutz, one of the most influential medieval exegetes, the Old Testament prophets represent those who hunger and thirst for righteousness.[36] Through the prophets, God repeatedly condemns the unjust and the oppressor ("they sell the righteous for silver, and the needy for a pair of sandals—they who trample the head of the poor into the dust of the earth," Amos 2:6–7) and commands the Israelites to practice justice toward the most vulnerable:

> Is not this the fast that I choose:
>> to loose the bonds of injustice,
>> to undo the thongs of the yoke,
> to let the oppressed go free,
>> and to break every yoke?
> Is it not to share your bread with the hungry,
>> and bring the homeless poor into your house ... ?   (Isa 58:6–7)

This strand of the prophetic tradition calls for God's righteousness to be made manifest in human societies. Using this prophetic lens in relation to the beatitude leads to the view that Jesus blesses those who hunger for "the

---

34. Chromatius of Aquileia, *Sermons and Tractates on Matthew*, trans. Thomas P. Scheck, ACW 75 (New York: The Newman Press, 2018), Tractatus 17.5.2, 5.4; Bernard of Clairvaux, *Sermons on Conversion*, trans. Marie-Bernard Saïd (Kalamazoo, MI: Cistercian Publications, 1981), 62–63.

35. Craig S. Keener, *A Commentary on the Gospel of Matthew* (Grand Rapids: Eerdmans, 1999), 169–70.

36. Rupert of Deutz, *De gloria et honore filii hominis super Mattheum*, see Stoll, *De Virtute*, 195.

realization of God's goodness in the world."[37] Isaiah's reference to the hungry highlights a connection between those who hunger and those who hunger for justice. The former need the latter; the latter feed the former. In the nineteenth century, John MacEvilly made plain this connection between actual hunger and hunger for justice when he paraphrased the beatitude, "Blessed are they who are subjected to hunger and thirst, because justice is refused them."[38] Mark Allan Powell paraphrases it more succinctly as those "starved for justice."[39] The hungry are hungry for food *and* for the justice that would right the imbalances that keep them hungry.

The balance between human and divine agency, a recurring theme for the Beatitudes, comes back into view here. Does God bring about justice for the hungry, or do human beings? For some interpreters, hungering for God's justice means longing for what only God can achieve—"the final salvation that only God can effect" (so Kingsbury). For Dietrich Bonhoeffer, longing for righteousness means longing for "the forgiveness of all sin, for complete renewal, for the renewal too of the earth and the establishment of God's law."[40] But as James might remind us, faith (in God's justice) without works is dead (Jas 2:17); thus Yiu Sing Lúcás Chan writes that longing for God's righteousness necessarily involves seeking "the right conduct required by God as a response to the unrighteous human conditions."[41]

---

37. Gerald Vann, *The Divine Pity: A Study in the Social Implications of the Beatitudes* (New York: Sheed and Ward, 1946), 108–9; see also Glen Stassen, "The Beatitudes as Eschatological Peacemaking Virtues," in *Character Ethics and the New Testament: Moral Dimensions of Scripture*, ed. Robert L. Brawley (Louisville: Westminster John Knox, 2007), 251.

38. John MacEvilly, *An Exposition of the Gospels* (Dublin: W. B. Kelly; London: Simpkin, Marshall & Co., 1876), 77. William Domeris explains, blessed are "those who hunger and thirst because there is no justice," in Domeris, "'Blessed are you . . .' (Matthew 5:1–12)," *Journal of Theology for South Africa* 73 (1990): 71.

39. Mark Allan Powell, "Matthew's Beatitudes: Reversals and Rewards of the Kingdom," *CBQ* 58 (1996): 468. An unknown ninth-century interpreter, the composer of *The Heliand* (a Saxon harmony of the four gospels), interpreted the fourth beatitude as those who judge justly and fairly (*The Heliand: The Saxon Gospel*, trans. G. Ronald Murphy [Oxford: Oxford University Press, 1992], 46).

40. Jack Dean Kingsbury, *Matthew as Story* (Philadelphia: Fortress, 1986), 107; Dietrich Bonhoeffer, *The Cost of Discipleship* (New York: Simon & Schuster, 1995), 111. Cabasilas's brief meditation on the beatitude describes how Christ rendered justice and destroyed "the tyrant" and "the usurper" and "his unjust dominion" (6.11d, in Cabasilas, *The Life in Christ*, trans. Carmino J. deCatanzaro [Crestwood, NY: St. Vladimir's Seminary Press, 1974], 185).

41. Yiu Sing Lúcás Chan, *The Ten Commandments and the Beatitudes* (Lanham, MD: Rowman & Littlefield, 2012), 187. So also Keener, *Commentary on the Gospel of Matthew*, 169–170; and A.-M. Carré, who declared that it is an affront to the gospel to remain indifferent to the

Longing for God's justice: doing justice (outward acts of righteousness)

This is a natural conclusion. If one longs for God's justice to be done—and God has described rather clearly what that might look like in a human society such as Israel—then one will take whatever small steps one can to bring about that justice. In this respect, hungering for God's righteousness means an ardent desire for God's will that translates into action in accord with that will. Seventeenth-century writer Hendrik Niclaes (ca. 1501–1580) urged his readers to hunger after God by seeking to accomplish God's will with a humble heart and a pure love.[42] Seven centuries before Hendrik, a woman named Dhuoda (d. 843?) wrote to instruct her son, telling him that hungering for God's righteousness means making just laws, not taking advantage of the poor, and rendering legal judgments with mercy.[43]

Dhuoda's intertwining of justice and mercy reveals the long tradition of connecting those two attributes. But it also points to the order of the Beatitudes once again, since the blessing on the merciful (Matt 5:7) follows immediately after the blessing on those who hunger for justice (Matt 5:6). For the many interpreters who attend to the order of the Beatitudes, a hunger for justice leads naturally to acts of mercy.[44] For some, mercy also needs justice in order to be practiced rightly. Theophylact of Ochrid, for example, proposed that righteousness precedes mercy to show that one can't "give alms from what has been acquired by theft and extortion."[45] Stanley Jones understood the two beatitudes as pairs because each needs the correction of the other: "Righteousness unmodified by mercy is a hard, unlovely, Pharisaical, sour-visaged thing.... Mercy without righteousness is mushy."[46] Leo the Great, who understood the beatitude as a reference to fasting, insisted that fasting should not

---

distress of others (Carré, *Quand arrive le bonheur: Les Béatitudes*, 2nd ed. [Paris: Les Éditions du Cerf, 1974], 75–76).

42. Hendrik Niclaes, *The first exhortation of H. N. to his children, and to the Family of Love: Likewise H. N. upon the Beatitudes, and the Seven Deadly Sins* (London: For Giles Calvert, 1656), 193.

43. Dhuoda, *Handbook for her Warrior Son* 4.8, ed. and trans. Marcelle Thiébaux (Cambridge: Cambridge University Press, 1998), 159.

44. E.g., Ambrose of Milan, *Commentary of Saint Ambrose on the Gospel According to Saint Luke* 5.56, 5.57, 5.68, trans. Íde M. Ní Riain (Dublin: Halcyon, 2001), 136, 139.

45. Theophylact of Ochrid, *The Explanation by Blessed Theophylact of the Holy Gospel According to St. Matthew*, vol. 1 of *Blessed Theophylact's Explanation of the New Testament*, trans. Christopher Stade (House Springs, MO: Chrysostom Press, 1994), 45.

46. E. Stanley Jones, *The Christ of the Mount: A Working Philosophy of Life* (New York: Abingdon, 1931), 73–74.

be merely abstinence from food but should lead to good works, citing Matt 5:6: "Let works of piety [righteousness], therefore, be our delight and let us be filled with those kinds of good which feed us for eternity." As examples, he named giving to the poor, clothing the naked, and helping the sick, infirm, orphans, and widows.[47]

I began this chapter with a consideration of the Greek *dikaiosynē*. Modern interpreters sometimes appeal to the Greek concept (and its Hebrew equivalent *ṣĕdāqâ*) to make the case that righteousness includes human action that "accords with God's nature, will, and coming kingdom."[48] Jewish theologian Pinchas Lapide made the same point by appealing to the Hebrew word *ṣĕdāqâ* underlying the Greek *dikaiosynē*. Lapide took *ṣĕdāqâ* as both God's kindness toward humans and human fairness toward one another—the good deeds we owe to our fellow humans "as their rightful portion of the richness of unmerited gifts with which God showers the world."[49]

Hungering for God's righteousness in the heart (inward righteousness)

"And yet in our world," wrote Leo Tolstoy drily (or perhaps despairingly), "everybody thinks of changing humanity, and nobody thinks of changing himself."[50] For some interpreters, hungering for righteousness means longing for God's righteousness to be made manifest not (only) in the world but in one's own heart.

Viewing hunger for righteousness as longing for an inward, individual transformation becomes particularly prevalent during (and after) the Reformation. To be sure, pre-Reformation interpreters were not unaware of the connection between personal holiness and outward acts of justice. In the early fifth century, Jerome noted that "we are never sufficiently just," and so must al-

---

47. Leo the Great, *Sermons* 40.4 (*NPNF²* 12:155); see also Leo the Great, *Sermons* 95.6 (*NPNF²* 12:204). Witetschek argues that Gos. Thom. 69.2 is a parallel to Matt 5:6 but with a purpose clause—i.e., it commends fasting for the benefit of others; Witetschek sees a parallel in Origen's *Hom. Lev.* 10.2 (Witetschek, "Going Hungry," 379, see also 384).

48. Jonathan T. Pennington, *The Sermon on the Mount and Human Flourishing: A Theological Commentary* (Grand Rapids: Baker Academic, 2017), 90, original italics removed. So also R. T. France, *The Gospel of Matthew*, NICNT (Grand Rapids: Eerdmans, 2007), 167.

49. Pinchas Lapide, *The Sermon on the Mount: Utopia or Program for Action?*, trans. Arlene Swidler (Maryknoll: Orbis Books, 1986), 21–22.

50. Leo Tolstoy, "Some Social Remedies," in *Pamphlets* (Christchurch, Hants: The Free Age Press, 1900), 71.

ways hunger for justice to permeate our own lives and actions.[51] And Jerome's contemporary, Augustine, fought his famous battle against the Pelagians over the necessity of God's grace to heal the fallen human heart. As the prophet Jeremiah complained, "The heart is deceitful above all things, and desperately wicked" (Jer 17:9 KJV).

Still, the question of righteousness became a special problem during the Reformation, when an Augustinian monk named Martin Luther began to wrestle with the yawning gap between divine and human righteousness. Luther distinguished between two types of righteousness, one inward and one outward. The first type is "the principal Christian righteousness by which a person becomes pious and acceptable to God" (the Christian *coram Deo*, or "before God"), and the second type is "outward righteousness before the world, which we maintain in our relations with each other" (the Christian *coram hominibus*, or "before the neighbor").

For Luther, the subject of the beatitude is the second type—the Christian before the neighbor. Thus Luther's understanding of the beatitude was surprisingly active. The "righteous and blessed" person is the one "who continually works and strives with all his might to promote the general welfare and the proper behavior of everyone and who helps to maintain and support this by word and deed, by precept and example."[52] The Reformer may have been influenced by his predecessor William Tyndale, who likewise understood the righteousness of Matt 5:6 not as righteousness before God, but as "the outward righteousness before the world, and true and faithful dealing with each other."[53]

In another place, Luther also used the beatitude to refer to a Christian's desire to grow in faith or trust in Christ. When Luther wrote a pastoral letter to a woman (identified only as M.) to reassure her of God's forgiveness, he quoted the beatitude, saying that it referred to all those, like M., who would like to be stronger in their faith.[54] In the mid-twentieth century, German scholar Rudolf

---

51. Jerome, *Commentary on Matthew*, trans. Thomas P. Scheck, FC 117 (Washington, DC: Catholic University of America, 2008), 76. Augustine also insisted (contra Pelagius) that even the most righteous human being is not immune from sin, and so "must still hunger and thirst" for God's righteousness and grace (*Spirit and the Letter* 65, quoted in Robert Louis Wilken, "Augustine," in *The Sermon on the Mount through the Centuries: From the Early Church to John Paul II*, ed. Jeffrey P. Greenman, Timothy Larsen, and Stephen R. Spencer [Grand Rapids: Brazos, 2007], 55n18).

52. Martin Luther, *The Sermon on the Mount*, vol. 21 of *Luther's Works*, ed. Jaroslav Pelikan (St. Louis: Concordia, 1956), 26.

53. William Tyndale, *The Work of William Tyndale*, ed. G. E. Duffield (Philadelphia: Fortress, 1965), 200.

54. Martin Luther, *Luther: Letters of Spiritual Counsel*, trans. Theodore G. Tappert, LCC 18

Bultmann picked up this second emphasis of Luther's when he insisted that righteousness in Matt 5:6 cannot mean any form of human striving but refers to "those who long to have God pronounce the verdict 'righteous' as His decision over them in the judgment."[55] Bultmann is a good representative of a standard Lutheran view of the beatitude, which typically refers not to Luther's own writing on the beatitude but to approaches of later Lutheran interpreters.

Because of the word *righteousness* in the beatitude, Protestant interpretations for at least a century after the Reformation were profoundly shaped by evolving Protestant views—and Catholic responses—on justification, sanctification, and grace. Interpreters, especially later Protestant interpreters, began to read the beatitude through the lens of Paul, as debates over justification by faith in Romans influenced how people understood the fourth beatitude.

One of the post-Reformation issues concerned the nature of the sinful human being in relation to a righteous God. What happened when a person became a Christian, whether through conversion or baptism? And what did that person need to do in order to receive salvation? Catholics and Protestants agreed on the two components in that equation: humans were sinful, and God was righteous. Additionally, they agreed that God's grace effected the salvation of a human person.

They disagreed, of course, over the role of good works. They also disagreed about what grace *did* to a person. Catholic teaching is indebted to Augustine, who taught that grace is infused into a justified person, healing their fallen human nature and enabling them to will and to do the good. When God justifies a person, God *makes* that person good. A Christian's responsibility is then to cooperate with God's saving grace ("faith working through love") and thereby they "increase in that justice received through the grace of Christ and are further justified."[56] Justification was thus "a lifelong process in which the Christian progresses in a journey towards God."[57]

(Philadelphia: Westminster, 1955), 103. On this aspect of Luther's thought, see Stephen J. Chester, *Reading Paul with the Reformers: Reconciling Old and New Perspectives* (Grand Rapids: Eerdmans, 2017), 196–97.

55. Rudolf Bultmann, *The Message of Jesus, the Kerygma of the Earliest Church and the Theology of Paul*, vol. 1 of *Theology of the New Testament*, trans. Kendrick Grobel (London: SCM, 1952), 273.

56. Chester, *Reading Paul*, 70–74, 78–79. Quotation is from Schroeder, *Canons and Decrees of the Council of Trent*, 36 (Sixth Session, Chapter 10), quoted in Chester, *Reading Paul*, 101. I'm grateful to Stephen Chester for walking me through some of these distinctions, as well as for assisting me with the discussion of imputed and imparted righteousness.

57. Chester, *Reading Paul*, 101–2.

Luther, on the other hand, saw justification not as a transformation, and certainly not as a gradual process, but as a "joyous exchange" between the sinful human being and Christ. Righteousness was not infused into a person; it was *imputed* or reckoned to them.[58] For Luther, righteousness was always "alien"; it never became the property of the believer but always remained that of Christ— but paradoxically became perfectly received by the believer through union with Christ, a gift received through faith alone, requiring no good works to bring it to completion.[59] Calvin likewise rejected the view that grace is infused into a person, arguing that people participate in Christ by faith, through which they receive Christ's righteousness and are counted righteous by God.[60]

So when Catholic and Protestant interpreters in the Reformation and post-Reformation centuries talked about hungering for "righteousness," they used the same word but meant different things. To use Stephen Chester's term, they were using different grammars.[61] Indeed, even later Reformers did not always mean the same thing by the term justification (or righteousness) as their Protestant predecessors meant.[62]

By the time debates over justification worked their way into the mid-seventeenth century, Protestant interpreters had begun to split righteousness into two categories: imputed and imparted. Imputed righteousness was Christ's righteousness, which is bestowed on human beings and which people are incapable of earning or achieving. Imparted righteousness tended to be used as a synonym for sanctification or regeneration, and thus appeared more often in Calvinist or Reformed writings. For most Protestant interpreters from the mid-seventeenth century onward, both kinds of righteousness were included in the beatitude. In other words, Christ declares blessed those who long both for their justification and their sanctification, for God's declaration of their innocence in the heavenly court and for growth in holiness through the assistance of God's grace.[63]

58. For the language of joyous exchange, so Chester, *Reading Paul*, 249. Stephen Chester notes that vocabulary of imputation goes back as far as the Vulgate, which occasionally translates the verb *logizomai* with *imputare*. In email correspondence, Chester writes that it is "simply erroneous to think that [the Refomers'] position is identical to typical later Protestant accounts of imputation. They use the same words but they do not necessarily mean exactly the same things as they will later."

59. Chester, *Reading Paul*, 190, 245.

60. Chester, *Reading Paul*, 270.

61. See Chester, *Reading Paul*, 61–80, 95–103.

62. I am grateful to Stephen Chester for clarifying this point in an email exchange.

63. Increase Mather, *Sermons Wherein Those Eight Characters of the Blessed Commonly Called the Beatitudes Are Opened and Applied in Fifteen Discourses* (Boston: B. Green, for Daniel Hench-

It's easy to protest that these later Reformation interpreters were committing classic eisegesis: reading sixteenth-century debates back into a first-century text. When Matthew wrote *dikaiosynē*, he knew of neither imputation nor impartation. Yet these interpreters were capturing, in their own way, themes that appeared in reflections on the beatitude's inner and outer aspects from the very beginning.

Both inner and outer righteousness

Earlier, the chapter explored John Calvin's view of the beatitude. Calvin treated "those who hunger" and "the poor in spirit" under the same rubric, viewing both as having a material component (actual material poverty or social lowliness) and a spiritual one (humility and dependence upon God). Jeremiah Burroughs politely suggested that Calvin, despite being a very good interpreter of Scripture, had not gone far enough this time. Burroughs represents those interpreters who see the longing of the beatitude as having both an inner (personal holiness) and outer (justice in the world) component.

Burroughs proposed that Christ is blessing those who long for the power of righteousness in their own hearts to prevail over sin, *and* those who long for righteousness to prevail in the world. Burroughs made an implicit connection between hungering for righteousness and the prayer of lament through an allusion to the martyrs crying out to God in Revelation 6:10: "They send up strong cries to God that righteousness might come into the world. How long, how long shall it be, holy and true?"[64] And Burroughs gave practical advice to those who felt they were hungering and thirsting after righteousness yet could not find it (124–130), reassuring his congregation that "God is a compassionate father" (129) and that Christ is a shepherd who seeks out even the sheep lost and caught in the briars (130).

Four centuries after Burroughs, Dominican priest and Peruvian theologian Gustavo Gutiérrez (b. 1928) agreed. Righteousness indicates "a relation-

---

man, 1718), Sermon 7. Similar views appear in Thomas Watson, *The Beatitudes: An Exposition of Matthew 5:1–10* (Carlisle, PA: Banner of Truth Trust, 2014), 129–30; William Hendriksen, *The Gospel of Matthew*, New Testament Commentary (Edinburgh: Banner of Truth Trust, 1973), 273–74. Lefèvre d'Étaples describes *justice* as those who long for their sanctification and propitiation (*Jacques Lefèvre d'Étaples et ses Disciples: Epistres et Evangiles pour le cinquante et deux dimenches de l'an*, ed. Guy Bedouelle and Franco Giacone [Leiden: Brill, 1976], 375).

64. Jeremiah Burroughs, *The Saints' Happiness* (Edinburgh: James Nichol, 1867; Soli Deo Gloria, 1988, 1992), 89–90, quotation on 91.

ship with the Lord—namely, holiness; and at the same time a relationship with human beings—namely, recognition of the rights of each person and especially the despised and the oppressed, or, in other words, social justice."[65] For some, this mirrors the internal and external righteousness of the two great love commandments, more often expressed as horizontal (love of neighbor) and vertical (love of God) aspects. For A.-M. Carré, for example, "total justice" is love of God and love of neighbor; it is friendship with God and with others.[66] This view brings us full circle to the material aspect with which we began, since justice expressed in the world—or love of the neighbor—typically involves concrete acts that address the real needs of those neighbors.

They/You will be filled

Both actual and symbolic bread

Just as reflections on the first half of the beatitude wrestle with the material and spiritual dimensions of hunger, interpretations of the second half—the promised reward—do the same. As with the first half, views of the second half also tend toward the spiritual aspect of being filled.

Elsewhere in Matthew and Luke, "being filled" (*chortazō*) refers to the contentment of eating actual bread. The great crowds eat the miraculously multiplied bread and are filled (Matt 14:20, 15:37; Luke 9:17). The prodigal son and the poor man, Lazarus, long to be filled but remain hungry (Luke 15:16, 16:21). And the brother of Jesus warns his congregation, "If a brother or sister is naked and lacks daily food, and one of you says to them, 'Go in peace; keep warm and eat your fill,' and yet you do not supply their bodily needs, what is the good of that?" (Jas 2:16).

Yet, as we have already seen, Scripture is also replete with metaphors of food and drink as divine or spiritual sustenance. In the Old Testament, eating and drinking often has "a spiritual and symbolic component" but is never merely spiritual; it's always "anchored in the physical materiality" of real food.[67] Modern scholar Benedict Green appealed to the merging of the material and the eschatological in Isaiah:

---

65. Gutiérrez, *The God of Life*, trans. Matthew J. O'Connell (Maryknoll, NY: Orbis Books, 1991, 1998), 120.

66. Carré, *Quand arrive*, 83.

67. Antonio Sicari, "The Hunger and Thirst of Christ," *Communio* 18 (1991): 592.

Thus says the Lord:
In a time of favor I have answered you,
   on a day of salvation I have helped you.
They shall feed along the ways,
   on all the bare heights shall be their pasture;
they shall not hunger or thirst,
   neither scorching wind nor sun shall strike them down,
for he who has pity on them will lead them,
   and by springs of water will guide them. (Isa 49:8, 9b–10)[68]

Likewise, in Isaiah 55 wine, milk, and bread symbolize God's eternal covenant with Israel. So also in Christian thought: after the Last Supper, bread is more than bread.[69]

Augustine explained the promised reward by pointing to the cessation of (spiritual) thirst in John 4, when Jesus promises the Samaritan woman living water so that she will never thirst again (John 4:10–15) (*De Serm. Dom.* 1.2.6).[70] Another woman from the region of Tyre and Sidon asks Jesus for crumbs from his table, by which she means not actual bread but the healing of her daughter (Mark 7:24–30).[71]

In Revelation, the exalted Son of Man (i.e., the risen Christ) urges the church in Laodicea to repent and recognize their need of him, so that he might "eat with you, and you with me" (Rev 3:20); and the One seated on the throne promises, "To the thirsty I will give water as a gift from the spring of the water of life" (Rev 21:6). The gospel writers borrowed imagery from Isaiah to portray the eschaton, the new age, as a banquet of rich foods and wine (e.g., Isa 25:6–8, 49:10–13; Matthew 7:11; Luke 13:29).

Thus for some writers, being filled has both a literal and a spiritual meaning. As John Calvin wrote, "God will supply everything we lack."[72] Only a very

---

68. Green, *Matthew, Poet*, 227.

69. Bonhoeffer is one of the few modern authors to understand the promise to be filled as a reference to the bread of the Eucharist. Bonhoeffer wrote, "They are blessed because they already enjoy this bread here and now, for in their hunger they are sustained by the bread of life, the bliss of sinners"; and, "They will eat the Bread of Life in the Messianic Feast" (Bonhoeffer, *Cost of Discipleship*, 111).

70. Augustine drew from John 4:34 and John 4:14; Augustine, *The Lord's Sermon*, 15.

71. Carré pointed out this story in parallel with the Samaritan woman at the well in his exegesis of the beatitude (Carré, *Quand arrive*, 77).

72. Calvin, *Sermons on the Beatitudes*, 40. Jacques Bénigne Bossuet wrote that being filled is the "fulfillment of all our longings" (Bossuet, *The Sermon on the Mount*, trans. F. M. Capes [Longmans, Green: 1900], 1).

few see the promised reward as wholly material and this-worldly. This is true even of Luke's beatitude; for example, Herman Hendrickx writes that Luke's promise that the hungry shall be filled has both an earthly and an eschatological referent. He suggests that the fulfillment promised by Jesus would be hollow if it failed to address "the depressing conditions" of the victimized and oppressed in this life; but, he also points out that eating one's fill has resonances with the imagery of the heavenly, messianic banquet.[73]

Spiritual

For many other writers, the primary meaning of the promised reward is spiritual. As always, a "now and not yet" paradigm shapes understandings of the beatitude's second half. God fills the hungry both now, in part, and perfectly in the next life. God satisfies the desires of hungry hearts in the here-and-now through the Spirit's presence, the assurance of forgiveness in Christ, and the gift of grace. "Nothing else but grace is bread," wrote Puritan Robert Harris, citing Isa 55:1.[74] And American theologian Jonathan Edwards declared, "There is enough in Christ . . . to equal the utmost strength of the desire. There is an ocean of it."[75] For some, being filled *now* refers to justification, whereas being filled *then* is the perfection of sanctification, the healing and full restoration of the image of God.[76]

Ultimately, being filled entails the full arrival of the kingdom of God in which God's will is always fully accomplished, in heaven as on earth.[77] This

73. Herman Hendrickx, *Ministry in Galilee (Luke 3:1–6:49)*, vol. 2A of *The Third Gospel for the Third World* (Collegeville, MN: Liturgical Press, 1997), 278–79. So also Powell, "Matthew's Beatitudes," 468.

74. Robert Harris, *The Way to True Happiness: Delivered in Twenty-Four Sermons upon the Beatitudes*, ed. Don Kistler (Morgan, PA: Soli Deo Gloria, 1998), 170. So also Watson, *The Beatitudes*, 148.

75. Jonathan Edwards, *Sermons and Discourses 1730–1733*, vol. 17 of *The Works of Jonathan Edwards*, ed. Mark Valeri (New Haven, CT: Yale University Press, 1999), 136.

76. E.g., D. Martyn Lloyd-Jones, *Studies in the Sermon on the Mount*, vol. 1 (Grand Rapids: Eerdmans, 1960), 82; John Peter Lange, *The Gospel According to Matthew*, vol. 16 of *A Commentary on the Holy Scriptures: Critical, Doctrinal, and Homiletical, with Special Reference to Ministers and Students*, trans. Philip Schaff, 12th ed. (New York: Charles Scribner's Sons, 1884), 102. Burroughs also applied the beatitude's promise ("they shall be filled") to the soul's justification before God, which by God's grace is the saint's sanctification; because of the power of God's righteousness and grace in the saint's life, the promise to be filled or blessed is also accomplished in the present (Burroughs, *Saints' Happiness*, 100–123).

77. Green commented, "the satisfaction transcends the object of desire," in Green, *Matthew, Poet*, 234.

illustrates the relatively common belief that all the promised rewards of the Beatitudes ultimately refer to the same thing: the inheritance of and entrance into the eschatological kingdom of God. If, as Augustine believed, our deepest desire is for our Creator, then God satisfies us, now and in the end, with nothing less than God's own self.[78]

Conclusion

"You open your hand," sings the psalmist, "satisfying the desire of every living thing" (Ps 145:16). When God declared through his prophet Isaiah that the exiles returning from Persia to their homeland "shall not hunger or thirst" on their journey (Isa 49:8–10), surely God meant that they would not starve as they traveled through the desert. But just as surely, the promise of provisions, alongside the poetic declaration that God will turn all the mountains into level roads (Isa 49:11; see also Isa 40:4), stands in for God's loving care and protection; indeed, it functions as a reference to the restoration of the covenant itself. For some Jewish readers as for the early Christians, the prophetic announcement of Israel's return from exile became a declaration of eschatological and not only this-worldly restoration.

For those readers who view the beatitude through a purely spiritual lens, perhaps Luke's version serves a corrective function, even a prophetic function, reminding us that hungering and thirsting for God cannot be neatly detached from the real hunger and thirst of the impoverished and suffering. Nor will Matthew let us forget that hunger and thirst is equally a scriptural metaphor for longing for God and for God's justice, for the full outpouring of the kingdom of God that is only now glimmering on the horizon.

The two beatitudes converge at just this point: hungering for justice for the hungry, longing for a world in which there are no more children who starve to death because they have no bread, longing for God's kingdom to come with its abundant banquet table laid for all. Perhaps in Jesus's time, the meaning of Matthew and Luke overlapped closely, since the literally hungry were the ones longing for God's redemption, and the first followers of Jesus were the hungry.

---

78. Kyriaki Karidoyanes FitzGerald and Thomas FitzGerald, *Happy in the Lord: The Beatitudes for Everyday: Perspectives from Orthodox Spirituality* (Brookline, MA: Holy Cross Orthodox Press, 2000), 95. So also Aquinas, who took being filled as a reference to the eschaton and the beatific vision (Aquinas, *Commentary on Matthew*, C.5 L.2.428).

The challenge of the two versions in our time is what to do when the two categories are more separate. How will you ever hunger and thirst for righteousness, asks American writer Paul Louis Metzger, if you take clean water for granted?[79] In 1977, when evangelical theologian Ron Sider first published *Rich Christians in an Age of Hunger*, it galvanized and scandalized a generation of evangelical Christians to consider and respond to their complicity in unjust economic structures.[80] His challenge remains apt. It has become even more pressing in a time of globalization (with its unequal blessings) and an ever-widening gap between rich and poor.

Sider urges rich, Western Christians to make changes in their personal lives, in their churches, and in the structures of society.[81] "All we need to do," he writes,

> is truly obey the One we rightly worship. But to obey will mean to follow. And he lives among the poor and oppressed, seeking justice for those in agony. In our time, following in his steps will mean simple personal lifestyles. It will mean transformed churches with a corporate lifestyle consistent with worship of the God of the poor. It will mean costly commitment to structural change in secular society. . . . Together we must strive to be a biblical people ready to follow wherever Scripture leads. We must pray for the courage to bear any cross, suffer any loss and joyfully embrace any sacrifice that biblical faith requires in an Age of Hunger.[82]

He ends on a note of hope: the hungry *will* be filled. The thirst of the thirsty *will* be quenched. Those who hunger for justice will see justice done.

> We know that the Sovereign of the universe wills an end to hunger, injustice and oppression. The resurrection of Jesus is our guarantee that, in spite of the massive evil that sometimes almost overwhelms us, the final victory will surely come. Secure on that solid rock, we will plunge into this unjust world, changing now all we can and knowing that the risen King will complete the victory at his glorious return.[83]

79. Paul Louis Metzger, *Beatitudes, Not Platitudes: Jesus' Invitation to the Good Life* (Eugene, OR: Cascade, 2018), 49–51.

80. Ronald J. Sider, *Rich Christians in an Age of Hunger*, rev. ed. (Downers Grove, IL: InterVarsity Press, 1984).

81. Sider, *Rich Christians*, 162.

82. Sider, *Rich Christians*, 223–24.

83. Sider, *Rich Christians*, 224.

7

Stretching Out the Hand

The Merciful

Blessed are the merciful, for they will receive mercy (Matt 5:7).

Hendrik Niclaes (ca. 1501–1580) was a merchant and a mystic. A native of Germany, he spent most of his life in Amsterdam and Emden (northwest Germany, today), where he established a religious order called the Family of Love. In his meditation on the fifth beatitude, written to encourage his beloved Family, he repeated the phrase "stretching out the hand" over and over again. He described mercy as stretching out an open hand with food for the poor, with loving hospitality, and with forbearance and forgiveness.[1] It is a gentle phrase that captures the wideness of the term mercy in the beatitude and elsewhere in Scripture.

It's also a phrase that hints at the potential power of an act of mercy. Think of the Persian king Ahasuerus stretching out his scepter to Esther to grant her permission to approach the throne (Esth 5:1–3). An open-palmed, outstretched hand sometimes means, "I decline to hurt you" or "I restrain my power over you." Mercy can be clemency. In this sense, mercy is not a "relatively bland" feeling of compassion but "life-or-death power."[2] When you are "at the mercy" of someone, you are entirely in their power, for good or for ill.

The metaphor of the outstretched hand also hints at the way mercy can indicate rescue or even salvation. In the Old Testament, God's "outstretched arm" indicates God's mighty power, and is associated especially with the exodus—God's rescue of the enslaved Israelites from Pharaoh in Egypt (e.g., Exod 6:6, Deut 5:15, 2 Kings 17:36).

1. Hendrik Niclaes, *The first exhortation of H. N. to his children, and to the Family of Love: Likewise H. N. upon the Beatitudes, and the Seven Deadly Sins* (London: For Giles Calvert, 1656), 199.

2. Sarah Ruden, *The Face of Water: A Translator on Beauty and Meaning in the Bible* (New York: Pantheon Books, 2017), 78.

It is an apt metaphor, then, for its capaciousness. The history of this beatitude reveals a similarly multilayered understanding of mercy, both spiritual and bodily, individual and social: "every kind of mercifulness."[3] It is seeking the good of our neighbor in every way.[4] When Catholic humanist Erasmus of Rotterdam paraphrased the fifth beatitude in the sixteenth century, he wrote that Jesus declares blessed those who "out of brotherly love consider another's misery their own, who are pained at the misfortunes of a neighbour, who shed tears for the calamities that strike other people, who feed the needy out of their own wealth, clothe the naked, warn the erring, teach the ignorant, forgive the sinner—in short, who use whatever resources they have to lift up and restore others."[5] The use of the verb form of *mercy* elsewhere in Matthew's Gospel bears witness to a similarly complex understanding; Matthew used mercy alongside the acts of healing the blind (Matt 9:27, 20:30–31), driving out demons (Matt 15:22, 17:15), and forgiving debts (Matt 18:33).

The second half of this beatitude receives more attention than usual. It's the only beatitude whose equation is perfectly balanced; the first half (shows mercy) matches its second half (receives mercy). It is this feature that tempts its interpreters to read it in reverse. That is, instead of declaring that the merciful will be shown mercy, it is often said that the merciful show mercy because they have already been shown mercy. The beatitude is set on a kind of continual loop, from mercy to mercy. It is precisely the danger of breaking this loop that is implied in the promised reward *they shall be shown mercy*. If it is the merciful who receive mercy, what about those who do *not* show mercy? The second half of this beatitude has posed a special challenge to interpreters, since it seems to impose a limit on God's grace. Does failing to show mercy to one's fellow human beings cause the withholding of divine mercy?

3. Juan Maldonado, *S. Matthew's Gospel, Chapters I to XIV*, vol. 1 of *A Commentary on the Holy Gospels*, trans. and ed. George J. Davie (London, UK: John Hodges, 1888), 136.

4. Mackintosh Mackay, *A practical exposition of the first ten verses of the fifth chapter of the Gospel by Matthew*, 2 vols. (Edinburgh: William Whyte & Co., 1840–1842), 2:17.

5. Erasmus of Rotterdam, *Paraphrase on Matthew*, vol. 45 of *Collected Works of Erasmus*, trans. Dean Simpson (Toronto: University of Toronto Press, 2008), 88. Puritan Nonconformist Thomas Watson wrote in 1660 that mercy includes exhorting and praying for sinners, protecting the reputation of others, forgiving debts, and forgiving those who wrong you (Watson, *The Beatitudes: An Exposition of Matthew 5:1–10* [Carlisle, PA: Banner of Truth Trust, 2014], 153–62).

Broadly speaking, the many meanings of mercy throughout history can be grouped into three main categories: helping the needy, forgiving the offender, and welcoming the outsider.

Almsgiving: material assistance to the needy

First and perhaps foremost, showing mercy is understood as almsgiving, or providing material assistance to the poor and needy. This understanding has its foundations in Judaism. Before Jesus preached the Beatitudes, Jewish teaching already considered almsgiving to be a central form of mercy.[6] "The one who dishonors the poor sins," wrote the author of Proverbs, "but the one who shows mercy to the poor is blessed" (Prov 14:21 LXX). The Greek language itself indicates almsgiving as a form of mercy, since the word for almsgiving (found in Matt 6:2–4) is *eleēmosynē*, a close relative of the adjective *eleēmōn* ("merciful") used in the beatitude in Matt 5:7.

It's no surprise, then, that many of the earliest Christian interpreters in both East and West understood the fifth beatitude as almsgiving, including Cyprian, bishop of Carthage in North Africa (ca. 200–258); Ambrose, bishop of Milan (ca. 340–397); and John Chrysostom, the golden-tongued archbishop of Constantinople (ca. 349–407).[7] This approach endured with no significant change during the medieval era. Likewise, Protestant Reformers, including Martin Luther, described giving alms or helping the poor as one of the aspects of mercy included in the beatitude, and later Protestant theologians followed in their footsteps. American theologian Jonathan Edwards, for example, discussed the beatitude in a sermon (preached on Deut 15:7–11) entitled "The Duty of Charity to the Poor."[8]

6. Hans Dieter Betz, *The Sermon on the Mount*, Hermeneia (Minneapolis: Fortress, 1995), 133n313; Jacques Dupont, *Les évangélistes*, vol. 3 of *Les Béatitudes* (Paris: Gabalda, 1973), 606–17.

7. Cyprian, *Treatises* 12.3.1 (ANF 5:531); Ambrose of Milan, *Commentary of Saint Ambrose on the Gospel According to Saint Luke* 5.57–8, trans. Íde M. Ní Riain (Dublin: Halcyon, 2001), 136; Chrysostom, *Homilies on the Gospel of Saint Matthew* 15.6 (NPNF¹ 10:94); Augustine, *The Lord's Sermon on the Mount* 1.2.7, trans. John J. Jepson, ACW 5 (Mahwah, NJ: Paulist, 1948), 15.

8. Jonathan Edwards, *Sermons and Discourses 1730–1733*, vol. 17 of *The Works of Jonathan Edwards*, ed. Mark Valeri (New Haven, CT: Yale University Press, 1999), 381. For Luther, see Martin Luther, *The Sermon on the Mount*, vol. 21 of *Luther's Works*, ed. Jaroslav Pelikan (St. Louis: Concordia, 1956), 30. See also Increase Mather, *Sermons Wherein Those Eight Characters of the*

Every misery: a broad understanding of "almsgiving"

We usually think of almsgiving simply as giving money or other material assistance to the poor, and this is certainly the heart of it. But for Christian writers throughout history, "almsgiving" was a broad umbrella term for all kinds of material and spiritual help to those in need. As one writer put it, "Not a misery escapes the attention, the tenderness of the people of the beatitudes."[9] Another suggested that mercy is giving alms in imitation of God, whose bounty gives alms to creation—alms of being, life, intelligence, beauty.[10]

For many Christians, the parable of the sheep and the goats in Matthew 25 has named the kind of merciful acts that fall under the heading of "almsgiving": giving food and drink to the hungry and thirsty, offering hospitality to strangers, providing clothing to those without enough clothes to wear, caring for the sick, and visiting prisoners (Matt 25:31–46). Over time, this list expanded and was codified in the Catholic tradition in the corporal and spiritual works of mercy, which recognizes that mercy to the poor includes spiritual or emotional help as well as material or bodily assistance.[11] Evangelist Billy Graham shared this same insight when he wrote that mercy includes caring for the bodily needs of others (food, shelter) and for their social needs (friendship).[12]

Contemporary scholars have broadened the definition of mercy even further to include structural issues of injustice. So, to return to the categories of Matthew 25, these commentators focus on the structures that keep so many hungry or without access to clean water, or on any immigration system that makes it difficult to welcome strangers, or on a criminal justice system that (for example) disproportionately imprisons black men in America. In this view, in the words of Mark Allan Powell, the merciful "favor the removal of everything

---

Blessed Commonly Called the Beatitudes Are Opened and Applied in Fifteen Discourses (Boston: B. Green, for Daniel Henchman, 1718), Sermon 8.

9. A.-M. Carré: "Pas une misère n'échappe à l'attention, à la tendresse du peuple des beatitudes" (Carré, *Quand arrive le bonheur: Les Béatitudes*, 2nd ed. [Paris: Les Éditions du Cerf, 1974], 63). "For the way of showing mercy is manifold," writes John Chrysostom (Chrysostom, *Homilies on the Gospel of Saint Matthew* 15.6 [*NPNF*¹ 10:94]).

10. Jean François Anne Thomas Landriot, *Les Béatitudes évangéliques*, 2 vols. (Paris: Palmé, 1866–1867), 2:229.

11. E.g., Yiu Sing Lúcás Chan, *The Ten Commandments and the Beatitudes* (Lanham, MD: Rowman & Littlefield, 2012), 197–98; Kyriaki Karidoyanes FitzGerald and Thomas FitzGerald, *Happy in the Lord: The Beatitudes for Everyday: Perspectives from Orthodox Spirituality* (Brookline, MA: Holy Cross Orthodox Press, 2000), 108–9; Leo the Great, *Sermons* 78.4 (*NPNF*² 12:194).

12. Billy Graham, *The Secret of Happiness: Jesus' Teaching on Happiness as Expressed in the Beatitudes* (Garden City, NY: Doubleday, 1955), 61–65.

that prevents life from being as God intends: poverty, ostracism, hunger, disease, demons, debt."[13]

Chilean theologian Segundo Galilea described mercy in terms of solidarity with the suffering. This solidarity leads to commitment toward and involvement with the needy and afflicted.[14] Galilea likely drew the notion of solidarity from a document emerging from the Catholic Church's Second Vatican Council called *Gaudium et Spes [Joy and Hope]* (its English title is, less succinctly, "Pastoral Constitution of the Church in the Modern World"). The document begins, "The joys and the hopes, the griefs and the anxieties of the men of this age, especially those who are poor or in any way afflicted, these are the joys and hopes, the griefs and anxieties of the followers of Christ." The theme of solidarity anticipates the theme of mercy as "weeping with those who weep" (Rom 12:15) (more on that below).

Justice and mercy

This recent focus on solidarity and structures broadens the concept of almsgiving out even further, all the way to community development. But we can also return to an ancient exegetical practice that had already helped to illustrate the need for mercy to attend to justice—the practice of considering the order of the Beatitudes as a clue for how to interpret them. The blessing on the merciful, of course, comes just after the blessing on those who hunger and thirst for justice. This implies that mercy is the natural result of hungering for justice.

For Ambrose of Milan (339–397), for example, mercy (which means giving to the poor) is the natural result of the virtue of justice or righteousness described in the previous beatitude. As support, he quoted from a psalm: "He has given to the poor; his righteousness [*dikaiosynē*] endures forever" (Ps 111:9 LXX).[15] Not long after Ambrose, the North African theologian Au-

---

13. Mark Allan Powell, "Matthew's Beatitudes: Reversals and Rewards of the Kingdom," *CBQ* 58 (1996): 471. Glen Stassen captured the wide range of mercy by describing it as any act of deliverance, whether from the bondage of need, illness, or guilt (Stassen, "The Beatitudes as Eschatological Peacemaking Virtues," in *Character Ethics and the New Testament: Moral Dimensions of Scripture*, ed. Robert L. Brawley [Louisville: Westminster John Knox, 2007], 251).

14. Segundo Galilea, *The Beatitudes: To Evangelize as Jesus Did*, trans. Robert R. Barr (Maryknoll, NY: Orbis Books, 1984), 50–51.

15. Ambrose, *Comm. Luke* 5.57–8, in *Gospel According to Saint Luke*, 136. Similarly, Cornelius à Lapide: "hunger for justice disposes one to mercy, for one who desires to increase in justice and holiness performs the works of mercy" (Cornelius à Lapide, *The Holy Gospel According to*

gustine of Hippo (354–430) connected the two beatitudes by describing the believer as a beggar standing at God's door hungering for justice. Augustine told his congregation, "The way you treat your beggar [at your door] is the way God treats his."[16] In other words, warned Augustine, if you turn away a beggar from your door, God may turn you away from his door when you come begging for his mercy (*they shall not receive mercy*). Later, Augustinian monk Martin Luther concurred: mercy is righteousness in action.[17] For Luther, the mercies that flow from a righteous life include forgiving the sinful or frail, and doing good to those who are poor or needy.[18]

Some writers propose one other way of understanding the relationship between mercy and justice. Rather than flowing out of justice, mercy could be a necessary complement or counterbalance to justice. In the thirteenth century, influential theologian Thomas Aquinas wrote, "justice without mercy is cruelty, while mercy without justice is the mother of laxity."[19] Puritan clergyman (and eventual Harvard president) Increase Mather wrote that hunger and thirst after righteousness can be overdone, leading a person to become "sinfully severe," so that the fourth beatitude needs mercy to balance it.[20]

For some, this counterbalancing relationship between the two beatitudes results in practical advice. A medieval noblewoman named Dhuoda commented on the two beatitudes by instructing her young son William on his potential future role as a judge. If William were to sit someday in a court of law and render judgment, she advised, he must "use mercy and clemency," because "mercy transcends justice"—a truth that was, for her, reflected in the order of the Beatitudes.[21]

Saint Matthew, vol. 1 of *The Great Commentary of Cornelius à Lapide*, trans. Thomas W. Mossman, rev. ed. [Fitzwilliam, NH: Loreto, 2008], 228).

16. Augustine, Sermon 53A.10, in Augustine, *Essential Sermons*, ed. Boniface Ramsey, trans. Edmund Hill, The Works of Saint Augustine: A Translation for the 21st Century (Hyde Park, NY: New City Press, 2007), 81.

17. Luther, *Sermon on the Mount*, 30.

18. Luther, *Sermon on the Mount*, 30.

19. Aquinas cited Prov 3:3 and Ps 85:10 as support, in Thomas Aquinas, *Commentary on the Gospel of Matthew, Chapters 1–12*, ed. The Aquinas Institute, trans. Jeremy Holmes and Beth Mortensen, Biblical Commentaries 33 (Lander, WY: The Aquinas Institute for the Study of Sacred Doctrine, 2013), C.5 L.2.429.

20. Mather, *Sermons Wherein*, 8. John MacEvilly: mercy and justice "supplement each other" (MacEvilly, *An Exposition of the Gospels* [Dublin: W. B. Kelly; London: Simpkin, Marshall & Co., 1876], 78).

21. Dhuoda, *Handbook for her Warrior Son* 4.8, ed. and trans. Marcelle Thiébaux (Cambridge: Cambridge University Press, 1998), 159.

Today, reflections on the relationship between mercy and justice occur (quite apart from the Beatitudes) in a variety of settings, from the criminal justice system to global development and poverty alleviation efforts. One important voice is John Perkins, founder of the Christian Community Development Association (CCDA). Beginning in the 1960s, Perkins urged American Christians to help the poor more effectively. He laments, "By focusing on the symptoms rather than on the underlying disease, [Christian ministries] are often hurting the very people we are trying to help."[22]

The book *When Helping Hurts* takes up Perkin's challenge and urges North American congregations to address poverty in less harmful ways, in ways that empower rather than shame. The authors advocate for Christians to focus on what they call development and rehabilitation rather than relief.[23] One way to avoid paternalism, described in the book, is a practice called asset-based community development (ABCD)—beginning with a community's assets rather than its needs, and seeking the highest level possible of a community's participation in finding solutions to its own problems.[24]

Of course, understanding mercy as almsgiving, no matter how broadly construed, largely assumes that the merciful are those capable of giving help, rather than those who require it. For most interpreters of the beatitude, this is an assumption that goes relatively unexamined. However, attention is occasionally given to the social context of the hearers of this beatitude, whether the rich or the poor.

Woe to the rich

On the one hand, interpreters who address the rich with this beatitude have especially stern warnings for them. The rich must spend their money on mercy rather than frivolous things. Works of mercy must be done simply (with no ulterior motive), freely, cheerfully, liberally, and constantly. They are reminded

---

22. John Perkins, foreword (2009) to *When Helping Hurts: How to Alleviate Poverty without Hurting the Poor . . . and Yourself*, by Steve Corbett and Brian Fikkert (Chicago: Moody Publishers, 2009, 2012), 10.

23. Corbett and Fikkert, *When Helping Hurts*, 100–113.

24. Corbett and Fikkert, *When Helping Hurts*, 119–31, 140.

that when they give to the poor, they are giving to Christ, as in Matthew 25.[25] One preacher warned his congregation, "a rich man without mercy is an intolerable abuse." Another clergyman echoed his warning in even more dire terms: "Such as are cruel to the poor, let me tell you, you unchristian yourselves."[26] Although these more targeted applications generally accept the assumption that the beatitude addresses those who are able to give, they also sharpen the point in ways reminiscent of similar reflections on the first beatitude and its accompanying Lukan woe ("But woe to you who are rich, for you have received your consolation," Luke 6:24). One might also wonder if these preachers felt that the rich needed a little extra prodding to give generously to the poor.

What if I'm too poor to give alms?

On the other hand, a few interpreters notice that not all the hearers of this beatitude will be able to give alms or any kind of material assistance, but may in fact be in need of such assistance themselves. This observation tends to press interpreters to view mercy through other lenses, different from, or wider than, simply almsgiving. Contemporary scholar Benedict Green suggested that the evangelist Matthew himself saw almsgiving as only one small, limited aspect of mercy, in large part because almsgiving (in its traditional form) assumes a well-to-do person giving to a poor person, whereas Matthew seems to envisage that if one follows Jesus one will likely not remain rich much longer.[27]

Surprisingly few interpreters address the social context of the hearers of this fifth beatitude, so two examples will suffice, one Catholic and one Protestant. Spanish Jesuit Juan Maldonado agreed with Green: almsgiving is only one aspect of mercy. Since not everyone is able to be generous in almsgiving ("the Apostles, who had left all, could not be"), the merciful must also mean those who forgive injuries.[28] Nonconformist Welsh minister Matthew Henry, who authored an enormously popular six-volume biblical commentary in 1706, wrote that if one is not oneself wealthy enough to give liberally, then one must show mercy by having compassion on the suffering and being willing to help however one can.[29]

---

25. Robert Harris, *The Way to True Happiness: Delivered in Twenty-Four Sermons upon the Beatitudes*, ed. Don Kistler (Morgan, PA: Soli Deo Gloria, 1998), 198–204, 205–6, 209.

26. James Buck, *A Treatise of the Beatitudes, or, Christ's Happy Men* (London: printed by B.A. and T.F. for Iohn Clark, and Wil. Cooke, 1637), 190; Watson, *The Beatitudes*, 169.

27. H. Benedict Green, *Matthew, Poet of the Beatitudes* (Sheffield: Sheffield Academic, 2001), 215.

28. Maldonado, *S. Matthew's Gospel*, 1:136.

29. Matthew Henry, *Matthew to John*, vol. 5 of *An Exposition of the Old and New Testament* (New York: Revell, n.d. [1708–1710?]), comment on Matt 5:7, section V.

Compassion: is mercy feeling or doing?

Henry's reference to compassion raises the question of whether mercy is primarily an emotion (compassion), or an action, or both. The history of interpretation is surprisingly uniform on this point: for readers throughout history, it is both.

Christians insisted from relatively early in the tradition that mercy is not action alone but actions that are undergirded and prompted by an interior orientation. The merciful *feel* something for the suffering, whether compassion, sorrow, or a kind of emotional solidarity, a "suffering-with." For some, feelings of compassion are what give rise to the acts of mercy. As Thomas Aquinas put it, mercy is first of all to "have a miserable heart at the misery of others" and then to desire to drive their misery away.[30] In other words, it is compassion or "suffering-with" the other that moves a person to try to help relieve the other's suffering. As one writer put it (in 1665), when a merciful person sees his neighbor "oppressed with wrongs or miseries," he is so sensitive to his neighbor's suffering that it's as if "that very cross of affliction were engraven in his heart."[31]

For these writers, one must voluntarily choose both to enter into another person's suffering and to seek to relieve it. Long before Aquinas, Gregory of Nyssa (ca. 335–395) was one of the earliest to emphasize this dimension of mercy when he defined it as "a voluntary sorrow that joins itself to the suffering of others" and "the loving disposition towards those who suffer distress."[32] Gregory also described mercy as concrete acts of help and charity toward the needy and suffering. But he saw interior compassion as the necessary prerequisite for those material actions: "For unless mercy softens the soul, a man cannot arrive at healing the ills of his neighbour, since mercy is defined as the opposite of cruelty."[33]

This twofold understanding of mercy as emotion and action continued into the medieval era, in both East and West. As a representative of the Byzantine or Eastern stream of thought, Theophylact of Ochrid wrote that the mercy

---

30. Aquinas, *Commentary on Matthew*, C.5 L.2.430. For Aquinas on compassion, see Thomas Aquinas, *Summa Theologica: Complete English Edition in Five Volumes*, trans. Fathers of the English Dominican Province (Westminster, MD: Christian Classics, 1948), 2.2.30.1.

31. E. M., *Ashrea: Or, the Grove of the Beatitudes, Represented in Emblemes* (London: Printed for W. P. at Grayes-Inn Gate in Holborne, 1665; Reprint: English Emblem Books 18; Yorkshire, England: Scolar Press, 1970), C3, 54.

32. Gregory of Nyssa, *The Lord's Prayer; The Beatitudes*, trans. Hilda C. Graef, ACW 18 (Mahwah, NJ: Paulist, 1954), 133.

33. Gregory of Nyssa, *The Lord's Prayer*, 132.

of Matthew's beatitude includes both almsgiving and "tears of compassion."[34] Representing the Western monastic tradition, Bernard of Clairvaux drew on the solidarity and unity of the body of Christ when he described the merciful as those who "quickly grasp truth in their neighbors, extending their own feelings to them and conforming themselves to them through love, so that they feel *their* joys or troubles as their own. . . . They *rejoice with them that do rejoice, and weep with them that weep*" (Rom 12:15).[35]

Likewise, a compassionate response to suffering remains a significant aspect of the Protestant Reformers' reflections on mercy. In John Calvin's exegesis of the beatitude, he understood mercy first and fundamentally as suffering with a neighbor's afflictions, or what we might today call empathy: "We must assume their identity, as it were, so as to be deeply touched by their suffering and moved by love to mourn with them." Mercy, he wrote, "is the grief we experience from the sadness of others."[36] This is in part because of Calvin's conviction that giving grudgingly to the poor is not blessed; instead, he agreed with Aquinas that the mercy of Matthew's beatitude is a compassion that moves one to action.[37]

Jeremiah Burroughs followed in Calvin's footsteps and elaborated even further: he described the workings of mercy in the heart as (first) compassion toward the suffering, which (second) gives rise to a desire to help them, and then (third) requires a thoughtful plan for how to help. This plan of attack should include a willingness to lend or give away whatever one has in order to help, a willingness to pardon wrongs, and finally an empathetic solidarity with the person

34. Theophylact of Ochrid, *The Explanation by Blessed Theophylact of the Holy Gospel According to St. Matthew*, vol. 1 of *Blessed Theophylact's Explanation of the New Testament*, trans. Christopher Stade (House Springs, MO: Chrysostom Press, 1994), 45.

35. Bernard of Clairvaux, *The Steps of Humility* 3.6, trans. George Bosworth Burch (Cambridge, MA: Harvard University Press, 1942), 133. Reginius: "The merciful is he who . . . counts others' misery his own, and is sad at their grief as at his own" (quoted in Thomas Aquinas, *St. Matthew*, vol. 1 of *Catena Aurea: A Commentary on the Four Gospels Collected out of the Works of the Fathers*, trans. John Henry Newman [London: The Saint Austin Press, 1999], 152). Jacques Bénigne Bossuet named mercy as a form of love: "The most beautiful fruit of love is to be touched by the ills of others" (Bossuet, *The Sermon on the Mount*, trans. F. M. Capes [Longmans, Green: 1900], 20).

36. John Calvin, *Sermons on the Beatitudes: Five Sermons from the Gospel Harmony, Delivered in Geneva in 1560* (Carlisle, PA: Banner of Truth Trust, 2006), 42, 63.

37. Calvin, *Sermons on the Beatitudes*, 43. It also includes having compassion on those who sin or have gone astray (Calvin, *Sermons on the Beatitudes*, 46). See also Harris, *Way to True Happiness*, 183, 184, 192.

suffering (as in Rom 12:15). Burroughs wrote, "mercy causes one to put himself into the same state, to be in bonds with those that are in bonds, and to weep with those that weep."[38] Burroughs also pointed out to his congregation that they would not be moved to mercy if they didn't see suffering.[39] In other words, for Burroughs, it is not enough to practice charity from a distance. True mercy, the mercy of the Beatitudes, has to draw close enough to *see* suffering, to weep with those who weep. Thomas Watson even declared, "It is a kind of cruelty (says Quintilian) to feed one in want and not to sympathize with him."[40] Conversely, compassion without concrete acts is no good either, as James makes clear (Jas 2:14–17). Anglican Charles Gore pointed out, "Compassion which does nothing is in the New Testament regarded as a form of pernicious hypocrisy."[41]

Forgiveness

If the first major strand concentrates on concrete acts of compassionate help, the second major strand turns its attention to a more internal act: forgiving the offender. (Forgiving itself can have a material aspect, since the "debts" to be forgiven—as in Matt 6:12—could be spiritual or financial.) Here, as usual, Augustine's method of linking a beatitude to a spiritual gift and to a petition of the Lord's Prayer proves influential, since the blessing on the merciful lines up with the petition "Forgive us our debts, as we also have forgiven our debtors" (Matt 6:12) (*De Serm. Dom.* 2.11.38).[42] Of course, Augustine was not the first to understand mercy as forgiveness. In the Old Testament, God's mercy typically indicates God's slowness to anger, graciousness, and forgiveness (e.g., Exod 33:19, 2 Chron 30:9, Neh 9:17, Ps 51:1). But Augustine's abiding influence firmly establishes forgiveness as one aspect of the beatitude's blessing on the merciful.

This strand rarely stands on its own. For many interpreters throughout history, mercy includes both almsgiving (broadly construed) and forgiveness.

38. Jeremiah Burroughs, *The Saints' Happiness* (Edinburgh: James Nichol, 1867; Soli Deo Gloria, 1988, 1992), 135–36.

39. Burroughs, *Saints' Happiness*, 151.

40. Watson, *The Beatitudes*, 164.

41. Charles Gore, *The Sermon on the Mount: A Practical Exposition* (London: John Murray, 1907), 38.

42. Augustine, *The Lord's Sermon*, 126; Thomas Aquinas, *The Three Greatest Prayers: Commentaries on the Lord's Prayer, the Hail Mary, and the Apostles' Creed* (Manchester, NH: Sophia Institute Press, 1990), 148; Leo the Great, *Sermons* 49.5 (NPNF² 12:162).

As forgiveness, mercy can simply mean forgiving those who have wronged us, but it can also mean forbearance or gentleness in relation to people's wrongdoing in general, even when one isn't directly harmed.[43] Hendrik Niclaes wrote that the merciful not only forgive others when wronged but also "upbraid no man with his sins."[44]

For others, mercy is especially manifested as forgiveness or kindness shown toward one's enemies. In this way, the beatitude becomes linked to Jesus's command to love the enemy and pray for the persecutor (Matt 5:44).[45] Gene Davenport wrote, "The meek and the mourner are not released from their Darkness [Matt 4:16] so that they may become new Lords of the Darkness," but must "earnestly . . . seek the oppressor's well-being."[46]

In the early twenty-first century, Yiu Sing Lúcás Chan considers mercy through a wider social lens, interpreting it in relation to the punishment of criminal offenders. For Chan, both the life sentence and the death penalty "are in principle and in reality contradicting what a merciful society demands."[47] Much like the interpreters who widened out the meaning of almsgiving to include structural issues, Chan explores the meaning of mercy not merely as a personal or individual act but as a quality that may also apply to a society or a nation.

This, of course, taps into the wider debate about who the Beatitudes are for, or to which arenas they apply (see chapter 1). Are they meant only for Christians, or do they have more universal application? Do they shape the life of the church, or should they also affect the world? Are they about character or actions toward others? By and large, until the fundamentalist-modernist

43. Thomas Aquinas wrote that mercy is also compassion for those who fall into sin (Aquinas, *Commentary on Matthew*, C.5 L.2.430).

44. Niclaes, *The first exhortation*, 199. For William Tyndale, to be merciful means "not to make a grievous sin of every small trifle" (Tyndale, *The Work of William Tyndale*, ed. G. E. Duffield [Philadelphia: Fortress, 1965], 201). For R. T. France, mercy is "a generous attitude which is willing to see things from the other's point of view and is not quick to take offense" (France, *The Gospel of Matthew*, NICNT [Grand Rapids: Eerdmans, 2007], 168).

45. *Incomplete Commentary on Matthew [Opus Imperfectum]*, ed. Thomas C. Oden, trans. James A. Kellerman, Ancient Christian Texts 1 (Downers Grove, IL: IVP Academic, 2010), 86; Clement of Alexandria, *Stromata* 2.18 (*ANF* 2:367).

46. Gene Davenport, *Into the Darkness: Discipleship in the Sermon on the Mount* (Eugene, OR: Wipf & Stock, 1988, 2003), 87; see also 90, where he equated mercy with agape love. Davenport was echoing (whether consciously or not) language from Martin Luther King Jr.'s sermon "Loving Your Enemies" (sermon delivered at Dexter Avenue Baptist Church, Montgomery, Alabama, November 1957 [MLKEC, INP, Martin Luther King, Jr. Estate Collection, In Private Hands, ET-1; Atl-5A & 5B]).

47. Chan, *Ten Commandments*, 199.

split at the turn of the twentieth century, interpreters assumed that they were primarily for Christians, but that they had relevance for how Christians lived in the world. They assumed that the Beatitudes were both about inner character and about how people with such characters loved their neighbors.

Welcome of sinners and outsiders

The third major strand is a more recent understanding of mercy, one that appears primarily in the twentieth and twenty-first centuries. It overlaps in part with the previous strand (mercy as forgiveness) because of its connection to Jesus's association with sinners (Matt 9:10–13). But it places the accent mark not on forgiveness but on welcome. In this view, mercy entails the welcome and embrace of the outsider.

Matthew's Gospel itself provides the backdrop for this view. Twice in Matthew, Jesus quotes from the prophet Hosea: "I desire mercy, not sacrifice" (Hos 6:6). The first time, he uses the verse to rebuke the Pharisees for asking his disciples why Jesus ate with tax collectors and sinners (Matt 9:9–13). The implication, of course, was that Jesus should *not* be associating either with tax collectors, who were seen as collaborators with Roman imperial rule (and sometimes as cheats, skimming a little off the top of the taxes for themselves), or with "sinners"—those who might sully Jesus's reputation, lure him into sin himself, or endanger his ritual purity.

In later Christian thought, these two groups (tax collectors and sinners) come to represent any shunned, scorned, or feared outsider. Chan, for example, names the practice of hospitality toward immigrants as one of the most urgently needed practices of mercy for the contemporary world.[48] Joseph Ratzinger (by then Pope Benedict XVI) makes a similar connection when he interprets the beatitude in relation to Jesus's parable of the Good Samaritan (Luke 10:25–37). The parable, of course, reverses the theme of the inclusion of the outsider by portraying the hated and feared outsider as the one who fulfills the command to love the neighbor while the righteous insiders (the priest and the Levite) fail to do so. By naming the Samaritan as "the merciful" of Matt 5:7, Ratzinger narrates mercy as material assistance to anyone in need, as radical solidarity with the other, and as God's love extended to the alienated.[49]

---

48. Chan, *Ten Commandments*, 198.

49. Joseph Ratzinger (Pope Benedict XVI), *Jesus of Nazareth: From the Baptism in the Jordan to the Transfiguration*, trans. Adrian J. Walker (New York: Doubleday, 2007), 195–201.

This third strand—welcome of sinners and outsiders—also crops up in settings where the writers themselves are relative outsiders or come into contact with those considered to be on the margins of society. From his precarious position in the Confessing Church of Germany under Nazi rule, Dietrich Bonhoeffer may have been thinking of the Pharisees' accusing question in Matt 9:11 ("Why does your teacher eat with tax collectors and sinners?") when he wrote that the merciful pay no attention to their own honor but are "glad to incur reproach" by seeking out the company of "the down-trodden, the sick, the wretched, the wronged, the outcast and all who are tortured with anxiety."[50]

In another context of occupation, Isaac Allen noticed and quietly condemned the opposite tendency of his countrymen. Allen was an Anglican chaplain to British soldiers in India during the British imperial occupation. He observed in his comments on the fifth beatitude that in India he and his fellow Englishmen were more prone to the temptation to "be oppressors and unmerciful" to "foreigners" (i.e., the residents of India) than when at home in England.[51] And when artist Charles Connick (1875–1945) personified the Beatitudes as eight "saints of the Americas" in the rose windows of the Cathedral of St. Paul, Minnesota, he chose for the merciful Francis Solano (1549–1610), a Spanish Franciscan missionary in South America who became famous for refusing to abandon a ship when it ran aground because there were no lifeboats for the slaves. This returns again to the theme of solidarity that frequently accompanies reflections on the merciful.

Extending God's offer of salvation
to outsiders (gentiles, etc.) and sinners

A variation on this third strand focuses not on how people should treat so-called sinners and outsiders, but how God does. This view draws attention to divine mercy toward sinful humanity, all of whom sin and fall short of God's glory (Rom 3:23; cf. Gen 6:5). For this group of writers, the greatest act of mercy is salvation: God's gracious decision to forgive sins, to have mercy on fallible and frail human beings. When A.-M. Carré considered the meaning of the merciful, he began by narrating God's rescue of Israel from slavery in

---

50. Dietrich Bonhoeffer, *The Cost of Discipleship* (New York: Simon & Schuster, 1995), 111.

51. Isaac Allen, *Reflection on Portions of the Sermon on the Mount. Intended Principally for Soldiers* (London: SPCK, 1848), 22.

Egypt. And in the New Testament, Christ is the embodiment of God's mercy-as-salvation. "In effect, Christ isn't 'merciful': *he is mercy*."[52]

God's offer of salvation through Christ presses some to an even more particular view of mercy; for some, mercy is especially God's welcome of gentiles into God's household alongside Israel. This connects to the theme of the welcome of outsiders since gentiles (non-Jews) were originally "aliens from the commonwealth of Israel, and strangers to the covenants of promise, having no hope and without God in the world" (Eph 2:12).

This understanding of mercy explains, for example, Benedictine monk Rupert of Deutz's (1076–1129) decision to associate the fifth beatitude with Mary Magdalene (who was understood in medieval thought as a symbol for the church of the gentiles) and with the apostles, since the "mystery" of God's mercy to the gentiles was made known by the apostles through their proclamation of the gospel to all the nations.[53] It also illuminates an otherwise even more puzzling (and controversial) connection made in the famous altarpiece in St. Bavo's Cathedral in Ghent, Belgium.

The Ghent altarpiece personifies the eight Matthean Beatitudes as eight groups of people from varying stations of life. The merciful are just judges (perhaps making a connection to mercy as protection of the vulnerable, as in Luke 18:1–8). But the merciful are also depicted as crusading knights.[54] It is hard to think of a more counterintuitive embodiment of mercy than soldiers who murdered and pillaged in the name of Christ and the church. Seen through the lens of mercy-as-salvation, the crusaders (at least in principle) were the bearers of divine mercy to people who had not heard the gospel. In that way, the Ghent altarpiece illustrates the not-uncommon view that the highest form of mercy is seeking the salvation of others. As Clarence Jordan, author of the *Cotton Patch Gospel*, put it, the compassionate desire to share one's riches with others extends especially to the riches of the kingdom of God.[55] But the al-

---

52. Carré, *Quand arrive*, 54–55, quotation on 55 ("En effet le Christ n'est pas 'miséricordieux': il est le miséricorde," italics original).

53. Rupert of Deutz, *Liber de Divinis Officiis*, vol. 3, ed. and trans. Helmut Deutz and Ilse Deutz (Freiburg: Herder, 1999), 288; see Brigitta Stoll, *De Virtute in Virtutem: zur Auslegungs- und Wirkungsgeschichte der Bergpredigt in Kommentaren, Predigten und hagiographischer Literatur von der Merowingerzeit bis um 1200* (Tübingen: Mohr Siebeck, 1988), 149.

54. See Rebekah Eklund, "The Blessed," Visual Commentary on Scripture, http://thevcs.org/blessed.

55. Clarence Jordan, *Sermon on the Mount*, rev. ed. (Valley Forge, PA: Judson, 1952), 31. See also Graham, *Secret of Happiness*, 65–69; Mather, *Sermons Wherein*, Sermon 8. George Hunsinger uses the beatitude to contemplate the possibility of universal salvation, in Hunsinger, *The Beatitudes* (Mahwah, NJ: Paulist, 2015), 64–67.

tarpiece also, more uncomfortably, forces its modern viewers to reckon with the shameful intertwining of evangelism and violence throughout the church's history. Mercy-as-salvation must not be practiced at the expense of other forms of mercy.

Imitation of God

More than any other strand in the beatitude's history, this emphasis on divine mercy leads to the theme of the imitation of God—a theme that appears often in explorations of the Beatitudes (especially, as we will see, in comments on the blessing on the peacemakers). Other biblical texts encourage this connection. Although Luke's Beatitudes don't include the blessing on the merciful, Luke's Sermon on the Plain includes the exhortation, "Be merciful, as your heavenly Father is merciful" (Luke 6:36). This makes clear what Matthew leaves implicit: Jesus's followers should be merciful in imitation of their merciful God. Interpreters cite Luke 6:36 over and over again to explain Matthew's beatitude, often using it to interpret mercy as forgoing revenge or not punishing people as they deserve, in imitation of God's restraint and forbearance.[56]

If mercy is forgiveness, then forgiveness also imitates God's forgiveness in advance, as it were: "forgive us . . . as we have forgiven" (Matt 6:12, Luke 11:4). In a certain sense, the sayings about forgiveness actually seem to be about God imitating us! But the instruction to forgive assumes God's prior forgiveness; the disciples are not instructed to show a form of mercy that God has not already reached out with first.

Indeed, for Paul John Isaak, imitation of God's mercy includes identifying with the suffering and feeling for or with them, since God likewise "did not remain aloof and detached" from our world but entered into it.[57] This solidarity with the sinful and suffering might also mean a willingness to suffer on their behalf. To explain the blessing on the merciful, Bernard of Clairvaux (ca. 1090–1153) used Adam as an example of someone who failed to show mercy at the right moment by refusing to take responsibility for Eve's (and his) sin. Bernard wrote that Adam should have told God, "mine only is the iniquity,

---

56. E.g., Cabasilas, *The Life in Christ* 6.11e, trans. Carmino J. deCatanzaro (Crestwood, NY: St. Vladimir's Seminary Press, 1974), 185–86. Ellen Gould White cited 1 John 4:19: "We love, because He first loved us" (White, *Thoughts from the Mount of Blessing* [Mountain View, CA: Pacific Press Publishing Association, 1900, 1928], 37).

57. Paul John Isaak, "Luke," in *Africa Bible Commentary*, ed. Tokunboh Adeyemo, 2nd ed. (Nairobi, Kenya: WordAlive; Grand Rapids: Zondervan, 2010), 1145.

mine all the sin, therefore on me alone let Thy vengeance fall."[58] Mercy would have meant Adam's willingness to suffer alone *all* the punishment that both he and Eve deserved, just as Christ bore the pain of the cross in place of sinful humanity. In another setting entirely, Dietrich Bonhoeffer hinted at this theme when he wrote, "If any man falls into disgrace, the merciful will sacrifice their own honour to shield him, and take his shame upon themselves."[59] For Bonhoeffer, as for Bernard, willingness to bear shame for the sake of another was a Christlike act (Heb 12:2). As a form of solidarity or empathy, being merciful can be costly.

Restoration of God's image

Imitation of God (I *behave* like God) sometimes crosses over into transformation of the person (I *become* like God). This is an especially prominent theme in Eastern thought, which tends to think of sanctification (growth in holiness) as growth in godlikeness, or *theōsis*—not merely an imitation of God's characteristics, but a taking on of them through transformation. This is often connected to the theme of the creation of humanity in the image of God (Gen 1:26–27). Although the image of God was marred by the fall, it was never erased altogether and is restored through God's grace and through actions that allow God's grace to flow into and heal the soul, polishing the stained mirror of the image of God and gradually restoring it to its original brilliance.

As Eastern theologian Gregory of Nyssa (ca. 335–395) wrote, since God is merciful, the fifth beatitude invites the hearer to become godlike: "If, therefore, the term 'merciful' is suited to God, what else does the Word invite you to become but God."[60] A Western thinker, Pope Leo the Great, followed a similar train of thought when he wrote that mercy (expressed through almsgiving) is a way that the image of the Creator may be seen in his creatures.[61] Centu-

---

58. Bernard of Clairvaux, "First Sermon for the Feast of All Saints. On the Eight Beatitudes," in *St. Bernard's Sermons for the Seasons and Principal Festivals of the Year*, vol. 3 (Westminster, MD: Carroll, 1950), 346, see also 347.

59. Gregory of Nyssa, *The Lord's Prayer*, 111.

60. Gregory of Nyssa, *The Lord's Prayer*, 131. Cyril of Alexandria (ca. 376–444) explained that those who give to others in need in turn "receive more truly what is our own—that holy and admirable beauty that God forms in people's souls, making them like himself, according to what we originally are" (Cyril of Alexandria, *Commentary on the Gospel of St. Luke*, trans. R. Payne Smith [Long Island, NY: Studion, 1983], Homily 109 on Luke 16:9–13).

61. Leo the Great, *Sermons* 95.7 (*NPNF*[2] 12:204).

ries later, even a Puritan preacher could contemplate the same theme; Robert Harris mused that since being merciful is natural to God but not humans, a person needs to be transformed by grace in order to be merciful as God is merciful (Luke 6:36): "For what is mercy but a piece of God's image, a spark of the divine nature?"[62]

Seeing mercy as the imitation of God helps us to see the wide understanding of mercy with which I began this chapter. God's mercy means forgiveness of sins; it means welcome of those estranged from God (which means all humanity) and the embrace of the gentiles who were once outside God's promises. Divine mercy means compassion for the poor and outrage at their mistreatment.

They will receive mercy

Mercy: what kind, when, and from whom?

At first glance, this beatitude appears perfectly balanced: give mercy, and receive mercy. But are the meanings of "mercy" in both cases the same? The first type of (offered) mercy is not always the same as the second type of (received) mercy. Nobody takes the beatitude to mean, "Blessed are the almsgivers, for they shall receive alms," but it can mean "Blessed are those who forgive, for they will be forgiven." The two types of mercy, then, do not appear to be exactly the same. Two questions remain about the beatitude's second half: from *whom* will the merciful receive mercy, and *when*? The answer to the first question turns out to be dependent on the second.

As usual, there is frequently a sense that the beatitude's promise is fulfilled partially or proleptically in the present. For some, this partial fulfillment is a form of reciprocity; one is judged, measure for measure, with the same judgment you show. Mercy from fellow human beings is then a practical result of showing mercy to them. Theophylact of Ochrid observed that when we show mercy to people, they are more likely to show mercy to us when we need it.[63] John Calvin also wrote that the promise assures us that if we have been merciful we will, in turn, receive help when we need it.[64] But neither theologian restricted the promise to the present life or to human mercy.

---

62. Harris, *Way to True Happiness*, 178, quotation 180.
63. Theophylact of Ochrid, *Gospel According to St. Matthew*, 45.
64. Calvin, *Sermons on the Beatitudes*, 44–45.

For Calvin as for Theophylact, the second and more important meaning of the beatitude's promise is eschatological: it ultimately refers to divine mercy at the last judgment. Occasionally, an interpreter proposes that this eschatological mercy spills over into the present time. Isaac of Nineveh wrote that when someone shows mercy to "his fellow man," they receive the divine mercy of the next life symbolically in this one when "our Lord delivers his soul from gloomy darkness . . . and brings it into contact with the light of life."[65]

For the most part, however, interpreters focus on the receiving of mercy in the next life. The beatitude might then be paraphrased, "How honored are those who give alms, forgive, and welcome outsiders, for God will receive them into eschatological glory." The earliest interpreters of the beatitude often specifically extended or paraphrased the beatitude to clarify that the promised mercy indicated divine mercy in the next life. The *Acts of Paul and Thecla*, an account of the miraculous acts of a young woman named Thecla converted by Paul and composed as early as 230 CE, quotes an extended version of the beatitude's second half: "they shall obtain mercy and shall not see the bitter day of judgement."[66]

In the *Apocalypse of Paul* (*Visio Pauli*), composed in the mid-third century, Paul sees the souls of human beings at the moment of their death, as they are received in heaven and judged to be either sinful or righteous. In one case, a heavenly voice quotes the beatitude and then declares the beatitude's implied opposite (its Lukan "woe," if you will): "whoever shall not have been merciful, neither shall God pity him." The unmerciful soul is then cast into the outer darkness (Matt 8:12, 22:13, 25:30) to await the final judgment. When another soul is led forward weeping, God declares, "For you never showed mercy, therefore you were handed over to such angels as have no mercy."[67] The author of the *Apocalypse of Paul* may simply have borrowed a line from the book of James, which echoes the fifth beatitude: "For judgment will be

---

65. Isaac of Nineveh, *Mystic Treatises by Isaac of Nineveh* 65.456, trans. A. J. Wensick (Amsterdam: Koninklijke Akademie van Wetenschappen, 1923), 305–6. Aquinas wrote that the reward begins in this life and is perfected in the future (Aquinas, *Commentary on Matthew*, C.5 L.2.431).

66. *Acts of Paul and Thecla*, in J. K. Elliott, *The Apocryphal New Testament* (Oxford: Clarendon Press, 1993), 365. For others who interpret the promised mercy as divine mercy on the day of judgment see also Chromatius of Aquileia, *Sermons and Tractates on Matthew*, trans. Thomas P. Scheck, ACW 75 (New York: The Newman Press, 2018), Tractatus 17.6.1; Erasmus, *Paraphrase on Matthew*, 88; Bossuet, *The Sermon on the Mount*, 2; Bonhoeffer, *Cost of Discipleship*, 112; Burroughs, *Saints' Happiness*, 140–41.

67. *Apocalypse of Paul*, in Elliott, *Apocryphal New Testament*, 626. Beryl Cohon notes a rabbinic parallel: "He who has mercy on his fellow-creatures obtains mercy from God" (Sab. 151b; quoted in Cohon, *Jacob's Well: Some Jewish Sources and Parallels to the Sermon on the Mount* [New York: Bookman Associates, 1956], 31).

without mercy to anyone who has shown no mercy" (Jas 2:13). In a way, James may be thought of as supplying the Lukan "woe" that Matthew's fifth beatitude lacks. Mercy to the merciful; judgment without mercy to the unmerciful. This understanding—that the promised mercy refers to divine mercy on the day of judgment—traverses through history as the dominant interpretation.

Problem of "merit": do the merciful earn salvation?

It also raises an immediate, pressing question: does God refuse to save those who have not been merciful in this life? It seems straightforwardly to say so. The authors of the *Acts of Paul and Thecla* and the *Apocalypse of Paul* seemed to think so. But it creates a certain tension with other scriptural teachings about God's mercy toward the undeserving. Indeed, it creates a rather serious problem for the view that God is *merciful*. Although James wrote "For judgment will be without mercy to anyone who has shown no mercy," he also immediately went on to say, "mercy triumphs over judgment" (Jas 2:13). To put it in the sharpest possible terms, does failure to help the poor or to forgive others lead to eternal damnation?

You may be thinking, *Of course not!* That is a reasonable reaction. But let's treat this question with the gravity that it deserves. After all, the beatitude declares that (only?) the merciful shall receive mercy: what, then, of the unmerciful? As Luke's Beatitudes reveal, each beatitude has its opposing partner, even if left unstated by Matthew. Woe to the unmerciful!

In a certain sense, the beatitude echoes a reciprocity on display elsewhere in Scripture, including in the Sermon on the Mount. Two chapters after the Beatitudes, Jesus warns, "Do not judge, so that you may not be judged. For with the judgment you make you will be judged, and the measure you give will be the measure you get" (Matt 7:1–2). The parable of the unmerciful slave in Matt 18:23–35 applies the same principle, this time as a warning for those who don't extend reciprocity in forgiving debts. The unmerciful slave represents the implied "woe" of the beatitude; the merciless person who refuses to extend mercy to another person who needs it is denied mercy on the day of divine judgment.

The unmerciful slave also illustrates the inverse of the beatitude, or its prior assumption that people are called to be merciful because they have *already* been shown divine mercy: "Should you not have had mercy on your fellow slave, as I had mercy on you?" (Matt 18:33).[68] This is a common theme in

---

68. E.g., Thomas Torrance, *The Beatitudes and the Decalogue* (London: Skeffington & Son, 1921), 52.

the history of interpretation. Many interpreters emphasize God's prior mercy by reversing the equation of the beatitude. Billy Graham paraphrased the beatitude to be a blessing on the people who "have obtained mercy from God and are so happy that they are merciful to others."[69]

An even more prominent strand in the history of interpretation draws on two parables: the Matthean parable of the sheep and the goats (Matt 25:31–46), and the Lukan parable of the rich man and Lazarus (Luke 16:19–31). The seriousness of the failure to help the poor is firmly established very early in the Christian tradition, not least because of passages like these two parables. Written no later than 135 CE (and possibly as early as 80 CE), *The Epistle of Barnabas* describes the path of eternal death in part as the way of those "who do not look out for the widow and the orphan . . . showing no mercy to the poor nor toiling for the oppressed . . . they turn their backs on the needy, oppress the afflicted, and support the wealthy. They are lawless judges of the impoverished, altogether sinful" (20.1–2).[70]

By the end of the fourth century, bishop Gregory of Nyssa had a long and venerable tradition to draw upon when he ended a sermon on the fifth beatitude with a scathing indictment of those who do not show mercy to the poor, citing the parables of the sheep and the goats, and the rich man and Lazarus. He concluded, "You have neglected the afflicted, you shall be neglected when you perish. . . . You have abhorred the poor, He who has been poor for your sake will abhor you."[71]

Grace and mercy

As you can imagine, the second half of the beatitude—and this early stream of interpretation—created tension for some post-Reformation Protestant interpreters, who worried that the beatitude (or a certain reading of it) edges dangerously close to the line of earning God's grace through good works. This

---

69. Graham, *Secret of Happiness*, 59. Cabasilas writes that we should show mercy because God first showed us mercy even though we didn't deserve it (as in Luke 1:79); he also quotes Luke 6:36 ("be merciful, just as your Father is merciful") (Cabasilas, *Life in Christ* 6.11e, 185–86).

70. *Epistle of Barnabas*, in *The Apostolic Fathers*, vol. 2, *Epistle of Barnabas. Papias and Quadratus. Epistle to Diognetus. The Shepherd of Hermas*, ed. and trans. Bart D. Ehrman, LCL 25 (Cambridge, MA: Harvard University Press), 2003.

71. Gregory of Nyssa, *The Lord's Prayer*, 142. See also Theophylact of Ochrid commenting on Matt 6:15 ("if you do not forgive others"): "God, Who is meek, hates nothing more than cruelty" (Theophylact of Ochrid, *Gospel According to St. Matthew*, 59).

possibility didn't seem to bother the magisterial Reformers; neither Luther nor Calvin commented on the problem of "works righteousness" in relation to the beatitude. Later Protestants, however, sometimes struggled with the meaning of the promised reward in relation to salvation by grace.

For example, Welsh Reformed preacher D. Martyn Lloyd-Jones (long-time minister of Westminster Chapel in London) devoted significant space to demonstrating that the beatitude's promised reward is not a violation of the gospel of grace. For him, the second half teaches not that God shows mercy-as-forgiveness only to those who are forgiving toward others, but that God extends mercy to the truly repentant, since only the truly repentant are willing to forgive others who trespass against them.[72] Evangelical Sherwood Wirt, an associate of Billy Graham, pointed out that the beatitude cannot be a simple *do this/get that* proposition, since Christ was merciful and obtained no mercy but instead was crucified mercilessly.[73]

Others see the beatitude's second half as a logical sequence, and its implied opposite as an equally logical outcome. Because the Lord is merciful, suggested Emanuel Swedenborg, the person who is not merciful "cannot be conjoined with the Lord, because he is unlike Him and not at all in His image."[74] It is not that God withholds mercy from the unmerciful as an act of punishment or retribution; the unmerciful simply cannot have any eternal share in a God who is merciful.

The Rev. W. Arnot used a vivid mechanical image to express a similar idea. He compared the beatitude to two wheels in a factory—a large upper wheel and a small lower wheel "which receives the motion." Although the larger wheel is the one that "communicates the motion," it will be stopped if the smaller wheel stands still. Arnot mused, "It is in some such way that God's

---

72. D. Martyn Lloyd-Jones, *Studies in the Sermon on the Mount*, vol. 1 (Grand Rapids: Eerdmans, 1960), 101–2.

73. Sherwood E. Wirt, *Magnificent Promise: A Fresh View of the Beatitudes from the Cross* (Chicago: Moody Press, 1964), 64. Dispensationalist Lewis Chafer solved the problem by assigning the Beatitudes to the future age of the millennial kingdom, not the present age of grace. (Lewis Sperry Chafer, *Systematic Theology*, vols. 4 and 5 [Dallas, TX: Dallas Seminary Press, 1948], 4:217, see also 5:104–5.)

74. Emanuel Swedenborg, *Words of Spirit and Life: The Spiritual Meaning of the Sermon on the Mount. From the Writings of Emanuel Swedenborg*, ed. Leonard Fox (Charleston, SC: Arcana Books, 1997), 15. See also Mackay, who argued vigorously that the beatitude does not indicate "the covenant of works" (Mackay, *A practical exposition*, 2:85). Mackay: "It is those on whom the gospel is taking effect, whom it is renewing, whom it is conforming to his own image and character, who shall *obtain* the mercy of God, the salvation of the gospel" (Mackay, *A practical exposition*, 2:106).

goodness and mercy impel us to forgive from the heart those that have tres-passed against us. The power is all from above. Yet, though we by our goodness do not set the beneficent machinery in motion, we may by our badness cause it to stand still. It is not our forgiveness accorded to an evil-doer that procures forgiveness to ourselves—the opposite is the truth; yet our refusal of forgive-ness to a brother prevents the flow of pardon to our guilty hearts."[75]

In that sense, then, these interpreters are highlighting what we might call the failure of faith to be active in love. Being unmerciful reveals the falsity of one's conversion, if you will—it shows that one has not received and inhabited God's grace. Good trees bear good fruit. Or as evangelical John Stott claimed, by bearing the marks of the Beatitudes, "we give evidence of what by God's free grace and gift we already are."[76] Gustavo Gutiérrez writes that all the prom-ises of the Beatitudes "are gifts of the Lord, fruits of his gratuitous love, and therefore call for a certain kind of behavior." In the case of mercy, the beatitude "declares happy those who will receive God's love, which is always a gift. But this gift demands in turn that the recipients be merciful to others."[77]

Perhaps the way out of the quandary is to play out the equation of mercy to its logical end—God shows mercy to the undeserving. In other words, even when we fail to show mercy to one another, we can hope that God's mercy exceeds our mercilessness, and pardons even that.

75. Quoted in Torrance, *Beatitudes*, 46.

76. John R. W. Stott, *Christian Counter-Culture: The Message of the Sermon on the Mount* (Downers Grove, IL: InterVarsity Press, 1978), 29.

77. Gustavo Gutiérrez, *The God of Life*, trans. Matthew J. O'Connell (Maryknoll, NY: Orbis Books, 1991, 1998), quotations on 128 and 124.

8

Such Powerful Light

The Pure in Heart

Blessed are the pure in heart, for they will see God (Matt 5:8).

The characters in Ted Chiang's short story "Hell Is the Absence of God" live in an alternative universe, one in which angels regularly visit the earthly realm, leaving behind both blessings (miraculous healings) and devastation (tornados, earthquakes, shattered glass). A man named Neil is trying to bring himself to love God after his wife dies in the wake of an angelic visitation and ascends to heaven. By the rules of this alternative world, he must love God for God's own sake—and for no other reason—to join his wife in heaven in the afterlife. There's one loophole: in the brief moment when an angel breaks into the earthly plane, heaven's light shines through. Seeing heaven's light is almost as dangerous as encountering an angel; it inevitably leaves the person literally eyeless. But it also guarantees that person access to heaven when they die. Neil devotes his life to the supremely dangerous hobby of chasing angels, hoping to catch a glimpse of heaven's light. When he does, Chiang describes what happens to him: "Like a thousand hypodermic needles the light punctured his flesh and scraped across his bones." In that moment, Neil loved God "with an utterness beyond what humans can experience for one another."[1]

Chiang's story isn't an interpretation of the beatitude. But its consideration of the power of the heavenly light is a dramatic fictional account of something that Christians have wondered ever since they began to try to make sense

1. Chiang suggests that the "terrifying power" of the angels came subconsciously from Annie Dillard's description of church as a setting in which people should be wearing crash helmets and life preservers and lashing themselves to the pews (Ted Chiang, *Stories of Your Life and Others* [New York: Vintage Books, 2016], 279). Dillard asks, "Does anyone have the foggiest idea what sort of power we so blithely invoke?" (Annie Dillard, *Teaching a Stone to Talk: Expeditions and Encounters* [New York: Harper Perennial, 1982, 2013], 52).

of the beatitude's promise: how can one see a powerful, holy God, and God's powerful and holy light, and stay alive?

They shall see God! How? (Isn't God invisible?) What kind of purity of heart enables this extraordinary vision? Will people see God in this life, or the next? The sixth beatitude's promised reward has occasioned some extraordinarily beautiful writing, as Christians strain to imagine what seems beyond imagining.

The beatitude's history is also a tantalizing tangle of rabbit holes—easy to fall into, hard to know when to emerge. Some early Christian writers used the beatitude as evidence in various controversies over the nature of the Trinity: Novatian against Sabellianism, Augustine against the anti-Nicene Homoians. The beatitude's promise even became a flash point in the tensions between the East and West.

Sustained reflection on the promise to see God continued well into the post-Reformation era among Catholic and Protestant alike. American Reformed theologian Jonathan Edwards's sermon on the pure in heart focuses single-mindedly and elegantly on what it means to see God. Puritan preacher Increase Mather offered a long and moving homily on the joys of seeing God in all his beauty and glory, describing it as the highest happiness that a creature is capable of.[2]

This is not to say that interpreters unanimously agreed on what purity of heart actually is. Instead, they offered a range of options. Frequently cited as inspiration or background for the beatitude is Psalm 24:3–4: "Who shall ascend the hill of the LORD? And who shall stand in his holy place? Those who have clean hands and pure hearts, who do not lift up their souls to what is false, and do not swear deceitfully."[3] These verses don't definitively explain what purity of heart is, but they do point to several themes we'll encounter in this chapter.

The motif of clean hands suggests purity of heart as absence of sin or wrongdoing (an association also suggested by David's repentant plea in Ps 51:10 after his double sins of rape and murder: "Create in me a clean heart, O God, and put a new and right spirit within me"). Some interpreters, especially the

---

2. Jonathan Edwards, *Sermons and Discourses 1730–1733*, vol. 17 of *The Works of Jonathan Edwards*, ed. Mark Valeri (New Haven, CT: Yale University Press, 1999), 59–86; Jeremiah Burroughs, *The Saints' Happiness* (Edinburgh: James Nichol, 1867; Soli Deo Gloria, 1988, 1992), 169–75; Increase Mather, *Sermons Wherein Those Eight Characters of the Blessed Commonly Called the Beatitudes Are Opened and Applied in Fifteen Discourses* (Boston: B. Green, for Daniel Henchman, 1718), Sermon 10. Hans Boersma explores how the beatific vision "flourished" among Puritan writers in his *Seeing God: The Beatific Vision in Christian Tradition* (Grand Rapids: Eerdmans, 2018), 315–53.

3. In the Dead Sea Scrolls, 4QBeatitudes contains similar language: a pure heart, clean hands, not swearing deceitfully, and not lifting up the soul (George J. Brooke, *The Dead Sea Scrolls and the New Testament* [Minneapolis: Fortress, 2005], 225).

medieval and the mystical, extended this insight into the cleansing not only of sin but of sinful desires as well, leading to an emphasis on purity of heart as *apatheia* (the absence or tempered control of desires such as lust and greed). The declaration that those with pure hearts "do not lift up their souls to what is false" (Ps 24:4b) gestures toward those who single-mindedly serve only God and no other gods. And the phrase "do not swear deceitfully" (Ps 24:4c) suggests characteristics such as integrity and honest dealings with others.

—

After a brief consideration of what "the heart" (Greek *kardia*) is, I'll outline three main options for what purity of heart is: holiness (defined especially as chastity and as *apatheia*, or detachment from emotions), single-minded devotion to God, and integrity. Because it's less obvious how one might become pure of heart (especially in relation to the overlap between purity of heart, holiness, and sinlessness), I'll then explore *how* one can attain purity of heart, according to our interpreters: in short, by God's grace, and by living into the previous five beatitudes. Next, I turn my attention to the issues raised by the beatitude's second half and explore the various ways interpreters suggest God might be seen in this life and in the next.

Blessed are the pure in heart

What is the heart? This might seem obvious. The heart, of course, is the emotional center of the human being, from which flow love, compassion, anger, and so on. Hearts are lifted up to worship; hearts fall in disappointment; hearts are broken. The heart is often contrasted today to the head (the intellect, or the mind). But this wasn't true for Matthew and his first-century audience.

In the Greek of the New Testament, the heart is not the location for deep emotion. Instead, it is the bowels. When Jesus is moved with compassion or pity (Matt 20:34, Mark 1:41), the word for being moved with compassion (*splanchnizomai*) literally means "to be moved in the bowels," a translation that doesn't play particularly well in contemporary English, since we tend to place compassion in the heart and not the intestines.

What, then, is the heart (*kardia*) in Matt 5:8? Jewish thinkers like the evangelist could speak of the heart as feeling, willing, and thinking.[4] In Matthew's

4. Dale Allison explains, "Jews spoke of the heart as feeling (e.g., Deut. 28:47; cf. Matt.

context, it seems to refer to "a person's inner self," including their desires and understanding.[5] Later interpreters frequently adopted this wide view of the heart, including in it the intellect, the will, and the emotions.

Who, then, are the pure in heart (or the "clean of heart" as in Rheims, NAB, Wycliffe)? Interpretations tend to fall into three main categories: (1) cleansing from sin or sinful desires, (2) single-minded devotion to God, and (3) integrity toward others. As usual, the three categories don't necessarily exclude one another. That is, exegetes sometimes use two or even all three categories at once to explain the meaning of the pure in heart.

I'll lay them out in roughly chronological order this time, since the first category is concentrated in pre-Reformation Catholic and Orthodox thought. Purity of heart as cleansing from or avoidance of sin has both an internal and external aspect. When considering outward or bodily sins, the tradition concentrates much of its energies on the virtue of chastity. When considering the internal aspect, or sinful desires, one influential set of writings depicts purity of heart as *apatheia*, or equanimity: the ability not to be controlled by one's desires. This emphasis appears especially in monastic reflection on the mystical contemplation of God.

The second and third categories emerge from predominantly Protestant (and/or modern) thought. They are tied to one another through their common emphasis on single-mindedness and the rejection of hypocrisy, in relation to God (through an exclusive seeking of God's will) and in relation to others (by dealing with one's fellow humans with integrity and honesty). The third (integrity) is typically used in tandem with the second, as an outworking or result of it: loyalty to God and refusal to worship idols manifests itself in honest dealings with others.

Cleansed from sin and/or sinful desires

Although Danish philosopher Søren Kierkegaard (1813–1855) drew his famous line (and book title) "Purity of heart is to will one thing" from Jas 4:8, rather than from Matt 5:8, his phrase has become something of a shorthand today for the beatitude, and it neatly captures this first strand of meaning. (Kierke-

---

5:27–28; 22:37), willing (e.g., Jer. 3:17), and thinking (e.g., Judg. 5:16; cf. Matt. 9:4)" (Allison, *The Sermon on the Mount: Inspiring the Moral Imagination* [New York: Crossroad, 1999], 51).

5. H. Benedict Green, *Matthew, Poet of the Beatitudes* (Sheffield: Sheffield Academic, 2001), 240. Elsewhere in Matthew, *kardia* occurs in 5:28, 6:21, 9:4, 15:8, 12:34, 13:15, and 13:19.

gaard did allude to the beatitude briefly, later in his book.)[6] The subtitle to Kierkegaard's book indicates his context for purity of heart: *Spiritual Preparation for the Office of Confession*. Although the motif of "willing one thing" fits more closely with the next category (exclusive devotion to God alone), Kierkegaard's link between purity of heart and the confession of sin places him in this first category.

Purity of heart is typically seen as a matter not only of action but also of desire. Chrysostom, for example, emphasized purity as control of the desires that give rise to sinful actions. Chrysostom drew on Aristotle's thought to describe purity as temperance, or the virtue of moderating the desires in order to desire good things in the right amount, neither too much nor too little.[7]

Although understanding purity of heart as avoidance of sin or sinful desire doesn't originate with Augustine, his exegetical innovation proves influential once again. His decision to match each beatitude with a gift of the Spirit from Isaiah 11 and a petition of the Lord's Prayer in Matthew 6 creates a set of associations that are not always obvious (see chapter 1). In this case, however, it creates (or illuminates) a logical link between purity of heart and resistance to sin, because Augustine lined up the pure in heart with the petition, "Lead us not into temptation" (*De Serm. Dom.* 2.11.38).[8]

For the next 1,400 years, it was common to describe purity of heart as avoidance of temptation and the desires that lead to sin. Chromatius of Aquileia (d. ca. 406) is representative; he described the pure in heart as "those who have given up the filth of sin, have purged themselves of all fleshly defilement, and by the works of faith and justice have pleased God."[9] Chromatius's dramatic description relies on a common biblical metaphor for sin as a stain that needs to be cleansed. To be pure in heart (or clean of heart), then, must mean not having the stain of sin on the heart. But Chromatius's reference to "fleshly defilement" points to another common aspect of this category of

6. Søren Kierkegaard, *Purity of Heart Is to Will One Thing: Spiritual Preparation for the Office of Confession*, trans. Douglas V. Steere (New York: Harper & Brothers, 1938, 1948), 53.

7. Chrysostom, *Homilies on the Gospel of Saint Matthew* 15.6 (NPNF¹ 10:94). Gerald Vann likewise referred to cleanness of heart as "temperateness" toward material things; not the absence of desires but discipline of them (Vann, *The Divine Pity: A Study in the Social Implications of the Beatitudes* [New York: Sheed and Ward, 1946], 165).

8. Augustine, *The Lord's Sermon on the Mount*, trans. John J. Jepson, ACW 5 (Mahwah, NJ: Paulist, 1948), 127.

9. Chromatius of Aquileia, *Sermons and Tractates on Matthew*, trans. Thomas P. Scheck, ACW 75 (New York: The Newman Press, 2018), Tractatus 17.6.3–4. So also Cornelius à Lapide, *The Holy Gospel According to Saint Matthew*, vol. 1 of *The Great Commentary of Cornelius à Lapide*, trans. Thomas W. Mossman, rev. ed. (Fitzwilliam, NH: Loreto, 2008), 220.

interpretation: a disproportionate emphasis on the sins of the body—that is, on sexual sins.

For the influential medieval theologian Thomas Aquinas, cleanness of heart is cleanness "from unworthy thoughts" but even more so "cleanness of body." By cleanness of the body, he seems to mean especially the "cleanliness" of chastity, since he referred in the same section to the way that "the moral virtues, especially chastity, advance one toward the contemplative life" and thus toward purity of heart.[10]

Especially chastity

When Aquinas used the term chastity (Latin *castitas*), it's unclear whether he meant celibacy (complete sexual renunciation) or proper restraint of sexual desire, which might include sexual activity within marriage. In another writing, he differentiated between chastity (*castitas*) and virginity (*virginitas*), or the state of never having engaged in sexual relations at all (ST II-II Q.151 and Q.152). The terminology can be a little tricky. What some people call chastity, others call celibacy. Today, some Christian traditions, including the Catholic Church, use chastity to refer to both fidelity in marriage and abstinence outside of marriage, while celibacy refers to the complete and permanent renunciation of sexual activity. Although some Christian writers do commend chastity as purity of heart, it is celibacy (or virginity) that becomes the exemplar. Why (and when) did *sexual* purity, especially celibacy, come to dominate discussions of purity of heart?

Christianity has always had an ascetic streak. That is, practices of self-denial or self-restraint have been part of Christian teaching from the very beginning. It's unclear whether this streak has any roots in the Second Temple Judaism from which Christianity emerged. While some assume that the Jewish group known as the Essenes practiced celibacy, other scholars have challenged this view. Rabbinic writings typically understand the command "be fruitful and multiply" (Gen 1:28) as an obligation for all Jews. On the whole, the endorsement of celibacy appears to be a minority view within the Judaism of the time.[11] Marriage was considered such a standard obligation for Jews that

10. Thomas Aquinas, *Commentary on the Gospel of Matthew, Chapters 1–12*, ed. The Aquinas Institute, trans. Jeremy Holmes and Beth Mortensen, Biblical Commentaries 33 (Lander, WY: The Aquinas Institute for the Study of Sacred Doctrine, 2013), C.5 L.2.435.

11. For representatives of the debate over celibacy in ancient Judaism, especially among the Essenes and in the Dead Sea Scrolls, see Pieter W. van der Horst and Silvia Castelli, "Celibacy in

Jesus (as a single man in a marrying culture) may have even had to defend himself against the charge that he was a eunuch by explaining that there were some men who renounced marriage and children for the greater good of the kingdom of God (Matt 19:12).[12]

The ancient pagan culture in which Christianity arose had its own tradition of sacred female virgins in the Vestal virgins—the priestesses who tended the fire of the goddess Vesta.[13] Greco-Roman culture also valued chastity as a virtue. As Virginia Burrus observes, "Chastity (*sophrosyne, pudicitia*) [was] the virtue most often cited by Greek and Roman men in their praises of women. It encompasses discretion, sobriety, and diligence, but is exemplified most typically and completely through a woman's exercise of self-control in the area of sexuality."[14] Of course, Burrus's observation—and the example of the Vestal virgins—points out how much chastity was (and is) a virtue associated with women rather than men.

When the apostle Paul wrote "it is well . . . to remain unmarried" (1 Cor 7:8), it was a relatively surprising claim for a Jewish writer, even a Hellenized one. What is perhaps more surprising is how widespread and how popular sexual renunciation became in Christian theology.[15] Elizabeth Clark points out that Christian Scripture (e.g., Gen 1:28) often assumes marriage and child-bearing as the norm so that early church writers sometimes "repositioned" those biblical passages or "recontextualized" them to promote asceticism and sexual renunciation.[16] Still, "ascetic impulses" are visible in the earliest extant Christian writings, including the letters of Paul and the gospels.[17]

Chastity became associated with purity of heart as early as the second century, when both chastity and celibacy were becoming ever more prized

---

Early Judaism," *RB* 109, no. 3 (2002): 390–402; Joseph E. Zias, "The Cemeteries of Qumran and Celibacy: Confusion Laid to Rest?," *DSD* 7, no. 2 (2000): 220–53; Paul Heger, "Celibacy in Qumran Hellenist Fiction or Reality? Qumran's Attitude toward Sex," *Revue de Qumrân* 26, no. 1 (2013): 53–90; and Eyal Regev, "Cherchez les femmes: Were the *yaḥad* Celibates?" *DSD* 15 (2008): 253–84.

12. Dale C. Allison Jr., "Eunuchs because of the Kingdom of Heaven (Matt 19:12)," *Theological Students Fellowship Bulletin* 8, no. 2 (1984): 4.

13. On Roman and pagan virginity, see Sissel Undheim, *Borderline Virginities: Sacred and Secular Virgins in Late Antiquity* (New York: Routledge, 2018).

14. Virginia Burrus, *Chastity as Autonomy: Women in the Stories of the Apocryphal Acts*, Studies in Women and Religion 23 (Lewiston, NY: Mellen, 1987), 4n4.

15. Roger Steven Evans, *Sex and Salvation: Virginity as a Soteriological Paradigm in Ancient Christianity* (Lanham, MD: University Press of America, 2003), xii.

16. Elizabeth A. Clark, *Reading Renunciation: Asceticism and Scripture in Early Christianity* (Princeton, NJ: Princeton University Press, 1999), 4.

17. Clark, *Reading Renunciation*, 25–26.

within Christian thought. Toward the end of the second century, a writing called *Acts of Paul and Thecla* portrays the apostle Paul preaching an extended version of the sixth beatitude:

> Blessed are the pure in heart, for they shall see God; blessed are those who have kept the flesh chaste, for they shall become a temple of God; blessed are the continent, for God shall speak with them; blessed are those who have kept aloof from this world, for they shall be pleasing to God; blessed are those who have wives as not having them, for they shall experience God; blessed are those who have fear of God, for they shall become angels of God.[18]

This lengthy expansion of the beatitude links purity of heart firmly to sexual abstinence. The heroine of *Acts of Paul and Thecla* is a Christian woman named Thecla, who renounces both her riches and her fiancé after hearing Paul's preaching.

Other apocryphal *Acts* purporting to be records of the apostles' ministries were written in the late second and early third centuries, and in all of them "women's chastity is of central importance."[19] The emphasis on *women's* sexuality helps us to see that purity of heart became associated with women's virginity in particular. For many patristic and medieval Christian thinkers, virginity signaled a special purity.

Scholars differ over the function of virginity for women in the early church. On the one hand, the high value that male Christian writers placed on female virginity could signal the patriarchal and sometimes misogynistic currents in antiquity, to which Christian thought is not immune.[20] On the other hand, some scholars point out that chastity could function as a form of power or agency for women, liberating them from the sometimes oppressive dominance of husbands and fathers. Burrus writes of the women in the apocryphal Acts, "Ironically, this virtue of chastity, which is most often seen as a buttress of marital life, is precisely what enables the women in the stories of the apocryphal *Acts* to break out of their marriages. From the point of view of

---

18. *Acts of Paul and Thecla* 1.5, in J. K. Elliott, *The Apocryphal New Testament* (Oxford: Clarendon Press, 1993), 365.

19. Burrus, *Chastity as Autonomy*, 2.

20. Susanna Elm: "If through asceticism a woman achieves 'male' virtue (*aretē*), and is thereby transformed into a 'manly woman', then she has not only achieved true equality with her male counterparts, but has been transformed into an ideal, complete human being" (Elm, *"Virgins of God": The Making of Asceticism in Late Antiquity* [New York: Clarendon Press, 1994], ix).

patriarchal marriage, 'chastity' is thus subverted. It becomes a means not to women's restriction or subjugation but to women's autonomy."[21]

Whatever empowering or restricting role chastity or virginity played in the lives of early Christian women, it's clear that purity of heart and chastity were already linked to one another approximately a century after Jesus first spoke the beatitude. But the connection didn't become dominant until two hundred years later, when a "great explosion of literature on virginity" occurred in the fourth century and continued through the sixth century.[22] By the fourth century virginity became viewed as a means to secure salvation—especially for women.[23]

In the medieval era, when beatitudes were usually understood as virtues, purity of heart was often (but not always) associated with the virtue of chastity, as in the late thirteenth-century treatise *Somme le roi*.[24] This explains the artist Jan van Eyck's decision to personify the pure in heart as the virgins (female martyrs and saints) in the famous Ghent altarpiece.[25] In perhaps the most well-known treatment of purity of heart in all literature, the poet Dante Alighieri depicts purity of heart in his *Purgatorio* as the virtue of Chastity and places it in opposition to the vice of Lust (*Purg.* 27.8).[26]

In the fourteenth century, the so-called Gawain-Poet provides an especially vivid example of the association between purity of heart and the virtue of chastity. His poem "Cleanness" (sometimes also translated "Purity") is a lengthy meditation on the beatitude. In it, the poet names three episodes of uncleanness that especially arouse God's anger: humanity's "willful and perverse

---

21. Burrus, *Chastity as Autonomy*, 4n4.

22. Evans, *Sex and Salvation*, xii.

23. Evans, *Sex and Salvation*, xiv.

24. Ellen Kosmer, "Gardens of Virtue in the Middle Ages," *Journal of the Warburg and Courtauld Institutes* 41 (1978): 304; Rosemond Tuve, "Notes on the Virtues and Vices," *Journal of the Warburg and Courtauld Institutes* 27 (1964): 46, 53. The Bedford Hours does the same (Tuve, "Notes on the Virtues," 67). Hugh of St. Victor associated it instead with opposition to the vice of gluttony (Brigitta Stoll, *De Virtute in Virtutem: zur Auslegung— und Wirkungsgeschichte der Bergpredigt in Kommentaren, Predigten und hagiographischer Literatur von der Merowingerzeit bis um 1200* [Tübingen: Mohr Siebeck, 1988], 158–59). Theophylact of Ochrid took purity of heart as chastity and temperance (Theophylact of Ochrid, *The Explanation by Blessed Theophylact of the Holy Gospel According to St. Matthew*, vol. 1 of *Blessed Theophylact's Explanation of the New Testament*, trans. Christopher Stade [House Springs, MO: Chrysostom Press, 1994], 46).

25. Rebekah Eklund, "The Blessed," Visual Commentary on Scripture, http://thevcs.org/blessed.

26. Dante Alighieri, *Purgatorio*, trans. Jean Hollander and Robert Hollander (New York: Anchor Books, 2003), 25–27.

sexual relations," which God punishes through the Flood (cf. Gen 6:4); the sexual sins of Sodom (Gen 19:4–5); and the idolatry of Zedekiah and Balthasar in the OT.[27] Of course, many biblical scholars today reject the view that either the Flood or the punishment of Sodom have to do with sexual sin, but the Gawain-Poet is firmly within the exegetical traditions of his time when he sees them as such, and when he connects sexual sin to impurity of heart. His third example, that of idolatry, points forward to and overlaps with the second main category of interpretation that I'll consider next.

While the view that purity of heart springs from sexual renunciation waned after the Reformation, it does endure in some modern-day Catholic thought. Servais Pinckaers, for example, named multiple elements of purity of heart but focused special and sustained attention on chastity.[28] Protestants loosen the link between celibacy and purity of heart for obvious reasons, given their rejection of enforced celibacy for clergy. Some Protestant interpreters, however, maintain a link to sexual purity more broadly by associating purity of heart with an avoidance of adultery and lust, often through noticing that the word "heart" appears both in the sixth beatitude ("pure of heart") and in the prohibition against lust in Matt 5:27–28 ("committed adultery with her in his heart").[29]

Apatheia *and the mystical contemplation of God*

Chastity is not the only interpretation of purity of heart to appear in a monastic context. In fact, another interpretation is even more important in monasticism, and we already encountered it above, when Aquinas claimed that the virtues (especially chastity) "advance one toward the contemplative life." In the Eastern monastic tradition, purity of heart became central because it enabled mystical contemplation of God. That is, purity of heart was understood as the prerequisite for contemplative prayer, which for many monks was their highest calling. The theme is not absent from Western monastic writing. Francis of Assisi, for example, wrote, "The truly pure in heart are those who despise the

---

27. Gawain-Poet, *Complete Works: Patience, Cleanness, Pearl, Saint Erkenwald, Sir Gawain and the Green Knight*, trans. Marie Borroff (New York: Norton, 2011), 36–39.

28. Servais Pinckaers, *The Pursuit of God's Happiness—God's Way: Living the Beatitudes*, trans. Mary Thomas Noble (New York: Society of St. Paul, 1998), 134–35, 141–44.

29. E.g., Billy Graham, *The Secret of Happiness: Jesus' Teaching on Happiness as Expressed in the Beatitudes* (Garden City, NY: Doubleday, 1955), 77–81.

things of earth and seek the things of heaven, and who never cease to adore and behold the Lord God living and true with a pure heart and soul."[30]

Earlier precedence for this approach appears in Leo the Great's claim that people will see God "through the unspeakable joy of eternal contemplation"; "the brightness of the true light" will then be seen by "minds that are bright and clean."[31] Still, it achieves much greater prominence in Eastern monastic thought.

In general, Byzantine or Eastern spirituality "equated 'purity of heart' with *apatheia*, freedom from the passions."[32] For example, Egyptian monk Evagrius Ponticus (346–399) wrote that when the mind turns away from the passion "and puts off the old man," the pure heart becomes able to see a vision of "another heaven [*allos ouranos*] . . . the vision of which is both light and the spiritual 'place.'"[33] Of course, renouncing the passions often went hand in hand with abstinence from food and from sex, but those were means to an end. The goal was *apatheia*.

The monk John Cassian (ca. 360–435) is often credited with introducing monasticism to western Europe after studying extensively under Christian monks in Egypt. Cassian's *Conferences* records a series of conversations between Cassian and his Egyptian teachers—"the great leaders of Eastern monasticism of his time."[34] In one such conversation, the Ethiopian monk Abba Moses describes the kingdom of heaven as the "ultimate goal" of contemplative prayer, and purity of heart as the "immediate goal," which makes the ultimate goal possible because "without purity of heart none can enter into that kingdom."[35]

If purity of heart is thus necessary for contemplative prayer, then what *is* purity of heart (and how does one achieve it)? For Abba Moses, it is *apatheia*,

---

30. Francis of Assisi, Admonition 16, in Francis of Assisi and Clare of Assisi, *Francis and Clare: The Complete Works*, trans. Regis Armstrong and Ignatius C. Brady (New York: Paulist, 1982), 32.

31. Leo the Great, *Sermons* 95.8 (*NPNF*² 12:205).

32. Allison, *Sermon on the Mount*, 51.

33. Evagrius Ponticus, Epistle 39, quoted in Alexander Golitzin, "'The Demons Suggest an Illusion of God's Glory in a Form': Controversy Over the Divine Body and Vision of Glory in Some Late Fourth, Early Fifth Century Monastic Literature," *Studia Monastica* 44, no. 1 (2002): 68.

34. Justo L. González, ed., *The Westminster Dictionary of Theologians*, trans. Suzanne E. Hoeferkamp Segovia (Louisville: Westminster John Knox, 2006), 193.

35. Cassian, Conf. 1.3–4, in Cassian, "The Conference of Cassian," in *Western Asceticism*, ed. Owen Chadwick, Library of Christian Classics Ichthus Edition (Philadelphia: Westminster, 1958), 196–97.

or "the soul's detachment." One achieves detachment from unruly desires through the ascetic disciplines such as fasting and celibacy. The purpose of these disciplines is "to free the heart from injury by bodily passions and to keep it free."[36] Evagrius Ponticus was one of the Egyptian monks who tutored Cassian, and Evagrius also equated purity of heart to *apatheia*. Like Abba Moses, he described purity of heart (and *apatheia*) as the result of the ascetic life. For Evagrius, perfect purity of heart develops in the soul after one has won victory over the demons who oppose the ascetic life.[37]

Protestant Reformers, including Martin Luther, objected to the connection between purity of heart and ascetic monasticism.[38] They pointed out that this made purity of heart unavailable to lay Christians and made it instead an esoteric pursuit for those in monastic cloisters. They also critiqued this approach for its focus on achieving an ecstatic experience of God that, again, appeared limited to only a few. Modern-day inheritors of the Lutheran tradition likewise reject interpretations that link purity of heart to contemplative experiences. Ulrich Luz, for example, worried about interpretations of the beatitude that "lead to a flight from the world or a private piety of the religiously gifted person," and preferred Reformation readings like Luther's, who exhorted his audience to "seek God in the wretched, the erring and toiling" rather than strive to the mystic heights.[39]

Luz (and Luther) was surely right that any interpretation that fences off the beatitude's reward and makes it available only to a few has gone astray. One might also object that this stream of Christianity had drunk too deeply from the water of Stoicism, in its conviction that the emotions hinder one's prayers. Yet its core insight holds true: that a heart or mind clouded with fear

36. Conf. 1.13, Cassian, "The Conf.erence," 202; Conf. 1.7, Cassian, "The Conference," 198.

37. Evagrius Ponticus, *The Praktikos; Chapters on Prayer*, trans. John Eudes Bamberger, Cistercian Studies Series 4 (Spencer, MA: Cistercian Publications, 1972), *Praktikos* 60, 81, 83. John Climacus (ca. 570–649) linked purity of heart to those who have achieved maturity/perfection by *apatheia* (John Climacus, *Scala Paradisi* 26 [PG 88:1092c]). Cabasilas treated the pure in heart as those who have abandoned evil thoughts and think only good and noble thoughts; those whose spirits successfully resist the desires of the body. (Cabasilas, *The Life in Christ* 6.11f, trans. Carmino J. deCatanzaro [Crestwood, NY: St. Vladimir's Seminary Press, 1974], 187). Dominican mystic Meister Eckhart described purity of heart as "separation and detachment from all material things," which enables union with God (Eckhart von Hochheim, *Meister Eckhart: Teacher and Preacher*, ed. Bernard McGinn [Mahwah, NJ: Paulist, 1986], 280).

38. Martin Luther, *The Sermon on the Mount*, vol. 21 of *Luther's Works*, ed. Jaroslav Pelikan (St. Louis: Concordia, 1956), 32–33.

39. Ulrich Luz, *Matthew 1–7*, trans. James E. Crouch, Hermeneia (Minneapolis: Fortress: 2007), 197.

or roiled with rage is less likely to see past its own preoccupations and enter into God's presence.

The theme of purity of heart as a cleansing from sin or sinful desires does appear in modified form in two different Protestant streams, one Reformed and one Wesleyan. In both cases, purity of heart is available not to a cloistered few but to all Christians. Rather than *apatheia*, purity of heart is a progressive cleansing from sin and sinful desires and growth in holiness or ability to do God's will. In other words, it's what is usually called sanctification—in the Wesleyan holiness tradition, "entire sanctification" and in the Reformed tradition, "regeneration."

Regeneration/Entire sanctification

Amanda Berry Smith (1837–1915) was born a slave in Maryland. She became an African Methodist Episcopal (AME) preacher who spoke at camp meeting revivals and the Women's Christian Temperance Union. She read the sixth beatitude through the lens of the Wesleyan doctrine of entire sanctification, the teaching that Christians are able to reach a state of holiness so that they no longer sin.[40]

Smith equated "the blessing of heart purity" with "the blessed light of full salvation," or the experience of sanctification. For Smith, purity of heart is achievable in this life, not only in the next. She also differentiated heart purity from salvation by works, insisting that one does not receive sanctification through works such as baptism by immersion or foot-washing.[41] Instead, heart purity is a blessing, received by the baptized person through prayer and the grace of the Spirit.

On the Reformed side, theologians who inherit Calvinist thought tend to associate purity of heart with regeneration, a concept that remains somewhat distinct from the broader category of sanctification. Regeneration is "the beginning of the spiritual life," as John Calvin wrote (*Inst.* II.iii.6). Calvin described regeneration variously as a rebirth, the creation of the "new Adam," the restoration of the image of God that had been damaged by the fall, and

---

40. Amanda Smith, *An Autobiography: The Story of the Lord's Dealings with Mrs. Amanda Smith the Colored Evangelist* (Oxford: Oxford University Press, 1988), 90, see also 86. A Nazarene preacher once told R. T. Kendall that this beatitude is "a key verse for [the Nazarene] doctrine of entire sanctification" (Kendall, *The Sermon on the Mount* [Oxford, UK: Monarch Books, 2011, 2013], 50).

41. Smith, *An Autobiography*, 84, 90–91.

the conversion of the will so that it begins to turn away from sin and toward God (*Inst.* II.iii.6; III.iii.9). For some Reformed thinkers, then, regeneration is a rebirth that makes it possible for a person to follow God and seek God's will, whereas sanctification is the continuance or ongoing work of that rebirth.[42]

But Calvin himself insisted that regeneration is not a one-time event but rather an ongoing process, a restoration that "does not take place in one moment or one day or one year." Instead, "through continual and sometimes slow advances God wipes out in his elect the corruptions of the flesh, cleanses them of guilt, consecrates them to himself as temples renewing all their minds to true purity" (*Inst.* III.iii.9). So some Reformed writers followed this path when they framed regeneration as a kind of progressive sanctification, or as something akin to Wesleyan entire sanctification, although Calvin himself wrote that "this warfare [against sin and guilt] will end only at death" (*Inst.* III.iii.9; see also *Inst.* III.iii.10–11).

Jonathan Edwards appears to view purity of heart in ways similar to Calvin, treating it as the regeneration of both rebirth and an ongoing process of cleansing. For Edwards, a pure heart is one that abhors sin, grieves over sin when it is committed, is freed "from the reigning power and dominion of [sin]," and continually seeks to cleanse itself from the "remainders" of sin. Those who are pure in heart delight in loving God and neighbor.[43] Evangelist Billy Graham, another inheritor of the Reformed tradition, connected purity of heart to spiritual rebirth and regeneration, focusing more on Calvin's first aspect—regeneration as the beginning of a new life made possible in Christ.[44]

For these Protestant thinkers, whether Calvinist or Wesleyan, purity of heart is initiated first by God's saving act in Christ, and then grasped or sought after by the Christian, through repentance and prayer. For both Protestant streams, the purpose or result of purity of heart is somewhat different from monastic practice: the goal is not contemplation of God or mystical experience of God, but rather increasing ability to be free from the power of sin and to more freely love God and neighbor unhindered from sinful desires. (The question of how one obtains purity of heart, anticipated here, will also be taken up a little later in this chapter.)

---

42. See Kenneth Stewart, "The Doctrine of Regeneration in Evangelical Theology: The Reformation to 1800," *Journal for Baptist Theology and Ministry* 8, no. 1 (Spring 2011): 44, 46, 48–49, 53.

43. Edwards, *Sermons and Discourses*, 78–81.

44. Graham, *Secret of Happiness*, 73.

The next two main strands might be viewed as two sides of the same coin: the purity of an undivided heart. A pure heart is whole, or single, in relation both to God (manifested as single-minded devotion to God) and in relation to the neighbor (manifested as a life of integrity and honesty before others).

Single-mindedly seeking God

If asceticism in general and sexual renunciation in particular dominates pre-Reformation interpreters, this second strand comes to dominate post-Reformation views. Fittingly, it is Martin Luther who laid the groundwork for this interpretation.

For Luther a pure heart is always "watching and pondering what God says and replacing its own ideas with the Word of God."[45] The highest purity is achieved not by ascetic practice but by faith—simply by believing in Christ. But it's not entirely passive either. Luther went on to say that purity of heart has two parts: "the Word of faith toward God, which purifies the heart, and the Word of understanding, which teaches him what he is to do toward his neighbor."[46] While both parts spring from divine agency, the second part results in human agency or action.

Luther's views of purity of heart are shaped in part by his reaction against monasticism and his insistence on justification by faith alone. As Mark Burrows writes, for Luther, "Christians attain a purity of life and a righteousness before God not because of outward religious profession (for example, as monks who sought perfection by fulfilling the *consilia evangelii* [evangelical counsels]) but on account of the Word of God which they come to hold inwardly in their heart through faith."[47] But Luther, the former Augustinian monk, was also reaching back to his predecessor Augustine, who preached that hearts are purified by "faith working through love."[48]

45. Luther, *Sermon on the Mount*, 34.

46. Luther, *Sermon on the Mount*, 34.

47. Mark S. Burrows, "Selections from Martin Luther's Sermons on the Sermon on the Mount," in *The Theological Interpretation of Scripture: Classic and Contemporary Readings*, ed. Stephen E. Fowl (Malden, MA: Blackwell, 1997), 252.

48. Augustine, Sermon 53.11, in Augustine, *Sermons III (51–94) on the New Testament*, vol. 3 of *The Works of Saint Augustine Part 3*, ed. John E. Rotelle, trans. Edmund Hill (Brooklyn, NY: New City Press, 1991), 71.

Many influential Protestant thinkers followed in Luther's footsteps, including Reformed theologian John Peter Lange (1802–1884), who described purity of heart as "that steady direction of the soul toward the divine life which excludes every other object from the homage of the heart."[49] Karl Barth, a twentieth-century Reformed theologian, saw it as reliance only on the Word of Jesus and nothing else (CD II/2.38.2).[50] To have a pure heart is to acknowledge that only God can heal, save, and deliver; and to accept God's forgiveness: "We shall see Him when we become wholly bereft" and cry out to God for help.[51]

The theme of complete surrender to God or exclusive devotion to God occasionally appears in contemporary Orthodox and Catholic thought as well. For example, Catholic Peruvian theologian Gustavo Gutiérrez (b. 1928) understands purity of heart as loyalty to God alone and therefore as the opposite of idolatry. A person who is pure in heart does not try to serve two masters (Matt 6:24) but instead loves God with the whole self (Deut 6:5).[52] The pure in heart are thus the opposite of the double-minded person described in the book of James (Jas 1:7–8, 4:8).[53]

---

49. John Peter Lange, *The Gospel According to Matthew*, vol. 16 of *A Commentary on the Holy Scriptures: Critical, Doctrinal, and Homiletical, with Special Reference to Ministers and Students*, trans. Philip Schaff, 12th ed. (New York: Charles Scribner's Sons, 1884), 103. Dietrich Bonhoeffer described the pure in heart as "those who have surrendered their hearts completely to Jesus that he may reign in them alone" (Bonhoeffer, *The Cost of Discipleship* [New York: Simon & Schuster, 1995], 112). See also Carl F. H. Henry, *Christian Personal Ethics* (Grand Rapids: Eerdmans, 1957), 480; Timothy D. Howell, *The Matthean Beatitudes in Their Jewish Origins: A Literary and Speech Act Analysis* (New York: Lang, 2011), 145.

50. Karl Barth, *Church Dogmatics*, ed. G. W. Bromiley and T. F. Torrance, trans. G. W. Bromiley (Peabody, MA: Hendrickson, 1958, 2004), 693.

51. Karl Barth and Eduard Thurneysen, *Come Holy Spirit: Sermons*, trans. George W. Richards, Elmer G. Homrighausen, and Karl J. Ernst (Grand Rapids: Eerdmans, 1933, 1978), 86–88, quotation on 88. Craig Keener, similarly: "those who recognize that God alone is their hope (Ps 73:2–28)" (Craig S. Keener, *A Commentary on the Gospel of Matthew* [Grand Rapids: Eerdmans, 1999], 170).

52. Gustavo Gutiérrez, *The God of Life*, trans. Matthew J. O'Connell (Maryknoll, NY: Orbis Books, 1991, 1998), 125. For an Orthodox example, see Kyriaki Karidoyanes FitzGerald and Thomas FitzGerald, *Happy in the Lord: The Beatitudes for Everyday: Perspectives from Orthodox Spirituality* (Brookline, MA: Holy Cross Orthodox Press, 2000), 124.

53. Gutiérrez, *God of Life*, 126. So also Davies and Allison, who write that purity of heart is integrity, a correlation between the inward and the outward, and seeking only God's will above all else (W. D. Davies and Dale C. Allison Jr., *A Critical and Exegetical Commentary on the Gospel According to Saint Matthew*, ICC 1 [London: T&T Clark, 1988], 1:456).

And seeking the things of God (compassion, justice, kindness)

Like Gutiérrez, Baptist Clarence Jordan (1912–1969) described purity of heart as a loyalty to God that dethrones all other masters, including wealth, racial prejudice, and militarism.[54] In this way, Jordan aptly captured Luther's second element of a pure heart ("what [one] is to do toward [one's] neighbor"). If purity of heart is single-minded devotion to God, then it also implies an active devotion to the things of God: compassion, justice, mercy—or what Benedict Green described as a "generous response to the total demands of God."[55]

This is a minor theme in the beatitude's exegesis—a small creek, if you will, meandering off a larger river. But it surfaces a few times in interesting ways and in various places. Like Jordan, Thomas Torrance wrote (while living in Chengtu, China) that purity of heart includes passion against injustice, inhumanity, tyranny, and oppression; the joy of seeing God (Matt 5:8b) includes the end of all these things and the establishment of God's justice.[56]

In the East, in the seventh century, the Syrian mystic Isaac of Nineveh (ca. 613–700) wrote that purity is "a heart full of compassion for the whole of created nature."[57] In one of Isaac's dialogues, a student asks for the sign of purity of heart, and the teacher answers, "When he sees all men in a good light, without any one appearing to him unclean or defiled," in fulfillment of Phil 2:3 ("Do nothing from selfish ambition or conceit, but in humility regard others as better than yourselves").[58] In the West, two centuries later, Dhuoda of Septimania wrote to her son that one aspect of purity of heart is cherishing and welcoming the poor with kindness. To that end, she instructed her son to keep his noble rank hidden so that with a pure heart he might show "brotherly compassion to the most humble."[59]

---

54. Clarence Jordan, *Sermon on the Mount*, rev. ed. (Valley Forge, PA: Judson, 1952), 32–33.

55. Green, *Matthew, Poet*, 240. So also Michael Crosby: "a person's total commitment to God's plan . . . manifested by doing good, by showing care," living generously and "alleviating the needs of others" (Crosby, *Spirituality of the Beatitudes: Matthew's Vision for the Church in an Unjust World*, rev. ed. [Maryknoll, NY: Orbis Books, 2005], 140–41).

56. Thomas Torrance, *The Beatitudes and the Decalogue* (London: Skeffington & Son, 1921), 66.

57. Quoted in Jim Forest, *The Ladder of the Beatitudes* (Maryknoll, NY: Orbis Books, 1999), 99.

58. Isaac of Nineveh, *Mystic Treatises by Isaac of Nineveh* 35.250, trans. A. J. Wensick (Amsterdam: Koninklijke Akademie van Wetenschappen, 1923), 168.

59. Dhuoda, *Handbook for her Warrior Son* 4.8, ed. and trans. Marcelle Thiébaux (Cambridge: Cambridge University Press, 1998), 155.

Integrity

Interpreters who see purity of heart as integrity often appeal to the psalmist, who wrote that those who have pure hearts "do not swear deceitfully" (Ps 24:4). For some, this means honest dealing with others, whether in personal relationships or—as John Calvin emphasized—in business transactions.[60] They are single-minded not only in their devotion to God but in their dealings with others; as Carl Henry put it, they have nothing to hide.[61] For medieval monk Bernard of Clairvaux, as for Dhuoda, the pure of heart follow the un-selfish, self-giving example of Jesus in Phil 2:3–8; they "do not seek their own advantage, but that of many."[62]

For most of the interpreters in this category, purity of heart is the opposite of hypocrisy.[63] The pure in heart are like the tax collector who cries out for God's mercy and unlike the Pharisee who thanks God that he is not like the sinful tax collector (Luke 18:9–14).[64] Identifying the tax collector as one who is pure in heart is an interesting move, since the tax collector calls himself a sinner, and it's the arrogant Pharisee who sees himself as righteous—as pure, perhaps?—before God. In this sense, purity of heart is not at all a lack of sin or even of sinful desires, but rather an acknowledgement of one's own helpless-ness, one's own failure to wriggle free from the grip of sin, and a wholehearted turning toward God for mercy. Purity of heart is telling the truth about one's own sinful state. Along these lines, Puritan preacher Robert Harris (1581–1658) had some gentle words for those who worry that they are hypocrites. We can't expect to be perfectly stable and pure in this life, he told his congregation. "But

60. John Calvin contrasted the pure in heart with those who weave "schemes of decep-tion" when doing business; the pure in heart rather "take no pleasure in cunning, but deal honestly with men" (John Calvin, *A Harmony of the Gospels Matthew, Mark and Luke*, vol. 1, ed. David W. Torrance and Thomas F. Torrance, trans. A. W. Morrison [Grand Rapids: Eerdmans, 1972], 171).

61. Henry, *Christian Personal Ethics*, 480.

62. Bernard of Clairvaux, *Sermons on Conversion*, trans. Marie-Bernard Saïd (Kalamazoo, MI: Cistercian Publications, 1981), 70.

63. Mather, *Sermons Wherein*, Sermon 9; William Tyndale, *The Work of William Tyndale*, ed. G. E. Duffield (Philadelphia: Fortress, 1965), 204; Samuel Collett, *A Paraphrase of the Fifth, Sixth, and Seventh Chapters of Matthew, with Proper Soliloquies at Every Period* (London: J. Williams, 1764), 18; D. Martyn Lloyd-Jones, *Studies in the Sermon on the Mount*, vol. 1 (Grand Rapids: Eerd-mans, 1960), 111; Robert Harris, *The Way to True Happiness: Delivered in Twenty-Four Sermons upon the Beatitudes*, ed. Don Kistler (Morgan, PA: Soli Deo Gloria, 1998), 237–46.

64. FitzGerald and FitzGerald, *Happy in the Lord*, 119–21.

as long as we have our faces set heavenward, though the wind may violently carry us sometimes off the path, it should not dismay us."[65]

Yiu Sing Lúcás Chan likewise saw purity of heart as the opposite of hypocrisy; it is "a sense of *integrity* between one's interior life and external actions." He named three examples: two models of integrity, and one of failure. First, he commended Pope Pius XI (1857–1939) as a model of integrity, that is, as a person who demonstrated the alignment of his commitments and his outer actions when he spoke out against the emerging powers of fascism and Nazism. Likewise, Chan praised El Salvador's Archbishop Óscar Romero for courageously defending the poor and challenging the injustices of his government. As for the failure, he criticized the Catholic leadership for their lack of integrity in relation to the sex abuse scandal.

Chan's critique stems from understanding integrity as a particular virtue, as defined by the virtue ethics tradition stemming from Aristotle. In that tradition, integrity has a number of sub-virtues associated with it, including truthfulness, prudence, and vigilance. By failing to be truthful (covering up sex abuse cases rather than bringing them into the light), prudent (exercising poor judgment in relation to abusive priests), and vigilant (failing to protect the vulnerable children in their care), the Catholic Church acted without integrity.[66]

—

What should we make of these various definitions? The first option, dominant throughout the patristic and medieval eras, narrated purity of heart as cleansing from sin and sinful desires. It seems sensible to assume that a pure heart is one that is free (or as free as possible) from sin. Elsewhere in the Sermon on the Mount, Jesus points out the ways that the desires of the heart (lust, anger) lead to sinful actions (adultery, murder) (Matt 5:21–30). So it also seems true to claim that a pure heart is one that is likewise kept free of these kinds of sinful desires. Conversely, what people do with their bodies affects the inner person. Whether and how we have sex or what and how we eat affects our inner lives, hearts, and souls.

In that sense, the traditional association of purity of heart with chastity rightly recognizes that the body and the inner self (the intellect, heart, etc.) are not separable from one another. Yet as we have also seen, the close at-

---

65. Harris, *Way to True Happiness*, 279–80.
66. Yiu Sing Lúcás Chan, *The Ten Commandments and the Beatitudes* (Lanham, MD: Rowman & Littlefield, 2012), 202–3, 206–7.

tention to sexual renunciation proved to be a double-edged sword especially for women—sometimes empowering, sometimes denigrating. The Christian tradition has sometimes overemphasized sexual practice and sexual sin, and that's a danger with this beatitude, too.

Kierkegaard's slogan (purity of heart is to will one thing) reminds us that a *pure* thing is a *single* thing, one that's not contaminated or mixed with anything else. A pure heart means not only the absence of some things (sin, sinful desires) but the presence of something, of *one* thing. And what is that one thing?

The second option provides the answer: a pure heart turns wholeheartedly toward God, and toward the things of God. The second and first options are thus compatible, even if they have a different emphasis. It's the third option (integrity) that points out the outward effect of the first two. A person whose heart is kept clean and oriented toward the love of God will deal in truth and kindness toward others. In other words, the love of God is not detachable from the love of neighbor; the two go hand in hand. And the third option also introduces a note of grace.

I, for one, am skeptical that I will ever achieve holiness in this life. Instead, like Paul, I often find myself in despair over my own choices and praying gratefully for God's rescuing grace (Rom 7:14–25). For that, the beatitude needs one more lens: the tax collector who acknowledges his failure before God and asks for God's mercy. If the first option (alone) puts us in danger of putting ourselves into the position of the self-righteous Pharisee of the parable, it's the third option that corrects this possibility, bringing us back to mercy.

How does one get purity of heart?

One final question remains. Is it possible to become truly pure of heart? If so, how? Even integrity—the perfect alignment of our inner commitments and our outer actions—can seem tricky to achieve, as Paul noticed in Romans 7. Unlike some of the other beatitudes, purity of heart is an inward characteristic rather than an action to be performed (like acts of mercy or mourning) or a state brought about whether one desires it or not (poverty, persecution).

We've already glimpsed one approach to obtaining purity of heart. In medieval monasticism, especially in mystical thought, one achieved purity of heart through ascetic practices, which trained one to disentangle the soul from the web of sinful desires that ensnare it and block it from ascending upward toward God. Protestant approaches instead shift the attainment of a pure heart from human to divine agency.

By faith: justification and participation in Christ

Of course, this isn't a purely Protestant innovation. The medieval monks recognized that one could never overcome sinful desire without God's grace. Long before the medieval era, Augustine wrote that one purifies the heart by faith, as in Acts 15:9 ("cleansing their hearts by faith").[67] For Augustine, of course, faith is not mere belief, but faith that manifests itself in love (Jas 2:19, Gal 5:6).[68]

Still, it was the Protestant Reformers who put the accent back onto God's action in relation to how people might become pure of heart. It is God's grace that cleanses the heart, as a gift, not as a result of any particular action (or any particular state of life, such as chastity).[69] Puritan preacher Increase Mather struck a common note when he wrote that perfect purity is only obtainable in heaven, but that purity of heart on earth comes about through being in Christ, because faith purifies the heart.[70]

Billy Graham associate Sherwood Wirt also linked purity of heart to Christ, but via the cross. For Wirt, purity of heart can only be achieved by taking up the cross and being crucified with Christ.[71] And preacher Lloyd-Jones similarly emphasized that only the Holy Spirit can cleanse the heart, but he also insisted that believers still have a responsibility to strive to be as close to God as possible (citing Rom 8:13).[72] Lloyd-Jones's balance of divine and human agencies returns us to a recurring theme of this chapter—visible, for example, in the discussion of entire sanctification just above. And it also returns us to Augustine.

Embody the previous five beatitudes

Recall Augustine's contention just a moment ago that purity of heart is achieved by faith—but by a faith (or a faithfulness, if you will) that is active in love. Thus Augustine, without any sense of contradiction, also wrote that your heart is purified if you perform the previous five beatitudes.[73] That is, if one

---

67. Augustine, Sermon 53.10, in Augustine, *Sermons III (51–94)*, 71.

68. Augustine, Sermon 53.10–11, in Augustine, *Sermons III (51–94)*, 71–72.

69. Thomas Watson, *The Beatitudes: An Exposition of Matthew 5:1–10* (Carlisle, PA: Banner of Truth Trust, 2014), 185–86.

70. Mather, *Sermons Wherein*, Sermon 9.

71. Sherwood E. Wirt, *Magnificent Promise: A Fresh View of the Beatitudes from the Cross* (Chicago: Moody Press, 1964), 80–81.

72. Lloyd-Jones, *Studies*, 115.

73. Augustine, Sermon 53A.11, in Augustine, *Essential Sermons*, ed. Boniface Ramsey, trans.

strives to become poor in spirit (humble), mournful (repentant), meek (over-coming evil with good), thirsty for God's righteousness (loving and doing the good), and merciful (aiding the needy), then one will necessarily become pure in heart, because all those previous actions and inner attitudes will purify the heart, cleansing it and orienting it wholly toward love of God and neighbor.

When Augustine preached on the Beatitudes, he exhorted his listeners to clean out "the room of your heart" to make space for God so that when God enters there will be nothing there "to cause him displeasure." But he also had a reassuring word for his congregation. Augustine was not only a theologian, he was a pastor. He knew that it is not so easy to clean out the room of the heart. So he continued, "But perhaps you may find difficulty in cleaning out your heart; call [God] in, he won't refuse to clean out a place for himself, and he will agree to stay with you. . . . I agree, there's nothing greater than God; don't worry, all the same, about not having enough room; receive him, and he enlarges your living space."[74]

They will see God

The promise "they will see God" uncovers a tension in the scriptural witness-es.[75] "No one has ever seen God," wrote John straightforwardly (John 1:18;

Edmund Hill, *The Works of Saint Augustine: A Translation for the 21st Century* (Hyde Park, NY: New City Press, 2007), 81; see also Augustine, Sermon 53.9, in in Augustine, *Sermons III (51–94)*, 268. See also Leo the Great, who wrote that a pure heart is a heart "free of possessiveness . . . capable of mourning . . . thirsts for what is right . . . merciful . . . loving . . . undivided" (Leo the Great, *Sermons* 95.8 [*NPNF²* 12:205]). Clarence Jordan writes that the pure heart is a result of having taken the steps of all the previous beatitudes; the result is God forming a new nature in us (Jordan, *Sermon on the Mount*, 32).

74. Augustine, Sermon 53A.11, in Augustine, *Essential Sermons*, 81. Origen: since "the strength of our will is not sufficient to procure the perfectly pure heart," we should pray Psalm 51:10 ("Create in me a clean heart") (Origen, *Against Celsus* 7.33 [*ANF* 4:624]). Some interpreters follow Augustine's lead but identify one particular beatitude (or two or three) that purifies the heart. Contemporary author Susan Muto connects purity of heart especially to the first beatitude, describing both poverty of spirit and purity of heart as the two "unitive" beatitudes that "draw us to an intimate, unitive relationship with the Trinity" (Susan Muto, "Blessed Are the Poor in Spirit and the Pure of Heart," in *New Perspectives on the Beatitudes*, ed. Francis A. Eigo [Villanova, PA: Villanova University Press, 1995], 130). Muto also claims that the pure of heart "embody all the dispositions that flow from the beatitudes" (Muto, "Blessed," 153).

75. For a list of the texts that represent the tension between the impossibility of seeing God and the promise that we will, see Dale C. Allison Jr., *Studies in Matthew: Interpretation Past and*

1 John 4:12; see also 1 Tim 6:15–16). Colossians, 1 Timothy, and Hebrews describe God as invisible (Col 1:15, 1 Tim 1:17, Heb 11:27). All these texts imply that it's only in the next life when "we will see [God] as he is" (1 John 3:2; see also Heb 12:14, Rev 22:4).

But other scriptural texts suggest that the pure of heart can see God—or some aspect of God—in *this* life. When Moses asks God, "Show me your glory," God first tells Moses, "you cannot see my face; for no one shall see me and live" (Exod 33:20). God then proceeds to show Moses the LORD's "back" as the LORD passes by. God clarifies: "you shall see my back; but my *face* shall not be seen" (Exod 33:23, emphasis added). Even this detail has puzzled some interpreters, since if we back up a few verses in Exodus chapter 33, we see the author claiming that "The LORD used to speak to Moses face to face, as a man speaks to his friend" (Exod 33:11; see also Gen 32:30).

Of course, the author of Exodus could simply be using "face to face" as a metaphor. Other texts further complicate the issue. The psalmist wrote, "the upright shall behold his face" (Ps 11:7; see also Ps 17:15).[76] The prophet Isaiah reported that he saw God seated on a throne (Isa 6:1). The prophet Ezekiel was more cautious; although he wrote that he saw in one of his visions "something that seemed like a human form" seated on a heavenly throne, he concluded, "This was the appearance of the likeness of the glory of the LORD" (Ezek 1:28), putting three modifiers of distance between himself and the LORD.[77] When Moses, Aaron, and the seventy elders of Israel ascended Mount Sinai and "they saw the God of Israel," the narrator felt compelled to add, "And upon the nobles of the children of Israel [God] laid not his hand" (Exod 24:9–11). They did see God and live, but the narrator seems to think this is an anomaly: God, who by all rights should have struck them down, refrained.[78]

The most influential text of all—when it comes to the exegesis of the beatitude's promise—comes from the hand of Paul, who wrote, "For now we see in a mirror, dimly, but then we will see face to face. Now I know only in

---

Present (Grand Rapids: Baker Academic, 2005), 44–45n7, and 46n14; see also discussion in Green, *Matthew, Poet*, 241–45.

76. Dale Allison takes this to be a claim not about seeing per se, but about experiencing God in the Jerusalem temple (Allison, *Studies in Matthew*, 59).

77. Cf. 2 *Enoch* 39:5–6. See Alexander Golitzin, "The Vision of God and the Form of Glory: More Reflections on the Anthropomorphite Controversy of AD 399," in *Abba: The Tradition of Orthodoxy in the West: Festschrift for Bishop Kallistos (Ware) of Diokleia*, ed. John Behr, Andrew Louth, and Dimitri Conomos (Crestwood, NY: St. Vladimir's Seminary Press, 2003), 280.

78. I'm grateful to Ben Quash for pointing out this text to me.

part; then I will know fully, even as I have been fully known" (1 Cor 13:12). Or, in the terser and more elegant rendering of the King James: "For now we see through a glass, darkly; but then face to face."

Now, as through a glass, darkly; but then face to face

Only a very few modern interpreters propose that the promise "they will see God" is fulfilled *only* in this life. Conversely, until the modern age, it's very difficult to find anyone who thought that the promise will be fulfilled only in the next. As Dale Allison points out, many modern commentators assume that the promise is eschatological—that is, that it refers solely to the vision of God in the afterlife or at the eschaton—and has no bearing in this life.[79]

Most interpreters throughout history have taken their cue from 1 Cor 13:12 and seen the promise—like all the promises of the Beatitudes—as pointing to both the present (in part, darkly) and the future (in full, face to face). Thus the promise to see God has a partial or proleptic fulfillment, one that anticipates the greater joy of seeing God in the heavenly realm, at the return of Christ, or in the new age. For Jeremiah Burroughs, for example, the pure in heart glimpse God in this life in God's effects or God's works, in God's Word and God's Son, but all these are only "some glimmerings of God, some little sight of it."[80]

The one exception to this proves to be the mystics, who strove to attain the full contemplation of God "face to face" in this life. For example, Byzantine monk Symeon the New Theologian (949–1022) wrote that the person who has attained the Beatitudes and become pure of heart "is indeed enabled to see Him by contemplation. . . . His mind sees strange visions and is wholly illuminated and becomes like light. . . . He sees himself wholly united to the light." Symeon concluded, "Let us not wait to see Him in the future, but strive to contemplate Him now."[81]

Even for the mystics, however, contemplation of God in this life by some is the forerunner to the beatific vision given to all in the next. As poet and preacher John Donne mused, in a somewhat different key, the pure in heart are already in "present possession" of the blessing of seeing God, since this

79. Allison, *Studies in Matthew*, 43–44. For an exploration of the beatific vision, see Boersma, *Seeing God*.

80. Burroughs, *Saints' Happiness*, 172. As Allison points out, "The notion that God cannot be perceived directly but only through 'effects' is already well developed in Philo" and can be traced back to Plato (Allison, *Studies in Matthew*, 57n57).

81. Symeon the New Theologian, Sermon 2.12, 14 in *Discourses*, 56, 58.

world and the next world are "the same House" to the pure in heart: "so the Joy . . . which the pure in heart have here, is not a joy severed from the Joy of Heaven, but a Joy that begins in us here, and continues, and accompanies us thither, there flowes on."[82] For Donne, as for most Christian writers, the joy had in the present is inchoate (or not fully formed), and its full consummation will be in heaven when we see God there.[83]

Interpreters throughout history were well aware of the tension in Scripture regarding whether God can or cannot be seen. Gregory of Nyssa patiently listed all the verses that propose that God cannot be seen, but then pointed out that Christ would never "set forth what outstrips hope" or exceeds human nature.[84] Christ doesn't make empty promises or fill his listeners with false hope. So if the promise "they will see God" comes true, when and how does it come to fruition?

New Testament scholar Dale Allison sorts the options for what it means to see God into seven categories: christological interpretations, a mystical encounter, a metaphor for insight, in perfected self and neighbor, in present and future experience, and an embodied deity.[85] He points out that the categories aren't mutually exclusive; many writers name more than one, and some (like Augustine and Jeremiah Burroughs) manage to include the first six.[86] I'm indebted to Allison's thorough study. I've also chosen a slightly different way of grouping the many options: three ways of seeing God that pertain both to this life and the next, and three ways of seeing God that pertain only to seeing in the world to come. The first way of seeing now and then is bodily; the second way is spiritual or intellectual. The third is bodily, but of someone else's body (rather than God's body): seeing God in the restored image of God in oneself and one's neighbor. The three ways of seeing God in the eschaton that I'll consider all include a bodily element, whether through seeing the glorious body of the risen Christ, becoming transformed "like the angels," or seeing with the eyes of one's own glorious resurrected body.

---

82. Donne, Sermon 13, in John Donne, *The Sermons of John Donne*, vol. 7, ed. Evelyn M. Simpson and George R. Potter (Berkeley: University of California Press, 1962), 340; see also Boersma, *Seeing God*, 313.

83. Donne, Sermon 13, in Donne, *Sermons*, vol. 7, 341.

84. Gregory of Nyssa, *The Lord's Prayer*, trans. Hilda C. Graef, ACW 18 (Mahwah, NJ: Paulist, 1954), 145.

85. Allison, *Studies in Matthew*, 45–60.

86. Allison, *Studies in Matthew*, 60, 62.

Now (and then): bodily

Controversy over whether God has a body—and thus whether the Trinity could be seen with physical eyes—arose very early in the Christian tradition and continued for several centuries. The Alexandrian theologian Origen (ca. 184–253) was one of the first to launch an attack on the view, apparently held by some, that God is corporeal.[87] In 399 CE, a fellow Alexandrian, the Patriarch Theophilus, wrote an Easter letter also condemning the teaching that God has a bodily human form. This aroused so much ire among Egyptian monks that a group of "angry ascetics" stormed Theophilus's home in protest.[88] Around the same time, the monk Cassian (whom we encountered earlier in this chapter) wrote one of his *Conversations* in part to defend Theophilus against the view of these same Egyptian monks.[89] In the West, Augustine joined his Eastern brother Origen in firmly rejecting the idea that God is in any way corporeal or has "a bodily face." For Augustine, God is seen with the eyes of the heart, not the eyes of the body.[90]

The efforts of Origen, Theophilus, and Augustine demonstrate that belief in God's corporeal nature was relatively widespread in the first few centuries of the church.[91] For example, an early fourth century Christian, perhaps writing in Palestine, used Matt 18:10 and the sixth beatitude to claim that "[God] has shape, and He has every limb primarily and solely for beauty's sake, and not for use. . . . But He has the most beautiful shape on account of man, that the pure in heart may be able to see Him."[92] Similarly, the Eastern Orthodox priest Timothy of Constantinople (d. 523) wrote that the vision of God granted through mystical contemplation is a bodily vision, not simply a spiritual one. For Timothy, the Trinity "is by nature invisible" but "can be seen with the eyes

---

87. Golitzin, "The Vision of God," 288.

88. Golitzin, "The Vision of God," 273. See also Golitzin, "The Demons Suggest," 13–43.

89. Golitzin, "The Vision of God," 286–87. A series of episcopal synods in the East condemned the Messalians of Syro-Mesopotamia for their belief that the Trinity could be seen with physical eyes (Golitzin, "The Demons Suggest," 76).

90. Augustine, Sermon 53.7, in Augustine, *Sermons III (51–94)*, 267–68; see also Augustine, Letter 148.2.9, 148.3.11, in *Augustine: Political Writings*, ed. E. M. Atkins and R. J. Dodaro (Cambridge: Cambridge University Press, 2001), 500–501.

91. The belief that God has a visible body appears to be relatively widespread in Jewish thought (in the OT, in Second Temple texts, and in rabbinic Judaism), as well as in early Christian thought; see Allison, *Studies in Matthew*, 45–48.

92. *Pseudo-Clementine Recognitions* 17.7 (ANF 8:319–20). See also discussion of this text in Allison, *Studies in Matthew*, 46.

of the flesh by those who have come into what they call *apatheia*; and to such people alone occurs the vision seen by them bodily."[93]

This may be a startling idea to encounter, especially for Western Christians. The notion that God is invisible and cannot be seen runs deep. In Eastern Christianity, however, the picture remained more complex for centuries, even to the present day.

In general, the term "beatific vision" refers to the direct and unmediated perception of God enjoyed by those who are in heaven as opposed to the indirect and mediated understanding of God that's possible in the earthly world. For the Western traditions, the vision of God in all its fullness in the afterlife is typically understood as a *perception* rather than visible sight. Even when Thomas Aquinas proposed that in the beatific vision we will see God's very essence (or being), he meant that we will perceive God's being in an intellectual sense, not a bodily one.[94] Like Catholic teaching, Protestant teaching typically emphasizes God as invisible, as in the hymn composed by Free Church of Scotland minister Walter Chalmers Smith: "Immortal, invisible, God only wise, / In light inaccessible hid from our eyes."

Theologians in the Eastern churches, however, hold open the possibility that one particular aspect of God might be visibly seen. The differences between East and West flow from a disagreement over the very nature of God, a disagreement that emerged from early monastic thought especially in Egypt (so above) and erupted again in the early fourteenth century.

By the fourth century, Christian thinkers had already distinguished between the divine persons (*hypostaseis*) and the divine essence (*ousia*). This was a necessary distinction that undergirded the doctrine of the Trinity: the term *hypostasis* indicates the distinct identities of Father, Son, and Spirit; and the divine essence is what is shared in common by all three (thus, one God rather than three).

Almost a thousand years before Palamas, another Gregory (of Nyssa) had posited an additional category: the divine energy or energies (*energeia*). Aristotle used the term *energeia* to mean "an activity or operation characteristic of a living being."[95] Gregory of Nyssa proposed that the pure in heart become able

93. Timothy of Constantinople, *Haeresis* 86.48–49, quoted in Francois P. Viljoen, "Interpreting the *visio Dei* in Matthew 5:8," *HvTSt* 68, no. 1, Art. #905 (January 2012): 2.

94. Thomas Aquinas, *Summa Theologica: Complete English Edition in Five Volumes*, trans. Fathers of the English Dominican Province (Westminster, MD: Christian Classics, 1948), I-II, q.4, a.3; see Boersma, *Seeing God*, 415.

95. Richard B. Steele, "Transfiguring Light: The Moral Beauty of the Christian Life According to Gregory Palamas and Jonathan Edwards," *SVTQ* 52, no. 3–4 (2008): 416.

to see *not* God's essence but rather God's energies—e.g., God's "operations" in the world, such as God's wisdom and goodness.[96] This picks up a thread from the Old Testament theophanies: Moses and Isaiah saw God's glory, not YHWH's essence or being.

Gregory Palamas (1296–1359) adopted and developed this concept of divine energies. For Palamas, God's energies are "all of God's activities taken together"; they are "the workings of God in, on, and through his creatures."[97] Another name for the divine energies might simply be grace: "God Himself, communicating Himself and entering into ineffable union with man."[98] Palamas, then, distinguished between God's essence (or being) and God's energies (or activity in the world)—a distinction rejected by Western Christianity. For Palamas, God's essence cannot be seen, and the divine persons cannot be seen; but the divine energy *can* be seen by those who contemplate the divine reality.[99]

The divine energy is sometimes also referred to as the divine light, or as *uncreated* light, to indicate that it emanates from the eternal God (rather than being a *created* light, or a part of God's creation). In Orthodox belief, the uncreated light is what the disciples Peter, James, and John saw radiating from Jesus at his transfiguration (Matt 17:1–9, Mark 9:2–10, Luke 9:28–36). This belief in the ability to see the divine light is called hesychasm, and hesychasts are the contemplatives who claim to be able to see the divine light. As Alexander Golitzin explains, "local Church councils held in Constantinople a thousand years after Nicea upheld the possibility of the vision of the 'uncreated light' of Mt. Thabor [the site of the transfiguration] and declared this the official teaching of the Byzantine Church."[100]

Although the controversy over God's energies took shape in the early fourteenth century with the writings of Gregory Palamas, hesychasm has its roots in the writings of the Egyptian monks and other Desert Fathers and Mothers of the fourth, fifth, and sixth centuries.[101] Hesychast monks asserted that the

---

96. Gregory of Nyssa, *The Lord's Prayer*, 147.

97. Steele, "Transfiguring Light," 416.

98. Vladimir Lossky, *In the Image and Likeness of God*, ed. John H. Erickson and Thomas E. Bird (Crestwood, NY: St. Vladimir's Seminary Press, 1974, 2001), 59.

99. For more on the distinction, see the lucid explanation in Steele, "Transfiguring Light," 413–17.

100. Golitzin, "The Demons Suggest," 55. Dominican mystic Meister Eckhardt connected the uncreated light ("a light that is uncreated and not capable of creation and . . . is in the soul") to unmediated comprehension of God "as he is in himself" (von Hochheim, *Meister Eckhart*, 198).

101. Steele, "Transfiguring Light," 409.

apatheia achieved through ascetic discipline (i.e., purity of heart) "gradually enabled them to see, in this life, with their bodily eyes, the same divine light" that the disciples witnessed at the transfiguration.[102] What the hesychasts see in this life through contemplation, all believers will behold "on the eighth day," in the future resurrection age.[103]

Seeing the divine light is not the same thing as seeing bright light radiating from the sun. Instead, Palamas wrote that eyes that see the divine light see "in a way superior to that of natural sight. . . . This mysterious light, inaccessible, immaterial, uncreated, deifying, eternal, this radiance of the Divine nature, this glory of the divinity, this beauty of the heavenly kingdom, is at once accessible to sense perception and yet transcends it."[104] The vision of God's energies, then, is neither strictly spiritual nor merely bodily. Symeon the New Theologian likewise summed up the contradiction and mystery of seeing God: in the visions of the pure heart, it is "in a shape without shape and a form without form that he is seen invisibly, and comprehended incomprehensibly."[105] Still, Palamas's understanding of divine light was largely rejected in the West precisely "because it postulated the possibility of seeing God with corporeal eyes."[106]

Of course, the vision of God as mystical contemplation of God is a theme in both Eastern and Western monasticism. Guigo II (a late twelfth-century Carthusian monk) used the sixth beatitude as an example of the process by which monks ascend from earth to heaven in a four-step process (what Guigo called the monk's ladder): study of Scripture, meditation, prayer, and contemplation. The monk's goal is contemplation, or seeing God, "when the mind is in some sort lifted up to God and held above itself, so that it tastes the joys of everlasting sweetness."[107] But for Guigo, unlike Palamas and the hesychasts, the vision of God's glory is purely a spiritual one, not in any way a bodily or physical one.

---

102. Steele, "Transfiguring Light," 412. Ascetic practices enable but do not automatically result in the vision of the divine light (Steele, "Transfiguring Light," 435).

103. Lossky, *In the Image*, 60.

104. Gregory of Palamas, *Triads*, 3.1.22, 80, quoted in Steele, "Transfiguring Light," 418–19.

105. Symeon the New Theologian, *Discourses* 10; quoted in Golitzin, "The Vision of God," 297.

106. F. T. Tomoioagă, "The Vision of Divine Light in Saint Gregory Palamas's Theology," *Acta Theologica* 35, no. 2 (2015): 144, citing Vladimir Lossky, *In the Image*, 62.

107. Guigo II, *The Ladder of Monks: A Letter on the Contemplative Life, and Twelve Meditations*, trans. Edmund Colledge and James Walsh (Garden City, NY: Image Books, 1978), 82.

Now (and then): spiritual/intellectual

With the eyes of the heart

By contrast, for most Western exegetes throughout history (as well as a few Eastern ones), seeing God in this life and in the next is not a bodily vision but a spiritual one. Origen, for example, said that when God appeared to Abraham, Isaac, and Jacob, they saw the LORD with the pure heart, not with their bodily eyes.[108] Similarly, when Jerome noticed that Isaiah claimed to have seen "the LORD sitting on a throne, high and lofty" (Isa 6:1), he concluded that although fleshly eyes are not able to see any member of the Trinity in their divinity, "the eyes of the mind" can see God when God so wills. For Jerome this was true for Isaiah as for Abraham (Gen 18:1–3), Jacob (Gen 32:30), and Ezekiel (Ezek 1:26–27).[109]

Writers frequently referred to seeing God with the eyes of the heart, the mind, or the soul. Origen and Augustine wrote about "the eyes of the heart"; Jerome and Erasmus about "the eyes of the mind." Ephrem the Syrian referred to "the luminous eye" (that is, the inner eye illumined by faith). Jonathan Edwards preferred "the eye of the soul."[110] The phrase, in all its variations, might originate from the letter to the Ephesians, when Paul wrote, "I pray that the God of our Lord Jesus Christ, the Father of glory, may give you a spirit of wisdom and revelation as you come to know him, so that, with the eyes of your heart enlightened, you may know what is the hope to which he has called you" (Eph 1:18).[111] Paul's connection between "the eyes of your heart" and a spirit

108. Origen, *Against Celsus* 6.4 (*ANF* 4:575).

109. Jerome, *Commentary on Isaiah*; *St. Jerome's Translation of Origen's Homilies 1–9 on Isaiah*, trans. Thomas P. Scheck, ACW 68 (Mahwah, NJ: The Newman Press, 2015), 151. See also Ephrem the Syrian, *St. Ephrem's Commentary on Tatian's Diatessaron* 6.1, trans. Carmel McCarthy (Oxford: Oxford University Press, 1993), 109.

110. Origen, *Against Celsus* 6.4 (*ANF* 4:575); Augustine, Sermon 53.6, in Augustine, *Sermons III (51–94)*, 68; Jerome, *Commentary on Isaiah*, 151; Erasmus of Rotterdam, *Paraphrase on Matthew*, vol. 45 of *Collected Works of Erasmus*, trans. Dean Simpson (Toronto: University of Toronto Press, 2008), 89. According to Martin Hogan, Ephrem often used the "luminous eye" to talk about the "pure eye of faith, which can see the divine mystery hidden in what is visible" (Hogan, *The Sermon on the Mount in St. Ephrem's Commentary on the Diatessaron* [Bern: Lang, 1999], 36); see also Sebastian Brock, *The Luminous Eye: The Spiritual World Vision of Saint Ephrem*, Cistercian Studies Series 124 (Kalamazoo, MI: Cistercian Publications, 1992), 71–74. For Jonathan Edwards, see Edwards, *Sermons and Discourses*, 63.

111. A.-M. Carré, *Quand arrive le bonheur: Les Béatitudes*, 2nd ed. (Paris: Les Éditions du Cerf, 1974), 200. Carré cites Eph 1:18 and Eph 5:8.

of wisdom is telling, since this form of seeing is closely associated with understanding or knowing God. As Erasmus wrote, "What the sun is to unclouded eyes, God is to unclouded minds"—that is, to a pure heart.[112]

Recall from earlier in this chapter that the heart is not the seat of the emotions in the biblical imagination. Instead, the heart included the will and the intellect. This explains why ancient writers used the phrases "the eyes of the heart" and "the eyes of the mind" interchangeably. For them, to see God with these nonphysical "eyes" meant to know and understand God. We use sight in this way when we say, "I see your point."[113]

Scripture often uses blindness and seeing, darkness and light, as metaphors for discernment, understanding, or knowledge. Think of the phrase "their eyes were opened," which Scripture uses to indicate Adam and Eve recognizing their nakedness (Gen 3:7; cf. Gen 3:5), Balaam becoming able to see the angel of the LORD blocking his path (Num 22:31), and the two disciples on the road to Emmaus suddenly recognizing Jesus in their midst (Luke 24:31). You're familiar with this idea if you've ever sung, "Open the eyes of my heart, Lord" or "I once was blind, but now I see."[114]

Toward the end of the second century, Clement of Alexandria (ca. 150–215) proposed that the pure in heart are those whose souls have been purified by Christ and who have attained the knowledge of God, which is the vision of God promised in the beatitude.[115] Similarly, Origen (185–254) interpreted the beatitude's promise to see God as the ability to know and understand God with the mind. When the saints reach the heavenly abode, their rational minds will be perfected, so that they will perfectly and purely comprehend God through their purity of heart.[116]

Augustine (354–430), then, had a couple hundred years of precedent before him when he aligned the sixth beatitude with the spiritual gift of understanding, embedding this identification even more deeply in the Western tradition (*De Serm. Dom.* 1.4.11, 2.11.38).[117]

Augustine acknowledged that Scripture sometimes speaks of seeing God "face to face," but he proposed that "the face of God is the knowledge of God."

---

112. Erasmus, *Paraphrase on Matthew*, 89.

113. See the helpful discussion in Allison, *Studies in Matthew*, 54–56.

114. Paul Baloche, "Open the Eyes of My Heart" (CCLI: 2298355); John Newton, "Amazing Grace" (composed ca. 1772).

115. Clement of Alexandria, *Stromata* 4.6 (ANF 2:416); Clement of Alexandria, *Stromata* 5.1 (ANF 2:446).

116. Origen, *De Principiis* 1.1.9 (ANF 4:245); Origen, *De Principiis* 2.11.7 (ANF 4:299).

117. Augustine, *The Lord's Sermon*, 20, 127.

To see God's face means "to know the love of Christ that surpasses knowledge" and to "be filled with the fullness of God" (Eph 3:19).[118] This knowledge is not merely what we would today call "head knowledge," but is the sort of knowing that suffuses one's whole being.

Even former Augustinian Martin Luther found a way to follow this path while reshaping it around his views of God. Luther wrote that the promise to see God means that the person who grasps the gospel and has faith in Christ will immediately see that God is a gracious and friendly Father.[119] Purity of heart, then, means understanding or correctly perceiving God's true character. Some modern interpreters continue to adopt this view, including Clarence Jordan (1912–1969) and Reformed evangelical D. A. Carson (b. 1946).[120]

This line of thought appeared in the East as well. Isaac the Syrian or Isaac of Nineveh (ca. 613–700) discussed the beatitude in relation to the revelations and visions given to those who practice solitude, writing, "Revelation of those things which are apperceived intellectually, is received through purity [of heart]."[121] Much like Origen and Gregory, Isho'dad of Merv (d. ca. 852), bishop of the Assyrian Church of the East, described seeing God as "the light and revelation which the soul receives inwardly by knowledge about Him."[122]

Delight: to know him is to love him

You might recall at this point that "knowing" is sometimes a metaphor in Scripture for intimate knowledge, as in "Adam knew his wife Eve, and she conceived" (Gen 4:1). To construe seeing God as knowing God is not to restrict the vision of God to a purely intellectual exercise, one that leaves the heart or soul untouched. Ethiopian monk Abba Moses (330–405) taught that

---

118. Augustine, Sermon 53.7, 16, in Augustine, *Sermons III (51–94)*, 69, 74. So also fifteenth-century Augustinian monk and mystic Walter Hilton (d. 1396): once cleansed from sin, and fully grasping and believing God's forgiveness, the pure in heart then see God "with the inner eye that is understanding, cleansed and illumined through the grace of the Holy Spirit to see the truth" (Walter Hilton, *The Scale of Perfection*, trans. John P. H. Clark and Rosemary Dorward [Mahwah, NJ: Paulist, 1991], Book 2.11).

119. Luther, *Sermon on the Mount*, 37.

120. Jordan, *Sermon on the Mount*, 34; D. A. Carson, *The Sermon on the Mount: An Evangelical Exposition of Matthew 5–7* (Grand Rapids: Baker Books, 1978), 26.

121. Isaac of Nineveh, *Mystic Treatises* 35.250, p. 168.

122. Viljoen, "Interpreting the *visio Dei*," 4; Allison, *Studies in Matthew*, 55. Allison points out that Dionysius bar Salibi (d. 1171) wrote "almost identical words" (Allison, *Studies in Matthew*, 55n53).

when a person is pure of heart, their soul "attains the true knowledge of God and feeds upon his beauty."[123]

Some 1,300 years after Abba Moses, it was the man known as America's first theologian who made this point even more clearly. Following Augustine (et al.), Congregationalist preacher and revivalist Jonathan Edwards (1703–1758) insisted that "God is a spiritual being, and he is beheld with the understanding."[124] For Edwards, to see God "is to have an immediate and certain understanding of God's glorious excellency and love," as opposed to indirect and mediate knowledge.[125] The sight of God is an intellectual pleasure that is suited to humanity's nature as a creature endowed with reason and understanding.[126] For Jonathan Edwards, the faithful on earth already begin to see God in God's Word and in "the face of Jesus Christ."[127] This is equally true in the eschaton, when seeing God is perfected but remains an intellectual form of sight.

For Edwards as for Augustine, this is no dry, passionless view of the intellect. To see God is to delight in God. Edwards compared the joy of seeing God to swimming in the boundless ocean of God's love: "The love of so glorious a Being is infinitely valuable, and the discoveries of it are capable of ravishing the soul above all other loves."[128]

The restored image of God

The third possibility is an embodied one of sorts, but in a completely different sense from the first option. It draws on the teaching that "God created humankind in his image" (Gen 1:27a). This implies that one may see God (that is, God's image) when looking at a human being—any human being! Of course, the obstacle to this is the doctrine of the fall, which teaches that after the disobedience of Adam and Eve, the image of God in every person became distorted or damaged.

Purity of heart thus becomes understood as the repair or restoration of the original image of God that resides within humanity. As Gregory of Nyssa wrote, "if a man's heart has been purified from every creature and all unruly af-

---

123. Cassian, Conf. 1.8, in "The Conference," 200.
124. Edwards, *Sermons and Discourses*, 63.
125. Edwards, *Sermons and Discourses*, 64.
126. Edwards, *Sermons and Discourses*, 67.
127. Edwards, *Sermons and Discourses*, 74–75.
128. Edwards, *Sermons and Discourses*, 67.

fections, he will see the Image of the Divine Nature in his own beauty."[129] And, we might add, in the beauty of others as well. So wrote Jeremiah Burroughs, who declared that one of the numerous ways the faithful see God during their lifetimes is in the glorious image of God in other Christians. For Burroughs this is not so much because the image of God itself has been restored, but because those with pure hearts become capable of seeing it.[130]

Some interpreters, like Paschasius Radbertus, even speculate that the beatitude is sixth because of God's creation of humanity in God's image on the sixth day.[131] As Anselm reportedly taught, "Purity of heart comes properly in the sixth place, because on the sixth day man was created in the image of God, which image was shrouded by sin, but is formed anew in pure hearts by grace."[132]

A few other writers further the analogy by comparing the image of God to a mirror that has become warped or stained. Becoming pure in heart means, in part, to cleanse and restore that mirror to its original flawless polish. For the writers who draw on this metaphor, seeing God in the restored image of God is possible first in this life, through becoming (more and more) pure in heart, and then in the world to come, when "the likeness to God originally given to Adam and Eve but then obscured through sin will be perfectly regained."[133] For these writers, through spiritual rebirth and God's regenerating grace (to borrow a Calvinist term), the soul becomes clean and bright, "pure as a mirror," and thus reflects the God who looks into the soul.[134] Dietrich Bonhoeffer

129. Gregory of Nyssa, *The Lord's Prayer*, 148. In a comment on Song of Solomon 6:3, Gregory of Nyssa wrote that the soul that is cleansed "of every material concern and thought" becomes "a supremely vivid image of the prototypical Beauty" (*Cant.* 15.439.12–16; Boersma, *Seeing God*, 146). For more on Gregory of Nyssa's connection between the Beatitudes and the image of God, see Rebekah Eklund, "Blessed are the Image-Bearers: Gregory of Nyssa and the Beatitudes," *AThR* 99, no. 4 (Fall 2017): 729–40.

130. Burroughs, *Saints' Happiness*, 165–66. See also Mather, *Sermons Wherein*, Sermon 10.

131. For Radbertus, the *imago Dei* is restored in the heart of the believer when it is freed from all the vices and the bonds of this world (Stoll, *De Virtute*, 188–89).

132. Quoted in Aquinas's *Catena* as "*Glossa Ordinaria*" (*Gloss.*), ascribed in the marginal notes of J. H. Newman to Anselm, in Thomas Aquinas, *St. Matthew*, vol. 1 of *Catena Aurea: A Commentary on the Four Gospels Collected out of the Works of the Fathers*, trans. John Henry Newman (London: The Saint Austin Press, 1999), 153.

133. Allison, *Studies in Matthew*, 58.

134. E.g., Evagrius Ponticus (John Eudes Bamberger, introduction to Evagrius Ponticus, *The Praktikos*, xci); Symeon the New Theologian, Sermon 31.7 in *Discourses*, 332; Jacques Bénigne Bossuet, *The Sermon on the Mount*, trans. F. M. Capes (Longmans, Green: 1900), 22; Alfred G. Mortimer, *The Laws of Happiness; or, The Beatitudes as Teaching Our Duty to God, Self, and Neighbor* (E. and J. B. Young, 1888), 71–72, 77.

renarrated in a Christological key: those who will see God are those "whose hearts have become a reflection of the image of Jesus Christ."[135]

Earlier, in the chapter on the merciful, we saw that some interpreters reversed the beatitude's equation, such that those who have been shown mercy are those who show mercy in turn. The same logic is at work in an interesting strand of interpretation that popped up mostly among the Puritans. For them, those who see God shall become perfectly pure in heart. This conclusion depends, at least in part, on the connection between purity of heart and the restored image of God.

Puritan Nonconformist Thomas Watson wrote in 1660 that God's purity is "the pattern and prototype of all holiness." Because humanity was created in God's image, they have a "created purity" that shares in God's holiness.[136] In the eschaton, the vision of God is "a transforming sight. . . . [T]he saints by beholding the brightness of God's glory shall have a tincture of that glory upon them."[137] This actually borrowed a more medieval understanding of light as a substance that travels from the eye to the object being seen and then returns physically to the eye of the observer.[138] (A modern physicist might appreciate that explanation!) By looking at something (in this case, God), one is changed by that thing.

Jeremiah Burroughs and John Trapp appealed to 2 Cor 3:18 to make the same case: "And all of us, with unveiled faces, seeing the glory of the Lord as though reflected in a mirror, are being transformed into the same image from one degree of glory to another; for this comes from the Lord, the Spirit" (2 Cor 3:18). Burroughs also quoted from 1 John: "we will be like him, for we will see him as he is" (1 John 3:2).[139] For Burroughs, this indicates the connection between seeing and becoming like him. To see is not only to perceive but to be transformed by that sight. As American Puritan Jonathan Edwards mused, the glimpses of God that people get in this life transform them in part into the

---

135. Bonhoeffer, *Cost of Discipleship*, 112.

136. Watson, *The Beatitudes*, 185–86.

137. Watson, *The Beatitudes*, 215.

138. Jennifer Sliwka, "Illusive and elusive: The (im)possibility of seeing in Michael Simpson's flat surface paintings" (paper presented at the Theology, Modernity, and Visual Arts colloquium, Art Institute of Chicago, May 23, 2019). Sliwka cites Suzannah Biernoff, *Sight and Embodiment in the Middle Ages* (Basingstoke: Palgrave Macmillan, 2002), 97; and Margaret R. Miles, *Image as Insight: Visual Understanding in Western Christianity and Secular Culture* (Boston: Beacon Press, 1986), 96.

139. Burroughs, *Saints' Happiness*, 168; John Trapp, *Commentary or Exposition on All the Books of the NT* (London: Richard D. Dickinson, 1865), 49, quoted in Allison, *Studies in Matthew*, 58.

image of God's glory, but the perfect sight of God in the eschaton—the beatific vision—"will transform them perfectly."[140]

Invisible God, visible Son

The incarnation further complicates the question of what it means to see God. In John's Gospel, Jesus claims, "Whoever has seen me has seen the Father" (John 14:9). Some readers take their cue from this verse and explain that the beatitude's promise means seeing God incarnate in the person of Jesus of Nazareth.[141] To explain why only the pure in heart are able to see God (whereas everyone could see Jesus), these interpreters often suggest that only those with pure hearts could see God in Jesus, or could recognize Jesus as the Messiah during his lifetime.[142] (For some, this also explains why not everyone could recognize Jesus after his resurrection, until their eyes—i.e., their eyes of faith—were opened.)

Roman scholar Novatian (ca. 200–258) pointed out that Christ would not have promised seeing God as a *future* reward if people had already seen the Father when they saw the Son.[143] So another possibility is that the beatitude's promise refers to seeing Jesus at his Second Coming as the risen and exalted Lord.[144] This isn't true for Novatian, who argued that the promise is to see the Father, not the Son. (Novatian took seeing in a spiritual sense, not a bodily one.) For some, though, the promise to see God means the ability to

---

140. Edwards, *Sermons and Discourses*, 71.

141. E.g., John Burr, *The Crown of Character: A Study of the Beatitudes of Our Lord* (James Clarke & Co., 1932), 94. For Robert Harris, we see God most clearly in the Son (Heb 1:3) and then also in the Word (Harris, *Way to True Happiness*, 285). A.-M. Carré pointed also to Matt 13:16—"la gloire de Dieu sur la face d'un homme [the glory of God in the face of a man]" (Carré, *Quand arrive*, 202).

142. So Carré, *Quand arrive*, 202; Origen, *Homilies on Luke*, trans. Joseph T. Lienhard, FC 49 (Washington, DC: Catholic University of America Press, 2009), 15.

143. Novatian, *Treatise Concerning the Trinity* 28 (*ANF* 5:639–40).

144. Robert H. Gundry, *Matthew: A Commentary on His Handbook for a Mixed Church under Persecution*, 2nd ed. (Grand Rapids: Eerdmans, 1995), 71; David P. Scaer, *The Sermon on the Mount: The Church's First Statement of the Gospel* (St. Louis, MO: Concordia, 2000), 88; Adolf Schlatter, *Der Evangelist Matthäus: Seine Sprache, sein Ziel, seine Selbständigkeit* (Stuttgart: Calwer Verlag, 1959), 139. I owe these citations to Allison, *Studies in Matthew*, 49n27. Allison also notes that the Acts of Thomas appears to equate seeing God with seeing Jesus, in its modified version of the third beatitude: "Blessed are you meek, because you will see the face of the Lord"—with "the Lord" in the next line named as Jesus (Acts of Thomas 94; quoted in Allison, *Studies in Matthew*, 49n27).

see Christ in his true identity, even at the eschaton or in the heavenly realm. In Augustine's treatise *On the Trinity*, at the last judgment the wicked will only see Christ as the Son of Man, not Christ in his equality with the Father (*De Trin.* 1.12.28, 30; 8.4.6–7).[145]

For other readers, like Gregory Palamas, the transfiguration provides the key to unlock the beatitude's promise. What exactly did the disciples see when they saw Jesus "transfigured" (Greek *metamorphoō*), when "his face shone like the sun, and his clothes became dazzling white" (Matt 17:2)? This could be a spiritual seeing: they recognized Jesus as the glorious Son of Man (see Matt 16:28, Dan 7:13–14), or as the Son of God. Origen of Alexandria (185–254) proposed that Christ only took Peter, James, and John with him onto the mountain because only those three had the spiritual capacity at the time to see his glory, or the brilliance of his divinity.[146] For Origen, seeing Christ's glory was not a bodily vision but was "a spiritual apprehension of Christ, for which spiritual vision is required."[147]

Others see the transfiguration as indicating a more literal, visual sight of God's glory. Did the disciples *see* the second person of the Trinity? Was the radiance of God visible, as the glory of God sometimes manifested visibly among Israel (Exod 40:34)?[148] As we've already seen, many Orthodox writers believed that the disciples visibly saw the uncreated, divine light emanating from Jesus. These two ways of understanding the transfiguration influence interpretations of the beatitude. Whatever the disciples saw in Jesus's radiance on Mt. Tabor corresponds to what the faithful will see in the heavenly vision of God.

---

145. Augustine, *The Trinity*, trans. Stephen McKenna, FC 45 (Washington, DC: Catholic University of America Press, 1963), 42–43, 46, 250–52. Matthew 5:8 (alongside Phil 2:5–7 and 1 Cor 15:24–28) was a key part of Augustine's argument against the anti-Nicene Homoians (those who argued that the Son is inferior to the Father because the Son is visible, whereas God is invisible). For Augustine, all the Persons of the Trinity, including the Son (in his divinity), can only be seen at the end-time (Michael René Barnes, "The Visible Christ and the Invisible Trinity: Mt. 5:8 in Augustine's Trinitarian Theology of 400," *Modern Theology* 19, no. 3 [July 2003]: 331–32).

146. Origen, *Against Celsus* 2.64 (*ANF* 4:457); Corine B. Milad, "Incarnation and Transfiguration: Origen's Theology of Descent," *JTI* 12, no. 2 (2018): 207–8. Origen also believed that Christ was capable of changing his form in order to accommodate the capacity of his viewers (Milad, "Incarnation and Transfiguration," 207).

147. Milad, "Incarnation and Transfiguration," 211.

148. Golitzin proposes that "Christ was himself the Glory that Moses had glimpsed" on Mt. Sinai, drawing from 1 Cor 2:8 and 2 Cor 3:7–4:6 (Golitzin, "The Vision of God," 281; see also Golitzin, "The Demons Suggest," 58). For a comparison of Aquinas and Gregory of Palamas on the transfiguration and the vision of God, see Boersma, *Seeing God*, 129–62.

Once again it was Puritan writers who overlapped with older Orthodox thought. Like Origen, Jonathan Edwards insisted that the vision of God's glory is primarily a spiritual or intellectual one. He wrote that the disciples present at the transfiguration "beheld a wonderful, outward glory in Christ's body, an inexpressible beauty in his countenance, but that outward glory and beauty delighted them principally as it was an expression or signification of the divine excellencies of his mind." Similarly, the saints in heaven see the "outward glory" of the resurrected body of Christ, which is an expression of God's spiritual glory, his divine holiness.[149] He concluded, "The beauty of [the risen] Christ's body that will be beheld with bodily eyes [in heaven] will be ravishing and delighting chiefly as it will express his spiritual glories."[150] Edwards's predecessor Thomas Watson agreed: the vision of God in glory is both intellectual (seeing God with the eyes of the mind) and material ("we shall with bodily eyes behold Jesus Christ, through whom the glory of God, his wisdom, holiness, and mercy, shall shine forth to the soul").[151]

Two options remain. Both are about the possibility of seeing God the Father—and not only the risen Christ—in the heavenly realm. Christian writers speculate about ways in which that might become possible in the eschaton. In other words, what might it be about the afterlife, or the next age, that enables the vision of God with bodily eyes?

Like the angels

This strand of thought takes its cue from two sayings of Jesus. In the first, Jesus instructs his disciples, "Take care that you do not despise one of these little ones; for, I tell you, in heaven their angels continually see the face of my Father in heaven" (Matt 18:10). In the second, Jesus teaches that "in the resurrection they neither marry nor are given in marriage, but are like angels in heaven" (Matt 22:30). Interpreters use the second saying as evidence that the faithful become like the angels, and the first saying as evidence that the angels in

149. Edwards, *Sermons and Discourses*, 62–63.

150. Edwards, *Sermons and Discourses*, 62–63. For a comparison of Edwards and Gregory of Palamas, see Steele, "Transfiguring Light," 403–5, 431–39; see also Boersma, *Seeing God*, 354–55, 398–401.

151. Watson, *The Beatitudes*, 214.

heaven see God's face. When placed together, these texts indicate (for some) that the pure in heart become like the angels in heaven and that's why they're able to see God.[152]

The eyes of the resurrected body

Another more common proposal derives from the Christian teaching of the resurrection of the body. When Jesus rose from the dead, the Gospels insist that he did so in his earthly body, nail holes and all; but that it was also somehow a transformed body, capable of disappearing and appearing at will (Luke 24:31, 36; John 20:19, 26). The apostle Paul wrestled mightily with this conundrum in 1 Corinthians 15. What will the resurrection body be like? Whatever it's like, the foundational Christian belief that the next age will include raised bodies and not only souls leads some Christian writers to speculate about the capacities of those resurrected eyes.

In the fourth century, Hilary of Poitiers (ca. 310–367) and Chromatius of Aquileia (d. ca. 406) wrote that the pure in heart are enabled to see God in the next life once they are "changed into immortality" (1 Cor 15:53) at the resurrection and can behold God with their transformed, immortal eyes.[153] Around the same time, Augustine (354–430) insisted that the resurrected saints will "see God *in* the body," but he admitted that since he didn't know exactly what kind of bodies the saints will have, it's not easy to say whether seeing will be the same sense as it is on earth.[154]

Although Augustine suggested that the saints won't actually need bodily eyes in order to see God (that is, to see God in a spiritual sense), he also

152. E.g., Clement of Alexandria, *Exhortation to the Heathens* 11 (ANF 2:202–4). Pseudo-Clementine wrote that people cannot see God "as long as they are men" because "God is seen by the mind, not by the body"; at the resurrection of the dead, people are made like the angels (Matt 22:30) and therefore become able to see God (*Pseudo-Clementine Recognitions* 3.30 [ANF 8:122]). Evagrius Ponticus: "By true prayer a monk becomes another angel [*isangelos*; or: like an angel, cf. Luke 20:36], for he ardently longs to see the face of the Father in heaven" (*Chapters on Prayer* 113). Augustine quoted Matt 18:10 alongside 1 Cor 13:12 and 1 John 3:2 to defend the idea that in the city of God, in our immortal bodies, we shall see as the angels see (Augustine, *City of God* 22.29, trans. Henry Bettenson [New York: Penguin Books, 1972, 2003], 1082). For others, see Viljoen, "Interpreting the visio Dei," 6, and Allison, Studies in Matthew, 48n23.

153. Hilary of Poitiers, *Commentary on Matthew* 4.7, trans. D. H. Williams, FC 125 (Washington, DC: Catholic University of America, 2012), 61; Chromatius of Aquileia, *Sermons and Tractates on Matthew*, Tractatus 17.6.4–5.

154. Augustine, *City of God* 22.29, p. 1082.

wondered if the risen faithful might also have the ability to see God with their perfected physical eyes, that is, "to see the immaterial."[155] Augustine proposed that risen bodies will likely be capable of this feat: "in the future life, wherever we turn the spiritual eyes of our bodies we shall discern, by means of our bodies, the incorporeal God directing the whole universe."[156]

—

What to make of this confusion of options? The possibility of seeing Christ's resurrected body at the eschaton rightly captures the Gospels' insistence that Jesus was raised not as a ghost but in the same body with which he lived—and Paul's insistence that the same will be true for us as well. As for the possibility of seeing God (whether Father or Spirit or the Trinity as a whole) in some bodily or visual sense, perhaps I'm too much of a Westerner to wrap my head around that one. When Scripture says that God is invisible (Col 1:15, 1 Tim 1:17, Heb 11:27), I'm inclined to follow that lead.

More importantly, the promise of the beatitude does not exhort us (primarily) toward seeking ecstatic experiences of God. For most of us, the vision of God is not to be had through mystical contemplation. Instead, it's to be had in the faces of our neighbors. Catherine of Siena, the first woman declared to be a "Doctor" of the church, once wrote: "The soul who comes to know herself in you finds her greatness wherever she turns, even in the tiniest things, in people and in all created things."[157]

What Catherine grasped is what Scripture implies: that the most promising ways we can see God in this life are through seeing God's image in every human being we encounter (Gen 1:26–27), and through seeing Jesus in the poor (Matt 25:31–46). There's an old monastic tradition of welcoming every guest at the door as if that person is Christ. It takes practice to see people this

155. Augustine, *City of God* 22.29, p. 1084.

156. Augustine, *City of God* 22.29, pp. 1086–87. For similar reflections, see also Augustine, Letter 148.4.16 in *Augustine: Political Writings*, 503. For an exploration of Augustine's view of the vision of God, see Roland J. Teske, "St. Augustine and the Vision of God," in *Augustine: Mystic and Mystagogue*, ed. Joseph C. Schnaubelt, Frederick van Fleteren, and Joseph Reino (New York: Lang, 1994), 207–308. John Donne also discussed Augustine's views in Donne, Sermon 13 in *Sermons*, vol. 7, 342–46. John Burr writes that God may be seen in God's creation (Burr, *Crown of Character*, 89), but this appears to be a minority view; perhaps the tradition shies away from this claim to avoid pantheism.

157. Catherine of Siena, "Your Greatness is Everywhere," in *Passion for the Truth; Compassion for Humanity*, ed. Mary O'Driscoll (New York: New City Press, 2008), 72.

way, especially if the guests at the door are strangers, or are homeless, or are people we were raised to be suspicious of. We have to dust off our hearts and uncloud our minds. It takes a pure heart to look at every person we encounter every day and see the glory and beauty of God's image flung forth. We *will* see God—if only we are pure enough to know where to look.

Conclusion

Reading sermon after sermon on what it might be like to see God taught me how deeply this hope is embedded in the Christian imagination. For all these theologians and preachers, seeing God will be an astonishing experience that overwhelms the viewer's whole self. The vision of God conjures up a holy fear, but only the kind of "fear" that in Scripture connotes reverential, trembling awe in the presence of divine holiness. Writers for two centuries have fumbled to convey the breathtaking beauty in store for the pure in heart. Most of all, the vision of God is about joy.

The vision of God is the *telos*—the ultimate end and true purpose—of human existence. To see God is for the self finally to come to rest, cleansed and made whole. As Edwards wrote, "There is no darkness can bear such powerful light."[158]

158. Edwards, *Sermons and Discourses*, 71.

9

The Heart of God

The Peacemakers

Blessed are the peacemakers, for they will be called children of God (Matt 5:9).

Israel's great king Solomon was known as a man of peace. Even his name means peace, since the Hebrew word for peace is *shalom* (you can see how *Solomon* is related to *shalom*). For the book of Chronicles, this is the reason why he, and not his father David, built the LORD's temple in Jerusalem. God informed David, the great warrior-king, that he has too much blood on his hands to build God's house (1 Chron 22:8, 28:3). David's son Solomon would build it instead. It's no surprise, then, that medieval Irish commentaries usually name Solomon as the exemplar of the seventh beatitude.[1] Not only did he bring peace to Israel, he built the temple that symbolized and ritually enacted peace between Israel and God. When Jesus is called the Son of David, this could suggest that he's like David's son Solomon—the man of *shalom*.

Franciscan Sister Rosemary Lynch (1917–2011) was neither as famous nor as powerful as Solomon. She moved to Las Vegas, Nevada, in the late 1970s and lived there until her death. In Las Vegas, she founded an organization to promote nonviolence called Pace e Bene (Italian for "peace and good"). Sister Rosemary pursued peace on a national (and international) scale by organizing nonviolent protests against nuclear weapons testing in Nevada. But she was also a peacemaker on a smaller scale when she befriended many of the people working at the test site and developed genuinely warm friendships with them.[2]

---

1. Brigitta Stoll, *De Virtute in Virtutem: zur Auslegungs- und Wirkungsgeschichte der Bergpredigt in Kommentaren, Predigten und hagiographischer Literatur von der Merowingerzeit bis um 1200* (Tübingen: Mohr Siebeck, 1988), 181.

2. Jim Forest, *The Ladder of the Beatitudes* (Maryknoll, NY: Orbis Books, 1999), 119–25.

When Jesus blesses peacemakers like Solomon and Sister Rosemary, he uses the word *eirēnē*, the Greek translation of the Hebrew *shalom*. *Shalom* means not only absence of conflict but also harmony and wholeness. Where there is *shalom*, there is also justice (Ps 72:1–7; Ps 85:10). *Shalom* is a sign of God's reign both now and in the new age, as in Isaiah's peaceable kingdom, where the wolf lives with the lamb and nobody hurts or destroys anybody else (Isa 11:6–9). To be peacemakers, then, means to actively participate in ushering in the world of *shalom*, making whole whatever is broken.

Indeed, for ancient writers peacemaking leaves nothing untouched by God's harmony, a conviction that produced the most creative application of the beatitude, not to warring people but to warring paragraphs. Origen (ca. 184–253) wrote that a peacemaker is (among other things) one who sees "abundance of peace in all the Scriptures, even in those which seem to be at conflict" and who is able to demonstrate "their concord and peace."[3] In Origen's view, God is the ultimate author of all Scripture, which means that no Scripture passages can genuinely contradict one another. Origen is keenly aware that some biblical texts are in tension with one another. Peacemakers have the ability to "show how texts that appear contradictory are in fact in harmony with each other."[4] This interpretation, creative as it was, never became popular. But it shows just how comprehensive Origen (and others) understood peacemaking to be. It brings to harmony anything in discord—even texts!

For most of our interpreters throughout history, one form of peace must come first, and that is peace with God. Let's call that the vertical dimension of peacemaking—establishing peace between human beings and God. The remaining dimensions are horizontal—peace between people, where first we find a repeated emphasis on making peace within the self. A violent or agitated person has no chance of making peace with or among others. Then there is peace with those near (neighbors, family, friends) and with those far off (nations). In between the two lies the church—and many of our past interpreters

---

3. Origen, *Commentary on the Gospel of Matthew* 2 (ANF 9:413).

4. Stephen Westerholm and Martin Westerholm, *Reading Sacred Scripture: Voices from the History of Biblical Interpretation* (Grand Rapids: Eerdmans, 2016), 76. Echoing Origen, Cyril of Alexandria (ca. 376–444) wrote, "The peacemaker is the one who makes harmony known [in what is] to others an apparent war in the Scriptures—old with new, things pertaining to the law with things pertaining to the prophets, gospels with gospels" (Cyril of Alexandria, Frag. 38 on Matt 5:9, in *Lukas-Kommentare aus der griechischen Kirche*, ed. Joseph Reuss [Berlin: Akademie-Verlag, 1984], 164; author's translation).

considered the pressing problem of making peace among conflicted brothers and sisters, or among fractured factions of the universal church.

Peace at an individual or small-community level tends to be relatively straightforward, calling forth a host of practical advice. The more challenging and contentious cases concern peace in the political sphere. For centuries the beatitude was rarely applied at this broader level—until a feisty Augustinian monk came along. From the twentieth century onward, this beatitude is frequently invoked to plead for world peace, especially in times of war.

Vertical dimension: peace with God

The New Testament itself uses "peace" to describe God's salvation. As Paul wrote to the Christians in Rome, justification by faith means peace with God (Rom 5:1). Perhaps the most frequently quoted verse in the beatitude's history is also Paul's: "through [Christ] God was pleased to reconcile to himself all things, whether on earth or in heaven, by making peace through the blood of his cross" (Col 1:20). Peacemaking is God's work, achieved through Christ. The first task of the (human) peacemaker, then, is to reconcile with God, to receive God's gift of peace herself.

Peacemakers also facilitate this divine work by sharing the gospel and inviting others into the sphere of God's peace. For this reason, some writers (like Theophylact of Ochrid) describe the peacemakers as missionaries, or (like Rupert of Deutz) as the apostles, who brought God's peace to the nations.[5] Others viewed the peacemakers as Christians who seek to reconcile others with God, whether through preaching, missionary work, or individual witness.

Most interpreters throughout history, until recently, assumed that peace with God is prior to all other forms of peacemaking. Only the person at peace with God can treat her fellow humans peaceably, or can broker peace between his neighbors. This approach takes a variety of forms; the most common often draws its inspiration from Paul's claim that Christ "is our peace; in his flesh he has made both [Jews and gentiles] into one and has broken down the dividing wall, that is, the hostility between us" (Eph 2:14).

For writers like A.-M. Carré, this indicates that only the love of Christ can destroy the dividing walls of hostility between people. The peacemak-

---

5. For Rupert of Deutz, see Stoll, *De Virtute*, 196; for Theophylact, see Dale C. Allison Jr., *The Sermon on the Mount: Inspiring the Moral Imagination* (New York: Crossroad, 1999), 54.

er's service of love is "to solve, at their very source . . . the conflicts that tear apart humanity," which necessarily means transforming the heart with Christ's boundary-breaking power.[6] Likewise evangelist Billy Graham's view that peacemakers must first reconcile to God springs from his conviction that Christ has the power to transform people and break down the barriers that divide them.[7]

Joseph Ratzinger (Pope Benedict XVI) specifically connects Christianity with peaceable societies: "When men lose sight of God, peace disintegrates and violence proliferates to a formerly unimaginable degree of cruelty."[8] Like Graham and Carré, Ratzinger's view assumes God's power to bring peace into human hearts, but it's also underwritten by a broader anxiety over the secularization of Europe. His assumption that Christianity stabilizes society is complicated by the acknowledgement that Christianity itself has authorized violence and destabilized societies, whether by turning against other Christians or against non-Christians such as Muslims. So the assumption that Christians are always (or only) peacemakers is hard to sustain.

To be sure, authors like Graham, Carré, and Ratzinger build on the central Christian teaching that Christ pours a peace that surpasses understanding into the hearts of those who let him in (Phil 4:7). They likewise rely on an insight we see repeatedly throughout reflections on the beatitude—that out of the overflow of the heart the mouth speaks, the mind discerns, and the body acts (to extend Matt 12:34). When more recent authors point to non-Christian peacemakers like Gandhi, the Dalai Lama, and Kofi Annan,[9] they provide a needed reminder that people outside the church have been powerful peacemakers.

---

6. A.-M. Carré, *Quand arrive le bonheur: Les Béatitudes*, 2nd ed. (Paris: Les Éditions du Cerf, 1974), 134. The original quotation is "pour résoudre, à leur source même . . . les conflits qui déchirent l'humanité."

7. Billy Graham, *The Secret of Happiness: Jesus' Teaching on Happiness as Expressed in the Beatitudes* (Garden City, NY: Doubleday, 1955), 88; so also Ellen Gould White, *Thoughts from the Mount of Blessing* (Mountain View, CA: Pacific Press Publishing Association, 1900, 1928), 43; Segundo Galilea, *The Beatitudes: To Evangelize as Jesus Did*, trans. Robert R. Barr (Maryknoll, NY: Orbis Books, 1984), 76; Sherwood E. Wirt, *Magnificent Promise: A Fresh View of the Beatitudes from the Cross* (Chicago: Moody Press, 1964), 96.

8. Joseph Ratzinger (Pope Benedict XVI), *Jesus of Nazareth: From the Baptism in the Jordan to the Transfiguration*, trans. Adrian J. Walker (New York: Doubleday, 2007), 85.

9. E.g., John Dear, *Beatitudes of Peace: Meditations on the Beatitudes, Peacemaking and the Spiritual Life* (New London, CT: Twenty-Third Publications, 2016), 9–12, 83–87.

Horizontal dimensions: peace with others

Next are the horizontal dimensions: making peace with others both near and far, both individual and corporate. We'll begin with the smallest inner circle and expand outward.

Peace with self

This beatitude has action written into it: blessed are the peace-*makers*, not the peace-*filled*. Still, many argue that you can't make peace with others if you're not first at peace with yourself. Only the peaceful can make peace. But how does one become peaceful?

For many premodern interpreters, one became peaceful by practicing all the previous beatitudes. For Ambrose, for example, the justice of the fourth beatitude leads naturally to the mercy of the fifth (since justice must be balanced with mercy, and merciful acts flow out of a desire to see justice done), and mercy requires purity of heart (the sixth) to be practiced rightly. Finally, purity of heart is needed for peacemaking: "How can you purify the hearts of others unless you have first purified your own?" (*Comm. Luke* 5.57–8).[10] Thomas Aquinas saw the same chain but understood peace as the *effect* of all the preceding beatitudes: from humility, repentance, restraint, justice, mercy, and purity naturally flow peace.[11] Meekness seems especially appropriate, when it's regarded as the restraint of anger. It's easy to see how someone who easily loses their temper would struggle to be a peacemaker either with another person, or with another nation, if that person has the power to declare war or sign an armistice.

10. Ambrose of Milan, *Commentary of Saint Ambrose on the Gospel According to Saint Luke*, trans. Íde M. Ní Riain (Dublin: Halcyon, 2001), 136. See also D. Martyn Lloyd-Jones, *Studies in the Sermon on the Mount*, vol. 1 (Grand Rapids: Eerdmans, 1960), 117–24.

11. Thomas Aquinas, *Commentary on the Gospel of Matthew, Chapters 1–12*, ed. The Aquinas Institute, trans. Jeremy Holmes and Beth Mortensen, Biblical Commentaries 33 (Lander, WY: The Aquinas Institute for the Study of Sacred Doctrine, 2013), C.5 L.2.437. See also Symeon the New Theologian, Sermon 2.11 in *The Discourses*, trans. C. J. deCatanzaro (New York: Paulist, 1980), 55. Bernard of Clairvaux wrote that the previous five beatitudes reconcile man [sic] to himself and to his neighbors, so that he now can be reconciled to God (Bernard of Clairvaux, "First Sermon for the Feast of All Saints. On the Eight Beatitudes," in *St. Bernard's Sermons for the Seasons and Principal Festivals of the Year*, vol. 3 [Westminster, MD: Carroll, 1950], 350). So also Lily M. Gyldenvand, *Invitation to Joy* (Minneapolis: Augsburg, 1969), 86–87.

For others, the book of James provides the key: "our wisdom is to be 'first pure, then peaceful'" (Jas 3:17). So wrote Charles Spurgeon.[12] For him and for many others, James teaches that purity of heart is necessary for peacemaking, since "purity of heart disposes one to peace, both personally and in making peace for others."[13] The theme that peacemakers must first make peace in their own hearts occurs repeatedly among patristic thinkers (including Gregory of Nyssa, Clement of Alexandria, Jerome, and Ambrose of Milan) as well as Reformation-era writers (Erasmus, Luther).[14] Simon Tugwell distills their position: "True peace in ourselves is a product of purity of heart, and without true peace in ourselves we stand little chance of being peacemakers for anyone else."[15]

This approach assigns a high value to character rather than simply actions, a view shared by teachings elsewhere in the Sermon on the Mount (Matt 5:21–24). Readers repeatedly see peacemaking as both an attitude and an action, an inner stance that flows into an outward practice.

The other horizontal dimensions (concerning peace with others) embrace relationships small and large, from families to nations. Gregory of Nyssa captured this generous scope, writing that peacemaking is the complete annihilation of anything foreign to goodness; it means "to cast out hatred and

12. Charles Spurgeon, *Morning and Evening*, ed. Roy Clarke (Nashville: Nelson, 1994), March 17, evening.

13. Cornelius à Lapide, *The Holy Gospel According to Saint Matthew*, vol. 1 of *The Great Commentary of Cornelius à Lapide*, trans. Thomas W. Mossman, rev. ed. (Fitzwilliam, NH: Loreto, 2008), 228. See also Jeremiah Burroughs, *The Saints' Happiness* (Edinburgh: James Nichol, 1867; Soli Deo Gloria, 1988, 1992), 176; Francis Greenwood Peabody, "The Peace-Makers," *HTR* 12, no. 1 (January 1919): 55–56, 66.

14. So Clement of Alexandria, *Stromata* 4.6 (*ANF* 2:416). See also Gregory of Nyssa, *The Lord's Prayer; The Beatitudes*, trans. Hilda C. Graef, ACW 18 (Mahwah, NJ: Paulist, 1954), 165; Jerome, *Commentary on Matthew*, trans. Thomas P. Scheck, FC 117 (Washington, DC: Catholic University of America, 2008), 76; Ambrose of Milan, quoted in Thomas Aquinas, *St. Matthew*, vol. 1 of *Catena Aurea: A Commentary on the Four Gospels Collected out of the Works of the Fathers*, trans. John Henry Newman (London: The Saint Austin Press, 1999), 154; Erasmus of Rotterdam, *Paraphrase on Matthew*, vol. 45 of *Collected Works of Erasmus*, trans. Dean Simpson (Toronto: University of Toronto Press, 2008), 89; Martin Luther, *The Sermon on the Mount*, vol. 21 of *Luther's Works*, ed. Jaroslav Pelikan (St. Louis: Concordia, 1956), 39.

15. Simon Tugwell, *The Beatitudes: Soundings in Christian Traditions* (Springfield, IL: Templegate, 1980), 111, 156n1. See also Alfred G. Mortimer, *The Laws of Happiness; or, The Beatitudes as Teaching Our Duty to God, Self, and Neighbor* (E. and J. B. Young, 1888), 89–91.

abolish war, to exterminate envy and banish strife, to take away hypocrisy and extinguish from within resentment of injuries smouldering in the heart."[16]

Peace with those near: family and friends

Writers typically focus on the *making* part of peacemaking, rather than the *peace* part. That is, rather than mulling over what peace is, they dwell on how to resolve conflict. Nowhere is this more evident than in instructions on peacemaking among the near. Reflecting on making peace with family members, friends, and neighbors gives rise to a flurry of practical advice.

Be willing to forget things done against you.[17] Never cast someone's error "in their teeth."[18] Refuse to pass along gossip. If you do hear malicious gossip about a neighbor, seek to give it the best possible interpretation, or conceal it from others.[19] "Make use of the golden talent of silence."[20] If you're in the wrong, confess it instantly to the person you wronged.[21] Don't start a debate when your spouse is in a bad mood. Don't trust your own judgment while you're angry.[22] If you're a lawyer, refuse to plead "in an ill cause."[23]

Be willing to sacrifice in order to make peace. Yield first if you're in a quarrel. Do not return evil for evil, but return good for evil (Rom 12:17, 21; 1 Peter 3:9). The minister Robert Henley used the analogy of the "peace" created when a section of wood is placed between two pieces of metal to prevent heat from traveling between them; peacemakers are "'non-conductors' of bitterness, and wrath, and anger, and clamour, and evil-speaking, and all malice."[24]

Matthew's readers sometimes notice that two groups of people are called the children of God: the peacemakers (Matt 5:9) and people who love their

16. Gregory of Nyssa, *The Lord's Prayer*, 164.

17. Hilary of Poitiers, *Commentary on Matthew* 4.8, trans. D. H. Williams, FC 125 (Washington, DC: Catholic University of America, 2012), 62.

18. Hendrik Niclaes, *The first exhortation of H. N. to his children, and to the Family of Love: Likewise H. N. upon the Beatitudes, and the Seven Deadly Sins* (London: For Giles Calvert, 1656), 214.

19. Luther, *Sermon on the Mount*, 42. The prohibition against slander is found in many postReformation authors.

20. Robert Henley, *Saintliness: A Course of Sermons on the Beatitudes; Preached at St. Mary's Church, Putney* (London; Oxford: Rivingtons, 1864), 80.

21. Henley, *Saintliness*, 80.

22. Burroughs, *Saints' Happiness*, 182–87.

23. James Buck, *A Treatise of the Beatitudes, or, Christ's Happy Men* (London: printed by B. A. and T. F. for Iohn Clark, and Wil. Cooke, 1637), 275.

24. Henley, *Saintliness*, 78.

enemies (Matt 5:44). For some, then, being a peacemaker refers especially to making peace with enemies. The command not to return evil for evil links easily to instructions to make peace with enemies. Treat your enemies fairly and even lovingly. If you see a hindrance coming toward your enemy, you should warn him.[25] Paul summed up the spirit of much of the advice in this category: "If it is possible, so far as it depends on you, live peaceably with all" (Rom 12:18).

Peace among Christians

Paul gave advice about living harmoniously with enemies and outsiders, but he also highly valued peaceable relations within the church, among brothers and sisters in Christ. He pleaded for his congregations to be like-minded and unselfish, and to avoid quarrelling (1 Cor 1:10–11; Phil 2:1–4). He even intervened in a dispute between two women, asking them to reconcile in a letter read publicly for their whole congregation to hear (Phil 4:2–3). His metaphor of the church as Christ's body illuminates the importance of unity for Paul but also unearths a painful irony—how can a body be at war with itself?

For this body often is at war. Christians, of course, quarrel with one another in local congregations, which means peacemaking among Christians is a matter of making peace with those near (friends, neighbors, even family members). The line "How very good and pleasant it is when kindred live together in unity!" (Ps 133:1) is a popular verse for Christian writers who address peace among brothers and sisters in local congregations.

It's possible that Matthew himself intended this beatitude for Christians in his own community to resolve conflicts with one another, as some modern scholars argue.[26] The evangelist gave detailed instructions on reconciling conflicts among community members elsewhere in his gospel (Matt 5:22–26, 18:15–22). Surely the beatitude applies to conflicts in Matthew's community, and by extension to conflicts within other local church bodies. Still, the connection noted above between peacemaking and loving the enemy also suggests that Matthew had in mind a broader form of peacemaking. When Jesus tells his disciples, "Love your enemies and pray for those who persecute you," their enemies are identified as their persecutors (Matt 5:44–45).[27]

---

25. Niclaes, *The first exhortation*, 210.

26. So Hugh M. Humphrey, "Matthew 5:9: 'Blessed are the Peacemakers, For They Shall Be Called Sons of God,'" in *Blessed are the Peacemakers: Biblical Perspectives on Peace and its Social Foundations*, ed. Anthony J. Tambasco (New York: Paulist, 1989), 62–78.

27. Rudolf Schnackenburg, "Die Seligpreisung der Friedensstifter (Matt 5:9) im mattäischen

Sometimes, of course, the outsider, the persecutor, and even the enemy can be one's fellow Christians. Denominations and Christian communions fracture and fight with one another, which means peacemaking among Christians is also a matter of making peace with those further off, something more akin to making peace between nations than neighbors. The theme of peacemaking as guarding the unity of the church occurs occasionally before the Reformation. For example, Cyprian of Carthage, Jerome, and Chromatius proposed that peacemakers are those who guard the peace and unity of the church.[28] All three were concerned with heresy and schism rather than with interpersonal conflicts within local congregations.

After the Reformation, the issue of ecclesial peacemaking and heresy took on more urgency. The beatitude was applied especially to battles among splintering Protestant communions. In the Massachusetts Bay colony, Puritan minister Increase Mather (1639–1723) warned Christians that "divisions and animosities among Christians are very offensive to [God]." He warned that God will depart from a church where "Christians of the same communion" speak bitterly against one another.[29] On the other side of the ocean, Thomas Watson (ca. 1620–1686) was an English Puritan preacher who was eventually ejected from his clergy post for Nonconformity (for dissenting from the doctrine or practice of the Church of England). Two years before his ejection in 1662, he preached a sermon on the seventh beatitude in which he lamented that in Tertullian's time people said, "See how the Christians love one another," but in his own time people say, "See how the Christians snarl at one another."[30]

Kontext," *BZ* 26, no. 2 (1982): 167. This beatitude "nimmt das Hauptmotiv für das Gebot auf, und die der Verfolgten bezieht sicht auf die ärgste Belastung für diejenigen, die zur Feindesliebe aufgerufen werden [The blessing on the peacemakers takes up the main motive for the command to love the enemy, and the persecuted refers to the heaviest burden for those called to love the enemy]" (Schnackenburg, "Die Seligpreisung," 169).

28. Cyprian, *Treatises* 1.24 (*ANF* 5:429); see also Cyprian, *Treatises* 12.3.3 (*ANF* 5:533); Jerome, *Commentary on Matthew*, 76; Chromatius of Aquileia, *Sermons and Tractates on Matthew*, trans. Thomas P. Scheck, ACW 75 (New York: The Newman Press, 2018), 17.7.1.

29. Increase Mather, *Sermons Wherein Those Eight Characters of the Blessed Commonly Called the Beatitudes Are Opened and Applied in Fifteen Discourses* (Boston: B. Green, for Daniel Henchman, 1718), quotations from Sermons 11 and 12.

30. Thomas Watson, *The Beatitudes: An Exposition of Matthew 5:1–10* (Carlisle, PA: Banner of Truth Trust, 2014), 226, see also 234. Similarly, Robert Harris (1581–1658), famous Puritan preacher and president of Trinity College, Oxford, wrote, "It is for dogs to snap and bite at one another, not for sheep," and criticized Christians who are quick to scatter and divide (Robert Harris, *The Way to True Happiness: Delivered in Twenty-Four Sermons upon the Beatitudes*, ed. Don Kistler [Morgan, PA: Soli Deo Gloria, 1998], 303).

English Protestant John Norris (1657–1711) exegeted the beatitude by dwelling at length on disturbers of the peace within the church and wrote that only "*Absolute* and *Evident* Necessity" can justify war or schism. He named the Reformation as one such example, but condemned the unreasonableness of the (present) dissenters and separatists from the Church of England.[31] Jeremiah Burroughs, on the other hand, was an English Congregationalist and Nonconformist preacher who (like Watson) was suspended and deprived of his income in 1637 when he refused to obey instructions from his bishop. In his sermons on the beatitude, he deals at length with the question of schism, arguing carefully that the Nonconformists were not schismatics when they withdrew from congregations due to issues of conscience.[32]

The issue of noncomformity raised the kind of complex questions that Protestants (and, to some extent, Catholics) grappled with at length in reflections on the eighth beatitude (the blessing on the persecuted). Watson decried schismatics and heretics as peacebreakers—but as a Protestant *and* a Nonconformist, he himself could wear the label of a schismatic from the perspective of both the Church of Rome and the Church of England.[33] Indeed, Protestants split over whether Noncomformists broke the peace of the church (and were thus peacebreakers rather than peacemakers) or were following their consciences. Following the conscience (and maintaining the truth of the gospel) did not fall under the umbrella of schism or heresy, but into the domain of the pure in heart and the persecuted instead.

Today the body of Christ continues to fracture, despite efforts (like the Lutheran-Catholic Dialogue) to heal the wounds. A church called to make peace is itself broken and bleeding. The Anglican Communion, the Lutheran churches, and the Methodist Church are tearing themselves apart over the issue of human sexuality, an issue that highlights the tension between peace and purity. As John Stott declared, "The visible unity of the church is a proper Christian quest, but only if unity is not sought at the expense of doctrine. . . . We have no mandate from Christ to seek unity without purity."[34]

What counts as purity and right doctrine is deeply contested. Neither side claims to toss aside the truth of Scripture, to abandon the gospel, or to act with

---

31. John Norris, *Christian Blessedness: or, Discourses upon the Beatitudes*, vol. 1 of *Practical Discourses Upon the Beatitudes*, 5th ed. (London: S. Manship, 1707), 148, 162–63.

32. Burroughs, *Saints' Happiness*, 189–90. See also Buck, *A Treatise of the Beatitudes*, 190, 279–88, 293, 331–32.

33. Watson, *The Beatitudes*, 233.

34. John R. W. Stott, *Christian Counter-Culture: The Message of the Sermon on the Mount* (Downers Grove, IL: InterVarsity Press, 1978), 51.

impure motives. Nobody thinks they're the heretic or the peacebreaker! That's always a charge leveled from the other side. But the practical result of defending the truth is often that purity (or the perceived rightness of one's cause) is pursued at the expense of peace. Where Christians perceive that purity is at stake, it's often peace that's sacrificed, rather than the other way around. Far too often, Christians would rather break peace with one another than risk being in fellowship with other Christians whom they deem to have inadequate or "impure" doctrines.

We'll explore the relationship between peacemaking and persecution (and purity) even more in the next chapter.

Peace among nations: politics and war

Byzantine theologian Nicholas Cabasilas (ca. 1319–1392) wrote that those who worship Christ should strive for peace and "stop those who are rashly at war."[35] Cabasilas was relatively alone in his connection between the beatitude and war until about 1530, when Martin Luther began preaching on the Sermon on the Mount.

Premodern commentators rarely applied the peacemaking of Matt 5:10 to the political sphere, or to conflict among kings and countries. Luther applied *all* the Beatitudes to the public sphere. For him, the Beatitudes concerned not the Christian's life before God but the Christian's life before the neighbor.

Luther insisted that the seventh beatitude doesn't prohibit the waging of war altogether. But it does seriously limit it. He argued that "anyone who claims to be a Christian and a child of God, not only does not start war or unrest; but he also gives help and counsel on the side of peace wherever he can, even though there may have been a just and adequate cause for going to war."[36] For Luther, however, the prohibition against starting a war did not rule out the possibility of a just war; he argued elsewhere that "the sword can legitimately be used by rulers to protect the common good and serve the people."[37]

English Reformer William Tyndale (ca. 1494–1536) was likely influenced by Luther when he invoked the beatitude similarly in relation to warring rul-

---

35. Cabasilas, *The Life in Christ* 6.11g, trans. Carmino J. deCatanzaro (Crestwood, NY: St. Vladimir's Seminary Press, 1974), 187.

36. Luther, *Sermon on the Mount*, 40.

37. Lisa Sowle Cahill, *Blessed Are the Peacemakers: Pacifism, Just War, and Peacebuilding* (Minneapolis: Fortress, 2019), 198. For more on Luther's view of war, see Cahill, *Blessed Are the Peacemakers*, 191–99.

ers. If princes wish to be God's children ("they will be called children of God" [Matt 5:9]), they "must not only give no cause of war, nor begin any; but also (though he have a just cause) suffer himself to be entreated, if he that gave the cause repent; and must also seek all ways of peace, before he fight."[38] Also in England, around the same time, the beatitude was reportedly the personal motto of King James I (the one who commissioned the King James Version of the Bible), perhaps because he ended England's war with Spain in 1604 and managed to rule without going to war against another power.[39]

After Luther, it became relatively common for Protestant exegetes to apply the beatitude to war, either to appeal for restraint in war or to argue for pacifism (as the Anabaptists did). In 1738, for example, Irish Anglican priest Arthur St. George wrote that "peace-makers in national quarrels" are "doubly blessed."[40] (As an Irish Anglican, St. George had pressing reasons to be interested in peace among nations, and between Catholics and Protestants.) In the twentieth century, the beatitude took on special urgency, first amid the shocking destruction of World War II and then under the looming specter of nuclear war.

The Second World War marked a dramatic change in the tactics and tools of war. For perhaps the first time in human history, peacemaking on an international scale started to seem necessary to save all of humanity. From the 1940s onward, the beatitude has been used increasingly in anti-war movements. In 1943, French Jesuit Albert Bessières wrote scathingly about the proponents of "total war" (a military strategy that could be characterized as "win at all costs"). Bessières accused the total war theorists of opposing Jesus's beatitude with their own anti-beatitude: "*Heureux les belliqueux!*" ("Blessed are the bellicose!").[41]

One of the issues of "total war" was the specter of nuclear war. René Coste begins his chapter on the beatitude by lamenting the massive destruction at Hiroshima and Nagasaki.[42] Although tensions between the two main nuclear powers—the United States and the Soviet Union—had run cold since the late 1940s, the Soviet invasion of Afghanistan in 1979 worsened relations. After his

38. William Tyndale, *The Work of William Tyndale*, ed. G. E. Duffield (Philadelphia: Fortress, 1965), 205.

39. Jane T. Stoddart, *The New Testament in Life and Literature* (London: Hodder and Stoughton, 1914), 40.

40. Arthur St. George, *The Blessings of Christian Philosophy; Being a Treatise on the Beatitudes* (London: W. Innys & R. Manby, 1738), 269.

41. Albert Bessières, *Les Béatitudes et la civilization* (Paris: Éditions Spes, 1943), 112.

42. René Coste, *Le grand secret des béatitudes: une théologie et une spiritualité pour aujourd'hui* (Paris: Editions S.O.S., 1985), 229.

election in 1980, President Ronald Reagan increased American military budgets and heightened the rhetoric of the Cold War. It seemed possible that the world would go to war again, and that the phrase "total war" would turn out to be an understatement of the result.

This may explain why a spate of resources appeared in the 1980s that connected the beatitude (however loosely) to the nuclear disarmament movement. In 1981, the Christian Campaign for Nuclear Disarmament published a resource using the beatitude as its title: *Blessed are the Peacemakers*.[43] In 1982, the Coalition for Justice and Peace of the Diocese of Worcester (MA) published a pamphlet of "Meditations and Resources on Nuclear Disarmament" with the same title.[44] Pope John Paul II captured this connection when he referred to the seventh beatitude as the Magna Carta of the peace movement in an open-air Mass in El Salvador on March 6, 1983.[45] Another book published in 1983 called *Who Are the Peacemakers? The Christian Case for Nuclear Deterrence* used the beatitude instead to launch an attack against pacifism, arguing that pacifism only leads to a more dangerous and violent world.[46]

Connections between the beatitude and various anti-war movements continue today. Six decades after Bessières, in 2006, American Catholic John Dear penned his own sarcastic anti-beatitude: "Blessed are the warmakers."[47] Alfred de Zayas, former Secretary of the United Nations Human Rights Committee, echoes Dear's critique by supplying (in poetic form) a Lukan woe to the eighth beatitude: "Woe upon the men who would unleash a war / regardless of the risks, impervious to the law!"[48]

Especially toward the end of the twentieth century, both Catholic and Protestant interpreters in the West have increasingly used the beatitude as a springboard to discuss just war, peacemaking, and the relationship between the Sermon on the Mount and public policy. In 2017, Pope Francis, echoing his

43. Christian Campaign for Nuclear Disarmament, *Blessed are the Peacemakers* (London: Christian Campaign for Nuclear Disarmament, 1981).

44. Michael True, ed., *Blessed Are the Peacemakers: Meditations and Resources on Nuclear Disarmament* (Worcester, MA: Diocese of Worcester, 1982).

45. Humphrey, "Matthew 5:9," 75n1.

46. Jerram Barrs, *Who Are the Peacemakers?: The Christian Case for Nuclear Deterrence* (Westchester, IL: Crossway, 1983). See also Friedhelm Solms and Marc Reuver, *Churches as peacemakers: an analysis of recent church statements on peace, disarmament and war* (Rome: IDOC International, 1985).

47. Dear, *Beatitudes of Peace*, 20, 27–28.

48. Alfred de Zayas, "Beatitudes," in *Poets Against the War*, ed. Sam Hamill (New York: Thunder's Mouth Press/Nation Books, 2003), 57. The specific topic of the poem is President Bush's invasion of Iraq (the Gulf War).

predecessor John Paul II, referred to the Sermon on the Mount as the church's manual for peacemaking.[49] In the global South, Paul John Isaak points to the desperate need for peacemakers in the conflicts in Sudan and elsewhere in Africa. "Africa," he pleads, "is a bleeding continent."[50]

In the twenty-first century, theologians and practitioners who reflect on the beatitude—and on peacemaking more generally—have begun to adopt the language of peacebuilding, adopting a term that originated with peace studies pioneer Johan Galtung.[51] This shift aims to refocus attention away from war itself to broader questions of how to build peace in societies, both to prevent conflict and to rebuild communities in the aftermath of violent conflict. It also seeks to chart a third way that is neither just war theory nor pacifism.[52]

For example, Lisa Sowle Cahill's 2019 book *Blessed are the Peacemakers* describes peacebuilding as an alternative to the traditional categories (and sometimes impasse) of pacifism and just war. She proposes that "Christian just war theorists and pacifists are starting to converge on the practical priority of nonviolently transforming situations of armed military and societal conflict. Peacebuilders bring this commitment front and center, partnering with other religious traditions, civil society, and governmental and nongovernmental organizations to avoid and reduce violence and rebuild violence-torn societies."[53] Peacebuilding "aims to resolve injustice in nonviolent ways and to transform the structural conditions that generate deadly conflict."[54] Theologian Glen Stassen and others use the term "just peacemaking" to indicate a similar set of practices.[55]

49. Pope Francis, "Nonviolence: A Style of Politics for Peace" (2017 World Day of Peace message); see Gerald Schlabach, "Round Table Discussion: Just Peacemaking. A 'Manual' for Escaping Our Vicious Cycles," *Journal of Moral Theology* 7, no. 2 (2018): 86. See also Gerald Schlabach, "Pope Francis's Peacebuilding Pedagogy: A Commentary on his 2017 World Day of Peace Message," posted January 2, 2017, http://www.geraldschlabach.net/2017/01/02/wdp17/.

50. Paul John Isaak, "Luke," in *Africa Bible Commentary*, ed. Tokunboh Adeyemo, 2nd ed. (Nairobi, Kenya: WordAlive; Grand Rapids: Zondervan, 2010), 1145.

51. Galtung-Institut for Peace Theory and Peace Practice, "Johan Galtung," https://www.galtung-institut.de/en/home/johan-galtung/; and International Association for Humanitarian Policy and Conflict Research, "The Conceptual Origins of Peacemaking," http://www.peacebuildinginitiative.org/index34ac.html?pageId=1764.

52. I'm indebted to John Kiess for pointing me to helpful resources in the field of peacebuilding.

53. Cahill, *Blessed Are the Peacemakers*, viii.

54. "What is Strategic Peacebuilding?," Kroc Institute for International Peace Studies, University of Notre Dame, https://tinyurl.com/yc79hy9k; quoted in Cahill, *Blessed Are the Peacemakers*, 7.

55. E.g., Glen Stassen, ed., *Just Peacemaking: Ten Practices for Abolishing War*, 2nd ed. (Cleve-

Can soldiers be peacemakers?

Not long after the early church emerged, Christians concluded that certain vocations were simply incompatible with following Christ. Around the year 200 CE, a document called *The Apostolic Tradition* lists the professions forbidden to Christians. The banned professions included brothel keeper and astrologer. (One wonders what might be on such a list today, were one to be made.) *The Apostolic Tradition* doesn't allow anyone who desires to become a soldier to be baptized, but makes allowances for soldiers who have converted to Christ while in military service: they may remain in service, but may not kill.[56] Of course, a soldier who refused an order to kill would presumably not remain in the army much longer.

Can soldiers, then, be peacemakers? For the first three centuries of the church's life, the answer was largely no. The reasons for this were varied. They included the close intertwining of Roman military service and Roman religion, which made it practically impossible to be a soldier without committing idolatry. Even more central was the guiding hand of Jesus's command to love your enemies (Matt 5:43–44), which early Christian writers frequently cited in tandem with the commandment "You shall not murder" (Exod 20:13).[57] Explicit appeals to the beatitude itself were rare, but comments about Christians as people of peace and imitators of the Prince of Peace were common.

This negative assessment also had to do with Christian notions of God's exclusive lordship. As one early Christian in Carthage, North Africa, wrote, "One soul cannot serve two masters: God and Caesar."[58] That same Christian, Tertullian (ca. 155–240), appealed to the story of Jesus telling Peter to put

---

land, OH: The Pilgrim Press, 1998). Examples of peacebuilders for Cahill are Maggy Barankitse and her Maison Shalom center (Cahill, *Blessed Are the Peacemakers*, 337–38; see also Emmanuel Katongole, *Born From Lament* [Grand Rapids: Eerdmans, 2017], 225–42); and Myla Leguro and other staff at the Mindanao Peacebuilding Institute in the Philippines, "where Muslims, Christians, and indigenous peoples with a conflicted history can learn a different way to see one another and become partners for peace" (Cahill, *Blessed Are the Peacemakers*, 340; see Myla Leguro, "The Many Dimensions of Catholic Peacebuilding: Mindanao Experience," Catholic Peacebuilding Network, 2008, https://tinyurl.com/y9hmmtpf). Cahill also gives examples of local Baltimore organizations like Safe Steps (Catholic Charities); Leaders of a Beautiful Struggle; Showing Up for Racial Justice; and the Harriet Tubman House (Cahill, *Blessed Are the Peacemakers*, 355–56).

56. *Apostolic Tradition* 16; see George Kalantzis, *Caesar and the Lamb: Early Christian Attitudes on War and Military Service* (Eugene, OR: Cascade, 2012), 62.

57. Kalantzis, *Caesar and the Lamb*, 41–42, 46–55.

58. Tertullian, *On Idolatry* 19.3 (*ANF* 3:73); quoted in Kalantzis, *Caesar and the Lamb*, 39.

his sword away when the impetuous Peter decides to fight the soldiers who have come to arrest Jesus (John 18:10–11): "The Lord, by taking away Peter's sword, disarmed every soldier thereafter."[59] Origen of Alexandria (ca. 184–253) invoked Isaiah's vision of the eschatological age (Isa 2:4b): "No longer do we take the sword against any nation, nor do we learn [the art of] war any more since we have become sons of peace through Jesus."[60]

This consensus shifted with the conversion of the emperor Constantine to Christianity in 312. Just before Constantine's conversion, Christian rhetorician Lucius Caecilius Firmianus Lactantius (ca. 250–325) declared, "A just man may not be a soldier."[61] A few years later, Lactantius became an advisor to the newly converted emperor and "his outlook changed."[62] It became more difficult to sustain Tertullian's conviction that one could not serve God and Caesar now that the emperor was part of the church. Overall, Christians became increasingly comfortable with military service, a trend that continued in the West with only minor interruptions (Anabaptists and Quakers). Christians in the East never embraced war the way the Christian West did; unlike the Western Crusaders, they never developed a tradition of holy war, and "even well into the late medieval period, the Christian East would not accept soldiers who died in battle as martyrs."[63]

One of the architects of Western Christianity, Augustine (bishop of Hippo in modern-day Algeria [354–430]), was born into the newly Christianized empire and lived through its demise. He used the seventh beatitude, among other texts, to consider the still-fraught question of whether a peacemaker could be a soldier. He did so in two letters sent to soldiers.

The first letter, written in 417, was to Boniface, a Roman soldier who later became governor of the Roman province of Africa. Augustine framed the letter around what he saw as the heart of the Christian life: the command to love God and one's neighbor (Letter 189.1). One can, he concluded, fulfill these two commands while serving as a soldier. As support, he cited several examples including King David, the centurion Cornelius (who was baptized by Peter [Acts 10:1–48]), and the Roman centurion whose faith is praised by Jesus

---

59. Tertullian, *On Idolatry* 19.3 (*ANF* 3:73); quoted in Kalantzis, *Caesar and the Lamb*, 39.

60. Origen, *Against Celsus* 5.33 (*ANF* 4:558); quoted in Kalantzis, *Caesar and the Lamb*, 39.

61. Lactantius, *The Divine Institutes, Books I–VII*, trans. Mary Francis McDonald, FC 49 (Washington, DC: Catholic University of America Press, 1964), 6.20.15–17; quoted in Kalantzis, *Caesar and the Lamb*, 53. On the example of Cornelius, see Kalantzis, *Caesar and the Lamb*, 66–68.

62. See Kalantzis, *Caesar and the Lamb*, 53n48.

63. Kalantzis, *Caesar and the Lamb*, 200.

(Matt 8:8–10) (Letter 189.4). Everyone has a particular gift, wrote Augustine (1 Cor 7:7); some fight invisible spiritual enemies, while others fight "visible barbarians" (Letter 189.5). He quoted the beatitude to tell Boniface, "Peace ought to be what you want, war [is] only what necessity demands. . . . Be a peacemaker, therefore, even in war, so that by conquering them you bring the benefit of peace even to those you defeat" (Letter 189.6).[64]

The second letter was written ca. 429/430 to Darius, a high-ranking official in the Roman army. Augustine also quoted the beatitude to Darius, and went on to praise "warriors who are both very brave and very faithful" for their role in defeating "an untamed enemy" and "pacifying the provinces." He continued by saying that the greater glory belongs to those who "war with words"—that is, those who achieve peace "not through war but through peace itself." Aiming for peace through bloodshed, he concluded, is a necessity; but aiming for peace by avoiding blood being shed is a joy (Letter 229.2).[65]

Augustine, then, made allowances for the necessity of war, even while arguing for the higher good of avoiding violence.[66] His exhortation to "be a peacemaker, even in war" is a terse summary of the just war tradition that he helped to develop. Augustine wasn't the first to formulate a theory of just war (he was influenced by both Cicero and Ambrose), but he was so influential that the Western just war tradition, "in both its Christian and secular varieties, traces its roots . . . to Augustine."[67]

From Augustine until the Reformation, if the beatitude appeared at all in relation to war (and it did so rarely) it was typically in a context that assumed just war rather than the pacificism of the early church. When Dhuoda of Septimania (d. 843?) wrote instructions to her "warrior son," she told him that if he practiced the meekness of the third beatitude (that is, if he restrained his anger and didn't lose his temper), then he would act peaceably and would deserve to be called a peacemaker (*Handbook* 4.8).[68] Like Augustine before her, Dhuoda

64. Augustine, "Letter 189 to Boniface," in *Augustine: Political Writings*, ed. E. M. Atkins and R. J. Dodaro (Cambridge: Cambridge University Press, 2001), 215–17.

65. Augustine, "Letter 229 to Darius," in *Augustine: Political Writings*, 225–26.

66. See also Augustine, "Letter 138 to Marcellinus," in *Augustine: Political Writings*, 38–39.

67. John Mark Mattox, *Saint Augustine and the Theory of Just War* (London: Continuum, 2006), 2. For the influence of Cicero and Ambrose, see Mattox, *Saint Augustine*, 14–23. For a concise summary of just war theory in Christianity, see Cahill, *Blessed Are the Peacemakers*, 8–13; on Augustine, see ibid., 91–137.

68. Dhuoda, *Handbook for her Warrior Son*, ed. and trans. Marcelle Thiébaux (Cambridge: Cambridge University Press, 1998), 149. Around the same time in history (first half of the ninth century), an unknown author interpreted the beatitude in light of Saxon warrior culture; given that his audience was mainly men who were warriors, he took the beatitude as a blessing on

assumed that her son could be a soldier *and* a peacemaker, so long as he behaved virtuously in war (and in peaceable relations with his fellow soldiers).

Almost exactly a thousand years later, Isaac Allen wrote reflections on the Beatitudes "chiefly for the use of [British] troops in India" in 1848. When he commented on the peacemakers, he began with a lament for the spirit of revenge and "the unholy love of strife, which has drenched nations in blood."[69] But Allen was writing *for* soldiers, not in opposition to them. So when he instructed them to apply the beatitude to their circumstances, he urged the soldiers not to quarrel among themselves, as "they are a band of brothers" defending the honor of the sovereign (by which he did not mean God).[70] When Harvard theology professor Francis Greenwood Peabody wrote an essay on the peacemakers in 1919, shortly after the end of World War I, he praised both soldiers and industrialists as peacemakers—the soldiers for reestablishing peace, and the industrialists for helping to rebuild society.[71]

Christians today are divided over whether peacemakers (that is, Christians) can be soldiers. Many Christians and church bodies accept this possibility, typically by making a case for just war. For some, the command to love the neighbor means sometimes going to the armed defense of that neighbor. For others, the command "You shall not kill" is absolute and has no exceptions: one cannot make peace by killing. If the sixth commandment is negative (you shall *not*), and Jesus's command to love the enemy is positive (you *shall*); it suggests that one actively expresses love for enemies through blessing and not cursing them, through praying for them, and through cultivating "piety, justice, love of humanity (*philanthrōpia*), faith, and hope."[72] For some Christians, today as in the first three centuries of the church's life, loving enemies excludes military service in which one might be asked to kill them. But for others, love must include justice, which might include the necessary evil of restraining the hostile or aggressive from harming the weak and vulnerable.[73]

---

those who "do not want to start any fights or court cases by their own actions"—leaving open, of course, the possibility that the warrior could fight in battles started by the actions of others (*The Heliand: The Saxon Gospel*, trans. G. Ronald Murphy [Oxford: Oxford University Press, 1992], 46).

69. Isaac Allen, *Reflection on Portions of the Sermon on the Mount. Intended Principally for Soldiers* (London: SPCK, 1848), 25.

70. Allen, *Reflection*, 26.

71. Peabody, "The Peace-Makers," 51–52.

72. Justin Martyr, *Dialogue with Trypho* 110.3; quoted in Kalantzis, *Caesar and the Lamb*, 53.

73. Allen Verhey, *Remembering Jesus: Christian Community, Scripture, and the Moral Life* (Grand Rapids: Eerdmans, 2002), 415–17, 464.

Justice and peace

The theme that peace requires justice occurs fairly often in post-Reformation and modern-day musings on the beatitude. John Calvin preached (in relation to the beatitude) that merely settling disputes is not enough; they must be settled with justice.[74] Michael Crosby called the peacemakers the justice-makers, since "justice is the basis for peace."[75] Warren Carter contrasts the *Pax Romana* (bought at a price, ensuring the domination of the elite and the economic exploitation of everyone else) with God's peace, which establishes justice for the weak and needy.[76] And Yiu Sing Lúcás Chan pointed out that peace and justice are closely associated with one another in both the Old and New Testaments.[77]

The necessity of making peace justly led some past interpreters to reflect on what tools or methods are permissible to peacemakers. Jeremiah Burroughs, in a sermon on the beatitude, laid out some rules for making peace "between man and man": never use violence unless it is absolutely necessary and all other means have been tried, and if violence is necessary use the minimum amount of force.[78] In another sermon on the beatitude, Burroughs urged two warring branches of the English church (Independency and Presbytery) not to resort to the civil law to try to settle their dispute, since that wouldn't make genuine peace.[79]

Sustained reflection on how to make peace through just means is urgently needed today. More and more, peacemakers must consider not only how to make peace but how to create the conditions that make violence less likely, and how to rebuild societies when violence leaves such a wide swath of destruction

---

74. John Calvin, *Sermons on the Beatitudes: Five Sermons from the Gospel Harmony, Delivered in Geneva in 1560* (Carlisle, PA: Banner of Truth Trust, 2006), 56–57.

75. Michael H. Crosby, *Spirituality of the Beatitudes: Matthew's Vision for the Church in an Unjust World*, rev. ed. (Maryknoll, NY: Orbis Books, 2005), 159.

76. Warren Carter, *Matthew and the Margins: A Socio-Political and Religious Reading* (Sheffield: Sheffield Academic, 2000), 136.

77. Yiu Sing Lúcás Chan, *The Ten Commandments and the Beatitudes* (Lanham, MD: Rowman & Littlefield, 2012), 211, 213.

78. Burroughs, *Saints' Happiness*, 182–85.

79. Burroughs, *Saints' Happiness*, 189. Matthew Henry focused on peacemaking as inviting others to become reconciled with God, and he warned that Christ did not intend for Christianity to spread through violence, coercion, by means of the law, or through "intemperate zeal" (Matthew Henry, *Matthew to John*, vol. 5 of *An Exposition of the Old and New Testament* [New York: Revell, n.d. [1708–1710?]], comment on Matt 5:9; section VII).

in its wake, crippling transportation, health systems, and education. The world needs more peacemakers.

They will be called sons of God

Earlier in this chapter, Origen referred to "sons of peace," which combines the first half of the beatitude "blessed are the peacemakers," with its second half "for they shall be called sons of God." Why are the peacemakers called the sons of God? (For the Greek "sons" [*huioi*], most English translations choose the gender-neutral "children.") To be a "son of X" means to display the qualities of X. James and John, the "sons of thunder" (Mark 3:17), were presumably thunderous men. In Jesus's parable of the dishonest manager, the children of this age are compared to the children of light (Luke 16:8; for Christians as children of light, see also John 12:36, Eph 5:8, 1 Thess 5:5). The children of this age are those who belong to the present evil age (Gal 1:4) and mirror its characteristics; the children of light belong to the God who is light and in whom there is no darkness (1 John 1:5), so they themselves also shed light into the world. God is a God of peace (Rom 15:33, 16:20; Phil 4:9); so are all his children. Those who make peace imitate and mirror their Father. They are recognized or claimed as God's children because they resemble God.[80]

As usual, the question is when: *when* shall the peacemakers be called the children of God? In this case, the beatitude functions as a clear exhortation for this life. The peacemakers are called to strive for peace now and are acknowledged as God's children whenever they succeed. But like all the beatitudes, this one is also taken to be an eschatological promise, since human beings can never perfectly bring about God's peace in this life. Any peace achieved here can only echo the *shalom* to come (1 Cor 15:53–54).[81]

This beatitude is seventh in Matthew's order, and the number seven, as the number of perfection or completion, cries out for theological interpretation. Surprisingly, given how much premodern commentators loved numbers (including the number seven), only a few interpreters commented on the ob-

---

80. In an interesting variation on this theme, Paschasius Radbertus took the sixth beatitude (pure in heart, Matt 5:9) as a reference to the creation of humanity in the image of God on the sixth day. In the purified heart of the believer, the *imago Dei* is restored (Stoll, *De Virtute*, 188, see also 202).

81. So Augustine, Sermon 53A.12, in Augustine, *Essential Sermons*, ed. Boniface Ramsey, trans. Edmund Hill, The Works of Saint Augustine: A Translation for the 21st Century (Hyde Park, NY: New City Press, 2007), 82.

vious correlation between peace and the seventh day of rest. Thomas Aquinas wrote that "peace is placed in the seventh beatitude, just as rest in the seventh day (Gen 2:2)." For Rupert of Deutz, the beatitude points to the Sabbath rest of the new age which has begun with Christ.[82] (Jewish tradition had already connected Sabbath rest with the eternal rest of the new age, a belief echoed in Heb 4:1–10.) In the late nineteenth century, John le Gay Brereton's exegesis connected the six days of creation to the first six beatitudes, and the seventh day of rest to the seventh beatitude. "The establishment of Peace is the actual restoration of the original Sabbath, and the seventh Beatitude, 'Blessed are the Peacemakers,' not only answers to, but is identical with the Seventh Day."[83]

With few exceptions, modern scholars typically dismiss the idea that the order or number of the Beatitudes have any significance. There are a few exceptions. Baptist Charles Spurgeon (who often closely followed medieval exegesis) noticed another aspect of the number seven, and he speculated, "Perhaps the Savior placed the peacemaker seventh on the list because the peacemaker most closely resembles the perfect man Jesus Christ."[84]

Whether or not the order was intentional, this beatitude comes late in Jesus's list. Perhaps it is no coincidence that it comes after meekness (self-restraint), mercy, mourning, and justice. Jesus's promise makes clear that whatever else the peacemakers are, they are the ones who show us God's heart.

Conclusion

R. T. Kendall's chapter on the peacemakers is called "Making friends." Kendall was born in Kentucky in 1935 and spent twenty-five years as senior minister at Westminster Chapel, an evangelical free church in London just down the street from Buckingham Palace. He proposes that peacemakers are the ones who bring together two people who are "poles apart theologically, culturally, socially, financially, politically and even sexually." Peacemakers make these unlikely matches by saying, "I'd like you to meet this person" or "I want you to become friends with this person."[85]

---

82. Thomas Aquinas, *Commentary on Matthew*, C.5 L.2.442; for Rupert, see Stoll, *De Virtute*, 196.

83. J. le Gay Brereton, *Genesis and the Beatitudes: The Spiritual Creation of Man* (Sydney: Turner & Henderson; London: James Speirs, 1887), 11. In other respects, Brereton's exegesis is utterly quirky.

84. Spurgeon, *Morning and Evening*, March 17, evening.

85. R. T. Kendall, *The Sermon on the Mount* (Oxford, UK: Monarch Books, 2011, 2013), 58.

He practices what he preaches, describing friendships he forged with President Yasser Arafat, Rabbi David Rosen, and Dr. Saab Erekat (at the time, the Palestinians' chief negotiator with the Israelis).[86] Kendall could have appealed to St. Francis of Assisi, who is frequently hailed as a peacemaker not only because he rejected all forms of violence, but also because he befriended Sultan Malik-al-Kamil of Egypt during the Fifth Crusade—a small but profound act of peace during a time of horrific violence instigated by Christians.[87]

Making friends across boundaries is one of the most urgent peacemaking needs of our time. It's needed, for example, in religiously plural contexts like the United States. Indian scholar T. Johnson Chakkuvarackal notes that the blessing on the peacemakers "has unique importance" in another religiously plural context: in India, where it functions as "a challenge to make initiative between warring religious groups."[88] A deeply religious nation, India is majority Hindu, but there are also significant populations of Muslims, Christians, and Sikhs, as well as smaller groups of Buddhists, Jains, and Zoroastrians. Peacemaking with one's neighbors takes on a new flavor when one's neighbors could be "Hindus, Muslims, Christians, Buddhists, Jains, Zoroastrians, Dalits."[89] Elsewhere in the world, people seeking to calm tension between Jews, Christians, and Muslims in Israel and Palestine have invoked the beatitude, including the Christian Peacemaker Teams and Palestinian Christian Audeh Rantisi.[90]

Making friends—and making peace—across political boundaries might be even more challenging. Can we consider "stretching out the hand" in mercy and friendship to a Brexiteer or a Remainer, to a Democrat or a Republican? Sister Rosemary dedicated her whole life to opposing nuclear weapons, but she also sought friendships with those who worked to develop them.[91] The temptation to demonize our opponents is so strong. It will take real courage to see God's image in someone we bitterly disagree with, or in someone who holds a view that is deeply offensive to us, and to reach out to them with an offer of friendship rather than a fist. Friendship does not mean papering over those

---

86. Kendall, *Sermon on the Mount*, 55.

87. Forest, *Ladder*, 113–18.

88. T. Johnson Chakkuvarackal, "The Message of the Sermon on the Mount in the Multi-Religious Context of India," *Indian Journal of Theology* 43, no. 1 & 2 (2001): 43.

89. Chakkuvarackal, "The Message of the Sermon on the Mount," 43.

90. Audeh G. Rantisi with Ralph K. Beebe, *Blessed are the Peacemakers: A Palestinian Christian in the Occupied West Bank* (Grand Rapids: Zondervan, 1990).

91. Another example is Peace Catalyst International, which aims to make peace between Muslims and Christians (https://www.peacecatalyst.org/).

differences or politely ignoring views that should be challenged or changed; true friendship never does.

One final peacemaking need, and perhaps the most pressing of all, is named in a recent, creative application of the beatitude by Catholic theologian Yiu Sing Lúcás Chan. Shortly before his untimely death, Chan named one application of this beatitude as the urgent imperative "to make peace with the Earth."[92] Catholic activist John Dear agrees: "If more and more of us . . . practice nonviolence, and see how every facet of life on earth affects Mother Earth, we can help make inroads of peace, cut the roots of war, lessen the violent catastrophe from climate change, and finally make peace with Mother Earth itself."[93]

92. Chan, *Ten Commandments*, 216.

93. John Dear, *They Will Inherit the Earth: Peace and Nonviolence in a Time of Climate Change* (Maryknoll, NY: Orbis Books, 2018), 95.

10

Mischief-Makers and Bandits

The Persecuted

Blessed are those who are persecuted for righteousness' sake, for theirs is the kingdom of heaven (Matt 5:10).

Blessed are you when people revile you and persecute you and utter all kinds of evil against you falsely on my account. Rejoice and be glad, for your reward is great in heaven, for in the same way they persecuted the prophets who were before you (Matt 5:11–12).

Blessed are you when people hate you, and when they exclude you, revile you, and defame you on account of the Son of Man. Rejoice in that day and leap for joy, for surely your reward is great in heaven; for that is what their ancestors did to the prophets (Luke 6:22–23).

Woe to you when all speak well of you, for that is what their ancestors did to the false prophets (Luke 6:26).

In the year 203 CE, two women were in prison in the city of Carthage in North Africa (modern-day Tunisia), awaiting execution. One was from a wealthy family. Her father had come to visit her, to beg her to deny that she was a Christian so that she could return home and raise her newborn baby. She refused. Her name was Perpetua. The second woman was a slave, and she was pregnant. Her name was Felicity; she also refused to deny that she was a Christian. The night before they died, Perpetua had a vision that their deaths would defeat Satan, the ancient enemy of God. According to the account of their martyrdom, they died calmly and courageously in the gladiatorial ring, Perpetua herself guiding the gladiator's sword to her throat.[1]

Fourteen hundred miles away and 101 years later, a young woman named Euphemia was arrested in Chalcedon (near modern-day Istanbul) for refusing to sacrifice to the god Ares, the god of war. A convert to Christianity, she insisted that the Roman emperor (Diocletian at the time) must be disobeyed if his orders were contrary to God. She was tortured and then turned over to the arena of the gladiators, where she was killed by a lion.[2]

Fourteen hundred years after that, Elizaveta Skobtsova (1891–1945) was a Russian noblewoman who fled to Paris after the Bolshevik revolution (and after a brief stint as mayor of a town called Anapa in southern Russia). She eventually took vows as an Orthodox nun and took the name Maria. Her home was a soup kitchen and a shelter for refugees and other people in need. She was arrested for smuggling Jews out of Paris during the Nazi occupation and was taken to the Ravensbrück concentration camp. She reportedly took the place of a Jewish prisoner who was slated to be sent to the gas chamber, and died as Russian troops were approaching to liberate the camp.[3]

These four women represent the persecuted. Their stories reveal a good deal about this eighth beatitude and its close association with the early martyrs. Mother Maria Skobtsova's story is more complex; Orthodox writer Jim Forest uses it to illuminate both humility (the first beatitude) and hunger for justice (the fourth).[4] But she also, of course, illustrates the eighth. Her humility (her willingness to renounce her own rights) and her hunger for righteousness (her risky protection of the vulnerable Jews and other refugees) manifested itself in courageous action for the materially hungry and poor and led to her persecution and death. In this way, she shows how intertwined the Beatitudes can be when they take shape in human lives.

———

Depending on how you count them, this chapter considers one or two (or three) beatitudes: (1) Matthew's eighth beatitude: "Blessed are those who are persecuted for righteousness' sake, for theirs is the kingdom of heaven" (Matt

1. Joseph J. Walsh, ed., *What Would You Die For? Perpetua's Passion* (Baltimore, MD: Apprentice House, 2006), 61–95.

2. Jim Forest, *The Ladder of the Beatitudes* (Maryknoll, NY: Orbis Books, 1999), 140.

3. Forest, *Ladder*, 71–74.

4. For the poor in spirit, see Forest, *Ladder*, 26.

5:10); and (2) Matthew's ninth beatitude (or his extension of the eighth), paralleled by Luke's fourth plus his corresponding woe: "Blessed are you when people revile/hate you"; "Woe to you when all speak well of you" (Matt 5:11–12; Luke 6:22–23, 26). In Matthew's account, this last beatitude shifts from third person ("Blessed are *they*") to second person ("Blessed are *you*"). (All of Luke's blessings are in the second person, so there's no shift in his account.) For some interpreters, the change signals a shift in audience from the crowds to the disciples. For others, the verbs *revile* and *utter* indicate that the ninth beatitude refers to verbal persecution such as slander whereas the eighth refers to physical persecution such as confiscation of property, arrest, or martyrdom.

The eighth beatitude offers the same promise as the first: "for theirs is the kingdom of heaven." That's where I'll end, bringing this last chapter full circle. I'll first consider a question that deals with a difference between the eighth and ninth beatitudes: to be blessed, must one be persecuted for righteousness, for justice, or for Jesus? Then I'll take you on a tour through the troubled history witnessed by this beatitude's interpreters. Two key events shape this beatitude: first, the era of the martyrs; second, the Reformation and its aftermath. Reflections on the eighth beatitude are relatively straightforward until the Reformation era. The martyrs—like Perpetua, Felicity, and Euphemia—are hailed as the exemplars of the persecuted, and the faithful are urged to imitate them. This is still true today, of course. But another layer is added beginning around the turn of the sixteenth century.

Not all the beatitudes undergo noticeable changes during the Reformation. This one does. From the 1500s through the end of the 1700s, several generations of Reformers and their successors focused sustained attention on this beatitude. They wrote reams about it; they applied it to themselves. *They* were the new martyrs; they circled back to that earlier era to make sense of their own situation. To a lesser extent, Catholics, especially in England, also wrote about themselves as the new martyrs.[5]

This chapter considers the special dilemma faced by Christians once they stand on both sides of the beatitude, as both persecuted and persecutor. Along the way, I'll explore two proposed relationships between the eighth beatitude and the first seven beatitudes. Are the seven the cause of persecution, or are the seven the qualities needed to face persecution well? The first question we'll consider has to do with what kinds of persecution are blessed—and which kinds aren't.

5. Brad S. Gregory, *Salvation at Stake: Christian Martyrdom in Early Modern Europe* (Cambridge, MA: Harvard University Press, 1999), 4, 116–19, 250–314.

For righteousness, for justice, or for Jesus?

You may notice that the eighth and ninth beatitudes name two different reasons why persecution is a blessed state: for the sake of righteousness or justice (Matt 5:10), or for being hated on account of Jesus (Matt 5:11, Luke 6:22).

These qualifiers are crucial. Nobody argues that it's good simply to be persecuted or hated. Instead, *for what* are you being reviled or attacked? The Good News translation spells it out: for doing "what God requires." This is a way of explaining the word *righteousness* in the clause "for righteousness' sake" (Matt 5:10). As with the fourth beatitude, righteousness (*dikaiosynē*) indicates God's holiness, including God's covenant faithfulness, which God's people are called to imitate: "Be holy as I am holy" (1 Pet 1:16, quoting Lev 11:44–45, 19:1). Righteousness is both a characteristic of God and a human behavior. Love of neighbor is righteousness just as much as love of God is.

Given this understanding of righteousness, most interpreters until the twentieth century (or so) assumed that the phrase "for righteousness' sake" was synonymous with "for Jesus's sake." The early followers of Jesus were persecuted for the countercultural standards they adopted in their efforts to live in a manner worthy of a righteous God (Eph 4:1), and because of their association with a controversial figure—a crucified criminal who had once been accused of being in league with Satan (Matt 10:22, 25).[6] The two—for righteousness' sake, for Jesus's sake—went hand in hand.

Shouldn't righteous conduct be cause for praise, not for malice? In the first century a Christian way of life could lead to misunderstandings and even social scorn. Peter captured this observation when he reminded a congregation of gentile Christian converts that they once indulged in "what the Gentiles like to do"; his list includes sexual promiscuity, drunkenness, and idolatry. Their gentile neighbors, Peter pointed out, "are surprised that you no longer join them in the same excesses of dissipation, and so they malign you" (1 Pet 4:3–4).[7]

Some interpreters see this theme continuing today. Catholic theologian Hans Urs von Balthasar wrote of the eighth beatitude, "[T]he more compellingly the truth of the Christian message shines forth, the more wildly it is refused as an intolerable claim."[8] One might also think of Christian de Chergé and the other Cistercian monks of Tibhirine in Algeria, who were kidnapped and eventually

6. Charles Quarles, *Sermon on the Mount: Restoring Christ's Message to the Modern Church* (Nashville: B & H Academic, 2011), 71–72.

7. NRSV: "and so they blaspheme."

8. Hans Urs von Balthasar, *Man Is Created*, vol. 5 of *Explorations in Theology*, trans. Adrian Walker (San Francisco: Ignatius Press, 2015), 452.

killed.[9] As Jane Foulcher narrates their story, their commitment to humility (the virtue of the first beatitude) was a commitment to self-giving love for their neighbors: "love required that they bend before the other."[10] In their humility, they participated in the sufferings of Christ and were ultimately martyred.

The Cistercian monks also illustrated another way to understand righteousness, which is to recall that premodern interpreters usually saw the eighth beatitude as the pinnacle and goal of all the beatitudes. This led to a common assumption that being persecuted "for righteousness' sake" meant being persecuted because one embodied the previous seven beatitudes. This seems a little counterintuitive. Why punish humility, or persecute gentleness, or pursue the merciful? But this theme fits in with the repeated emphasis on the Beatitudes as countercultural—indeed, as so counter to the culture that they arouse hostility and hatred. In this sense, the eighth beatitude is simply the result of the first seven. This theme can be seen scattered in writings throughout history.[11]

The great preacher John Wesley colorfully illustrated the point in a sermon preached in 1739. Why are the faithful persecuted? For Wesley, it's largely because the world misunderstands or dislikes the qualities represented by the Beatitudes and practiced by the faithful: "Because they are meek: 'Tame, passive fools, just fit to be trampled upon!' . . . Because they are pure in heart: 'Uncharitable creatures, that damn all the world, but those that are of their own sort! Blasphemous wretches, that pretend to make God a liar, to live without sin!'" But the greatest reason they are persecuted is because they are peacemakers (that is, peacemakers between humanity and God) who seek to spread their religion ("their errors") to others.[12]

In our own time, New Testament scholar Warren Carter argues that the Beatitudes envision a "just way of life" that challenges the status quo. This challenge to the status quo naturally arouses opposition in those who benefit from the way things are: "The empire will certainly strike back."[13] Car-

---

9. Jane Foulcher, *Reclaiming Humility: Four Studies in the Monastic Tradition*, Cistercian Studies 255 (Collegeville, MN: Liturgical Press, 2015), 243–306.

10. Foulcher, *Reclaiming Humility*, 306.

11. E.g., Michael H. Crosby, *Spirituality of the Beatitudes: Matthew's Vision for the Church in an Unjust World*, rev. ed. (Maryknoll, NY: Orbis Books, 2005), 177, 194.

12. John Wesley, Sermon 23.3.3, in Wesley, *The Nature of the Kingdom: Wesley's Messages on the Sermon on the Mount*, ed. Clare George Weakley Jr. (Minneapolis: Bethany House Publishers, 1979), 94–95. Also available at http://wesley.nnu.edu/john-wesley/the-sermons-of-john-wesley -1872-edition/sermon-23-upon-our-lords-sermon-on-the-mount-discourse-three.

13. Warren Carter, *Matthew and the Margins: A Socio-Political and Religious Reading* (Shef-

ter's comments were anticipated a century earlier by the Swedish Pietist P. P. Waldenström (1838–1917), who connected the eighth beatitude not backward to the other seven but forward to Jesus's sayings about salt and light (Matt 5:13–15), which immediately follow the Beatitudes. Waldenström told his congregation, "The reason why [Jesus's followers] must be prepared to suffer such persecution is precisely because they are the salt of the world and the light of the world. If the prophets had simply remained silent and let everything they saw pass by without further comment, then they could have been left in peace."[14] When the prophets, John the Baptist, and Jesus criticized people for sin, hypocrisy, and false righteousness, "the salt burned in their wounds."[15] Modern-day prophets like John Wycliff, Jan Hus, Peter Waldo, and Martin Luther in turn suffered for the sake of righteousness.[16] From Waldenström's perspective at least, the "empire"—the reigning powers of the day—struck back against them, too.

Carter's description of the Beatitudes as a "*just* way of life" reminds us that the Greek word *dikaiosynē* can also mean justice. Not many English translations of Matt 5:10 choose this path, but it gives the beatitude a different ring. Blessed are those persecuted for "doing right," as the New Living Translation puts it. Dietrich Bonhoeffer represented this more recent view: the clause "for righteousness' sake" in Matt 5:10 "does not refer to the righteousness of God, but to suffering for a just cause."[17] Long before Bonhoeffer, the Jesuit Cornelius à Lapide suggested that righteousness meant a wide variety of things, including defending the rights of orphans.[18]

---

field: Sheffield Academic, 2000), 136. See also R. T. France, *The Gospel of Matthew*, NICNT (Grand Rapids: Eerdmans, 2007), 170.

14. P. P. Waldenström, "You Are the Salt and the Light of the World," in *The Swedish Pietists: A Reader. Excerpts from the Writings of Carl Olof Rosenius and Paul Peter Waldenström*, ed. and trans. Mark Safstrom (Eugene, OR: Pickwick, 2015), 216.

15. Waldenström, "You Are the Salt," 217.

16. Safstrom, *The Swedish Pietists*, 217.

17. Dietrich Bonhoeffer, *The Cost of Discipleship* (New York: Simon & Schuster, 1995), 113. Elsewhere, Bonhoeffer wrote, "Jesus cares for those who suffer for a just cause even if it is not exactly for the confession of his name" (Bonhoeffer, Church and World 1.349, in *Ethics*, vol. 6 of *Dietrich Bonhoeffer Works*, ed. Clifford J. Green, trans. Reinhard Krauss, Charles C. West, and Douglas W. Stott [Minneapolis: Fortress, 2005], 346). See also John Dear, *Beatitudes of Peace: Meditations on the Beatitudes, Peacemaking and the Spiritual Life* (New London, CT: Twenty-Third Publications, 2016), 101–9.

18. Cornelius à Lapide, *The Holy Gospel According to Saint Matthew*, vol. 1 of *The Great Commentary of Cornelius à Lapide*, trans. Thomas W. Mossman, rev. Michael J. Miller (Fitzwilliam, NH: Loreto, 2008), 224.

A short story by nineteenth-century author Lily Watson illustrates a similar point. In her story about the eighth beatitude, a rich young woman in London renounces her life of leisure to go live among and serve the poor. Her plan is met with bitter opposition from her family, who declare her "selfish, deluded, preposterous" and ungrateful.[19] She loses her friends, her family, and her future fiancé. "But she sees the fruit of her work increasing year by year. Year by year she loves it more."[20] For Lily Watson as for Lapide, the persecuted are blessed because they pursue all kinds of justice "for the sake of God."[21]

Bonhoeffer—and other twentieth-century interpreters—went further. For them, the persecuted, regardless of whether they are Christians, are blessed for pursuing any just cause. This view has occasioned some minor resistance. Welsh Protestant preacher D. Martyn Lloyd-Jones (1899–1981) was nervous about people being persecuted "for a cause" and warned that being persecuted for political beliefs is not covered by the beatitude.[22] He seems, in fact, to have taken a direct jab at people like Bonhoeffer who ended up in prison in Nazi Germany, suggesting that these people were being persecuted not for righteousness but for their political views.[23] For the most part, though, modern interpreters argue that those persecuted for Jesus's sake and for pursuing justice are blessed.

Martin Luther King Jr. invoked the beatitude in this way in his 1964 Nobel Peace Prize acceptance speech when he referred to all those who fight for human dignity, equality, peace, and justice as "these humble children of God [who] were willing to suffer for righteousness' sake."[24] Others placed in this category include the Freedom Riders and other nonviolent protestors

---

19. Lily Watson, *A Garden of Girls: Stories Illustrating the Beatitudes* (London: Religious Tract Society, 1893), 150.

20. Watson, *Garden of Girls*, 158.

21. Lapide, *The Holy Gospel According to Saint Matthew*, 225.

22. D. Martyn Lloyd-Jones, *Studies in the Sermon on the Mount*, vol. 1 (Grand Rapids: Eerdmans, 1960), 132.

23. Lloyd-Jones, *Studies*, 132–33.

24. Martin Luther King Jr., "Acceptance Speech" (Nobel Peace Prize, December 10, 1964), https://www.nobelprize.org/prizes/peace/1964/king/26142-martin-luther-king-jr-acceptance -speech-1964/. John Dear: Blessed are those who stand up for justice, for their work "against poverty, the death penalty, nuclear weapons, the war on Iraq"; as examples, Dear names Gandhi, King, Dorothy Day, Archbishop Romero, and Sister Ita Ford (John Dear, "The Beatitudes of Peace," *National Catholic Reporter* [November 21, 2006], https://www.ncronline.org/blogs /road-peace/beatitudes-peace). George Hunsinger separates the issue of being persecuted for Jesus (the ninth and last beatitude) from the issue of being persecuted for "doing what is right" (the eighth beatitude) (George Hunsinger, *The Beatitudes* [Mahwah, NJ: Paulist, 2015], 94).

during the civil rights movement, Ruby Bridges (the first African American student at an all-white public school in New Orleans in 1960), and Fannie Lou Hamer (who was beaten and jailed for her advocacy for voting rights for African Americans).[25]

Persecution by the state: the martyrdom era

The examples of Bonhoeffer and Martin Luther King Jr. show how dangerous it can be to stand for justice in an unjust world. Both died for the cause of righteousness; both are sometimes called martyrs.

Jesus, of course, was also a martyr. He teaches that anyone who wants to follow him must likewise take up their cross (Matt 10:38, 16:24; Mark 8:34; Luke 9:23). Many early Christians did not take this metaphorically. The ninth beatitude ("blessed are you *when*") assumes that Jesus's followers will be persecuted, hated, excluded, defamed, and slandered—a prediction that had likely already come true by the time Matthew and Luke wrote their gospels. Tradition has it that most of the original apostles died as martyrs. In light of Jesus's crucifixion, dying for one's faith became viewed as the pinnacle of Christian conviction. By dying for Christ's sake, one imitated Christ and participated in his death, witnessed to the resurrection and the truth of the gospel, and even defeated the powers of Satan himself (as in Rev 12:10–11).[26] Theirs was the kingdom of heaven. For this reason, the beatitude becomes closely associated with the martyrs of the church's early centuries. In Ambrose of Milan's words, martyrdom is "the very palm and crown of the Beatitudes" (*Comm. Luke* 5.61).[27]

Before the conversion of the Roman emperor Constantine, Christian reflections on the beatitude focused, understandably, on persecution at the hands of the Roman Empire. An early Christian treatise called the Didascalia (ca. 200–250) devotes a chapter to the Christian duty to care for those fleeing or facing persecution, citing Matt 5:11 in support of this duty. Clement of Alexandria (ca. 150–215) used the beatitude to praise the martyrs and to condemn those who deny Christ in order to avoid persecution.[28]

---

25. Carole Boston Weatherford, *The Beatitudes: From Slavery to Civil Rights*, ill. Tim Ladwig, Eerdmans Books for Young Readers (Grand Rapids: Eerdmans, 2010), n.p.

26. See, e.g., Perpetua's visions of her martyrdom, in Walsh, ed., *What Would You Die For?*, 68–70, 82; see also Middleton, *Radical Martyrdom*, 6, 79–82, 88–93.

27. Ambrose of Milan, *Commentary of Saint Ambrose on the Gospel According to Saint Luke*, trans. Íde M. Ní Riain (Dublin: Halcyon, 2001), 137.

28. Clement of Alexandria, *Stromata* 4.6 (*ANF* 2:416).

Origen (185–254), in a treatise aptly titled "Exhortation to Martyrdom" (ca. 235), encouraged his mentor Ambrose and the presbyter Protectetus, who were both imprisoned during the persecutions of the emperor Maximinus, to remember "the great reward laid up in heaven for those who are persecuted and reviled for righteousness' sake" (Matt 5:10–12, Luke 6:23), "just as the apostles once rejoiced when they were counted worthy to suffer dishonor for His name."[29] Cyprian (d. ca. 248), a bishop in third-century Carthage, turned to Jesus's exhortations to rejoice and be glad in persecutions to argue that the loss of earthly possessions is not to be feared but is "even to be desired," since the Lord himself announces that these things are blessed (Luke 6:22–23).[30] Cyprian was born in Carthage in North Africa around the same time that Perpetua and Felicity were executed by Roman gladiators in that same city. Half a century later, Cyprian, too, died there as a martyr.

The confidence of Origen and Cyprian that the persecuted are honored by God reveals an uncomfortable truth about this beatitude. Unlike "Blessed are the merciful," which easily translates into an instruction to be merciful, it doesn't seem possible for this beatitude to function as a command. Does Jesus really mean, Be persecuted? He seems rather to mean that those who are persecuted—not of their own choice—are blessed in the midst of their suffering. Some Christians did seek out martyrdom, to the astonishment of Roman rulers and the consternation of some of their peers.[31] The legacy of the martyrs as the exemplars of the persecuted endures even today.

After Constantine's conversion, of course, martyrdom (more or less) ceased in the West, at least until Christianity's collision with Islam. Reflections on the beatitude by medieval commentators in the West reveal an ongoing nostalgia for the age of martyrdom. For Thomas Aquinas (1225–1274), Matthew's eighth beatitude "refers to those who will die as martyrs." Invoking the common view that the Beatitudes are steps toward perfection, alongside

29. Origen, *An Exhortation to Martyrdom, Prayer, First Principles: Book IV, Prologue to the Commentary on the Song of Songs, Homily XXVII on Numbers*, trans. Rowan Greer (New York: Paulist, 1979), 43.

30. Cyprian, "On the Lapsed," in Cyprian, *Treatises* 3.12 (*ANF* 5:440).

31. For studies of the so-called martyrdom era (ca. 30–313 CE), including the phenomenon of voluntary martyrdom, see G. W. Bowersock, *Martyrdom and Rome* (Cambridge University Press, 1995); W. H. C. Frend, *Martyrdom and Persecution in the Early Church: A Study of a Conflict from the Maccabees to Donatus* (Oxford: Basil Blackwell, 1965); Paul Middleton, *Radical Martyrdom and Cosmic Conflict in Early Christianity* (London: T&T Clark, 2006); Candida Moss, *The Myth of Persecution: How Early Christians Invented a Story of Martyrdom* (New York: HarperOne, 2013).

the observation that this is the last beatitude and thus the final step on the ladder, Aquinas concluded that martyrdom is the ultimate perfection.[32] But for most medieval Christians, this perfection seemed out of reach. Bernard of Clairvaux (ca. 1090–1153) described persecution as "the privilege of the holy martyrs," but the monk also suggested, wistfully perhaps, that this privilege is largely unavailable, since "nowadays . . . none or only very few have to suffer persecution."[33] In the early fifteenth century, on the cusp of the Reformation, English mystic Margery Kempe (ca. 1373–1438) "fantasized about being a martyr for Christ."[34]

Viewing martyrs as the exemplars of the eighth beatitude continues today in Catholic teaching. It appears in Protestant writing as well, often in reference to more recent martyrs, whether missionaries who have died bringing the gospel around the globe or Christians who have been killed for their faith in places like Syria and Nigeria. Given that most Western Christians rarely risk their lives for Christ in a literal sense, contemporary Western writers sometimes construe martyrdom as dying to self, just as "taking up your cross" can now mean the willingness to give up material comfort or suffer social scorn for Christ's sake.[35]

The Reformers as the new martyrs

Viewing the persecuted as the martyrs took on new life in the writings of the Protestant Reformers.[36] It's easy to see why. Czech reformer Jan Hus was

---

32. Anton ten Klooster, *Thomas Aquinas on the Beatitudes: Reading Matthew, Disputing Grace and Virtue, Preaching Happiness* (Leuven: Peeters, 2018), 113–14, citing Thomas Aquinas, *Commentary on the Gospel of Matthew, Chapters 1–12*, ed. The Aquinas Institute, trans. Jeremy Holmes and Beth Mortensen, Biblical Commentaries 33 (Lander, WY: The Aquinas Institute for the Study of Sacred Doctrine, 2013), C.5 L.2.443, 444. See also Thomas Aquinas, *Summa Theologica: Complete English Edition*, 5 vols., trans. Fathers of the English Dominican Province (Westminster, MD: Christian Classics, 1948), II.II 124.1–4.

33. Bernard of Clairvaux, "First Sermon for the Feast of All Saints. On the Eight Beatitudes," in *St. Bernard's Sermons for the Seasons and Principal Festivals of the Year*, vol. 3 (Westminster, MD: Carroll, 1950), 351.

34. Gregory, *Salvation at Stake*, 30.

35. Yiu Sing Lúcás Chan, *The Ten Commandments and the Beatitudes* (Lanham, MD: Rowman & Littlefield, 2012), 223.

36. Occasionally (but rarely) the theme appears in Catholic writings as well during the Reformation and Counter-Reformation eras. Robert Southwell wrote "an epistle of comfort" to priests and Catholic laypeople, applying the blessing for the persecuted both to the early

burned at the stake in 1415. In 1523, two of Luther's followers, Henricus Vos and Johannes van den Esschen, were first stripped of their priestly robes by a Catholic bishop and then handed over to the local civil authorities to be burned to death in the market square of Brussels.[37] A few years later, in 1536, William Tyndale, who ran afoul of the Catholic Church for translating the Bible into English, was executed in Valvoorde near Brussels; he was strangled and then his dead body was burned. All this was before the Catholic Queen Mary I of England systematically rounded up almost three hundred Protestants and burned them at the stake between 1553 and 1558.

It's no surprise, then, that the blessing on the persecuted was "dear to the heart of many who sympathized with John Wyclif"[38] (one of the forerunners to the later Reformation), and to so many of the other Reformers. They did not have to strain to see themselves as the persecuted—as the inheritors of the second- and third-century martyrs. In sermons preached on the eighth beatitude, the Reformers (and later, the Puritans) repeatedly compared themselves and their own times to that of the early martyrs.[39]

---

martyrs and to any who presently suffer imprisonment, banishment, or any other oppression in the defense of the Catholic faith (Southwell, *An epistle of comfort to the reuerend priestes, & to the honorable, worshipful, & other of the laye sort restrayned in durance for the Catholicke fayth* [Paris, 1587], 196).

37. Dick Akerboom and Marcel Gielis, "'A New Song Shall Begin Here . . .' The Martyrdom of Luther's Followers among Antwerp's Augustinians on July 1, 1523 and Luther's Response," in *More than a Memory: The Discourse of Martyrdom and the Construction of Christian Identity in the History of Christianity*, ed. Johan Leemans (Leuven: Peeters, 2005), 243–44.

38. David Lyle Jeffrey, "Dante and Chaucer," in *The Sermon on the Mount through the Centuries: From the Early Church to John Paul II*, ed. Jeffrey P. Greenman, Timothy Larsen, and Stephen R. Spencer (Grand Rapids: Brazos, 2007), 102.

39. Huldrych Zwingli (1484–1531) linked the renewal of the church in his own time with the era of the martyrs: "Born in blood, the church I think can be restored in no other way than again in blood" (Zwingli, *Sämtliche Werke* 7:341ff., quoted in John Howard Yoder, "The Christological Presuppositions of Discipleship," in *Being Human, Becoming Human: Dietrich Bonhoeffer and Social Thought*, ed. Jens Zimmerman and Brian Gregor [Eugene, OR: Pickwick Publications, 2010], 128). Puritan preacher Jeremiah Burroughs quoted Ignatius (ca. 35–107), bishop of Antioch who was martyred during the reign of Trajan: "I had rather be a martyr than a monarch." Burroughs also alluded to the early days of martyrdom when he claimed, "Certainly the church was never more fruitful than when it was watered with her own blood" (Jeremiah Burroughs, *The Saints' Happiness* [Edinburgh: James Nichol, 1867; Soli Deo Gloria, 1988, 1992], 221–22), which echoes Tertullian's famous line: "We multiply whenever we are mown down by you; the blood of Christians is seed" (*Apologeticus* 50.13, in Tertullian, *Apology; de Spectaculis; Minucius Felix*, trans. T. R. Glover, LCL [Cambridge, MA: Harvard University Press, 1953], 227). Thomas Watson quoted Basil: "'The church is founded in blood and by blood it increases.' . . . The gospel has always flourished in the ashes of martyrs" (Thomas Watson, *The Beatitudes: An Exposition*

The Reformers often collapsed the distance between themselves and the first century by applying Jesus's warnings and promises directly to their situation. When William Tyndale wrote eloquently and at length on Matt 5:11, it's clear that he was thinking of his own time, perhaps even of himself, especially when he referred to innocent Christians who are condemned to death, excommunicated, and "deprived of the fellowship of holy church."[40] Martin Luther took Jesus's blessing on those who are reviled (Matt 5:11) as a blessing on the Reformers who were slandered by the pope, the bishops, and the princes; blessed are *they* when the pope rails against them and threatens them with excommunication.[41] Similarly, John Calvin applied Jesus's warning that the disciples "will be rejected, and driven out, and their name will be accursed" (Luke 6:22) to the Reformers' excommunication from the Roman Catholic Church.[42] Christ's blessings on the persecuted were given directly to them, to encourage them in their trials, especially as they suffered the pain of excommunication.

Reformer Menno Simons (1496–1561) also applied Jesus's warnings to the disciples that they would be persecuted and thrown out of synagogues directly to the Münsterite Anabaptists and their expulsions from other churches.[43] Simons, father of the Mennonites, opened his treatise *The Cross of the Saints* (ca. 1554) by quoting Jesus's blessing on those who are persecuted for righteousness' sake.[44] While Simons was still a priest, the civil authorities executed many of the Anabaptists in Münster, including one of Simons's brothers. After leaving the priesthood, Simons became a key Anabaptist leader; one of the few

of *Matthew 5:1–10* [Carlisle, PA: Banner of Truth Trust, 2014], 322). Increase Mather compared the early church martyrs to the Waldensians (Increase Mather, *Sermons Wherein Those Eight Characters of the Blessed Commonly Called the Beatitudes Are Opened and Applied in Fifteen Discourses* [Boston: B. Green, for Daniel Henchman, 1718], Sermon 14–15).

40. William Tyndale, *The Work of William Tyndale*, ed. G. E. Duffield (Philadelphia: Fortress, 1965), 207.

41. Martin Luther, *The Sermon on the Mount*, vol. 21 of *Luther's Works*, ed. Jaroslav Pelikan (St. Louis: Concordia, 1956), 48–50. He applied Matt 5:12 to the "slander and hostility" directed to pastor Conrad Cordatus for his commitment to Reformation faith (Martin Luther, *Luther: Letters of Spiritual Counsel*, trans. Theodore G. Tappert, LCC 18 [Philadelphia: Westminster, 1955], 169).

42. John Calvin, *Sermons on the Beatitudes: Five Sermons from the Gospel Harmony, Delivered in Geneva in 1560* (Carlisle, PA: Banner of Truth Trust, 2006), 67, 70; and John Calvin, *A Harmony of the Gospels Matthew, Mark and Luke*, vol. 1, ed. David W. Torrance and Thomas F. Torrance, trans. A. W. Morrison (Grand Rapids: Eerdmans, 1972), 5.11, p. 173.

43. Menno Simons, "The Cross of the Saints," in *The Complete Writings of Menno Simons*, ed. John Christian Wenger, trans. Leonard Verduin (Scottdale, PA: Herald Press, 1956), 583.

44. Simons, "The Cross of the Saints," 582.

to escape execution, he was forced to flee from the authorities until his death in 1561. Simons named specific accusations leveled against the Mennonites ("utter all kinds of evil against you" [Matt 5:11]), as well as the violent persecutions they endured: homes seized or torn down, tortured, hanged, burned alive at the stake, feet cut off.[45]

Katharina Schütz Zell (ca. 1498–1562), one of the mothers of the Reformation and the wife of Lutheran Reformer Matthew Zell, likewise applied Jesus's warnings that his followers would be excluded from fellowship and killed to her own situation. She wrote a letter of consolation and exhortation to a group of evangelically-minded women in Kentzingen whose husbands had left the city along with their priest (when he was expelled for "evangelical leanings") and then been denied reentry.[46] She encouraged them in the midst of their suffering, naming specific dangers that they and their husbands may encounter, including "imprisonment in towers, chains, drowning, banishment" and even death.[47] For these things, she said, they are blessed because of Christ's promise in the beatitude, since they are suffering "for Christ's sake."[48]

All these examples highlight one significant difference between the time of the early martyrs and the Reformers: they were persecuted not by a pagan government, but by other Christians—in Zell's case, by the Roman Catholic Church, and in Simons's case by Catholics and fellow Protestants. For it was not long before Protestants turned against each other too, and then returned the favor by persecuting Catholics wherever they gained the upper hand. A.-M. Carré used the beatitude as an occasion to lament that ever since the fourth century and the edict of Constantine, persecuted Christians have "changed camps" and turned around to become the persecutors.[49]

This painful irony—Christians as both persecuted and persecutor—dominated reflections on the eighth beatitude for several hundred years. Protestant writers sometimes used the thinly veiled metaphor of Cain and Abel to voice their dismay over being hunted down by a "sibling" but also to claim the moral high ground as the righteous Abel murdered by his envious brother Cain. Martin Luther used the metaphor in a ballad he wrote to commemorate the deaths

---

45. Simons, "The Cross of the Saints," 599.

46. Ronald K. Rittgers, *The Reformation of Suffering: Pastoral Theology and Lay Piety in Late Medieval and Early Modern Germany* (Oxford: Oxford University Press, 2012), 136.

47. Katharina Schütz Zell, *Church Mother: The Writings of a Protestant Reformer in Sixteenth-Century Germany*, ed. and trans. Elsie McKee (Chicago: University of Chicago Press, 2006), 51.

48. Zell, *Church Mother*, 50, 56.

49. A.-M. Carré, *Quand arrive le bonheur: Les Béatitudes*, 2nd ed. (Paris: Les Éditions du Cerf, 1974), 181.

of his two followers killed in Brussels. In the ballad he declared, "The Spirit cannot silent be: / Good Abel's blood out-poured / Must still besmear Cain's forehead."[50] Menno Simons, caught between Catholics and other Reformers, was more mournful about his situation. He lamented that those who are swift to shed blood and to persecute are not only Catholics but also "those who boast of the holy Word" (i.e., the other Reformers, including Lutherans and Zwinglians).[51] Simons pointed out the painful paradox: if they boast of God's Word, "Why do they then not fear God and His Word? Why . . . are they then still such terrible, ravenous wolves . . . ?"[52]

Rejoice and be glad

Despite these laments, the Reformers also recognized that this is the only beatitude that comes with a command: *Rejoice!* The exhortation to rejoice in persecutions has led interpreters to wonder why being persecuted and hated should lead to joy rather than to sorrow. The first, most obvious, reason is named in the beatitude itself: "for in the same way they persecuted the prophets who were before you" (Matt 5:12). Being persecuted placed them in a long, honorable line stretching back not only to the early martyrs and apostles, but to the Old Testament prophets. Another reason was that God permits such suffering.

Permitted by God for good purposes

Jerome (347–420), the brilliant mind behind the Latin Vulgate, was a little skeptical about this. He knew that "when Christ is its cause, reviling should be wished for," but he admitted that he didn't know anyone who could fulfill the words to rejoice and exult "when our reputation is torn to pieces by abusive speech."[53] Others were more positive. During the emperor Maximinus's persecutions, Jerome's predecessor Origen (185–254) suggested ("at least we

---

50. Akerboom and Gielis, "'A New Song,'" 259. See also Simons, "The Cross of the Saints," 588–89.

51. Simons, "The Cross of the Saints," 600.

52. Simons, "The Cross of the Saints," 601.

53. Jerome, *Commentary on Matthew*, trans. Thomas P. Scheck, FC 117 (Washington, DC: Catholic University of America, 2008), 77.

must suppose") "that the present temptation has come about as a testing and trying of our love for God."[54]

The Reformers picked up this ball and ran with it. The beatitude's background in Isaiah became especially appropriate for those hated by their own people (that is, by fellow Christians): "Your own people who hate you and reject you for my name's sake have said, 'Let the LORD be glorified, so that we may see your joy'; but it is they who shall be put to shame" (Isa 66:5). Luther's ballad for his two followers executed in Brussels confidently fulfilled the command to "rejoice and be glad" in the face of persecution. Instead of lamenting their deaths, Luther wrote, "A new song here shall be begun – / The Lord God help our singing! Of what our God himself hath done, / Praise, honor to him bringing. / At Brussels in the Netherlands / By two boys, martyrs youthful / He showed the wonders of his hands / Whom he with favor truthful / So richly hath adorned."[55]

Similarly, Katharina Schütz Zell told the women of Kentzingen that since they were suffering for Christ's sake they should receive their suffering with rejoicing as a fatherly gift sent to God's "best loved children [cf. Heb 12:6–7; Lk 16:8].... Yes, even if you are put in chains for Christ's sake, how happy you are! [cf. Mt 5:11]."[56] She concluded her letter by quoting the blessings on those who mourn and are persecuted (Matt 5:4, 10).[57] In a later generation of Reformers, John Wesley (1703–1791) reassured his listeners that even persecution is a tool in God's hands which he uses to enlarge his kingdom and achieve his gracious ends.[58]

A century earlier, Puritan Jeremiah Burroughs (1599–1646) argued that God uses persecution to achieve "many holy ends"—to demonstrate his power so that the saints may exercise their love, faith, patience, and humility ("Surely if I had not been brought into this low estate I should never have had the exercise of these graces"); to test the hearts of the faithful; to weed out the hypocrites; and to conform the saints to Christ, who suffered and entered into glory.[59] Burroughs was careful to say that God permits persecution but does not cause it. Instead, two parties are held responsible (by Burroughs and other writers): worldly men and the devil.

---

54. Origen, Exhortation 6, *An Exhortation to Martyrdom*, 45.

55. Akerboom and Gielis, "'A New Song,'" 256.

56. Zell, *Church Mother*, 50, 52.

57. Zell, *Church Mother*, 56.

58. Wesley, Sermon 23.3.5, in *Nature of the Kingdom*, 96–97.

59. Burroughs, *Saints' Happiness*, 206–9, quotation on 208; see also Watson, *The Beatitudes*, 289.

Sign of opposition from Satan

For the early Christians, the willing death of a martyr struck a decisive blow against the power of Satan. Origen claimed that Christians who "lay down their lives for the cause of godliness, shall utterly destroy the army of the wicked one," because "the demons perceive that those who meet death victoriously for the sake of religion destroy their authority."[60] The Reformers and their followers applied this principle to persecution in general; they were persecuted (if not always martyred) because Satan tries to destroy the gospel and the faithful who seek to spread it.

In Luther's words, Jesus warns his followers that "they should and must suffer persecution" because the devil will work hard to block them from entering the kingdom of God.[61] In fact, the fierceness of the persecution against them is paradoxically a sign of their success, because it reveals the devil's opposition to their preaching of the gospel: "the devil cannot bear it otherwise, nor will he stop egging people on against the Gospel, so that all the world is incensed against it."[62] In his ballad praising the Brussels martyrs, he wrote, "The ancient foe is filled with hate / That he was thus defeated / By two such youngsters – he, so great! . . . To God their Faith they gave thanks / That they would soon be rescued / From Satan's scoffs and mumming pranks."[63]

If persecution was a sign of Satan's opposition, then it was a mark of true godliness. Repeatedly throughout history, interpreters of the beatitude have viewed persecution as a mark of the true Christian—especially over against other Christians who claimed the name but were (in their view) not genuine disciples of Christ.

Mark of the true Christian

Due in part to this beatitude, Christians have long seen persecution as a mark of the true disciple, heir to the prophets and apostles. In the eleventh century,

---

60. Origen, *Against Celsus* 8.44 (ANF 4:655).

61. Luther, *Sermon on the Mount*, 45.

62. Luther, *Sermon on the Mount*, 51.

63. Akerboom and Gielis, "'A New Song,'" 257; see also Robert Kolb, "From Hymn to History of Dogma: Lutheran Martyrology in the Reformation Era," in *More than a Memory: The Discourse of Martyrdom and the Construction of Christian Identity in the History of Christianity*, ed. Johan Leemans (Leuven: Peeters, 2005), 295, 312–13. Similarly, John Calvin wrote that persecution is inevitable because of the assaults of Satan and because "the flesh cannot abide the teaching of the Gospel" (Calvin, *Harmony of the Gospels* 5.10, p. 172).

Ælfric of Eynsham (ca. 955–1025) pondered the eighth beatitude at great length and concluded that "persecution is the surest sign of fidelity to Christ in both words and works."[64] But it was the Reformers who wielded this theme as a shield against their detractors.

Because Jesus promised his disciples that they would be persecuted and driven out, the Reformers viewed their persecution and even excommunications as a mark that they were genuine disciples of Christ. John Calvin, for example, wrote that Christ gave Matt 5:11 and Luke 6:22 as "a comfort to the faithful" (by which he meant his own congregation), because Christ made suffering for righteousness' sake "the mark by which Christ distinguishes His martyrs from the wicked and the evil-doers."[65] Christ's blessing on the persecuted should give them the courage not to fear papal excommunication, because they're not being separated from Christ but are rather being marked as his.[66]

This is a common theme among the magisterial Reformers, but it's even more true of the so-called radical Reformers, as well as the later Puritan Nonconformists, who had to defend themselves on all sides. For example, Dietrich Philips, one of the leaders of the Anabaptists in Münster, needed to defend the Anabaptist pastors as the "correct ministers" of the Word of God, even though they hadn't been ordained by bishops in the apostolic succession (in other words, by bishops who could trace their ordinations in an unbroken line back to the apostle Peter). In his treatise "The Church of God" (ca. 1650), Philips used the beatitude to argue that the "true minister[s] of the divine Word" are easily recognized not only by their orthodox teachings and their godly lives, but also by "the persecution which they must suffer for the sake of truth and righteousness."[67] In Philips's treatise, the seventh and final ordinance of the true church of God is that "all Christians must suffer and be persecuted."[68]

---

64. Derek A. Olsen, *Reading Matthew with Monks: Liturgical Interpretation in Anglo-Saxon England* (Collegeville, MN: Liturgical Press, 2015), 169.

65. Calvin, *Harmony of the Gospels*, 5.10, p. 172.

66. Calvin, *Harmony of the Gospels*, 5.11, p. 173. Menno Simons described persecution as the reward of "all true servants of God" (Simons, "The Cross of the Saints," 592). In 1764, Samuel Collett wrote that persecution of the faithful is "the greatest proof of their sincere love and reverence of God" (Samuel Collett, *A Paraphrase of the Fifth, Sixth, and Seventh Chapters of Matthew, with Proper Soliloquies at Every Period* [London: J. Williams, 1764], 21). See also Robert Harris, *The Way to True Happiness: Delivered in Twenty-Four Sermons upon the Beatitudes*, ed. Don Kistler (Morgan, PA: Soli Deo Gloria, 1998), 381–83; Watson, *The Beatitudes*, 285; Wesley, Sermon 23.3.7 in *Nature of the Kingdom*, 98.

67. Dietrich Philips, "The Church of God," in *Spiritual and Anabaptist Writers*, ed. George H. Williams (Philadelphia: Westminster, 1957), 241.

68. Philips, "The Church of God," 251–52.

Conversely, this suggests that Christians who aren't being persecuted are perhaps not being faithful or true to the gospel. This implication has sometimes led to uneasiness in the modern Western church, which is largely not a persecuted church. As Clarence Jordan (1912–1969) asked his fellow American Christians, "What are the things we do that are worth persecuting?"[69] Christians who lose their saltiness (Matt 5:13), wrote Jordan, are no longer worth persecuting.[70] For Jordan, "saltiness" meant speaking out against and resisting race prejudice, national pride, militarism, and exploitation.[71]

On the other side of the world, Chinese preacher Wang Mingdao (1900–1991) used the beatitude to explain why "many so-called Christians" were not persecuted by the world but were instead praised "as reasonable Christians."[72] He had in mind liberal scholars of his time, including Chinese theologians who adopted the social gospel.[73] For Mingdao, the Chinese Christians who were driven underground by the government and who were looked down on by society were the true church: their persecutions demonstrated their fidelity.

Only *for righteousness' sake: but who decides?*

In a memorable phrase, Augustine declared that the clause "for the sake of righteousness" in Matt 5:10 is what "distinguishes the martyr from the bandit."[74] Likewise the apostle Peter warned that suffering "as a mischief maker" is not blessed (1 Pet 4:15). This is the heart of the matter. Who gets to decide what counts as righteousness? What is righteousness to one is heresy to another.

When Augustine wrote those words, he was embroiled in what came to be known as the Donatist controversy. The Donatists argued that the validity of the church's sacraments depended on the purity or holiness of the minister. If the minister was impure, then the sacrament was invalid. For example, Donatists believed that ministers who had renounced their faith under threat of

---

69. Clarence Jordan, *Sermon on the Mount*, rev. ed. (Valley Forge, PA: Judson, 1952), 40.

70. Jordan, *Sermon on the Mount*, 41.

71. Jordan, *Sermon on the Mount*, 41.

72. Quoted in John Y. H. Yieh, "Reading the Sermon on the Mount in China: A Hermeneutical Inquiry into Its History of Reception," in *Reading Scriptures in China*, ed. Chlöe Starr (London: T&T Clark, 2008), 153.

73. Yieh, "Reading the Sermon," 150, 153.

74. Augustine, Sermon 53A.13, in Augustine, *Essential Sermons*, ed. Boniface Ramsey, trans. Edmund Hill, The Works of Saint Augustine: A Translation for the 21st Century (Hyde Park, NY: New City Press, 2007), 83.

persecution should not be allowed to return to the church and administer the sacraments; their apostasy (denial of Christ) made them unworthy. Augustine countered that the sacrament's grace was not dependent on the worthiness of the minister, and it was Augustine's case that won the day. The Donatists were deemed heretics.

Augustine conceded that heretics like the Donatists did suffer persecution. But, he insisted that heretics are *not* included in Christ's blessing or the promised reward of the kingdom, because they're suffering for their wrongdoing, not for the sake of justice. Those who break the unity of the church are excluded from the beatitude: "Nor may schismatics promise themselves any share in this reward, because in like manner where charity is not, justice cannot be; *for the love of neighbor worketh no evil.* If they had this charity they would not rend *the body of Christ which is the church*" (*De Serm. Dom.* 1.5.13).[75]

Augustine's principle reappears repeatedly in writings on the eighth beatitude. Instead of rejecting Augustine's principle, the Reformers embraced it (as did the Catholics who faced off against them). Augustine's *de facto* exclusion of schismatics and heretics from the blessing on the persecuted meant that the Reformers needed to justify their break with the church by arguing that they were members of the true church. Their excommunication was a signal of their righteousness, not of their errors. The seventeenth-century Puritan Robert Harris, for example, cited Augustine's argument against the Donatists to distinguish between punishment ("an act of justice" exercised against sin and disorder) and persecution ("an act of malice, ignorance, or both" exercised against truth and righteousness).[76] For Harris, of course, the Puritans were being persecuted for the truth, not punished for their disorder.

John Calvin also sided with Augustine: heretics do not fall under the blessing for the persecuted. Calvin, like Harris, saw himself as a guardian of the true church, not a heretic. On the other hand, Calvin firmly rejected the idea that the Anabaptists were being persecuted for righteousness, saying that they suffered instead for their errors.[77] One is not a martyr, he said tartly, if one "suffers persecution for his own fault."[78] He compared the Anabaptists to the fourth-century Donatists, writing that they "plague the Church with their insane ideas, and bring dishonor on the Gospel by boasting that they bear the

75. Augustine, *The Lord's Sermon on the Mount*, trans. John J. Jepson, ACW 5 (Mahwah, NJ: Paulist, 1948), 22–23, italics original.

76. Harris, *Way to True Happiness*, 413, see also 416.

77. Calvin, *Sermons on the Beatitudes*, 60–61.

78. Calvin, *Harmony of the Gospels* 5.12, p. 173.

marks of Christ when they are justly condemned."[79] The Anabaptist Menno Simons, for his part, did believe that he and his fellow Anabaptists bore the marks of Christ and his true church. But he had his own small stone to cast, too, writing that he and his followers were not like the Münsterite Anabaptists, who were seditious rebels.[80]

Catholics and Protestants were certainly not the first Christians to turn against one another in violent persecution. Christians had been persecuting one another as early as the fourth-century controversy between the Arians and the Nicenes over the nature of Christ's humanity and divinity. The Nicene bishop Athanasius of Alexandria was exiled five times (ca. 296–298) during his duels with the Arian bishops. He did not mince words concerning his treatment: "persecution is a device of the Devil."[81] This belief echoed down through the centuries and appeared with vigor in the writings of the Reformers. It also presented the magisterial Reformers with a dilemma. What's the line between persecution and punishment, or correction? The marks of two other beatitudes come into play here. Christians on opposite sides often found themselves torn between peace and purity—that is, between maintaining peace and unity in the church on the one hand, and guarding the purity, or right teaching of the church, on the other.

Schism: peacemaking and persecution

For some sixteenth-century Catholic leaders, Jesus's blessing on the peacemakers was evidence that the Reformers were not righteous, and were not blessed, because they were sowing discord in the church; they were peacebreakers, not peacemakers. Calvin acknowledged that his Catholic opponents quoted the blessing on the peacemakers against the Reformers because they caused trouble and strife in the world.[82] But he replied by emphasizing the phrase "for righteousness" to establish why they could not come to terms with the Roman Catholic Church despite the lack of peace: "God forbid that we should have peace at

---

79. Calvin, *Harmony of the Gospels* 5.12, p. 173. Calvin was not entirely unjustified in these claims; some of the earliest Anabaptists were violent, despite their present association with pacificism.

80. Simons, "The Cross of the Saints," 602–3, 609.

81. Athanasius, *Defence of His Flight* 23 (*NPNF*² 4:263). Tertullian suggested instead that "persecution comes to pass . . . by the devil's agency, but not by the devil's origination," since God allows persecution in order to test faith (Tertullian, *De Fuga* 9.2 [*ANF* 4:117]).

82. Calvin, *Sermons on the Beatitudes*, 59.

such a price!"[83] For many past interpreters, purity of heart should flow naturally into peacemaking (a conclusion drawn from the order of the Beatitudes). For Calvin, purity preempts peace. How could he abandon what he saw as the truth of the gospel in order to heal the schism caused by the Reformers?

He had a point. After all, Luther and the original Reformers had been expelled. They couldn't violate their consciences and confess things they didn't believe to be true in order to be readmitted to the church, thus restoring peace. Christian teaching has always insisted that one must follow one's conscience. To declare "Here I stand, I can do no other" is a long-honored part of Christian conviction—as Perpetua and Felicity demonstrated.

On the other hand, Perpetua and Felicity did not harm others for their convictions; they died for them. The gospels suggest that it's the business of the angels, not of the human faithful, to weed the garden of the church (Matt 13:24–30). This means Calvin had a more difficult case to make when it came to the Reformers turning to persecute other Reformers, as when Calvin lamented the bloodshed against the French Protestants but approved the execution of Spanish humanist Michael Servetus as a heretic in 1553. Augustine himself used the principle of love for the enemy (Matt 5:44) to plead for merciful treatment of the Donatist heretics. He appealed to his fellow Christians in Africa not to torture or execute even the Donatists who had attacked or killed Catholic priests.[84]

Standing firm in one's conscience and convictions does no violence and expels nobody. This theme anticipates a later element of the chapter, when we'll consider the qualities needed to face persecution well—qualities that include a refusal to take revenge or to use violence to achieve one's aims.

Woe to the persecutor

It also anticipates our next theme. Luke's version of the final beatitude pronounces a woe to those who are praised all the time, in contrast to those who are falsely accused and reviled. We might take a page from his book and consider the flip side of Matthew's blessing on the persecuted: *Woe to the persecutor!* Can a Christian intent on correcting heresy avoid becoming a persecutor? Can we identify a line between persecution and correction?

83. Calvin, *Sermons on the Beatitudes*, 60.

84. Augustine, "Letter 134: To Apringius" and "Letter 139: To Marcellinus," in *Augustine: Political Writings*, ed. E. M. Atkins and R. J. Dodaro (Cambridge: Cambridge University Press, 2001), 66, 68. On the willingness to kill heretics, see Gregory, *Salvation at Stake*, 74–96.

Jeremiah Burroughs offered a terse definition of persecution: "A pertinacious following of one to do him hurt, tending to his destruction."[85] Cornelius à Lapide defined persecution as "persistently following someone to trample him down, which allows him no place of peace or security but harasses and oppresses the innocent by every possible means, both calumnies and tortures, hurting them with both words and whips."[86] Neither Burroughs nor Lapide was speaking theoretically. Both witnessed in their own lifetimes the persecution of fellow Christians in England, whether of Protestants (for Burroughs) or of Catholics (for Lapide).

In a later generation of Reformers, Robert Harris wrote of his own time (early seventeenth-century England), "Never did the church of God show so much charity, mercy, and love as in times of persecution."[87] This sounds like wishful thinking when one surveys the actual historical record of the church during times of persecution! Surely Harris was thinking of the blessings of the persecuted, not the behavior of the persecutors—the "ravening wolves" lamented by Menno Simons.

The challenge is where to draw the lines. How much diversity of doctrine is or should be acceptable within the church? The term *adiaphora* is shorthand in the Christian tradition for nonessentials, for matters open to debate among Christians. People of good faith don't always agree on what counts as adiaphora and what counts as heresy.

My own tradition, the Evangelical Covenant Church (ECC), has long sought to have a "roomy tent" concerning how much Christians can disagree over certain doctrines and still remain in fellowship with one another in the church. In other words, it's generally put a lot of things under the umbrella of adiaphora and very few things into the category of heresy. It hasn't always lived up to this principle (and is struggling mightily to do so today). It's a principle expressed by early Covenanter C. V. Bowman in 1910 (who referred to the ECC with its original name, the Mission Friends):

> But concerning church order, the Mission Friends have a principle. . . . Namely this: they held that the local church shall consist only of believing members but, at the same time, to have room for all true believers no matter what their viewpoints are on controversial doctrines. It is this principle that really distinguishes Mission Friends from other

85. Burroughs, *Saints' Happiness*, 203.
86. Lapide, *The Holy Gospel According to Saint Matthew*, 224.
87. Harris, *Way to True Happiness*, 388.

Christian denominations, and which justifies their existence as a particular church.[88]

A church with wide boundaries has to navigate the tensions within rather
than expel those who differ—a worthy task for a *catholic* (universal) church
that embraces variety and difference.

Some will protest that the church must respond to heresy, even if narrowly
defined. In other words, how does a church protect its essential boundary
lines? As historian Brad Gregory writes of the Reformation era, both Catholics
and Reformers believed that "Heresy imperiled souls." Furthermore, "[here-
sy's] frequent links to sedition made its suppression even more urgent."[89] Are
there heresies that threaten the church's existence (or imperil souls) and that
must therefore be corrected or eliminated? In its responses to such a list of
items (which, in my view, should be a very small list), a church might remember the definitions of Burroughs and Lapide, and insist that Christians must
never seek to hurt, destroy, or trample down even the heretic.

It also benefits the church to remember and to lament the painful and horrific
history of when it became the persecutor not only of other Christians but of outsiders, especially of Muslims (during the Crusades) and of Jews (throughout most
of Christian history).[90] For the Reformed writer Marilynne Robinson, having
once been the persecuted ought to translate into present-day Reformed Christians
having sympathy for those currently persecuted, whether they be Muslim or immigrant or any other being pursued, as Burroughs says, to their destruction. One
thinks of the common refrain in Scripture: *Remember that you were once slaves in
Egypt* (Deut 5:15; 15:15; 16:12; 24:18, 22; see also Lev 19:34). Likewise, *Remember
that you were once the persecuted.* True, being persecuted is not, in and of itself, a
sign of righteousness: but the history of this beatitude reminds us that being the
persecutor is never a mark of the disciple seeking to live by the Beatitudes.

Responding to persecution with the first seven beatitudes

The pressing question of how to avoid becoming a persecutor lingers just
beneath the surface of reflections on the Beatitudes but rarely rises to the

88. C. V. Bowman, "About the Principles of the Mission Friends," in *Covenant Roots: Sources
and Affirmations,* ed. Glenn P. Anderson (Chicago: Covenant Press, 1980), 85–86.
89. Gregory, *Salvation at Stake,* 88.
90. See, e.g., Hunsinger, *Beatitudes,* 113–16.

surface. Another question does receive attention, which is how one should respond to persecution. What kind of qualities are required to bear persecution well?

One early question was whether one was allowed to run away. Christians disagreed, especially in the early period of martyrdoms. The theologian Tertullian (ca. 155–220) quoted Matthew's eighth beatitude as part of his argument that believers should not flee persecution because persecution is always, ultimately, God's will.[91] Origen and Athanasius disagreed. Origen appealed both to the beatitude and to Jesus's instructions in Matt 10:23 ("When they persecute you in one town, flee to the next") to demonstrate that Christians should avoid persecution when possible.[92] The bishop Athanasius wrote a defense of his own decision to flee from persecution (ca. 357), not from the state but from three Arian bishops. Athanasius insisted that saints such as Jacob (who fled Esau), David (who fled from Saul), and Peter and Paul (who both hid or fled for fear) were not condemned.[93] He cited the beatitude to support his claim that those who fled were still declared blessed by Christ.[94]

Another theme is far more important and widespread. Christians throughout history have insisted that those who are persecuted must respond to their persecution with the characteristics of the first seven beatitudes: humility, nonretaliation, mercy, nonviolence, forgiveness. Symeon the New Theologian (949–1022) points to Jesus's command to rejoice, and concludes that a person needs all the previous beatitudes to bear persecution with joy; otherwise, persecution would prompt "vengeful thoughts."[95] German mystic Hendrik Niclaes (ca. 1501–1580) instructs his followers on the necessity to show patience and love to adversaries and persecutors "for to amend them."[96] (Niclaes

91. Tertullian, *De Fuga* 1.7 (ANF 4:120).

92. Origen, *Commentary on the Gospel of Matthew* 10.23 (ANF 9:429). Origen, *Against Celsus* 1.65 (ANF 4:425); Origen, *Against Celsus* 8.44 (ANF 4:656).

93. Athanasius, *Defence of His Flight* 18 (NPNF² 4:261).

94. Athanasius, *Defence of His Flight* 19 (NPNF² 4:261–62). After Athanasius, it's a relatively uncommon theme in the exegetical history. In the mid-seventeenth century, Hendrik Niclaes spent a good deal of time defending the right of those persecuted in one land to flee to another (Hendrik Niclaes, *The first exhortation of H. N. to his children, and to the Family of Love: Likewise H. N. upon the Beatitudes, and the Seven Deadly Sins* [London: For Giles Calvert, 1656], 218, 222). John Wesley also cites Jesus's instructions to flee to another town to avoid persecution (Wesley, *Nature of the Kingdom*, 99).

95. Symeon the New Theologian, *The Discourses*, trans. C. J. deCatanzaro (New York: Paulist, 1980), Sermon 31.8, p. 333.

96. Niclaes, *The first exhortation*, 219.

anticipates Martin Luther King Jr., who writes a century later that only love for the enemy has the power to transform them.)[97]

The theme is especially prominent in Reformation-era writings. Some Reformers (and later Protestants) consider the clause "for righteousness' sake" and add another dimension to it—the righteousness of the person being persecuted. Persecution is only blessed if the cause is good *and* the person who suffers is good, too.[98] Puritan Robert Harris claimed that Christ gives the blessing on the persecuted last because it shows "God's usual way of dealing with His people, which is not to give them up to persecution till they are prepared to bear it by being made poor in spirit, pure in heart, meek, merciful, peaceable, and the rest."[99]

Two men on opposite sides of the Catholic-Protestant split dwelt at length on this theme. Erasmus of Rotterdam (1466–1536) was a Dutch humanist and Catholic priest who endured attacks both from fellow Catholics (for his calls for reforms within the church) and from Protestants (for his refusal to break with the Roman Catholic Church).[100] This context, and his desire to make peace within the strife-torn church, is evident in his 1522 paraphrase of the Beatitudes (written one year after Luther's excommunication). Erasmus closely associated the peacemakers with the persecuted. When you're persecuted, he wrote, you must still be a peacemaker, even toward your persecutor. Even if you can't achieve peace because your efforts are rejected, you're still blessed when persecuted as long as you refuse revenge and continue to seek peace.[101]

In Erasmus's paraphrase of the eighth beatitude, Jesus tells his followers, "I demand even more of you: . . . that you treat with mercy your blind

---

97. Martin Luther King Jr., "Loving Your Enemies" (sermon delivered at Dexter Avenue Baptist Church, Montgomery, Alabama, November 1957 [MLKEC, INP, Martin Luther King, Jr. Estate Collection, In Private Hands, ET-1; Atl-5A & 5B]).

98. Harris, *Way to True Happiness*, 380–81; Mather, *Sermons Wherein*, Sermon 14.

99. Harris, *Way to True Happiness*, 380. Similarly, Thomas Watson wrote that, in order to receive this blessing, one must suffer with patience, courage, cheerfulness, and with prayer for the persecutors (Watson, *The Beatitudes*, 295–96). See also John Wesley, Sermon 23.3.12–13, in Wesley, *Nature of the Kingdom*, 100–101.

100. Calvin pointed out that peacemakers who are fair and refuse to take sides end up making everyone angry, especially the rich who are accustomed to being favored (Calvin, *Sermons on the Beatitudes*, 57–58, quotation on 59).

101. Erasmus of Rotterdam, *Paraphrase on Matthew*, vol. 45 of *Collected Works of Erasmus*, trans. Dean Simpson (Toronto: University of Toronto Press, 2008), 90. For more on Erasmus's irenicism, see Lisa Sowle Cahill, *Blessed Are the Peacemakers: Pacifism, Just War, and Peacebuilding* (Minneapolis: Fortress, 2019), 250–56.

persecutors rather than be angry at them, that you bless those who curse you."[102] You are blessed in persecution, Erasmus said, if you reject anger and revenge, forsake pleasures of this world, thirst only for justice and godliness, desire to relieve the misfortunes of all and serve the advantage of all, keep your mind free from vice and delight only in God, and desire to foster and repair harmony.[103]

A century later, Jeremiah Burroughs (1600–1646) had his hands full dealing with various quarrels in the English churches: not only between the Catholics and Anglicans, but also the Independents and Presbyterians. In a sermon on the seventh beatitude, he appealed to the latter two sides not to violently oppose the other.[104] Drawing on the verb *revile* in Matt 5:11, he wrote that the faithful must never revile anyone, not even the wicked.[105] The faithful must never do anything that would give others cause to revile them; they should strive to walk in holiness.[106]

One can imagine Christians like Erasmus and Burroughs making common cause to insist that Christians on both sides of a dispute live by the rules of *all* the Beatitudes when they disagree. Indeed, both Burroughs and Erasmus wrote lengthy meditations toward the end of their lives pleading for peace in the church.[107] Both men knew that peacemaking is especially needed in times of persecution.

I'll finish with a story about someone who embodied this principle in her own life and in our own time. It's about a woman of the nomadic Rendille people in northern Kenya. Her name is Ndubaayo. When Ndubaayo became a Christian, "people called her names and her husband almost divorced her." This did not dissuade her. Instead, she "made a list of all of the people who had persecuted her since she became a Christian and she invited them to her home, killed the only lamb she had, and fed them a feast."[108] That's what it looks like to respond to persecution with the qualities of the first seven beatitudes. To her belongs the kingdom of heaven.

---

102. Erasmus, *Paraphrase on Matthew*, 92.

103. Erasmus, *Paraphrase on Matthew*, 92.

104. Burroughs, *Saints' Happiness*, 188–93.

105. Burroughs, *Saints' Happiness*, 229–31.

106. Burroughs, *Saints' Happiness*, 235.

107. Jeremiah Burroughs, *Irenicum to the Lovers of Truth and Peace: Heart-Divisions Opened in the Causes and Evils of them, with Cautions that we may not be hurt by them, and Endeavors to Heal them* (1653); and Erasmus, *On Mending the Peace of the Church* (1533).

108. Ann Voskamp, "When the Word Becomes Words," *Christianity Today* 62, no. 10 (December 2018), 60.

Theirs is the kingdom

The promise to the persecuted and to the poor (in spirit) is the same: "for theirs is the kingdom of heaven" (or "kingdom of God," in Luke). At least, it *looks* exactly the same. But for some premodern interpreters, there was one small but significant wrinkle.

Remember that premodern interpreters typically viewed the Beatitudes as an ascending scale or a ladder. One climbed the rungs one by one, advancing further upward toward God. For many of these interpreters, the rewards or promises also increased proportionally as one advanced higher on the ladder of the Beatitudes. This created a problem; how can the reward of the eighth be the same as the first, if it's the highest (and the first is the lowest)? At least some early writers concluded that since the eighth reward is the greatest, it must be different from the first.

The first and second kingdoms

Ambrose of Milan proposed that the first kingdom promised in Matt 5:3 signifies the moment when the saints shake off their mortal body and go to meet Christ in the air (as in 1 Thess 4:17), and the second heavenly kingdom promised in Matt 5:10 is the new creation inherited after the resurrection of the body (as in Rev 21:1) (*Comm. Luke* 5.61).[109] Another writer, the Benedictine abbot Rupert of Deutz (ca. 1075–1129), argued that the first kingdom was received in this life, but the second kingdom of the eighth beatitude was given after the resurrection.[110]

Augustine took a different tack. He treated the eighth as a return to, and perfection of, the first. Instead of being the end-point of a linear line or set of steps, it's the end-point of an arc which curves all the way around and becomes a circle. Recall that for Augustine the true number of the beatitudes is seven, because the eighth is the recapitulation of the first: "The eighth maxim returns, as it were, to the beginning, because it shows and commends what is complete and perfect. . . . Seven in number, therefore, are the things which lead to perfection. The eighth maxim throws light upon perfection and shows what it consists of" (*De Serm. Dom.* 1.3.10).[111]

---

109. Ambrose, *Gospel According to Saint Luke*, 137.

110. Brigitta Stoll, *De Virtute in Virtutem: zur Auslegungs- und Wirkungsgeschichte der Bergpredigt in Kommentaren, Predigten und hagiographischer Literatur von der Merowingerzeit bis um 1200* (Tübingen: Mohr Siebeck, 1988), 194.

111. Augustine, *The Lord's Sermon*, 18.

Now and not yet

Gregory of Nyssa also made use of the mystical significance of the number eight, but for a somewhat different purpose. For Gregory, the eighth beatitude is the "summit" of the Beatitudes, its highest peak. The resurrection happens in a certain sense on the eighth day, since Jesus was raised on the first day of the week (and the first day of the week is also an eighth day—seven days plus one). As the day of resurrection, "the eighth day" became shorthand for the eschaton, the eternal day of the new age. For this reason, then, "the eighth Beatitude contains the re-instatement in heaven of those who had fallen into servitude, and who are now from their slavery recalled to the Kingdom."[112]

These two interpreters—Augustine and Gregory—laid down a track that Western and Eastern Christians followed for a long time. The eighth beatitude is repeatedly described as the summit, crown, and consummation of the Beatitudes. Likewise, most interpreters throughout history see the inheritance of the kingdom in both beatitudes as a matter of the "now and not yet"—a promise fulfilled both in this life in part and then in full in the next: "grace here, and glory hereafter."[113] The present tense (theirs *is* the kingdom) means that the poor and persecuted receive glimpses of the kingdom now. "God stoops down to touch those who are persecuted."[114]

Conclusion

Claiming that one is being persecuted can be powerful rhetoric, a tool against a perceived enemy. As New Testament scholar Candida Moss observes, identifying an opponent as a persecutor in public discourse today can be "discursive napalm. It obliterates any sense of scale or moderation. . . . The language of martyrdom and persecution is often the language of war. It forces a rupture between 'us' and 'them' and perpetuates and legitimizes an aggressive posture toward 'the

---

112. Gregory of Nyssa, *The Lord's Prayer; The Beatitudes,* trans. Hilda C. Graef, ACW 18 (Mahwah, NJ: Paulist, 1954), 166.

113. Richard Watson, *Exposition of the Gospels of St. Matthew and St. Mark* (London: John Mason, 1833), 68. John Farrer used a very similar phrase in Farrer, *Sermons on the Mission and Character of Christ, and on the Beatitudes* (Oxford: Oxford University Press, 1804), 252. For Chrysostom, only a future eschatological reward can explain why God allows the righteous to suffer and the wicked to flourish in this life (Chrysostom, *Twenty-One Homilies on the Statutes* 1 [*NPNF*¹ 9:339–340]).

114. R. T. Kendall, *The Sermon on the Mount* (Oxford, UK: Monarch Books, 2011, 2013), 64.

other' and 'our enemies,' so that we can 'defend the faith.'"[115] She's thinking of public figures, on both the left and the right, who use the rhetoric of persecution to claim the rightness of their cause and to demonize the other side.

Moss's reminder suggests that Christians today should be slow to use the language of persecution to describe their own situations; they should pause to consider whether they're truly being persecuted (hurt, destroyed, trampled down) for righteousness' sake. It's not hard to think of cases of genuine persecution outside the Western world: Syria, Palestine, Nigeria, India, Sri Lanka.[116] It's also easy to think of people being persecuted for other faiths, like Muslims in China and Myanmar. In the United States, Muslims and Jews have been the subject of hostile attacks, both in the past and in increasing amounts today.

Contemporary Christian theologian Carl Trueman (b. 1967) urges Christians to remember that "The aim of theological conflict among Christians is not to win, not to beat one's opponents mercilessly into a bloodied wreck, but to establish the nature of truth and to convince as many as possible of the truth. This requires," he continues, "a personal openness on our part which is driven by a love and concern for those with whom we disagree."[117] He confesses that this has not always been easy for him in his own theological life: "I have found an uncompromising attitude to truth to be easier to manage over the years than an uncompromising attitude to love."[118]

Like Trueman, we often find fighting for purity easier than making peace. But the challenge of the Beatitudes is to honor both.

---

115. Moss, *The Myth of Persecution*, 13–14.

116. E.g., for the persecution of Indian Christians, see Vanlalchhawna Khiangte, *Matthean Beatitudes in Socio-Historical Context: Their Implications for Contemporary Christian Discipleship* (New Delhi: Christian World Imprints, 2016), xxxv, 252–73.

117. Carl Trueman, "Editorial: What Has Boxing to do with Jerusalem?" *Themelios* 27, no. 1 (Autumn 2001): 2.

118. Trueman, "Editorial," 3.

CONCLUSION

The yellowing notebook for my college Philosophy of Religion class contains this plaintive inscription: *Sunday school was never this complicated.* You may now be thinking, *The Beatitudes were never this complicated.* It's true that the Beatitudes are more complex than they first appear. They are (like all of Scripture) inexhaustibly rich. The deeper you dig, the more they yield. But I hope that as we have traveled together through them and heard their stories, you've experienced this complexity as depth and beauty and not as a burden.

Throughout this book I've tried to avoid the word *meaning*, in the sense that it's hard to say that a beatitude *means* anything apart from a context in which that meaning might be practiced, and apart from lives in which the Beatitudes might mean something. (This is, in part, why I began each chapter with a story.) I made a case in chapter 1 that the Beatitudes are best understood in their wider narrative contexts in Matthew and Luke: they only make sense as part of a wider story about God and God's Son Jesus. As Kavin Rowe writes, "[W]e cannot understand the sense ideas or practices have apart from the stories that make them intelligible as things to think/do in the first place."[1]

Now I also want to make a case that the Beatitudes can be known most fully not by reading about them but through seeing what they look like in human lives. Perhaps it's better to say not that the Beatitudes mean something but that they hope to transform someone, that they aim to transform *us*. I didn't expect to be changed by writing a book on the Beatitudes, but I was. I thought often about how I experience and express anger, whether I am a gentle person, how I spend money, how I treat people who are poor or homeless, when and how I pray, and whether I ever suffer for a commitment to justice. "How can

---

1. C. Kavin Rowe, *One True Life: The Stoics and Early Christians as Rival Traditions* (New Haven, CT: Yale University Press, 2016), 200.

one communicate the flame of the beatitudes," wonders René Coste, "if one does not oneself burn?"[2]

Christin Lore Weber writes of the Beatitudes, "If we approach their meaning through analysis we will fail to understand them. Instead we need to receive them with love . . . and hold them within us until they bear fruit in our lives. We cannot explain them; but we can tell stories about finding them enfleshed in the people and situations we encounter."[3] Taking Weber's cue, then, I want to finish with two stories—two performances of the Beatitudes, if you will.[4] The first story is about a girl named Lena.

Helena Jakobsdotter Ekblom (1784–1859) was born in Östergötland, Sweden, the same province from which the Eklund side of my family originated. At an early age she began to have visions of paradise, in which all the promises of the Beatitudes have come to fruition—she saw the poor rejoicing, laughing, and possessing the earth, crowned as sons and daughters of God. She started to preach about her visions, attracting crowds of impoverished peasants, who eagerly received her message, and the authorities, who did not.

Lena declared, in the words of the Beatitudes, good news to her fellow poor. As in Luke's Gospel, this message carried with it an implied corollary: "Woe to the rich who cause poverty, to those whose laughter is bought by tears, to those whose opulence is built on misery, to the mighty and powerful whose strength is founded on injustice, to those who despise and persecute and oppress the little ones of Jesus."[5] This implied corollary proved deeply challenging to both state and church authorities. As Jerry Ryan wrote, "Viewed through Lena's eyes, the existing order becomes intolerable, literally revolting."[6] Her preaching proved so disturbing that she was locked away for twenty years in

---

2. "Comment communiquer la flamme des Béatitudes, si on n'en brûle pas soi-même?" (René Coste, *Le grand secret des béatitudes: une théologie et une spiritualité pour aujourd'hui* [Paris: Editions S.O.S., 1985], 280).

3. Christin Lore Weber, *Blessings: A WomanChrist Reflection on the Beatitudes* (San Francisco: Harper & Row, 1989), 3.

4. See Allen Verhey, "Scripture as Script and as Scripted: The Beatitudes," in *Character Ethics and the New Testament: Moral Dimensions of Scripture*, ed. Robert L. Brawley (Louisville: Westminster John Knox, 2007), 19–34. Verhey suggests three possible "performances" of the Beatitudes in sermon, in prayer, and in actions (ibid., 30–31). For examples of embodied stories about the Beatitudes, see Anne Sutherland Howard, *Claiming the Beatitudes: Nine Stories from a New Generation* (Herndon, VA: Alban Institute, 2009); and Jim Langford, *Happy Are They: Living the Beatitudes in America* (Liguori, MO: Triumph Books, 1997).

5. Jerry Ryan, "Lena Ekblom: The Folly of the Beatitudes," *Cross Currents* 48, no. 1 (Spring 1998): 90.

6. Ryan, "Lena Ekblom," 91.

Vadstena, in a castle converted into an insane asylum. One summer while writing this book, I visited the Vadstena castle and imagined Lena chained by her ankle to one of its thick stone walls.

Even there, where she found herself among the poorest of the poor, the humiliated and abandoned, Lena continued to preach. She preached of God's unshakeable love for them, assuring them that even "in their cells they delight in the freedom of the sons of God, that they are the heirs of the promise" (Matt 5:9, 10).[7] After twenty years she was released, but she would not stop preaching the good news of the Beatitudes—good news for the poor, bad news for the powerful. She was arrested again, but on the way back to Vadstena, she and her escort passed through a town devastated by plague, and the guards fled in terror. Lena, however, stayed there, tending the sick, comforting the mourners. When the plague subsided, she was so beloved by the local people that nobody dared to arrest her again. When she grew old and unable to work, she moved into a shelter for the poor in her home village. Lena performed the Beatitudes in her preaching and in her life—she blessed the poor and was poor; she comforted and she wept.

The second story is about a woman whom I will call Anna. She has been, by turns, a community organizer and a preacher, a minister and a companion of the impoverished. For many years she brought a peaceful, generous, and resilient spirit to a neighborhood riven by gun violence and racial injustice. She also became a mother to two daughters, one of whom was diagnosed with autism after a period of anguished struggle to understand why every stage of her development was fraught with so much difficulty. As with her other vocations, she has borne this one with grace, gentleness, and strength. Knowing her, I have not had to look far to see what a peacemaker looks like, or how strong meekness is, or what poverty of spirit might be, or how to mourn in a way that calls beauty into the darkness.

When the Beatitudes take root in lives, they flower in different ways. Both of these women live on both sides of the Beatitudes: mourning and comforting, making peace and needing it, offering mercy and receiving it. "So we will honor the humiliated," wrote Allen Verhey, "and be humble ourselves. So we will comfort those who mourn, and weep ourselves in aching acknowledgement that it is not yet God's future. So we will meekly serve the meek. We will hunger for justice—and work for it."[8]

The Beatitudes occupy the same space we do: the time in which it is not yet God's future. For pastor and theologian Sam Wells, the first part of each be-

---

7. Ryan, "Lena Ekblom," 92.
8. Verhey, "Scripture as Script and as Scripted," 31.

atitude is a description of the cross (poor, thirsty, meek, merciful, persecuted), and the second half is a description of the resurrection (comfort, mercy, the kingdom of God). Wells writes that we live right in the middle of the first half and the second half. We dwell in the comma between "Blessed are you who weep now" and "for you will laugh."[9] Life in the middle of the cross and the resurrection is not easy, but it is joyful. It is deeply painful but also beautiful. And so are the Beatitudes.

I've found that the Beatitudes, like Jesus's parables, are deceptively simple. As Origen says (in the words of Stephen and Martin Westerholm), "the presence of mysteries in the divine text is hardly accidental: . . . the struggle to understand them is one of the divinely appointed means for bringing believers to maturity."[10]

Perhaps one of the main functions of the Beatitudes is to make us wonder about them—to move us to talk to each other about what poverty is, and what poverty of spirit is, and whether they're the same or different, and why they're both declared blessed by Jesus. The more you wrestle with the Beatitudes, the more they pull you into their depths. The deeper you dig, the more they yield.

9. Samuel Wells, "Dwelling in the Comma," in *Learning to Dream Again: Rediscovering the Heart of God* (Grand Rapids: Eerdmans, 2013), 135–41. Mary Cornwallis (who was one of the first women to write a commentary on the gospels) wrote that the Beatitudes are intended "to cheer and support us in our pilgrimage through this valley of tears" (Mary Cornwallis, *Observations, Critical, Explanatory, and Practical, on the Canonical Scriptures*, vol. 4 [London: Baldwin, Cradock & Joy, 1817], 2).

10. Stephen Westerholm and Martin Westerholm, *Reading Sacred Scripture: Voices from the History of Biblical Interpretation* (Grand Rapids: Eerdmans, 2016), 79, citing Origen, *Hom. Num.* 27.1.7; *Cels.* 3.45. Or as Rowan Williams suggests (in the words of Ben Quash), "Christ's confusing teachings . . . are *generatively*, perhaps even *deliberately*, underdetermined" (Ben Quash, *Found Theology: History, Imagination and the Holy Spirit* [London: Bloomsbury, 2013], 75).

BIBLIOGRAPHY

Primary Sources

Acts of Paul and Thecla. Translated by Alexander Walker. Vol. 8, pages 487–92 in Roberts and Donaldson, eds., *Ante-Nicene Fathers*.

Adams, Hannah. *Letters on the Gospels*. Cambridge, MA: Hillard & Metcalf, 1824.

Ainsworth, Percy C. *The Heart of Happiness: The Blessed Life as Revealed in the Beatitudes*. New York: Revell, 1910.

Mother Alexandra. "Blessed Are the Persecuted." *Diakonia* 22, no. 2 (1989): 81–88.

Alleine, Theodosia. *The life & death of Mr. Joseph Alleine . . .* London: for Nevil Simmon, at the Princes-Arms in St. Pauls Church-yard, 1672.

Allen, Isaac. *Reflection on Portions of the Sermon on the Mount. Intended Principally for Soldiers*. London: SPCK, 1848.

Allestree, Richard. *Forty sermons whereof twenty one are now first publish'd, the greatest part preach'd before the King and on solemn occasions*. Oxford; London: R. Scott, G. Wells, T. Sawbridge, R. Bentley, 1684.

Allison, Dale C., Jr. *The Sermon on the Mount: Inspiring the Moral Imagination*. New York: Crossroad, 1999.

———. *Studies in Matthew: Interpretation Past and Present*. Grand Rapids: Baker Academic, 2005.

Alt, Franz. *Peace Is Possible: The Politics of the Sermon on the Mount*. Translated by Joachim Neugroschel. New York: Schocken Books, 1985.

Amalar of Metz. *On the Liturgy*. Vol. 2, books 3–4. Translated and edited by Eric Knibbs. Dumbarton Oaks Medieval Library. Cambridge, MA: Harvard University Press, 2014.

Ambrose of Milan. *Commentary of Saint Ambrose on the Gospel According to Saint Luke*. Translated by Íde M. Ní Riain. Dublin: Halcyon, 2001.

———. *De Nabuthae [On Naboth]: A Commentary, with an Introduction and Trans-*

lation. Translated by Martin R. P. McGuire. Washington, DC: Catholic University of America Press, 1927.

Anselm. *Homiliae et Exhortationes.* In vol. 158 of Patrologia Latina. Edited by J.-P. Migne. 221 vols. Paris, 1844–1855.

Aphrahat. *Demonstrations.* Catholic Theological Studies of India 3. Translated by Kuriakose Valavanolickal. Kerala, India: HIRS Publications, 1999.

Arnold, Eberhard. *God's Revolution: Justice, Community, and the Coming Kingdom.* Farmington, PA: Plough Publishing House, 1984, 1997.

Arnold, Frank S. *The Octave of Blessing; a Present-day Application of the Beatitudes.* Chicago: Theodore Reese, 1895.

Athanasius. *Defence of His Flight (Apologia de Fuga).* Translated by M. Atkinson. In vol. 4 of Schaff and Wace, ed., *The Nicene and Post-Nicene Fathers,* Series 2, 254–65.

———. *Letters.* Edited by Archibald Robertson. Translated by John Henry Newman. In vol. 4 of Schaff and Wace, ed., *The Nicene and Post-Nicene Fathers,* Series 2, 495–581.

Augsburger, Myron S. *The Expanded Life: The Sermon on the Mount for Today.* Nashville: Abingdon, 1972.

Augustine. *Augustine: Political Writings.* Edited by E. M. Atkins and R. J. Dodaro. Cambridge: Cambridge University Press, 2001.

———. *City of God.* Translated by Henry Bettenson. New York: Penguin Books, 1972, 2003.

———. *Commentary on the Lord's Sermon on the Mount: With Seventeen Related Sermons.* FC 11. Washington, DC: Catholic University of America Press, 2001.

———. *Confessions.* Translated by Henry Chadwick. Oxford: Oxford University Press, 1991.

———. *Essential Sermons.* Edited by Boniface Ramsey. Translated by Edmund Hill. The Works of Saint Augustine: A Translation for the 21st Century. Hyde Park, NY: New City Press, 2007.

———. *Expositions on the Book of Psalms.* Edited by A. Cleveland Coxe. Vol. 8 of Schaff, ed., *The Nicene and Post-Nicene Fathers,* Series 1, 1–683.

———. *The Harmony of the Gospels.* Translated by S. D. F. Salmond. In vol. 6 of Schaff, ed., *The Nicene and Post-Nicene Fathers,* Series 1, 65–236.

———. *The Lord's Sermon on the Mount.* Translated by John J. Jepson. ACW 5. Mahwah, NJ: Paulist, 1948.

———. *On Christian Teaching.* Translated by R. P. H. Green. Oxford World's Classics. Oxford: Oxford University Press, 1997.

———. *Sermons III (51–94) on the New Testament. The Works of Saint Augustine*

Part 3. Vol. 3. Edited by John E. Rotelle. Translated by Edmund Hill. Brooklyn, NY: New City Press, 1991.

———. *Sermons on Selected Lessons of the New Testament*. Translated by R. G. MacMullen. In vol. 6 of Schaff, ed., *The Nicene and Post-Nicene Fathers*, Series 1, 237–545.

———. *The Trinity*. Translated by Stephen McKenna. FC 45. Washington, DC: Catholic University of America Press, 1963.

Aymer, Margaret. "The Beatitudes and the Accra Confession." In Roncace and Weaver, *Global Perspectives*, 223–24.

Baarda, Tjitze. "The Beatitudes of 'The Mourning' and 'The Weeping': Matthew 5:4 and Luke 6:21b." In *Studies in the Early Text of the Gospels and Acts: The Papers of the First Birmingham Colloquium on the Textual Criticism of the New Testament*, edited by David G. K. Taylor, 168–91. Atlanta: Society of Biblical Literature, 1999.

Bacon, Benjamin W. *The Sermon on the Mount: Its Literary Structure and Didactic Purpose*. London: Macmillan, 1902.

Baker, John. *Celebrate Recovery Updated Participant's Guide Set, Volumes 1–4: A Recovery Program Based on Eight Principles from the Beatitudes*. Rev. ed. Grand Rapids: Zondervan, 2016.

Balthasar, Hans Urs von. *Man Is Created*. Vol. 5 of *Explorations in Theology*. Translated by Adrian Walker. San Francisco: Ignatius Press, 2015. Originally published as *Homo Creatus Est*. Johannes Verlag, 1986.

Barbu, Liviu. "The 'Poor in Spirit' and Our Life in Christ: An Eastern Orthodox Perspective on Christian Discipleship." *Studies in Christian Ethics* 22, no. 3 (2009): 261–74.

Barclay, William. *The Old Law and the New Law*. Philadelphia: Westminster, 1972.

———. *Plain People Look at the Beatitudes*. Nashville: Abingdon, 1965.

Barnes, Michael René. "The Visible Christ and the Invisible Trinity: Mt. 5:8 in Augustine's Trinitarian Theology of 400." *Modern Theology* 19, no. 3 (July 2003): 329–55.

Barraud, C. W. *Meditations on the Mysteries of Our Holy Faith, Together with a Treatise in Mental Prayer. Based on the Work of the Venerable Father Louis de Ponte, S. J.* New York: Benziger, 1916.

Barrett, George W. *Christ's Keys to Happiness*. New York: The World Publishing Company, 1970.

Barrs, Jerram. *Who Are the Peacemakers?: The Christian Case for Nuclear Deterrence*. Westchester, IL: Crossway, 1983.

Barth, Karl. *Against the Stream: Shorter Post-War Writings (1946–52)*. New York: Philosophical Library, 1954.

————. *Church Dogmatics*. Edited by G. W. Bromiley and T. F. Torrance. Translated by G. W. Bromiley. Peabody, MA: Hendrickson, 1958, 2004.

————. *Die Lehre von Gott*. Vol. II/2 of *Die Kirchliche Dogmatik*. Zürich: Evangelischer Verlag A. G. Zollikon, 1942.

Barth, Karl, and Eduard Thurneysen. *Come Holy Spirit: Sermons*. Translated by George W. Richards, Elmer G. Homrighausen, and Karl J. Ernst. Grand Rapids: Eerdmans, 1933, 1978.

Basil of Caesarea. *The Long Rules*. In *Saint Basil, Ascetical Works*, translated by M. Monica Wagner, 223–337. FC 9. New York: Fathers of the Church, 1950.

————. *Shorter Rules* cols. 1080–1305. Vol. 31 of *Patrologia Graeca*. Edited by J.-P. Migne. 162 vols. Paris, 1857–1886.

Bataillon, Louis Jacques. "Béatitudes et types de sainteté." *Revue Mabillon* 7 (1996): 79–104.

Baudrand, Barthélemy. *L'âme éclairée par les oracles de la sagesse, dans les paraboles et les béatitudes évangéliques*. Tours: Chez Mame et Compagnie, Imprimeurs-Libraires, 1830.

Bauman, Clarence. *The Sermon on the Mount: The Modern Quest for Its Meaning*. Macon, GA: Mercer University Press, 1985.

Baumgarten, Otto. *Der Krieg und die Bergpredigt*. Speech given in Berlin on 10 May 1915. Berlin: Carl Heymann, 1915.

The Beatitudes, Or the Blessings Promised by Our Lord in His Sermon on the Mount: Six Illustrations. London: Thomas Nelson & Sons, 1868.

Beckett, Thomas A. *The Sermon on the Mount*. London: H. R. Allenson, 1909.

Benfell, V. S., III. "'Blessed are They That Hunger after Justice': From Vice to Beatitude in Dante's Purgatorio." In *Seven Deadly Sins: From Communities to Individuals*, edited by Richard Newhauser, 185–206. Leiden: Brill, 2007.

Berenstain, Mike. *The Berenstain Bears: Blessed are the Peacemakers*. Grand Rapids: Berenstain Publishing, 2014.

Bernard of Clairvaux. "First Sermon for the Feast of All Saints. On the Eight Beatitudes." In *St. Bernard's Sermons for the Seasons and Principal Festivals of the Year, Vol 3*. Westminster, MD: Carroll, 1950.

————. *The Parables and the Sentences*. Edited by Maureen M. O'Brien. Translated by Michael Casey and Francis R. Swietek. Cistercian Fathers 55. Kalamazoo, MI: Cistercian Publications, 2000.

————. *Sermons on Conversion*. Translated by Marie-Bernard Saïd. Kalamazoo, MI: Cistercian Publications, 1981.

————. *The Steps of Humility*. Translated by George Bosworth Burch. Cambridge, MA: Harvard University Press, 1942.

Berner, Ursula. *Die Bergpredigt: Rezeption und Auslegung im 20. Jahrhundert.* 3rd ed. Göttingen: Vandenhoeck und Ruprecht, 1985.

Bessières, Albert. *Les Béatitudes et la civilisation.* Paris: Éditions Spes, 1943.

Best, E. "Matthew 5:3." *NTS* 6 (1960/61): 255–58.

Betz, Hans Dieter. "Beatitudes, New Testament." *EBR* 3:675–80.

———. *The Sermon on the Mount.* Hermeneia. Minneapolis: Fortress, 1995.

Blomberg, Craig. "Beatitudes, Modern Europe and America." *EBR* 3:693–95.

———. "The Most Often Abused Verses in the Sermon on the Mount: And How to Treat Them Right." *Southwestern Journal of Theology* 46, no. 3 (Summer 2004): 1–17.

Blount, Brian K. "Righteousness from the Inside: The Transformative Spirituality of the Sermon on the Mount." In *The Theological Interpretation of Scripture: Classic and Contemporary Readings,* edited by Stephen E. Fowl, 262–84. Malden, MA: Blackwell, 1997.

Boehmer, Julius. "Die erste Seligpreisung." *JBL* 45, no. 3–4: 298–304.

Böhl, Felix. "Die Demut (הונע) als höchste der Tugenden: Bemerkungen zu Mt 5,3.5." *BZ* 20, no. 2 (1976): 217–23.

Bolo, Henry. *The Beatitudes: The Poor in Spirit, the Meek and Humble.* Translated by Madame Cecilia. London: Kegan Paul, Trench, Trübner & Co., 1906.

Bolz-Weber, Nadia. "Blessed Are the Unemployed, Unimpressive, and Under-represented." YouTube video. https://www.youtube.com/watch?v=ctcjNCrGyT8.

Bonaventure. *The Breviloquium.* Vol. 2 of *The Works of Bonaventure.* Translated by José de Vinck. Paterson, NJ: St. Anthony Guild Press, 1963.

———. *The Sunday Sermons of St. Bonaventure.* Vol. 12 of *The Works of St. Bonaventure.* Translated by Timothy J. Johnson. Saint Bonaventure, NY: Franciscan Publications, 2008.

Bonhoeffer, Dietrich. *The Cost of Discipleship.* New York: Simon & Schuster, 1995.

———. *Ethics.* Vol. 6 of *Dietrich Bonhoeffer Works.* Edited by Clifford J. Green. Translated by Reinhard Krauss, Charles C. West, and Douglas W. Stott. Minneapolis: Fortress, 2005.

Boreham, Frank W. *The Heavenly Octave: A Study of the Beatitudes.* Grand Rapids: Baker Books, 1936, 1968.

Bornhäuser, Karl. *Die Bergpredigt: Versuch einer zeitgenössischen Auslegung.* Gütersloh: Bertelsmann, 1923.

Bornkamm, Günther. *Jesus of Nazareth.* Translated by Irene McLuskey, Fraser McLuskey, and James M. Robinson. New York: Harper & Row, 1960.

Bossuet, Jacques Bénigne. *The Sermon on the Mount.* Translated by F. M. Capes. London: Longmans, Green, 1900.

Bouché, Anne-Marie. "The Spirit in the World: The Virtues of the Floreffe Bible Frontispiece: British Library, Add. Ms. 17738, ff. 3v–4r." In *Virtue and Vice: The Personifications in the Index of Christian Art*, edited by Colum Hourihane, 42–65. Princeton: Princeton University Press, 2000.

Bowman, John Wick. "An Exposition of the Beatitudes." *Journal of Bible and Religion* 15, no. 3 (1947): 162–70.

———. "Travelling the Christian Way—The Beatitudes." *RevExp* 54, no. 3 (1957): 377–92.

Boxall, Ian. *Matthew through the Centuries*. Wiley Blackwell Bible Commentaries. Malden, MA: Wiley Blackwell, 2019.

Brawley, Robert L. "Evocative Allusions in Matthew: Matthew 5:5 as a Test Case." *HvTSt* 59, no. 3 (2003): 597–619.

Brereton, J. le Gay. *Genesis and the Beatitudes: The Spiritual Creation of Man under Varying Conditions Harmoniously Unfolded from the First Section of Genesis and the Beatitudes of Our Lord*. Sydney: Turner & Henderson; London: James Speirs, 1887.

Bretscher, Paul G. *The World Upside Down or Right Side Up?* St. Louis, MO: Concordia, 1964.

Bridges, Jerry. *The Practice of Godliness*. Colorado Springs, CO: NavPress, 1983.

Broer, Ingo. *Die Seligpreisungen der Bergpredigt: Studien zu ihrer Überliefergung und Interpretation*. Bonn: Hanstein, 1986.

Brown, Michael Joseph. "Matthew." In *True to Our Native Land: An African American New Testament Commentary*, edited by Brian K. Blount, 85–120. Minneapolis: Fortress, 2007.

Brown, Raymond E. "The Beatitudes According to Luke." In *New Testament Essays*, edited by Raymond E. Brown, 265–71. London: Geoffrey Chapman, 1965.

———. *An Introduction to the New Testament*. The Anchor Bible Reference Library. New York: Doubleday, 1997.

Browne, John R. *The Great Sermon*. Boston, MA: Stratford, 1935.

Bruner, Frederick Dale. *The Christbook, Matthew 1–12*. Vol. 1 of *Matthew: A Commentary*. Revised and expanded ed. Grand Rapids: Eerdmans, 2004.

Buck, James. *A Treatise of the Beatitudes, or, Christ's Happy Men*. London: printed by B. A. and T. F. for Iohn Clark, and Wil. Cooke, 1637.

Buechner, Frederick. "Beatitudes." In *Whistling in the Dark: A Doubter's Dictionary*, 19–20. New York: HarperSanFrancisco, 1988, 1993.

Bultmann, Rudolf. *Theology of the New Testament*. Vol. 1. Translated by Kendrick Grobel. London: SCM, 1952.

Burleigh, Wm. H. "Blessed Are They That Mourn." *The Signs of the Times* 8, no. 10 (March 9, 1882): 109.

Burr, John. *The Crown of Character: A Study of the Beatitudes of Our Lord.* James Clarke & Co., 1932.

Burroughs, Jeremiah. *Irenicum to the Lovers of Truth and Peace: Heart-Divisions Opened in the Causes and Evils of them, with Cautions that we may not be hurt by them, and Endeavors to Heal them.* Edited by Don Kistler. Morgan, PA: Soli Deo Gloria, 1997.

———. *The Saints' Happiness.* Edinburgh: James Nichol, 1867; Soli Deo Gloria, 1988, 1992.

Burrows, Mark S. "Selections from Martin Luther's Sermons on the Sermon on the Mount." In *The Theological Interpretation of Scripture: Classic and Contemporary Readings,* edited by Stephen E. Fowl, 248–61. Malden, MA: Blackwell, 1997.

Bush, James. *The Choice: Or, Lines on the Beatitudes.* London: R. Saywell, 1841.

Cabasilas. *The Life in Christ.* Translated by Carmino J. deCatanzaro. Crestwood, NY: St. Vladimir's Seminary Press, 1974.

Caesarius of Arles. *Sermons.* Vol. 2. Translated by Mary Magdeleine Mueller. FC 47. Washington, DC: Catholic University of America, 1964.

Cahill, Lisa Sowle. *Blessed Are the Peacemakers: Pacifism, Just War, and Peacebuilding.* Minneapolis: Fortress, 2019.

———. "The Ethical Implications of the Sermon on the Mount." *Int* 41, no. 2 (April 1987): 144–56.

———. "Nonresistance, Defense, Violence, and the Kingdom." *Int* 38, no. 4 (October 1984): 380–97.

Calvin, John. *A Harmony of the Gospels Matthew, Mark and Luke.* Vol. 1. Edited by David W. Torrance and Thomas F. Torrance. Translated by A. W. Morrison. Grand Rapids: Eerdmans, 1972.

———. *John Calvin's Sermons on the Ten Commandments.* Translated and edited by Benjamin W. Farley. Grand Rapids: Baker Books, 1980.

———. *Sermons on the Beatitudes: Five Sermons from the Gospel Harmony, Delivered in Geneva in 1560.* Carlisle, PA: Banner of Truth Trust, 2006.

Carr, Arthur. *The Gospel according to St. Luke.* London: Rivingtons, 1875.

Carré, A.-M. *Quand arrive le bonheur: Les Béatitudes.* 2nd ed. Paris: Les Éditions du Cerf, 1974.

Carson, D. A. *The Sermon on the Mount: An Evangelical Exposition of Matthew 5–7.* Grand Rapids: Baker Books, 1978.

Carter, Warren. *Matthew and the Margins: A Socio-Political and Religious Reading.* Sheffield: Sheffield Academic, 2000.

———. *What Are They Saying about Matthew's Sermon on the Mount?* New York: Paulist, 1994.

Cassian. "The Conference of Cassian." In *Western Asceticism*. Library of Christian Classics Ichthus Edition. Edited by Owen Chadwick. Philadelphia: Westminster, 1958.

Madame Cecilia. *The Gospel According to St. Matthew*. Kegan Paul, Trench, Trübner & Co., 1906.

Cennick, John. *The Beatitudes, Being the Substance of a Discourse Delivered in Dublin, Dec. the 21st, 1753*. 2nd ed. London: M. Lewis, 1756.

Chafer, Lewis Sperry. *Systematic Theology*, Vols. 4 and 5. Dallas, TX: Dallas Seminary Press, 1948.

Chakkuvarackal, T. Johnson. "The Message of the Sermon on the Mount in the Multi-Religious Context of India." *Indian Journal of Theology* 43, no. 1 & 2 (2001): 42–49.

Chan, Yiu Sing Lúcás. *The Ten Commandments and the Beatitudes*. Lanham, MD: Rowman & Littlefield, 2012.

Charles, Elizabeth Rundle. *The Beatitudes: Thoughts for All Saints' Day*. London: Society for Promoting Christian Knowledge; New York: Young & Co., 1889.

Chaucer, Geoffrey. *The Complete Poetical Works of Geoffrey Chaucer*. Translated by John S. P. Tatlock and Percy MacKaye. New York: Free Press, 1912, 1940.

Chesto, Kathleen O. "Get a New Beatitude." *U.S. Catholic* 68, no. 1 (January 2003): 30–33.

Christian Campaign for Nuclear Disarmament. *Blessed are the Peacemakers*. London: Christian Campaign for Nuclear Disarmament, 1981.

Chromatius of Aquileia. *Sermons and Tractates on Matthew*. Translated by Thomas P. Scheck. ACW 75. New York: The Newman Press, 2018.

Chrysologus, Peter. *Selected Sermons*. Translated by George E. Ganss. FC 17. Washington, DC: Catholic University of America Press, 1953.

Chrysostom, John. *Homilies on Genesis 18–45*. Translated by Robert C. Hill. FC 82. Washington, DC: Catholic University of America Press, 1990.

———. *Homilies on the Gospel of Saint Matthew*. Translated by George Prevost. Vol. 10 of Schaff, ed., *The Nicene and Post-Nicene Fathers*, Series 1.

———. *Three Homilies (I.) Against Marcionists and Manichaeans, On the Passage 'Father, If it be Possible,' etc.* Translated by W. R. W. Stephens. In vol. 9 of Schaff, ed., *The Nicene and Post-Nicene Fathers*, Series 1, 201–32.

———. *Twenty-One Homilies on the Statutes*. Translated by W. R. W. Stephens. In vol. 9 of Schaff, ed., *The Nicene and Post-Nicene Fathers*, Series 1, 317–489.

Clare of Assisi. "First Letter to Blessed Agnes of Prague." In *Francis and Clare: The Complete Works*, translated by Regis Armstrong and Ignatius C. Brady, 190–94. New York: Paulist, 1982.

Clement of Alexandria. *Exhortation to the Heathens*. Edited by A. Cleveland Coxe. In vol. 2 of Roberts and Donaldson, eds., *Ante-Nicene Fathers*, 171–206.

———. *Stromata*. Edited by A. Cleveland Coxe. In vol. 2 of Roberts and Donaldson, eds., *Ante-Nicene Fathers*, 299–556.

———. *Who Is the Rich Man that Shall Be Saved?* Translated by William Wilson. In vol. 2 of Roberts and Donaldson, eds., *Ante-Nicene Fathers*, 589–604.

Climacus, John. *Scala Paradisi*. Vol. 88 of Patrologia Graeca. Edited by J.-P. Migne. 162 vols. Paris, 1857–1886.

Cohon, Beryl. *Jacob's Well: Some Jewish Sources and Parallels to the Sermon on the Mount*. New York: Bookman Associates, 1956.

Collett, Samuel. *A Paraphrase of the Fifth, Sixth, and Seventh Chapters of Matthew, with Proper Soliloquies at Every Period. In a Letter from a Father to a Son*. London: J. Williams, 1764.

Collins, Raymond F. "Beatitudes." In *Anchor Bible Dictionary, Vol. 1: A–C*, edited by David Noel Freedman, 629–31. New York: Doubleday, 1992.

Cornelius à Lapide. *The Holy Gospel According to Saint Matthew*. Vol. 1 of *The Great Commentary of Cornelius à Lapide*. Translated by Thomas W. Mossman. Revised by Michael J. Miller. Fitzwilliam, NH: Loreto, 2008.

Cornell, Thomas. "The Peacemakers." In *The Beatitudes in Modern Life*, edited by Margaret Garvey, 135–64. Chicago: Thomas More, 1989.

Cornwallis, Mary. *Observations, Critical, Explanatory, and Practical, on the Canonical Scriptures*. Vol. 4. London: Baldwin, Cradock & Joy, 1817.

Coste, René. *Le grand secret des béatitudes: une théologie et une spiritualité pour aujourd'hui*. Paris: Editions S.O.S., 1985.

Croatta, J. Severino. "Matthew 5:1–12. A Latin American Perspective." In *Return to Babel: Global Perspectives on the Bible*, edited by Priscilla Pope-Levison and John R. Levison, 117–23. Louisville: Westminster John Knox, 1999.

Crock, Clement Henry. *The Eight Beatitudes*. New York: Joseph F. Wagner, 1953.

Crosby, Michael H. "The Beatitudes: General Perspectives." In Eigo, *New Perspectives*, 1–43.

———. *Spirituality of the Beatitudes: Matthew's Vision for the Church in an Unjust World*. rev. ed. Maryknoll, NY: Orbis Books, 2005.

Crowder, Stephanie Buckhanon. "The Gospel of Luke." In *True to Our Native Land: An African American New Testament Commentary*, edited by Brian K. Blount, 158–85. Minneapolis: Fortress, 2008.

Cunningham, Dawn. "Elucidating Opposites: Virtues and a Diptych Associated with Giotto." *Religion and the Arts* 21 (2017): 309–34.

Cyprian. *Epistles*. Translated by Ernest Wallis. In vol. 5 of Roberts and Donaldson, eds., *Ante-Nicene Fathers*, 275–420.

———. *Treatises*. Translated by Ernest Wallis. In vol. 5 of Roberts and Donaldson, eds., *Ante-Nicene Fathers*, 421–564.

Cyril of Alexandria. *De Adoratione*. Vol. 68 of Patrologia Graeca. Edited by J.-P. Migne. 162 vols. Paris, 1857–1886.

———. *Commentary on the Gospel of St. Luke*. Translated by R. Payne Smith. Long Island, NY: Studion, 1983.

———. *Fragments*. In *Lukas-Kommentare aus der griechischen Kirche*. Edited by Joseph Reuss. Berlin: Akademie-Verlag, 1984.

Cyril of Jerusalem. *Catecheses*. In *The Works of Saint Cyril of Jerusalem*, Vol. 1. Translated by Leo P. McCauley and Anthony A. Stephenson. FC 61. Washington, DC: Catholic University of America Press, 1968.

D'Angelo, Mary R. "'Blessed the One Who Reads and Those Who Hear': The Beatitudes in Their Biblical Contexts." In Eigo, *New Perspectives*, 45–92.

Danker, Frederick W. *Jesus and the New Age: A Commentary on St. Luke's Gospel*. Rev. ed. Philadelphia: Fortress, 1988.

Dante Alighieri. *Purgatorio*. Translated by Jean Hollander and Robert Hollander. New York: Anchor Books, 2003.

———. *Purgatory*. Vol. 2 of *The Divine Comedy*. Translated by Mark Musa. New York: Penguin Books, 1981, 1985.

Davenport, Gene. *Into the Darkness: Discipleship in the Sermon on the Mount*. Eugene, OR: Wipf & Stock, 1988, 2003.

Davies, W. D., and Dale C. Allison Jr. *A Critical and Exegetical Commentary on the Gospel According to Saint Matthew*. ICC 1. London: T&T Clark, 1988.

———. "Reflections on the Sermon on the Mount." *Scottish Journal of Theology* 44, no. 3 (1991): 283–309.

Day, Dorothy. *Loaves and Fishes*. New York: Harper & Row, 1963.

Dear, John. "The Beatitudes of Peace." *National Catholic Reporter* (November 21, 2006). https://www.ncronline.org/blogs/road-peace/beatitudes-peace.

———. *Beatitudes of Peace: Meditations on the Beatitudes, Peacemaking and the Spiritual Life*. New London, CT: Twenty-Third Publications, 2016.

———. *They Will Inherit the Earth: Peace and Nonviolence in a Time of Climate Change*. Maryknoll, NY: Orbis Books, 2018.

Delling, Gerhard. "Die Bezeichnung 'Söhne Gottes' in der jüdischen Literatur der hellenistischen Zeit." In *God's Christ and His People: Studies in Honour of Nils A. Dahl*, edited by Jacob Jervell and Wayne A. Meeks, 18–28. Oslo: Universitetsforlag, 1977.

Dermer, E. C. *The Beatitudes: Studies for Lent*. Oxford: B. H. Blackwell; London: Simpkin, Marshall, Hamilton, Kent & Co., 1893.

Dhuoda. *Handbook for her Warrior Son.* Edited and translated by Marcelle Thié-baux. Cambridge: Cambridge University Press, 1998.

Dibelius, Martin. *The Sermon on the Mount.* New York: Charles Scribner's Sons, 1940.

Dodd, C. H. "The Beatitudes: A Form-Critical Study." In *More New Testament Studies*, edited by C. H. Dodd, 1–10. Grand Rapids: Eerdmans, 1968.

Dodds, Bill, and Michael J. Dodds. *Happily Ever After Begins Here and Now: Living the Beatitudes Today.* Chicago: Loyola Press, 1997.

Domeris, William. "'Blessed are you . . .' (Matthew 5:1–12)." *Journal of Theology for South Africa* 73 (1990): 67–76.

Donahue, John. "'Blessed are the Mourners': Lamentation and the Path to Justice." Paper presented at the Second Annual Marquette Scripture Conference: Biblical Ethics in the Twenty-First Century: In Memory of Rev. Yiu Sing Lúcás Chan, SJ, Marquette, MI, April 9, 2016.

Donihue, Anita Corrine. *When God Calls Me Blessed: Devotional Thoughts for Women from the Beatitudes.* Uhrichsville, OH: Barbour Books, 2002.

Donne, John. *The Sermons of John Donne.* Vol. 7. Edited by Evelyn M. Simpson and George R. Potter. Berkeley: University of California Press, 1962.

Douglass, Frederick. *Narrative of the Life of Frederick Douglass, an American Slave.* New York: Barnes & Noble Classics, 2003.

Dowsett, Rosemary M. "Matthew." In *The IVP Women's Bible Commentary*, edited by Catherine Clark Kroeger and Mary J. Evans, 517–41. Downers Grove, IL: InterVarsity Press, 2002.

Drobner, Hubertus R., and Albert Viciano, eds. *Gregory of Nyssa: Homilies on the Beatitudes. An English Version with Commentary and Supporting Studies.* Proceedings of the Eighth International Colloquium on Gregory of Nyssa (Paderborn, 14–18 September 1998). Leiden: Brill, 2000.

Duchrow, Ulrich. "Der Aufbau von Augustinus Schriften Confessiones und De Trinitate." *ZTK* 62, no. 3 (1965): 338–67.

Duguid, Iain M. *Hero of Heroes: Seeing Christ in the Beatitudes.* Phillipsburg, NJ: P&R Publishing, 2001.

Dupont, Jacques. *La bonne nouvelle.* Vol. 2 of *Les Béatitudes.* Paris: Gabalda, 1969.

———. *Les évangélistes.* Vol. 3 of *Les Béatitudes.* Paris: Gabalda, 1973.

———. *Le problème littéraire–Les deux versions du Sermon sur la montagne et des béatitudes.* Vol. 1 of *Les Béatitudes.* Bruges, Belgium: Abbaye de Saint-André, 1958.

Eckhart von Hochheim. *Meister Eckhart: The Essential Sermons, Commentaries, Treatises, and Defense.* Translated and edited by Edmund Colledge and Bernard McGinn. Mahwah, NJ: Paulist, 1981.

———. *Meister Eckhart: Teacher and Preacher*. Edited by Bernard McGinn. Mahwah, NJ: Paulist, 1986.

Edwards, Jonathan. *Sermons and Discourses 1730–1733*. Vol. 17 of *The Works of Jonathan Edwards*. Edited by Mark Valeri. New Haven, CT: Yale University Press, 1999.

Eigo, Francis A., ed. *New Perspectives on the Beatitudes*. Villanova, PA: Villanova University Press, 1995.

Eklund, Rebekah. "The Blessed." Visual Commentary on Scripture. http://thevcs.org/blessed.

———. "Blessed Are the Failures: Leaning into the Beatitudes." In *Theologies of Failure*, edited by Roberto Sirvent and Duncan B. Reyburn, 141–50. Eugene, OR: Cascade, 2019.

———. "Blessed are the Image-Bearers: Gregory of Nyssa and the Beatitudes." *AThR* 99, no. 4 (Fall 2017): 729–40.

———. *Jesus Wept: The Significance of Jesus' Laments in the New Testament*. LNTS. London: T&T Clark, 2015.

———. "Matthew, the Cross, and the Cruciform Life." In *Cruciform Scripture: Cross, Participation, and Mission*, edited by Nijay K. Gupta, Andy Johnson, Christopher W. Skinner, and Drew J. Strait, 3–21. Grand Rapids: Eerdmans, 2021.

———. "Octaves and Septenaries." *Studia Patristica* (forthcoming, 2021).

Elliott, J. K. *The Apocryphal New Testament*. Oxford: Clarendon Press, 1993.

Ephrem the Syrian. *St. Ephrem's Commentary on Tatian's Diatessaron*. Translated by Carmel McCarthy. Oxford: Oxford University Press, 1993.

Epistle of Barnabas. In *The Apostolic Fathers*, Volume 2: *Epistle of Barnabas. Papias and Quadratus. Epistle to Diognetus. The Shepherd of Hermas*. Edited and translated by Bart D. Ehrman. LCL 25. Cambridge, MA: Harvard University Press, 2003.

Erasmus of Rotterdam. *Paraphrase on Luke 1–10*. Volume 47 of *Collected Works of Erasmus*. Translated by Jane E. Phillips. Toronto: University of Toronto Press, 2016.

———. *Paraphrase on Matthew*. Volume 45 of *Collected Works of Erasmus*. Translated and annotated by Dean Simpson. Toronto: University of Toronto Press, 2008.

Evagrius Ponticus. *The Praktikos; Chapters on Prayer*. Translated by John Eudes Bamberger. Cistercian Studies Series 4. Spencer, MA: Cistercian Publications, 1972.

Farrer, John. *Sermons on the Mission and Character of Christ, and on the Beatitudes*. Oxford: Oxford University Press, 1804.

Felder, Cain Hope. *Troubling Biblical Waters: Race, Class, and Family*. Maryknoll, NY: Orbis Books, 1989.

Figura, Michael. "Der Heilige Geist als Tröster." *IKaZ* 20, no. 5 (1991): 393–404.

Findlay, J. Alexander. *The Realism of Jesus: A Paraphrase and Exposition of the Sermon on the Mount*. New York: George H. Doran, 1924?.

FitzGerald, Kyriaki Karidoyanes, and Thomas FitzGerald. *Happy in the Lord: The Beatitudes for Everyday: Perspectives from Orthodox Spirituality*. Brookline, MA: Holy Cross Orthodox Press, 2000.

Fitzmyer, Joseph A. *The Gospel According to Luke (I–IX)*. Anchor Bible 28. Garden City, NY: Doubleday, 1981.

Flusser, David. "Blessed are the Poor in Spirit . . ." *IEJ* 10, no. 1 (1960): 1–13.

Forest, Jim. *The Ladder of the Beatitudes*. Maryknoll, NY: Orbis Books, 1999.

France, R. T. *The Gospel of Matthew*. NICNT. Grand Rapids: Eerdmans, 2007.

Francis of Assisi. "The Admonitions." In *Francis and Clare: The Complete Works*, translated by Regis Armstrong and Ignatius C. Brady, 25–36. New York: Paulist, 1982.

Friedlander, Gerald. *The Jewish Sources of the Sermon on the Mount*. New York: Ktav, 1969.

Galilea, Segundo. *The Beatitudes: To Evangelize as Jesus Did*. Translated by Robert R. Barr. Maryknoll, NY: Orbis Books, 1984.

Gardiner, James. *A Practical Exposition of the Beatitudes, in the First Part of Our Saviour's Sermon on the Mount*. London: Bernard Lintott, 1712.

Gardner, Richard B. *Matthew*. Believers Church Bible Commentary. Scottdale, PA: Herald Press, 1991.

Garrison, William Lloyd. Preface to *Narrative of the Life of Frederick Douglass, an American Slave*, by Frederick Douglass. New York: Barnes & Noble Classics, 2003.

Garvey, Margaret. *The Beatitudes in Modern Life*. Chicago: Thomas More, 1989.

Gawain-Poet. *Complete Works: Patience, Cleanness, Pearl, Saint Erkenwald, Sir Gawain and the Green Knight*. Translated by Marie Borroff. New York: Norton, 2011.

Geldenhuys, Norval. *Commentary on the Gospel of Luke*. London: Marshall, Morgan & Scott, 1950.

Genuyt, François. "Les Béatitudes selon saint Matthieu (Mt 5,3–12)." *Lumière et vie* 47 (1997): 21–30.

Gioia, Dana. "Prayer at Winter Solstice." In *Pity the Beautiful*, 17. Minneapolis: Graywolf, 2012.

Goff, Michael. "Beatitudes, Hebrew Bible/Old Testament." *EBR* 3:673–75.

Gonnet, Giovanni. "L'incidence du Sermon de la Montagne sur l'ethique des

Vaudois [Waldensians] du Moyen Age." *Communio Viatorum* 29 (Autumn 1986): 119–27.

González, Justo L. *Luke.* Belief: A Theological Commentary on the Bible. Louisville: Westminster John Knox, 2010.

Good, Deirdre J. *Jesus the Meek King.* Harrisburg, PA: Trinity Press International, 1999.

Goodacre, Mark. *The Case Against Q: Studies in Markan Priority and the Synoptic Problem.* Harrisburg, PA: Trinity Press International, 2002.

Gore, Charles. *The Sermon on the Mount: A Practical Exposition.* London: John Murray, 1907.

Gould, Graham. "Basil of Caesarea and Gregory of Nyssa on the Beatitudes." *Studia Patristica* 23 (1989): 14–22.

Gourgues, Michael. "Sur l'articulation des béatitudes matthéenes (Mt 5.3–12): une proposition." *NTS* 44, no. 3 (1998): 340–56.

Graham, Billy. *The Secret of Happiness: Jesus' Teaching on Happiness as Expressed in the Beatitudes.* Garden City, NY: Doubleday, 1955.

Graham, Helen R. "Matthew 5:1–12. An Asian Perspective." In *Return to Babel: Global Perspectives on the Bible,* edited by John R. Levison and Priscilla Pope-Levison, 131–35. Louisville: Westminster John Knox, 1999.

Grawert, Friedrich. *Die Bergpredigt nach Matthäus auf ihre äussere und innere Einheit mit besond.* Marburg: N. G. Ehwert, 1900.

Green, H. Benedict. *Matthew, Poet of the Beatitudes.* Sheffield: Sheffield Academic, 2001.

Green, Joel B. *The Gospel of Luke.* NICNT. Grand Rapids: Eerdmans, 1997.

Greenman, Jeffrey P. "John R. W. Stott." In Greenman, Larsen, and Spencer, *Sermon on the Mount through the Centuries,* 245–80.

Greenman, Jeffrey P., Timothy Larsen, and Stephen R. Spencer, eds. *The Sermon on the Mount through the Centuries: From the Early Church to John Paul II.* Grand Rapids: Brazos, 2007.

Gregory of Nyssa. *Ascetical Works.* FC 58. Translated by Virginia Woods Callahan. Washington, DC: Catholic University of America Press, 1967.

———. *Gregory of Nyssa's Treatise on the Inscriptions of the Psalms: Introduction, Translation, and Notes.* Translated by Ronald E. Heine. Oxford: Clarendon Press, 1995.

———. *The Lord's Prayer; The Beatitudes.* ACW 18. Translated by Hilda C. Graef. Mahwah, NJ: Paulist, 1954.

Gregory of Palamas. *Ad Xenam de passionibus.* Vol. 150 of Patrologia Graeca. Edited by J.-P. Migne. 162 vols. Paris, 1857–1886.

————. *Homilies.* Vol. 151 of Patrologia Graeca. Edited by J.-P. Migne. 162 vols. Paris, 1857–1886.

Grobel, Kendrick. "How Gnostic is the Gospel of Thomas?" *NTS* 8, no. 4 (1962): 367–73.

Groeschel, Benedict. *Heaven in Our Hands: Receiving the Blessings We Long For.* Ann Arbor, MI: Charis, 1994.

Groothius, Douglas. *On Jesus.* Belmont, CA: Wadsworth, 2003.

Grundmann, Walter. *Das Evangelium nach Matthäus.* Evangelische Verlagsanstalt: Berlin, 1971.

Guelich, Robert. "The Matthean Beatitudes: 'Entrance Requirements' or Eschatological Blessing?" *JBL* 95 (1976): 415–34.

————. *The Sermon on the Mount: A Foundation for Understanding.* Waco, TX: Word, 1982.

Guigo II. *The Ladder of Monks: A Letter on the Contemplative Life, and Twelve Meditations.* Translated by Edmund Colledge and James Walsh. Garden City, NY: Image Books, 1978.

Gundry, Robert H. *Matthew: A Commentary on His Handbook for a Mixed Church under Persecution.* 2nd ed. Grand Rapids: Eerdmans, 1995.

Guroian, Vigen. *Incarnate Love.* 2nd ed. Notre Dame, IN: Notre Dame University Press, 2002.

————. "Liturgy and the Lost Eschatological Vision of Christian Ethics." *Annual of the Society of Christian Ethics* 20 (2000): 227–38.

Gutiérrez, Gustavo. *The God of Life.* Translated by Matthew J. O'Connell. Maryknoll, NY: Orbis Books, 1991, 1998.

————. "Option for the Poor." In *Mysterium Liberationis: Fundamental Concepts of Liberation Theology,* edited by Ignacio Ellacuría and John Sobrino, 235–50. Maryknoll, NY: Orbis Books, 1993.

Gyldenvand, Lily M. *Invitation to Joy.* Minneapolis: Augsburg, 1969.

Hagner, Donald A. *Matthew 1–13.* WBC 33A. Nashville: Nelson, 1993.

Hamm, M. Dennis. *The Beatitudes in Context: What Luke and Matthew Meant.* Wilmington, DE: Michael Glazier, 1990.

Hanson, K. C. "How Honorable! How Shameful! A Cultural Analysis of Matthew's Makarisms and Reproaches." *Semeia* 68 (1994): 81–111.

Harakas, Stanley Samuel. *Toward Transfigured Life: The "Theoria" of Eastern Orthodox Ethics.* Minneapolis: Light and Life, 1983.

Häring, Bernard. *The Blessed Beatitudes: Salt and Light.* Liguori, MO: Liguori, 1999.

Harnack, Adolf von. *What is Christianity?* Translated by Thomas Bailey Saunders. Philadelphia: Fortress, 1957, 1986.

Harris, Julie A. "The Beatitudes Casket in Madrid's Museo Arqueológico: Its Iconography in Context." *ZKunstG* 53, no. 1 (1990): 134–39.

Harris, Robert. *The Way to True Happiness: Delivered in Twenty-Four Sermons upon the Beatitudes.* Edited by Don Kistler. Morgan, PA: Soli Deo Gloria, 1998.

Hart, David Bentley. *The New Testament: A Translation.* New Haven, CT: Yale University Press, 2017.

Hauerwas, Stanley. "Living the Proclaimed Reign of God." *Int* 47, no. 2 (April 1993): 152–58.

Hays, Christopher M. *Luke's Wealth Ethics: A Study in Their Coherence and Character.* WUNT 2. Reihe 275. Tübingen: Mohr Siebeck, 2010.

Hays, Richard B. *Echoes of Scripture in the Gospels.* Waco, TX: Baylor University Press, 2016.

Heard, Gerald. *The Code of the Beatitudes: An Interpretation of the Beatitudes.* Eugene, OR: Wipf & Stock, 1941, 2008.

Heinrici, C. F. G. *Die Bergpredigt (Matth. 5–7; Luk. 6,20–49) quellenmässig und begriffsgeschichtliche Untersuchung.* Zurich: Gotthelf, 1900–1905.

The Heliand: The Saxon Gospel. Translated by G. Ronald Murphy. Oxford: Oxford University Press, 1992.

Hellwig, Monika K. "The Blessedness of the Meek, the Merciful, and the Peacemakers." In Eigo, *New Perspectives,* 191–216.

Hendrickx, Herman. *Ministry in Galilee (Luke 3:1–6:49).* Volume 2A of *The Third Gospel for the Third World.* Collegeville, MN: Liturgical Press, 1997.

———. *The Sermon on the Mount.* Rev. ed. London: Geoffrey Chapman, 1979, 1984.

Hendriksen, William. *The Gospel of Matthew.* New Testament Commentary. Edinburgh: Banner of Truth Trust, 1973.

Henley, Robert. *Saintliness: A Course of Sermons on the Beatitudes; Preached at St. Mary's Church, Putney.* London; Oxford: Rivingtons, 1864.

Henry, Carl F. H. *Christian Personal Ethics.* Grand Rapids: Eerdmans, 1957.

Henry, Matthew. *Matthew to John.* Vol. 5 of *An Exposition of the Old and New Testament.* New York: Revell, n.d. [1708–1710?].

Hilary of Poitiers. *Commentary on Matthew.* Translated by D. H. Williams. FC 125. Washington, DC: Catholic University of America, 2012.

Hildegard of Bingen. *Homilies on the Gospels.* Translated by Beverly Mayne Kienzle. Collegeville, MN: Liturgical Press, 2011.

Hilton, Walter. *The Scale of Perfection.* Translated by John P. H. Clark and Rosemary Dorward. Mahwah, NJ: Paulist, 1991.

Hinnebusch, Paul. *The Beatitudes: Seeking the Joy of God's Kingdom.* Boston: Pauline Books and Media, 2000.

Hinsdale, Mary Ann. "Blessed Are the Persecuted . . . Hungering and Thirsting for

Justice: Blessings for Those Breaking Boundaries." In Eigo, *New Perspectives*, 161–89.

Hogan, Martin. *The Sermon on the Mount in St. Ephrem's Commentary on the Diatessaron*. Bern: Lang, 1999.

Holladay, Carl R. "The Beatitudes: Happiness and the Kingdom." In *The Bible and the Pursuit of Happiness: What the Old and New Testaments Teach Us about the Good Life*, edited by Brent A. Strawn, 141–67. Oxford: Oxford University Press, 2012.

———. "The Beatitudes: Jesus' Recipe for Happiness." In *Between Experience and Interpretation: Engaging the Writings of the New Testament*, edited by Mary F. Hoskett and O. Wesley Allen Jr., 83–102. Nashville: Abingdon, 2008.

Holmes, Jeremy. "Aquinas' *Lectura in Matthaeum*." In *Aquinas on Scripture: An Introduction to His Biblical Commentaries*, edited by Thomas G. Weinandy, Daniel A. Keating, and John P. Yocum, 73-97. London: T&T Clark, 2005.

Hong, Sung Min. *Those Who Weep Shall Laugh: Reversal of Weeping in the Gospel of Luke*. Eugene, OR: Pickwick, 2018.

Hourihane, Colum, ed. *Virtue and Vice: The Personifications in the Index of Christian Art*. Princeton: Princeton University Press, 2000.

Howard, Anne Sutherland. *Claiming the Beatitudes: Nine Stories from a New Generation*. Herndon, VA: Alban Institute, 2009.

Howell, Timothy D. *The Matthean Beatitudes in Their Jewish Origins: A Literary and Speech Act Analysis*. New York: Lang, 2011.

Hughes, R. Kent. *The Sermon on the Mount: The Message of the Kingdom*. Wheaton, IL: Crossway, 2001.

Humphrey, Hugh M. "Matthew 5:9: 'Blessed are the Peacemakers, For They Shall Be Called Sons of God.'" In *Blessed are the Peacemakers: Biblical Perspectives on Peace and its Social Foundations*, edited by Anthony J. Tambasco, 62–78. New York: Paulist, 1989.

Hunsinger, George. *The Beatitudes*. Mahwah, NJ: Paulist, 2015.

Hunter, Archibald M. *A Pattern for Life: An Exposition of the Sermon on the Mount*. Rev. ed. Philadelphia: Westminster, 1965.

Ignatius. *Epistle to the Ephesians*. In vol. 1 of Roberts and Donaldson, eds., *Ante-Nicene Fathers*, 49–58.

Incomplete Commentary on Matthew [Opus Imperfectum]. Edited by Thomas C. Oden. Translated by James A. Kellerman. Ancient Christian Texts 1. Downers Grove, IL: IVP Academic, 2010.

Irenaeus. *Against Heresies*. Translated by Alexander Roberts and W. H. Rambaut. In vol. 1 of Roberts and Donaldson, eds., *Ante-Nicene Fathers*, 309–567.

Isaac of Nineveh. *Mystic Treatises by Isaac of Nineveh*. Translated by A. J. Wensick. Amsterdam: Koninklijke Akademie van Wetenschappen, 1923.

Isaacs, F. W. *The Beatitudes: As Learned by the Cross: Thoughts on the Seven Last Words of Our Lord*. Oxford; London: Mowbray & Co., 1896.

Isaak, Paul John. "Luke." In *Africa Bible Commentary*, edited by Tokunboh Adeyemo, 1229–1276. 2nd ed. Nairobi, Kenya: WordAlive; Grand Rapids: Zondervan, 2010.

James, Sara Nair. "Penance and Redemption: The Role of the Roman Liturgy in Luca Signorelli's Frescoes at Orvieto." *Artibus et Historiae* 22, no. 44 (2001): 119–47.

Jeffrey, David Lyle. "Dante and Chaucer." In Greenman, Larsen, and Spencer, *The Sermon on the Mount through the Centuries*, 81–107.

Jenkins, J. Marshall. *Blessed at the Broken Places: Reclaiming Faith and Purpose with the Beatitudes*. Nashville, TN: Skylight Paths, 2016.

Jenner, Thomas. *The Nanking Monument of the Beatitudes*. London: William Clowes & Sons, 1911.

Jeremias, Joachim. *The Sermon on the Mount*. Minneapolis: Fortress, 1963.

Jerome. *Commentary on Isaiah; St. Jerome's Translation of Origen's Homilies 1–9 on Isaiah*. Translated by Thomas P. Scheck. ACW 68. Mahwah, NJ: The Newman Press, 2015.

———. *Commentary on Matthew*. Translated by Thomas P. Scheck. FC 117. Washington, DC: Catholic University of America, 2008.

John of Damascus. *Exposition of the Orthodox Faith*. Translated by S. D. F. Salmond. In vol. 9 part 2 of Schaff, ed., *The Nicene and Post-Nicene Fathers*, Series 2, 1–101.

Johnson, Luke Timothy. *The Gospel of Luke*. SP 3. Collegeville, MN: Liturgical Press, 1991.

———. *Sharing Possessions: Mandate and Symbol of Faith*. London: SCM, 1981.

———. *Some Hard Blessings: Meditations on the Beatitudes in Matthew*. Allen, TX: Argus, 1981.

Jones, E. Stanley. *The Christ of the Mount: A Working Philosophy of Life*. New York: Abingdon, 1931.

Jordan, Clarence. *Sermon on the Mount*. Rev. ed. Valley Forge, PA: Judson, 1952.

Kalas, J. Ellsworth. *The Beatitudes from the Back Side*. Nashville: Abingdon, 2008.

Kapolyo, Joe. "Matthew." In *Africa Bible Commentary*, edited by Tokunboh Adeyemo, 1131–1196. Zondervan; ABC Editorial Board, Association of Evangelicals of Africa (AEA), 2006.

Karr, Mary. "Who the Meek Are Not." In *Sinner's Welcome*. New York: HarperCollins, 2006.

Kautsky, Karl Johann. *Foundations of Christianity: A Study in Christian Origins*. London: Routledge, 2015. English edition first published 1925 by G. Allen & Unwin.

Kealy, Seán P. *From Apostolic Times through the 19th Century*. Vol. 1 of *The Interpretation of the Gospel of Luke*. Lewiston, NY: Mellen, 2005.

———. *In the Twentieth Century*. Vol. 2 of *The Interpretation of the Gospel of Luke*. Lewiston, NY: Mellen, 2005.

———. *Matthew's Gospel and the History of Biblical Interpretation*. 2 vols. New York: Mellen Biblical, 1997.

Keener, Craig S. *A Commentary on the Gospel of Matthew*. Grand Rapids: Eerdmans, 1999.

Kendall, R. T. *The Sermon on the Mount*. Oxford, UK: Monarch Books, 2011, 2013.

Kertelge, Karl. "'Selig die Trauernden...' (Mt 5,4)." *IKaZ* 20, no. 5 (1991): 387–92.

Kessler, Colette. "Exégèse juive des béatitudes matthéennes." *Lumière et vie* 47 (1997): 51–61.

Khiangte, Vanlalchhawna. *Matthean Beatitudes in Socio-Historical Context: Their Implications for Contemporary Christian Discipleship*. New Delhi: Christian World Imprints, 2016.

Kierkegaard, Søren. *Purity of Heart is to Will One Thing: Spiritual Preparation for the Office of Confession*. Translated by Douglas V. Steere. New York: Harper & Brothers, 1938, 1948.

King, Henry Churchill. "The Fundamental Conditions of Happiness, as Revealed in Jesus' Beatitudes." *The Biblical World* 23, no. 3 (March 1904): 180–87.

King, Martin Luther, Jr. "Acceptance Speech." Nobel Peace Prize, December 10, 1964. https://www.nobelprize.org/prizes/peace/1964/king/26142-martin-luther-king-jr-acceptance-speech-1964/.

———. "Loving Your Enemies." Sermon delivered at Dexter Avenue Baptist Church, Montgomery, Alabama, November 1957. MLKEC, INP, Martin Luther King, Jr. Estate Collection, In Private Hands, ET-1; Atl-5A & 5B. https://kinginstitute.stanford.edu/king-papers/documents/loving-your-enemies-sermon-delivered-dexter-avenue-baptist-church.

Kingsbury, Jack Dean. *Matthew as Story*. Philadelphia: Fortress, 1986.

Kinoti, Hannah W. "Matthew 5:1–12. An African Perspective." In *Return to Babel: Global Perspectives on the Bible*, edited by Priscilla Pope-Levison and John R. Levison, 125–30. Louisville: Westminster John Knox, 1999.

Kissinger, Warren S. *The Sermon on the Mount: A History of Interpretation and Bibliography*. Metuchen, NJ: Scarecrow, 1975.

Kittel, Gerhard. "Die Bergpredigt und die Ethik des Judentums." *Zeitschrift für systematische Theologie* 2 (1924–25): 555–94.

Klauck, Hans-Josef, et al., eds. *Encyclopedia of the Bible and Its Reception*. Vol. 3, *Athena–Birkat ha-Minim*. Berlin: de Gruyter, 2011.

Kodjak, Andrej. *A Structural Analysis of the Sermon on the Mount*. Berlin: Mouton de Gruyter, 1986.

Kolbell, Erik. *What Jesus Meant: The Beatitudes and a Meaningful Life*. Louisville: Westminster John Knox, 2003.

Kosmer, Ellen. "Gardens of Virtue in the Middle Ages." *Journal of the Warburg and Courtauld Institutes* 41 (1978): 302–7.

Kovacs, Judith L. "Clement of Alexandria and Gregory of Nyssa on the Beatitudes." In *Gregory of Nyssa: Homilies on the Beatitudes*, edited by Hubertus R. Drobner and Albert Viciano, 311–29. Leiden: Brill, 2000.

Kreitzer, Beth, ed. *Luke*. Reformation Commentary on Scripture, New Testament 3. Downers Grove, IL: IVP Academic, 2015.

Krüger, Friedhelm. "Die Bergpredigt nach Erasmus." In *Bucer und seine Zeit*, edited by Marijn de Kroon and Friedhelm Krüger, 1–29. Wiesbaden: F. Stener Verlag, 1976.

Kvalbein, Hans. "Jesus and the Poor: Two Texts and a Tentative Conclusion." *Themeleios* 12, no. 3 (1987): 80–87.

Lachs, Samuel Tobias. *A Rabbinic Commentary of the New Testament: The Gospels of Matthew, Mark, and Luke*. Hoboken, NJ: Ktav, 1987.

Lactantius. *The Divine Institutes, Books I–VII*. Translated by Mary Francis McDonald. FC 49. Washington, DC: Catholic University of America Press, 1964.

Lagrange, M.-J. *Évangile selon Saint Luc*. 2nd ed. Paris: Gabalda, 1921.

Lambrecht, Jan. *"Eh bien! Moi je vous dis." Le discours-programme de Jésus (Mt 5–7; Lc 6,20–49)*. Lectio Divina 125. Paris: Les Éditions du Cerf, 1986.

Landriot, Jean François Anne Thomas. *Les Béatitudes évangéliques*. 2 vols. Paris: Palmé, 1866–67.

Lanfer, Peter Thacher. *Remembering Eden: The Reception History of Genesis 3:22–24*. Oxford: Oxford University Press, 2012.

Lange, John Peter. *The Gospel according to Matthew*. Vol. 16 of *A Commentary on the Holy Scriptures: Critical, Doctrinal, and Homiletical, with Special Reference to Ministers and Students*. Translated by Philip Schaff. 12th ed. New York: Charles Scribner's Sons, 1884.

Langford, Jim. *Happy Are They: Living the Beatitudes in America*. Liguori, MO: Triumph Books, 1997.

Lapide, Pinchas. *The Sermon on the Mount: Utopia or Program for Action?* Translated by Arlene Swidler. Maryknoll: Orbis Books, 1986.

Larsen, Timothy. "Charles Haddon Spurgeon." In Greenman, Larsen, and Spencer, *Sermon on the Mount Through the Centuries*, 181–205.

Lathbury, Clarence. *The Code of Joy: The Ten Requisites of Perfected Manhood.* Germantown, PA: The Swedenborg Publishing Association, 1902.

Lawson, LeRoy. *Blessed Are We: Experiencing Joy as the Beatitudes of Jesus Turn Our Priorities Upside Down.* Cincinnati, OH: Standard Publishing, 1998.

Lawson, William. *Good Christian Men Rejoice: The Meaning and Attainment of Happiness.* New York: Sheed and Ward, 1955.

Lechman, Judith C. *The Spirituality of Gentleness: Growing toward Christian Wholeness.* New York: Harper & Row, 1987.

Lefebure, Leo D. *The Buddha and the Christ: Explorations in Buddhist and Christian Dialogue.* Maryknoll, NY: Orbis Books, 1993, 1997.

Lefèvre, Jacques d'Étaples. *Jacques Lefèvre d'Étaples et ses Disciples: Epistres et Evangiles pour le cinquante et deux dimenches de l'an.* Edited by Guy Bedouelle and Franco Giacone. Leiden: Brill, 1976.

Légasse, Simon. "Les pauvres en esprit et les 'volontaires' de Qumran." *NTS* 8 (1962): 336–45.

———. *Les pauvres en esprit: Evangile et non-violence.* Paris: Les Éditions du Cerf, 1974.

Leo the Great. *Sermons.* Translated by Charles Lett Feltoe. In vol. 12 of Schaff, ed., *The Nicene and Post-Nicene Fathers,* Series 2, 115–205.

Leske, Adrian M. "The Beatitudes, Salt and Light in Matthew and Luke." *The SBLSP* 30 (1991): 816–39.

Le Sueur, Eustache. *Meekness.* 1650. Oil on panel. Charles H. and Mary F. S. Worcester Collection, Art Institute of Chicago. https://www.artic.edu/artworks/47159/meekness.

Lindsay, John, and John Court. *The New Testament of Our Lord and Savior Jesus Christ Carefully and Diligently Compared with the Original Greek.* London: R. Penny, 1736.

Linner, Rachelle. "Those Who Hunger and Thirst for Justice." In *The Beatitudes in Modern Life,* edited by Margaret Garvey, 69–96. Chicago: Thomas More, 1989.

Lis, Marek. "Beatitudes, Film." *EBR* 3:697.

Lischer, Richard. "The Sermon on the Mount as Radical Pastoral Care." In *The Theological Interpretation of Scripture: Classic and Contemporary Readings,* edited by Stephen E. Fowl, 294–306. Malden, MA: Blackwell, 1997.

Lloyd-Jones, D. Martyn. *Studies in the Sermon on the Mount.* Vol. 1. Grand Rapids: Eerdmans, 1960.

Loewen, Howard John. *One Lord, One Church, One Hope, and One God: Mennonite Confessions of Faith in North America. An Introduction.* Institute of Mennonite Studies, 1985.

Lohfink, Gerhard. "The Appeasement of the Messiah: Thoughts on Psalm 37 and the Third Beatitude." *TD* 44 (1997): 234–41.

Lohfink, Norbert. *Option for the Poor.* Translated by Linda M. Maloney. Berkeley, CA: BIBAL Press, 1987.

Long, Siobhán Dowling, and John F. A. Sawyer. *The Bible in Music: A Dictionary of Songs, Works, and More.* Lanham, MD: Rowman & Littlefield, 2015.

Long, Thomas. "The Christian Funeral and the Blessedness of Mourning." *The Yale ISM Review* 4, no. 2 (Fall 2018), http://ismreview.yale.edu/article/the-christian-funeral-and-the-blessedness-of-mourning/).

Lundbom, Jack R. *Jesus' Sermon on the Mount: Mandating a Better Righteousness.* Minneapolis: Fortress, 2015.

Luther, Martin. *Luther: Letters of Spiritual Counsel.* Translated by Theodore G. Tappert. LCC 18. Philadelphia: Westminster, 1955.

————. *The Sermon on the Mount.* Vol. 21 of *Luther's Works.* Edited by Jaroslav Pelikan. St. Louis: Concordia, 1956.

Luz, Ulrich. *Matthew 1–7.* Translated by James E. Crouch. Hermeneia. Minneapolis: Fortress, 2007.

————. *Studies in Matthew.* Translated by Rosemary Selle. Grand Rapids: Eerdmans, 2005.

M., E. [Edward Manning or Edward Mico?] *Ashrea: Or, the Grove of the Beatitudes, Represented in Emblemes: And, by the Art of Memory, To be read on our Blessed Saviour Crucifi'd.* London: Printed for W. P. at Grayes-Inn Gate in Holborne, 1665. Reprint: English Emblem Books 18. Yorkshire, England: Scolar Press, 1970.

Macchioro, Vittorio. "The Meaning of the First Beatitude." *JR* 12, no. 1 (1932): 40–49.

MacEvilly, John. *An Exposition of the Gospels.* Dublin: W. B. Kelly; London: Simpkin, Marshall & Co., 1876.

Mackay, Mackintosh. *A practical exposition of the first ten verses of the fifth chapter of the Gospel by Matthew: in forty one sermons, preached in the Parish Church of Dunoon.* 2 vols. Edinburgh: William Whyte & Co., 1840–1842.

Maldonado, Juan. *S. Matthew's Gospel, Chapters I to XIV.* Vol. 1 of *A Commentary on the Holy Gospels.* Translated and edited by George J. Davie. London, UK: John Hodges, 1888.

Malipurathu, Thomas. *"Blessed are you poor!": Exploring the Biblical Impulses for an Alternative World Order.* Delhi: Ishvani Kendra, 2014.

Martin, John A. "Dispensational Approaches to the Sermon on the Mount." In *Essays in Honor of J. Dwight Pentecost,* edited by Stanley D. Toussaint and Charles H. Dyer, 35–48. Chicago: Moody, 1985.

Mather, Increase. *Sermons Wherein Those Eight Characters of the Blessed Commonly Called the Beatitudes Are Opened and Applied in Fifteen Discourses*. Boston: B. Green, for Daniel Henchman, 1718.

Mayeski, Marie Anne. "The Beatitudes and the Moral Life of the Christian: Practical Theology and Biblical Exegesis in Dhuoda of Septimania." *Mystics Quarterly* 18, no. 1 (March 1992): 6–15.

McArthur, Harvey K. *Understanding the Sermon on the Mount*. New York: Harper & Brothers, 1960.

McCown, Chester S. "The Beatitudes in the Light of Ancient Ideals." *JBL* 46 (1927): 50–61.

McKenna, Megan. *Blessings and Woes: The Beatitudes and in the Sermon on the Plain in the Gospel of Luke*. Maryknoll, NY: Orbis Books, 1999.

McKnight, Scot. *The Sermon on the Mount*. The Story of God Bible Commentary. Grand Rapids: Zondervan, 2013.

Meier, John P. "Matthew 5:3–12." *Int* 44 (1990): 281–85.

Meiser, Martin. "Beatitudes, Christianity." *EBR* 3:688–90.

Menken, Maarten J. J. *Matthew's Bible: The Old Testament Text of the Evangelist*. Leuven: University Press, 2004.

Meredith, Anthony. "Gregory of Nyssa, *De Beatitudinibus*, Oratio I: 'Blessed are the Poor in Spirit, For Theirs Is the Kingdom of Heaven' (Mt 5,3)." In *Gregory of Nyssa: Homilies on the Beatitudes*, edited by Hubertus R. Drobner and Albert Viciano, 93–109. Leiden: Brill, 2000.

Merton, Thomas. *Blessed are the Meek: The Christian Roots of Nonviolence*. N.p., 1967. Reprinted from the May 1967 edition of Fellowship Magazine.

Metz, Johann Baptist. *Poverty of Spirit*. Translated by John Drury. Glen Rock, NJ: Newman Press, 1968.

Metzger, Paul Louis. *Beatitudes, Not Platitudes: Jesus' Invitation to the Good Life*. Eugene, OR: Cascade, 2018.

Michaelis, Christine. "Die Π-Alliteration der Subjektsworte der ersten 4 Seligpreisungen in Mt. 5:3–6 und ihre Bedeutung für den Aufbau der Seligpreisungen bei Mt., Lk. und in Q." *Novum Testamentum* 10, no. 2–3 (Apr–Jul 1968): 148–61.

Mitchell, Margaret M. "John Chrysostom." In Greenman, Larsen, and Spencer, *The Sermon on the Mount through the Centuries*, 19–42.

Morris, Leon. *Luke: An Introduction and Commentary*. TNTC. Leicester, England: InterVarsity Press; Grand Rapids: Eerdmans, 1974, 1988.

Mortimer, Alfred G. *The Laws of Happiness; or, The Beatitudes as Teaching Our Duty to God, Self, and Neighbor*. E. and J. B. Young, 1888.

Muessig, Carolyn. "Preaching the Beatitudes in the Late Middle Ages: Some Mendicant Examples." *Studies in Christian Ethics* 22, no. 2 (2009): 136–42.

Müller, Johannes. *Die Bergpredigt: verdeutscht und vergegenwärtigt.* 8th ed. München: C. H. Beck'sche Verlagsbuchhandlung, 1929.

Müller, Ludwig. *The Germanisation of the New Testament.* London: Friends of Europe, 1938.

Munson, Miriam Grove. "Humility, Charity, and the Beatitudes in Patience and The Scale of Perfection." *14th Century English Mystics Newsletter* 4, no. 3 (September 1978): 17–24.

Murphy, G. Ronald. *The Saxon Savior: The Germanic Transformation of the Gospel in the Ninth-Century Heliand.* Oxford: Oxford University Press, 1989.

Muto, Susan. "Blessed Are the Poor in Spirit and the Pure of Heart." In Eigo, *New Perspectives,* 129–59.

———. *Blessings that Make Us Be: A Formative Approach to Living the Beatitudes.* New York: Crossroad, 1982, 1984.

Nagai, Takashi. *The Bells of Nagasaki.* Translated by William Johnston. Tokyo: Kodansha International, 1984.

Newman, Barclay M. "Some Translational Notes on the Beatitudes. Matthew 5.1–12." *Bible Translator* 26 (1975): 106–20.

Niclaes, Hendrik. *The first exhortation of H. N. to his children, and to the Family of Love: Likewise H. N. upon the Beatitudes, and the Seven Deadly Sins.* Translated out of Base-Almayne into English. London: For Giles Calvert, 1656.

Nolland, John. *The Gospel of Matthew.* NIGTC. Grand Rapids: Eerdmans; Bletchley: Paternoster, 2005.

Norris, John. *Christian Blessedness: or, Discourses upon the Beatitudes.* Vol. 1 of *Practical Discourses Upon the Beatitudes.* 5th ed. London: S. Manship, 1707.

Novatian. *Treatise Concerning the Trinity.* Translated by A. Cleveland Coxe. In vol. 5 of Roberts and Donaldson, eds., *Ante-Nicene Fathers,* 611–644.

Okambawa, Wilfrid Kolorunko. *Les béatitudes: Le médicament pour le bonheur.* Dakar: Lux Africæ, 2015.

Olsen, Derek A. *Reading Matthew with Monks: Liturgical Interpretation in Anglo-Saxon England.* Collegeville, MN: Liturgical Press, 2015.

Oosterzee, Johannes Jacobus van. *The Gospel According to Luke: The Gospel of Universal Humanity.* Translated by Philip Schaff and Charles C. Starbuck. New York: Charles Scribner & Co., 1869.

Origen. *Against Celsus.* Translated by Frederick Crombie. In vol. 4 of Roberts and Donaldson, eds., *Ante-Nicene Fathers,* 395–669.

———. *Commentary on the Gospel of Matthew.* Translated by John Patrick. In vol. 9 of Roberts and Donaldson, eds., *Ante-Nicene Fathers,* 412–512.

———. *De Principiis*. Translated by Frederick Crombie. In vol. 4 of Roberts and Donaldson, eds., *Ante-Nicene Fathers*, 239–384.

———. *An Exhortation to Martyrdom, Prayer, First Principles: Book IV, Prologue to the Commentary on the Song of Songs, Homily XXVII on Numbers*. Translated by Rowan Greer. New York: Paulist, 1979.

———. *Homilies on Luke*. FC 49. Translated by Joseph T. Lienhard. Washington, DC: Catholic University of America Press, 2009.

The Orthodox Monastery of the Transfiguration. "Mother Alexandra." Accessed February 10, 2020. http://www.orthodoxmonasteryellwoodcity.org /about/foundress.

Pass, H. Leonard. *The Divine Commonwealth: A Study in the Beatitudes*. London; Oxford: A. R. Mowbray & Co., 1936.

Patrologia Graeca. Edited by J.-P. Migne. 162 vols. Paris, 1857–1886.

Patrologia Latina. Edited by J.-P. Migne. 221 vols. Paris, 1844–1855.

Patte, Daniel. *The Gospel According to Matthew: A Structural Commentary on Matthew's Faith*. Philadelphia: Fortress, 1987.

Patterson, Dorothy Kelley. *BeAttitudes for Women: Wisdom from Heaven for Life on Earth*. Nashville, TN: Broadman & Holman, 2000.

Peabody, Francis Greenwood. "The Peace-Makers." *HTR* 12, no. 1 (January 1919): 51–66.

Pelikan, Jaroslav. *Divine Rhetoric: The Sermon on the Mount as Message and as Model in Augustine, Chrysostom, and Luther*. Crestwood, NY: St. Vladimir's Seminary Press, 2001.

———. *The Melody of Theology*. Cambridge: Harvard University Press, 1988.

Pennington, Jonathan T. *The Sermon on the Mount and Human Flourishing: A Theological Commentary*. Grand Rapids: Baker Academic, 2017.

Perrin, Joseph Marie. *Gospel of Joy*. Westminster, MD: Newman, 1957.

Pertiné, Iván. *The Good Sense of Jesus: A Commentary on the Beatitudes*. Charlotte, NC: TAN Books, 2018. Original Spanish edition *La Sensatez Cristiana* (Agape Libros, 2016).

Peter Lombard. *The Sentences. Book 3: On the Incarnation of the Word*. Translated by Giulio Silano. Toronto, ON: Pontifical Institute of Mediaeval Studies, 2008.

Peterson, L. Elmer. *The Beatitudes: A Latter-Day Saint Interpretation*. Salt Lake City, UT: Deseret Book, 1964.

Peterson, Nils Holger. "Beatitudes, Music." *EBR* 3:696–97.

Philips, Dietrich. "The Church of God." In *Spiritual and Anabaptist Writers*, edited by George H. Williams, 228–62. First published ca. 1560 as *Van die Ghemeynte Godts* and later taken up into the *Enchiridion* (1563). Philadelphia: Westminster, 1957.

Pigot, Hugh. *The Blessed Life: A Course of Lectures on the Beatitudes: With Two Sermons on the War, Delivered in the Parish Church of Hadleigh.* London: J. H. & J. Packer, 1855.

Pinckaers, Servais. *The Pursuit of God's Happiness—God's Way: Living the Beatitudes.* Translated by Mary Thomas Noble. New York: Society of St. Paul, 1998.

———. *The Sources of Christian Ethics.* Edinburgh: T&T Clark, 2001.

Plummer, Alfred. *A Critical and Exegetical Commentary on the Gospel According to S. Luke.* 4th ed. Edinburgh: T&T Clark, 1901.

———. *An Exegetical Commentary on the Gospel According to S. Matthew.* London: Paternoster Row, 1909.

Pobee, John S. *Who Are the Poor?: The Beatitudes as a Call to Community.* World Council of Churches. Geneva: World Council of Churches, 1987.

Polycarp. *Epistle to the Philippians.* Translated by Alexander Roberts and James Donaldson. In vol. 1 of Roberts and Donaldson, eds., *Ante-Nicene Fathers,* 31–36.

Powell, Mark Allan. "Matthew's Beatitudes: Reversals and Rewards of the Kingdom." *CBQ* 58 (1996): 460–79.

Pseudo-Bede. *In Matthaei Evangelium Expositio Lib I.* Vol. 92 of Patrologia Latina. Edited by J.-P. Migne. 221 vols. Paris, 1844–1855.

Pseudo-Clementine. *Homilies.* Translated by Thomas Smith, Peter Peterson, and James Donaldson. In vol. 8 of Roberts and Donaldson, eds., *Ante-Nicene Fathers,* 223–346.

———. *Recognitions.* Translated by Thomas Smith. In vol. 8 of Roberts and Donaldson, eds., *Ante-Nicene Fathers,* 75–211.

Puech, Émile. "4Q525 et les pericopes des Beatitudes en Ben Sira et Matthieu." *RB* 98, no. 1 (1991): 80–106.

Quaintance, Chad. "The Blessed Life: Theological Interpretation and Use of the Beatitudes by Augustine, Calvin and Barth." PhD diss., Union Theological Seminary and Presbyterian School of Christian Education, 2003. ProQuest 3087209.

Quarles, Charles. *Sermon on the Mount: Restoring Christ's Message to the Modern Church.* Nashville: B & H Academic, 2011.

Quinn, Jenna. *Pure in Heart: A Memoir of Overcoming Abuse and Passing Jenna's Law.* Dallas, TX: Liberty House Publishing, 2017.

Rabanus Maurus. *De laudibus sanctae crucis* [In Praise of the Holy Cross]. Vol. 107 of Patrologia Latina. Edited by J.-P. Migne. 221 vols. Paris, 1844–55.

Ramsey, Paul. *Basic Christian Ethics.* London: SCM; Scribner's Sons, 1950.

Randall, Albert B. *Strangers on the Shore: The Beatitudes in World Religions.* New York: Lang, 2006.

Ranjar, Clifard Sunil. *Be Merciful Like the Father: Exegesis and Theology of the Sermon on the Plain (Luke 6,17–49).* Rome: Pontifical Biblical Institute, 2017.

Rantisi, Audeh G., with Ralph K. Beebe. *Blessed are the Peacemakers: A Palestinian Christian in the Occupied West Bank.* Grand Rapids: Zondervan, 1990.

Ratzinger, Joseph (Pope Benedict XVI). *Jesus of Nazareth: From the Baptism in the Jordan to the Transfiguration.* Translated by Adrian J. Walker. New York: Doubleday, 2007.

Raunio, Antti. "Beatitudes, Medieval Times and Reformation Era." *EBR* 3:690–93.

Reuss, Joseph, ed. *Lukas-Kommentare aus der griechischen Kirche.* Berlin: Akademie-Verlag, 1984.

———, ed. *Matthäus-Kommentare aus der griechischen Kirche.* Berlin: Akademie-Verlag, 1957.

Reynolds, Myra. "Material from English Literature Illustrative of the International Sunday-School Lessons." *Biblical World* 11 (1898): 49–52.

Roberts, Alexander, and James Donaldson, eds. *Ante-Nicene Fathers.* 1885–1887. 10 vols. Repr., Peabody, MA: Hendrickson, 1994.

Roncace, Mark, and Joseph Weaver, eds. *Global Perspectives on the Bible.* Boston: Pearson, 2014.

Rose, Scott, et al., with Leo J. O'Donovan. *Blessed Are the Refugees: Beatitudes of Immigrant Children.* Maryknoll, NY: Orbis Books, 2018.

Ruden, Sarah. *The Face of Water: A Translator on Beauty and Meaning in the Bible.* New York: Pantheon Books, 2017.

Rukundwa, Lazare S., and Andries G. Van Aarde. "Revisiting Justice in the First Four Beatitudes in Matthew (5:3–6) and the Story of the Canaanite Woman (Mt 15:21–28): A Postcolonial Reading." *HvTSt* 61, no. 3 (2005): 927–51.

Rupert of Deutz. *Liber de Divinis Officiis.* Vol. 3. Edited and translated by Helmut Deutz and Ilse Deutz. Freiburg: Herder, 1999.

Russell, William H. "The Eight Beatitudes in the School Program." *The Catholic Educational Review* 26 (1928): 193–202.

Ryan, Jerry. "Lena Ekblom: The Folly of the Beatitudes." *Cross Currents* 48, no. 1 (Spring 1998): 89–95.

Scaer, David P. *Discourses in Matthew: Jesus Teaches the Church.* St. Louis, MO: Concordia, 2000.

———. *The Sermon on the Mount: The Church's First Statement of the Gospel.* St. Louis, MO: Concordia, 2000.

Schaff, Philip, ed. *The Nicene and Post-Nicene Fathers,* Series 1. 1886–1889. 14 vols. Repr., Peabody, MA: Hendrickson, 1994.

————, ed. *The Nicene and Post-Nicene Fathers*, Series 2. 1886–1889. 14 vols. Repr., Peabody, MA: Hendrickson, 1994.

Schlabach, Gerald. "Pope Francis's Peacebuilding Pedagogy: A Commentary on his 2017 World Day of Peace Message." Posted January 2, 2017. http://www.geraldschlabach.net/2017/01/02/wdp17/.

————. "Round Table Discussion: Just Peacemaking. A 'Manual' for Escaping Our Vicious Cycles." *Journal of Moral Theology* 7, no. 2 (2018): 86–91.

Schlatter, Adolf. *Der Evangelist Matthäus: Seine Sprache, sein Ziel, seine Selbständigkeit*. Stuttgart: Calwer Verlag, 1959.

Schleusener, Jay. "'Patience,' Lines 35–40." *Modern Philology* 67, no. 1 (August 1969): 64–66.

Schlütz, Karl. *Isaias 11, 2 (die sieben Gaben des Hl. Geistes) in den ersten vier christlichen Jahrhunderten*. Münster: Aschendorff, 1932.

Schmitz, Hermann Joseph. *Les béatitudes de l'Évangile et les promesses de la démocratie sociale*. Translated by L. Collin. Paris: P. Lethielleux, 1902.

Schnackenburg, Rudolf. *All Things Are Possible to Believers: Reflections on the Lord's Prayer and the Sermon on the Mount*. Translated by James S. Currie. Louisville: Westminster John Knox, 1995.

————. *Die Bergpredigt: Utopische Vision oder Handlungsanweisung?* Edited by Rudolf Schnackenburg. Düsseldorf: Patmos, 1982.

————. "Die Seligpreisung der Friedensstifter (Matt 5:9) im mattaischen Kontext." *BZ* 26, no. 2 (1982): 161–78.

Schottroff, Luise, and Wolfgang Stegemann. *Jesus and the Hope of the Poor*. Translated by Matthew J. O'Connell. Maryknoll, NY: Orbis Books, 1986.

Schreiner, Susan E. "Martin Luther." In Greenman, Larsen, and Spencer, *The Sermon on the Mount through the Centuries*, 109–127.

Schuller, Robert. *The Be (Happy) Attitudes: Eight Positive Attitudes*. World Books, 1985, 1996.

Schweitzer, Albert. *The Kingdom of God and Primitive Christianity*. Translated by L. A. Garrard. New York: Seabury, 1968.

————. *The Mystery of the Kingdom of God: The Secret of Jesus' Messiahship and Passion*. Translated by Walter Lowrie. Buffalo, NY: Prometheus Books, 1985.

————. *The Quest of the Historical Jesus: A Critical Study of Its Progress from Reimarus to Wrede*. New York: Macmillan, 1968.

Schweizer, Eduard. *The Good News According to Matthew*. Translated by David E. Green. Atlanta: John Knox, 1975.

The Scofield Study Bible. New King James Version. New York: Oxford University Press, 2002.

Sheen, Fulton J. *The Cross and the Beatitudes*. Garden City, NY: Garden City Books, 1937, 1952.

Sicari, Antonio. "The Hunger and Thirst of Christ." *Communio* 18 (1991): 590–602.

Silvas, Anna M. *The Asketikon of St. Basil the Great*. Oxford: Oxford University Press, 2005.

Simons, Menno. "The Cross of the Saints." In *The Complete Writings of Menno Simons*, edited by John Christian Wenger, translated by Leonard Verduin, 581–622. Scottdale, PA: Herald Press, 1956.

Sloan, Robert Bryan. *The Favorable Year of the Lord: A Study of Jubilary Theology in the Gospel of Luke*. Austin, TX: Schola Press, 1977.

Smith, Amanda. *An Autobiography: The Story of the Lord's Dealings with Mrs. Amanda Smith the Colored Evangelist*. Oxford: Oxford University Press, 1988.

Smith, Harold. *Ante-Nicene Exegesis of the Gospels*. 2 vols. London: SPCK, 1925.

Smith, William. *Nine Discourses on the Beatitudes*. London: John, Francis, & Charles Rivington, 1782.

Snodgrass, Klyne. "A Response to Hans Dieter Betz on the Sermon on the Mount." *Biblical Research* 36 (1991): 88–94.

Solms, Friedhelm, and Marc Reuver. *Churches as peacemakers: an analysis of recent church statements on peace, disarmament and war*. Rome: IDOC International, 1985.

Southwell, Robert. *An epistle of comfort to the reuerend priestes, & to the honorable, worshipful, & other of the laye sort restrayned in durance for the Catholicke fayth*. Paris, 1587.

Spencer, Stephen R. "John Calvin." In Greenman, Larsen, and Spencer, *The Sermon on the Mount through the Centuries*, 129–52.

Spinoza, Baruch. *Tractatus theologico-politicus, Chapter 7*. In *History of Biblical Interpretation: A Reader*, by William Yarchin, 198–207. Peabody, MA: Hendrickson, 2004.

Spurgeon, Charles H. *The Beatitudes: Eight Sermons*. Pasadena, TX: Pilgrim Publications, 1978.

———. *Morning and Evening*. Edited by Roy Clarke. Nashville: Nelson, 1994.

St. George, Arthur. *The Blessings of Christian Philosophy; Being a Treatise on the Beatitudes*. London: W. Innys & R. Manby, 1738.

Stassen, Glen. "The Beatitudes as Eschatological Peacemaking Virtues." In *Character Ethics and the New Testament: Moral Dimensions of Scripture*, edited by Robert L. Brawley, 245–57. Louisville: Westminster John Knox, 2007.

———, ed. *Just Peacemaking: Ten Practices for Abolishing War*. 2nd ed. Cleveland, OH: The Pilgrim Press, 1998.

Stemberger, Günter. "Beatitudes, Rabbinic Judaism." *EBR* 3:686–88.

Stillingfleet, Edward. *A sermon preached November 5, 1673, at St. Margarets Westminst by Edward Stillingfleet.* 2nd ed. London: Robert White, for Henry Mortlock, 1674.

Stoddart, Jane T. *The New Testament in Life and Literature.* London: Hodder and Stoughton, 1914.

Stoll, Brigitta. *De Virtute in Virtutem: zur Auslegungs- und Wirkungsgeschichte der Bergpredigt in Kommentaren, Predigten und hagiographischer Literatur von der Merowingerzeit bis um 1200.* BGBE 30. Tübingen: Mohr Siebeck, 1988.

Stott, John R. W. *Christian Counter-Culture: The Message of the Sermon on the Mount.* Downers Grove, IL: InterVarsity Press, 1978.

Strecker, Georg. "Die Makarismen der Bergpredigt." *NTS* 17 (1970/71): 255–75.

———. *The Sermon on the Mount: An Exegetical Commentary.* Translated by O. C. Dean Jr. Edinburgh: T&T Clark, 1988.

Sugirtharajah, R. S. "Matthew 5–7: The Sermon on the Mount and India." In *Global Bible Commentary,* edited by Daniel Patte, 361–66. Nashville: Abingdon, 2004.

Swedenborg, Emanuel. *Words of Spirit and Life: The Spiritual Meaning of the Sermon on the Mount. From the Writings of Emanuel Swedenborg.* Edited by Leonard Fox. Charleston, SC: Arcana Books, 1997.

Symeon the New Theologian. *The Discourses.* Translated by C. J. deCatanzaro. New York: Paulist, 1980.

Talbert, Charles H. *Reading the Sermon on the Mount: Character Formation and Ethical Decision Making in Matthew 5–7.* Grand Rapids: Baker Academic, 2004.

Tamez, Elsa. *Bible of the Oppressed.* Maryknoll, NY: Orbis Books, 1982.

ten Klooster, Anton. "Dante and the Beatitudes: Moral Transformation in 'Purgatorio.'" *Incontri. Rivista europea di studi italiani* 34, no. 1 (2019): 122–27.

———. *Thomas Aquinas on the Beatitudes: Reading Matthew, Disputing Grace and Virtue, Preaching Happiness.* Leuven: Peeters, 2018.

Tertullian. *Against Marcion.* Translated by Peter Holmes. In vol. 3 of Roberts and Donaldson, eds., *Ante-Nicene Fathers,* 271–423.

———. *Apology; de Spectaculis; Minucius Felix.* Translated by T. R. Glover. LCL. Cambridge, MA: Harvard University Press, 1953.

———. *De Fuga in Persecutione [On Flight in Persecution].* Translated by S. Thelwall. In vol. 4 of Roberts and Donaldson, eds., *Ante-Nicene Fathers,* 116–25.

———. *On Idolatry.* Translated by S. Thelwall. In vol. 3 of Roberts and Donaldson, eds., *Ante-Nicene Fathers,* 61–77.

———. *Of Patience.* Translated by S. Thelwall. In vol. 3 of Roberts and Donaldson, eds., *Ante-Nicene Fathers,* 707–17.

Theodotus. *Excerpts*. Translated by William Wilson. In vol. 8 of Roberts and Donaldson, eds., *Ante-Nicene Fathers*, 39–50.

Theophylact of Ochrid. *The Explanation by Blessed Theophylact of the Holy Gospel According to St. Luke*. Vol. 3 of *Blessed Theophylact's Explanation of the New Testament*. Translated by Christopher Stade. House Springs, MO: Chrysostom Press, 1997.

———. *The Explanation by Blessed Theophylact of the Holy Gospel According to St. Matthew*. Vol. 1 of *Blessed Theophylact's Explanation of the New Testament*. Translated by Christopher Stade. House Springs, MO: Chrysostom Press, 1994.

Tholuck, Friedrich August. *Commentary on the Sermon on the Mount*. Translated from the 4th ed. by R. Lundin Brown. Edinburgh: T&T Clark, 1869.

Thomas Aquinas. *Commentary on the Gospel of Matthew, Chapters 1–12*. Translated by Jeremy Holmes and Beth Mortensen. Edited by The Aquinas Institute. Biblical Commentaries 33. Lander, WY: The Aquinas Institute for the Study of Sacred Doctrine, 2013.

———. *St. Matthew*. Vol. 1 of *Catena Aurea: A Commentary on the Four Gospels Collected out of the Works of the Fathers*. Translated by John Henry Newman. London: The Saint Austin Press, 1999.

———. *Summa Theologica: Complete English Edition in Five Volumes*. Translated by Fathers of the English Dominican Province. Westminster, MD: Christian Classics, 1948.

———. *The Three Greatest Prayers: Commentaries on the Lord's Prayer, the Hail Mary, and the Apostles' Creed*. Manchester, NH: Sophia Institute Press, 1990.

Thomson, James. *Exposition of the Gospel According to St. Luke, in a Series of Lectures*. Vol. 1. Edinburgh: Neill & Company, 1849.

Thurman, Howard. *Jesus and the Disinherited*. Nashville: Abingdon-Cokesbury Press, 1949.

Thurneysen, Eduard. *The Sermon on the Mount*. Translated by William Childs Robinson. Richmond, VA: John Knox, 1964.

Tiede, David L. *Luke*. Augsburg Commentary on the New Testament. Minneapolis: Augsburg, 1988.

Torrance, Thomas. *The Beatitudes and the Decalogue*. London: Skeffington & Son, 1921.

True, Michael, ed. *Blessed Are the Peacemakers: Meditations and Resources on Nuclear Disarmament*. Worcester, MA: Diocese of Worcester, 1982.

Trueman, Carl. "Editorial: What Has Boxing to do with Jerusalem?" *Themelios* 27, no. 1 (Autumn 2001): 1–4.

Trzyna, Thomas. *Blessed Are the Pacifists: The Beatitudes and Just War Theory.* Scottdale, PA: Herald Press, 2006.

Tugwell, Simon. *The Beatitudes: Soundings in Christian Traditions.* Springfield, IL: Templegate, 1980.

―――, ed. and trans. *The Nine Ways of Prayer of Saint Dominic.* Dublin: Dominican Publications, 1978.

Turner, David L. "Whom Does God Approve? The Context, Structure, Purpose, and Exegesis of Matthew's Beatitudes." *Criswell Theological Review* 6 (1992): 29–42.

Tuve, Rosemond. "Notes on the Virtues and Vices." *Journal of the Warburg and Courtauld Institutes* 27 (1964): 42–72.

Tyndale, William. *The Work of William Tyndale.* Edited by G. E. Duffield. Philadelphia: Fortress, 1965.

Vann, Gerald. *The Divine Pity: A Study in the Social Implications of the Beatitudes.* New York: Sheed and Ward, 1946.

Varner, William. *The Way of the Didache: The First Christian Handbook.* Lanham, MD: University Press of America, 2007.

Vaught, Carl G. *The Sermon on the Mount: A Theological Investigation.* Waco, TX: Baylor University Press, 2001.

Verhey, Allen. *Remembering Jesus: Christian Community, Scripture, and the Moral Life.* Grand Rapids: Eerdmans, 2002.

―――. "Scripture as Script and as Scripted: The Beatitudes." In *Character Ethics and the New Testament: Moral Dimensions of Scripture,* edited by Robert L. Brawley, 19–34. Louisville: Westminster John Knox, 2007.

Viljoen, Francois P. "Interpreting the *visio Dei* in Matthew 5:8." *HvTSt* 68, no. 1, Art. #905 (January 2012), 7 pages. http://dx.doi.org/10.4102/hts.v68i1.905.

Vinel, Françoise. "Grégoire de Nysse, *De Beatitudinibus,* Oratio III: 'Bienheureux les affligés, parce qu'ils seront consolés,' (Mt 5,5)." In *Gregory of Nyssa: Homilies on the Beatitudes,* edited by Hubertus R. Drobner and Albert Viciano, 139–47. Leiden: Brill, 2000.

Viviano, Benedict. "Eight Beatitudes at Qumran and in Matthew? A New Publication from Cave Four." *Svensk exegetisk årsbok* 58 (1993): 71–84.

―――. "The Sermon on the Mount in Recent Study." *Biblica* 78, no. 2 (1997): 255–65.

Vonnegut, Kurt. *A Man without a Country.* Edited by Daniel Simon. New York: Seven Stories Press, 2005.

Waldenström, P. P. "You Are the Salt and the Light of the World." In *The Swedish Pietists: A Reader. Excerpts from the Writings of Carl Olof Rosenius and Paul*

Peter Waldenström, ed. and trans. Mark Safstrom, 216–19. Eugene, OR: Pickwick, 2015.

Walker, Harold Blake. *Ladder of Light: The Meaning of the Beatitudes*. New York: Revell, 1951.

Wansbrough, Henry. "St. Luke and Christian Ideals in an Affluent Society." *New Blackfriars* 49, no. 579 (August 1968): 582–87.

Warner, Susan, and Anna Bartlett Warner. *The Golden Ladder; Stories Illustrative of the Eight Beatitudes*. London: Frederick Warne, 1887.

Watson, Lily. *A Garden of Girls: Stories Illustrating the Beatitudes*. London: Religious Tract Society, 1893.

Watson, Richard. *Exposition of the Gospels of St. Matthew and St. Mark*. London: John Mason, 1833.

Watson, Thomas. *The Beatitudes: An Exposition of Matthew 5:1–10*. Carlisle, PA: Banner of Truth Trust, 2014. Originally published as *The Beatitudes*. London: Ralph Smith, 1660.

Weatherford, Carole Boston. *The Beatitudes: From Slavery to Civil Rights*. Illustrated by Tim Ladwig. Eerdmans Books for Young Readers. Grand Rapids: Eerdmans, 2010.

Weber, Christin Lore. *Blessings: A WomanChrist Reflection on the Beatitudes*. San Francisco: Harper & Row, 1989.

Weeraperuma, Susunaga. *The Pure in Heart: Saluting Seven Saintly Women*. Delhi: ISPCK, 2003.

Weiss, Johannes. *Jesus' Proclamation of the Kingdom of God*. Edited and translated by Richard Hyde Hiers and David Larrimore Holland. Philadelphia: Fortress, 1971.

Welch, John W. *The Sermon on the Mount in the Light of the Temple*. Surrey, England: Ashgate, 2009.

Wellhausen, Julius. *Das Evangelium Lucae: Übersetzt und Erklärt*. Berlin: Georg Reimer, 1904.

———. *Das Evangelium Matthaei: Übersetzt und Erklärt*. Berlin: Georg Reimer, 1904.

Wells, B. Edward. *A Paraphrase with Annotations on the New Testament*. Vol. 1. London, 1730?.

Wells, Samuel. "Dwelling in the Comma." In *Learning to Dream Again: Rediscovering the Heart of God*, 135–41. Grand Rapids: Eerdmans, 2013.

Wenham, David. "How Do the Beatitudes Work? Some Observations on the Structure of the Beatitudes in Matthew." In *The Earliest Perceptions of Jesus in Context: Essays in Honor of John Nolland*, edited by Aaron W. White,

Craig A. Evans, and David Wenham, 201–12. London: Bloomsbury T&T Clark, 2018.

———. "The Rock on Which to Build: Some Mainly Pauline Observations about the Sermon on the Mount." In *Built Upon the Rock: Studies in the Gospel of Matthew*, edited by Daniel M. Gurtner and John Nolland, 187–206. Grand Rapids: Eerdmans, 2008.

Wesley, John. *The Nature of the Kingdom: Wesley's Messages on the Sermon on the Mount*. Edited and updated by Clare George Weakley Jr. Minneapolis: Bethany House Publishers, 1979.

West, Elizabeth. "Comparing Buddhism's Noble Eightfold Path and Jesus' Beatitudes." In Roncace and Weaver, *Global Perspectives*, 221–23.

White, Ellen Gould. *Thoughts from the Mount of Blessing*. Mountain View, CA: Pacific Press Publishing Association, 1900, 1928.

Wilken, Robert Louis. "Augustine." In Greenman, Larsen, and Spencer, *Sermon on the Mount through the Centuries*, 43–57.

———. "Gregory of Nyssa, *De Beatitudinibus*, Oratio VII: 'Blessed Are Those Who Are Persecuted for Righteousness' Sake, For Theirs Is the Kingdom of Heaven' (Mt 5,10)." In *Gregory of Nyssa: Homilies on the Beatitudes*, edited by Hubertus R. Drobner and Albert Viciano, 243–54. Leiden: Brill, 2000.

———. *The Spirit of Early Christian Thought: Seeking the Face of God*. New Haven, CT: Yale University Press, 2005.

Willard, Dallas. *The Divine Conspiracy: Rediscovering Our Hidden Life in God*. New York: HarperSanFrancisco, 1998.

Wilson, Richard. *The Journey of the Beatitudes*. Center City, MN: Hazelden, 1986.

Windisch, Hans. *The Meaning of the Sermon on the Mount: A Contribution to the Historical Understanding of the Gospels and to the Problem of their True Exegesis*. Philadelphia: Westminster, 1951.

Wintle, Brian. "Matthew." In *South Asia Bible Commentary*, edited by Brian Wintle, 1219–84. Open Door Publications; Zondervan; Langham Partnership, 2015.

Wirt, Sherwood E. *Magnificent Promise: A Fresh View of the Beatitudes from the Cross*. Chicago: Moody Press, 1964.

Witetschek, Stephan. "Going Hungry for a Purpose: On Gos. Thom. 69.2 and a Neglected Parallel in Origen." *JSNT* 32, no. 4 (2010): 379–93.

Wolterstorff, Nicholas. *Lament for a Son*. Grand Rapids: Eerdmans, 1987.

Wuellner, Flora Slosson. *Forgiveness, the Passionate Journey: Nine Steps of Forgiving through Jesus' Beatitudes*. Nashville: Upper Room Books, 2001.

Yancey, Philip. "General Schwarzkopf Meets the Beatitudes." *Christianity Today* 35, no. 7 (June 24, 1991): 72.

Yarchin, William. "Enlightenment Rationality for Understanding Scripture: Baruch Spinoza." In *History of Biblical Interpretation: A Reader*, ch. 18. Grand Rapids: Baker Academic, 2004.

Yieh, John Y. H. "Jesus as 'Teacher-Savior' or 'Savior-Teacher': Reading the Gospel of Matthew in Chinese Contexts." Paper delivered at The Society of Biblical Literature, November 2008. https://www.sbl-site.org/assets/pdfs /Yieh_TeacherSavior.pdf.

———. "Reading the Sermon on the Mount in China: A Hermeneutical Inquiry into Its History of Reception." In *Reading Scriptures in China*, edited by Chlöe Starr, 143–62. London: T&T Clark, 2008.

Yoder, John Howard. "The Christological Presuppositions of Discipleship." In *Being Human, Becoming Human: Dietrich Bonhoeffer and Social Thought*, edited by Jens Zimmerman and Brian Gregor, 127–51. Eugene, OR: Pickwick Publications, 2010.

———. *The Original Revolution: Essays on Christian Pacifism*. Scottdale, PA: Herald Press, 2003.

Young, Robin Darling. "Selections from John Chrysostom's Homilies on Matthew. Introduction." In *The Theological Interpretation of Scripture: Classic and Contemporary Readings*, edited by Stephen E. Fowl, 239–42. Malden, MA: Blackwell Publishers, 1997.

Zayas, Alfred de. "Beatitudes." In *Poets Against the War*, edited by Sam Hamill, 57–58. New York: Thunder's Mouth Press/Nation Books, 2003.

Zell, Katharina Schütz. *Church Mother: The Writings of a Protestant Reformer in Sixteenth-Century Germany*. Edited and translated by Elsie McKee. Chicago: University of Chicago Press, 2006.

Zias, Joseph E. "The Cemeteries of Qumran and Celibacy: Confusion Laid to Rest?" *DSD* 7, no. 2 (2000): 220–53.

Secondary Sources

Akerboom, Dick, and Marcel Gielis. "'A New Song Shall Begin Here . . .' The Martyrdom of Luther's Followers among Antwerp's Augustinians on July 1, 1523 and Luther's Response." In *More than a Memory: The Discourse of Martyrdom and the Construction of Christian Identity in the History of Christianity*, edited by Johan Leemans, 244–70. Leuven: Peeters, 2005.

Allison, Dale C., Jr. "Eunuchs because of the Kingdom of Heaven (Matt 19:12)." *Theological Students Fellowship Bulletin* 8, no. 2 (1984): 2–5.

———. "The History of the Interpretation of Matthew: Lessons Learned." *In die*

Skriflig 49, no. 1 (2015): Art. #1879, 13 pages. http://dx.doi.org/10.4102/ids.
v49i1.1879.

Ambrose of Milan. "On His Brother Satyrus." In Gregory Nazianzen and Ambrose,
Funeral Orations, edited by Martin R. P. McGuire, 157–259. FC 22. New
York: Fathers of the Church, 1953.

Aristotle. *The Ethics of Aristotle: The Nicomachean Ethics*. Translated by J. A. K.
Thomson. Revised by Hugh Tredennick. New York: Penguin Books, 1953,
1976.

———. *The Great Ethics of Aristotle*. Translated by Peter L. P. Simpson. New Brunswick: Transaction Publishers, 2014.

———. *Metaphysics, Books X–XIV. Oeconomica and Magna Moralia*. Translated
by G. Cyril Armstrong. Cambridge, MA: Harvard University Press, 1947.

———. *Nicomachean Ethics*. Translated by David Ross. Revised by Lesley Brown.
Oxford World Classics. Oxford: Oxford University Press, 2009.

———. *The Nicomachean Ethics*. Translated by H. Rackham. LCL 73. Cambridge,
MA: Harvard University Press, 1926, 1934.

Armitage, David J. *Theologies of Poverty in the World of the New Testament*. WUNT
2/423. Tübingen: Mohr Siebeck, 2016.

Aronstam, Robin Ann. "Penitential Pilgrimages to Rome in the Early Middle
Ages." *Archivum Historiae Pontificiae* 13 (1975): 65–83.

Augustine. *On Christian Doctrine*. Translated by D. W. Robertson Jr. New York:
Macmillan, 1958.

Baghos, Mario. "St. Basil's Eschatological Vision: Aspects of the Recapitulation of
History and the 'Eighth Day.'" *Phronema* 25 (2010): 85–103.

Baldovin, John F. *The Urban Character of Christian Worship: The Origins, Development, and Meaning of Stational Liturgy*. Orientalia Christiana Analecta 228.
Rome: Orientalia Christiana, 1987.

Balentine, Samuel E. Afterword to *The Origins of Penitential Prayer in Second Temple
Judaism*. Vol. 1 of *Seeking the Favor of God*, edited by Mark J. Boda, Dan-
iel K. Falk, and Rodney A. Werline, 193–204. Atlanta: Society of Biblical
Literature, 2006.

———. "'I Was Ready to Be Sought Out by Those Who Did Not Ask.'" In *The
Origins of Penitential Prayer in Second Temple Judaism*. Vol. 1 of *Seeking the
Favor of God*, edited by Mark J. Boda, Daniel K. Falk, and Rodney A. Wer-
line, 1–20. Atlanta: Society of Biblical Literature, 2006.

Bauerschmidt, Frederick Christian. "The Middle Ages." In *The Blackwell Companion to Catholicism*, edited by James J. Buckley, Frederick Christian Bauerschmidt, and Trent Pomplun, 49–62. Malden, MA: Wiley-Blackwell, 2011.

———. "Thomas Aquinas: The Unity of the Virtues and the Journeying Self." In

Unsettling Arguments: A Festschrift on the Occasion of Stanley Hauerwas's 70th Birthday, edited by Charles R. Pinches, Kelly S. Johnson, and Charles M. Collier, 25–41. Eugene, OR: Cascade, 2010.

Bautch, Richard J. *Developments in Genre between Post-Exilic Penitential Prayers and the Psalms of Communal Lament*. Leiden: Brill, 2003.

——. "Lament Regained in Trito-Isaiah's Penitential Prayer." In *The Origins of Penitential Prayer in Second Temple Judaism*. Vol. 1 of *Seeking the Favor of God*, edited by Mark J. Boda, Daniel K. Falk, and Rodney A. Werline, 83–99. Atlanta: Society of Biblical Literature, 2006.

Bedouelle, Guy, and Franco Giacone. *Jacques Lefèvre D'Étaples et ses Disciples*. Leiden: Brill, 1976.

Bélanger, Stéphanie. "Guyart, Marie." In Taylor, ed., *Handbook of Women Biblical Interpreters*, 224–27.

Berlin, Adele. "Qumran Laments and the Study of Qumran Literature." In *Liturgical Perspectives: Prayer and Poetry in Light of the Dead Sea Scrolls*, edited by Esther G. Chazon, Ruth Clements, and Avital Pinnick, 1–18. Leiden; Boston: Brill, 2003.

Bethge, Eberhard. *Dietrich Bonhoeffer: A Biography*. Revised and edited by Victoria J. Barnett. Minneapolis: Fortress, 2000.

Bier, Miriam J., and Tim Bulkeley, eds. *Spiritual Complaint: The Theology and Practice of Lament*. Eugene, OR: Pickwick, 2013.

Boase, Elizabeth. "Blurring the Boundaries: The Rhetoric of Lament and Penitence in Isaiah 63:7-64:11," in Bier and Bulkeley, *Spiritual Complaint*, 71–87.

Bockmuehl, Markus. "New Testament *Wirkungsgeschichte* and the Early Christian Appeal to Living Memory." In *Memory in the Bible and Antiquity*, edited by Loren Stuckenbruck, Stephen C. Barton, and Benjamin G. Wold, 341–68. Tübingen: Mohr Siebeck, 2007.

——. *Seeing the Word: Refocusing New Testament Study*. Grand Rapids: Baker Academic, 2006.

Boer, Roland, and Fernando F. Segovia, eds. *The Future of the Biblical Past: Envisioning Biblical Studies on a Global Key*. Atlanta: Society of Biblical Literature, 2012.

Boersma, Hans. "The Sacramental Reading of Nicene Theology: Athanasius and Gregory of Nyssa on Proverbs 8." *JTI* 10, no. 1 (2016): 1–30.

——. *Seeing God: The Beatific Vision in Christian Tradition*. Grand Rapids: Eerdmans, 2018.

Böttrich, Christfried. "The 'Book of the Secrets of Enoch' (2 En): Between Jewish Origin and Christian Transmission. An Overview." In *New Perspectives on*

2 Enoch: No Longer Slavonic Only, edited by Andrei A. Orlov and Gabriele Boccaccini, 40–67. Leiden: Brill, 2012.

Bowersock, G. W. *Martyrdom and Rome.* Cambridge University Press, 1995.

Bowman, C. V. "About the Principles of the Mission Friends." In *Covenant Roots: Sources and Affirmations,* ed. Glenn P. Anderson, 81–91. Chicago: Covenant Press, 1980.

Boyarin, Daniel. *Dying for God: Martyrdom and the Making of Christianity and Judaism.* Stanford, CA: Stanford University Press, 1999.

Brandt, Eric. "Smith, Amanda Berry." In Taylor, ed., *Handbook of Women Biblical Interpreters,* 450–52.

Breed, Brennan. *Nomadic Text: A Theory of Biblical Reception History.* Bloomington, IN: Indiana University Press, 2014.

Brock, Sebastian. *The Luminous Eye: The Spiritual World Vision of Saint Ephrem.* Cistercian Studies Series 124. Kalamazoo, MI: Cistercian Publications, 1992.

Brooke, George J. *The Dead Sea Scrolls and the New Testament.* Minneapolis: Fortress, 2005.

Burrus, Virginia. *Chastity as Autonomy: Women in the Stories of the Apocryphal Acts.* Studies in Women and Religion 23. Lewiston, NY: Mellen, 1987.

Cameron, Averil. *Byzantine Matters.* Princeton: Princeton University Press, 2014.

Carlile, J. C. *C. H. Spurgeon.* Westwood, NJ: Barbour & Co., 1987.

Catherine of Siena. *Passion for the Truth; Compassion for Humanity.* Edited by Mary O'Driscoll. New York: New City Press, 2008.

Cazelles, Henri. "'ashrê." *TDOT* 1:445–48.

Charry, Ellen T. *By the Renewing of Your Minds: The Pastoral Function of Christian Doctrine.* Oxford: Oxford University Press, 1997.

Chester, Stephen J. *Reading Paul with the Reformers: Reconciling Old and New Perspectives.* Grand Rapids: Eerdmans, 2017.

Chiang, Ted. *Stories of Your Life and Others.* New York: Vintage Books, 2016.

Clark, Elizabeth A. *Reading Renunciation: Asceticism and Scripture in Early Christianity.* Princeton, NJ: Princeton University Press, 1999.

Corbett, Steve, and Brian Fikkert. *When Helping Hurts: How to Alleviate Poverty without Hurting the Poor . . . and Yourself.* Chicago: Moody Publishers, 2009, 2012.

Cullen, Christopher M. *Bonaventure.* Oxford: Oxford University Press, 2006.

Deferrari, Roy J., and M. Inviolata Barry, with Ignatius McGuiness. *A Lexicon of Saint Thomas Aquinas.* Baltimore: J. D. Lucas, 1948, 1949.

Dillard, Annie. *Teaching a Stone to Talk: Expeditions and Encounters.* New York: Harper Perennial, 1982, 2013.

Douglas, Kelly Brown. *Stand Your Ground: Black Bodies and the Justice of God.* Maryknoll, NY: Orbis Books, 2015.

Duhigg, Charles. "The Real Roots of American Rage." *The Atlantic* (January/ February 2019). https://www.theatlantic.com/magazine/archive/2019/01 /charles-duhigg-american-anger/576424/.

Ekblad, Bob. *Reading the Bible with the Damned.* Louisville: Westminster John Knox, 2005.

Eklund, Rebekah. "Jesus of Nazareth." In *The State of New Testament Studies*, edited by Scot McKnight and Nijay K. Gupta, 139–60. Grand Rapids: Baker Academic, 2019.

Elm, Susanna. *"Virgins of God": The Making of Asceticism in Late Antiquity.* New York: Clarendon Press, 1994.

Eubank, Nathan. *Wages of Cross-Bearing and Debt of Sin: The Economy of Heaven in Matthew's Gospel.* Berlin: de Gruyter, 2013.

Evans, Robert. *Reception History, Tradition, and Biblical Interpretation: Gadamer and Jauss in Current Practice.* London: Bloomsbury T&T Clark, 2014.

Evans, Roger Steven. *Sex and Salvation: Virginity as a Soteriological Paradigm in Ancient Christianity.* Lanham, MD: University Press of America, 2003.

Feynman, Richard. *What Do You Care What Other People Think? Further Adventures of a Curious Character.* New York: Norton, 2018.

Flesher, LeAnn Snow. "The Use of Female Imagery and Lamentation in the Book of Judith: Penitential Prayer or Petition for Obligatory Action?" In *The Development of Penitential Prayer in Second Temple Judaism.* Vol. 2 of *Seeking the Favor of God*, edited by Mark J. Boda and Daniel K. Falk, 83–104. Leiden: Brill, 2007.

Flogaus, Reinhard. "Palamas and Barlaam Revisited: A Reassessment of East and West in the Hesychast Controversy of 14th Century Byzantium." *SVTQ* 42, no. 1 (1998): 1–32.

Foulcher, Jane. *Reclaiming Humility: Four Studies in the Monastic Tradition.* Cistercian Studies 255. Collegeville, MN: Liturgical Press, 2015.

Fowl, Stephen E. "Effective History and the Cultivation of Wise Interpreters." *JTI* 7, no. 2 (2013): 153–61.

———. *Engaging Scripture: A Model for Theological Interpretation.* Eugene, OR: Wipf & Stock, 1998.

Franks, Christopher A. *He Became Poor: The Poverty of Christ and Aquinas's Economic Teachings.* Grand Rapids: Eerdmans, 2009.

Freeburn, Ryan P. *Hugh of Amiens and the Twelfth-Century Renaissance.* Surrey, England: Ashgate, 2011.

Frend, W. H. C. *Martyrdom and Persecution in the Early Church: A Study of a Conflict from the Maccabees to Donatus.* Oxford: Basil Blackwell, 1965.

Gadamer, Hans-Georg. *Truth and Method.* Rev. ed. London; New York: Continuum, 2004.

Galtung-Institut for Peace Theory and Peace Practice. "Johan Galtung." https://www.galtung-institut.de/en/home/johan-galtung/.

Galtung, Johan. "Three Approaches to Peace: Peacekeeping, Peacemaking, and Peacebuilding." In vol. 2 of *Peace, War and Defense: Essays in Peace Research,* 282–304. Copenhagen: Christian Eljers, 1976.

———. "Twenty-Five Years of Peace Research: Ten Challenges and Some Responses." *Journal of Peace Research* 22, no. 2 (1985): 141–58.

Gassert, Philipp, and Daniel S. Mattern. *The Hitler Library: A Bibliography.* Westport, CT: Greenwood Press, 2001.

Golitzin, Alexander. "'The Demons Suggest an Illusion of God's Glory in a Form': Controversy Over the Divine Body and Vision of Glory in Some Late Fourth, Early Fifth Century Monastic Literature." *Studia Monastica* 44, no. 1 (2002): 13–43.

———. "The Vision of God and the Form of Glory: More Reflections on the Anthropomorphite Controversy of AD 399." In *Abba: The Tradition of Orthodoxy in the West: Festschrift for Bishop Kallistos (Ware) of Diokleia,* edited by John Behr, Andrew Louth, and Dimitri Conomos, 273–97. Crestwood, NY: St. Vladimir's Seminary Press, 2003.

González, Justo L., ed. *The Westminster Dictionary of Theologians.* Translated by Suzanne E. Hoeferkamp Segovia. Louisville: Westminster John Knox, 2006.

Gorman, Michael J. *Reading Revelation Responsibly.* Eugene, OR: Cascade, 2011.

Greene-McCreight, K. E. *Ad Litteram: How Augustine, Calvin, and Barth Read the 'Plain Sense' of Genesis 1–3.* New York: Lang, 1999.

Gregory, Brad S. *Salvation at Stake: Christian Martyrdom in Early Modern Europe.* Cambridge, MA: Harvard University Press, 1999.

Hart, Trevor. "Imagination and Responsible Reading." In *Renewing Biblical Interpretation,* edited by Craig Bartholomew, Colin Greene, and Karl Moller, 307–34. Cumbria, UK: Paternoster; Grand Rapids: Zondervan, 2000.

Harvey, John. *The Bible as Visual Culture.* Sheffield: Sheffield Phoenix, 2013.

Hawkins, Peter S. *Dante's Testaments: Essays in Scriptural Imagination.* Stanford, CA: Stanford University Press, 1999.

Hayes, Christine. "'The Torah was not Given to Ministering Angels': Rabbinic Aspirationalism." In *Talmudic Transgressions: Engaging the Work of Daniel Boyarin,* edited by Charlotte Elisheva Fonrobert, Ishay Rosen-Zvi, Aharon Shemesh, Moulie Vidas, and James Redfield, 123–60. Leiden: Brill, 2017.

Hays, Richard B. "The Palpable Word as Ground of *Koinōnia*." In *Christianity and the Soul of the University: Faith as a Foundation for Intellectual Community*, edited by Douglas V. Henry and Michael D. Beaty, 19–36. Grand Rapids: Baker Academic, 2006.

————. "Reading Scripture in Light of the Resurrection." In *The Art of Reading Scripture*, edited by Ellen F. Davis and Richard B. Hays, 216–38. Grand Rapids: Eerdmans, 2010.

Heger, Paul. "Celibacy in Qumran: Hellenist Fiction or Reality? Qumran's Attitude toward Sex." *Revue de Qumrân* 26, no. 1 (2013): 53–90.

Helm, Joe. "Jerry Falwell Jr. can't imagine Trump 'doing anything that's not good for the country.'" *Washington Post* (January 1, 2019). https://www.washingtonpost.com/lifestyle/magazine/jerry-falwell-jr-cant-imagine-trump-doing-anything-thats-not-good-for-the-country/2018/12/21/6affc4c4-f19e-11e8-80d0-f7e1948d55f4_story.html.

Heschel, Susannah. *The Aryan Jesus: Christian Theologians and the Bible in Nazi Germany*. Princeton: Princeton University Press, 2008.

Horgan, Maurya P. "Psalm Pesher 1 (4Q171=4QpPs^a=4QpPs37 and 45)." In *Pesharim, Other Commentaries, and Related Documents*. Vol. 6B of *The Dead Sea Scrolls: Hebrew, Aramaic, and Greek Texts with English Translations*, edited by James H. Charlesworth, 6–23. Louisville: Westminster John Knox; Tübingen: Mohr Siebeck, 2002.

International Association for Humanitarian Policy and Conflict Research. "The Conceptual Origins of Peacemaking." 2007–2008. http://www.peacebuildinginitiative.org/index34ac.html?pageId=1764.

Kalantzis, George. *Caesar and the Lamb: Early Christian Attitudes on War and Military Service*. Eugene, OR: Cascade, 2012.

Katongole, Emmanuel. *Born From Lament*. Grand Rapids: Eerdmans, 2017.

Katzenellenbogen, Adolf. *Allegories of the Virtues and Vices in Medieval Art: From Early Christian Times to the Thirteenth Century*. Toronto: University of Toronto Press, 1989.

Knight, Mark. "*Wirkungsgeschichte*, Reception History, Reception Theory." *JSNT* 33 (2010): 137–46.

Kolb, Robert. "From Hymn to History of Dogma: Lutheran Martyrology in the Reformation Era." In *More than a Memory: The Discourse of Martyrdom and the Construction of Christian Identity in the History of Christianity*, edited by Johan Leemans, 295–313. Leuven: Peeters, 2005.

Lambert, David A. *How Repentance Became Biblical: Judaism, Christianity, and the Interpretation of Scripture*. Oxford: Oxford University Press, 2016.

Lampe, G. W. H. "Martyrdom and Inspiration." In *Suffering and Martyrdom in the New Testament,* edited by William Horbury and Brian McNeil, 118–35. Cambridge University Press, 1981.

Lossky, Vladimir. *In the Image and Likeness of God.* Edited by John H. Erickson and Thomas E. Bird. Crestwood, NY: St. Vladimir's Seminary Press, 1974, 2001.

Lottin, D. O. "Les dons du Saint-Esprit chez les théologiens depuis P. Lombard jusqu'à S. Thomas d'Aquin." *RTAM* 1 (January 1929): 41–61.

Luz, Ulrich. "Reflections on the Appropriate Interpretation of New Testament Texts." In *Studies in Matthew,* translated by Rosemary Selle, 265–89. Grand Rapids: Eerdmans, 2005.

Lysen, Laura M. "Vicious Sorrow: The Roots of a 'Spiritual' Sin in the *Summa Theologiae*." *Studies in Christian Ethics* 30, no. 3 (2017): 329–47.

Massing, Michael. *Fatal Discord: Erasmus, Luther, and the Fight for the Western Mind.* New York: HarperCollins, 2018.

Mattox, John Mark. *Saint Augustine and the Theory of Just War.* London: Continuum, 2006.

McCambley, Casimir. "On the Sixth Psalm, Concerning the Octave by Saint Gregory of Nyssa." *GOTR* 32, no. 1 (1987): 39–50.

McKee, Elsie. "Zell, Katharina Schütz." In Taylor, ed., *Handbook of Women Biblical Interpreters,* 547–51.

Middleton, Paul. *Radical Martyrdom and Cosmic Conflict in Early Christianity.* London: T&T Clark, 2006.

Milad, Corine B. "Incarnation and Transfiguration: Origen's Theology of Descent." *JTI* 12, no. 2 (2018): 200–216.

Mitchell, Margaret M. *Paul, the Corinthians and the Birth of Christian Hermeneutics.* Cambridge: Cambridge University Press, 2010.

Moberly, R. W. L. "Theological Thinking and the Reading of Scripture: An *Auseinandersetzung* with Susannah Ticciati." *JTI* 10, no. 1 (2016): 103–16.

Moffat, Donald P. "The Profit and Loss of Lament: Rethinking Aspects of the Relationship between Lament and Penitential Prayer," in Bier and Bulkeley, *Spiritual Complaint,* 88–101.

Montefiore, C. G. *Ancient Jewish and Greek Encouragement and Consolation.* Bridgeport, CT: Hartmore House, 1971.

Moore, Michael S. "The Laments in Jeremiah and 1QH: Mapping the Metaphorical Trajectories." In *Uprooting and Planting: Essays on Jeremiah for Leslie Allen,* edited by John Goldingay, 228–52. New York: T&T Clark, 2007.

Morgan, Robert. "Susannah Heschel's Aryan Grundmann." *JSNT* 32, no. 4 (2010): 431–94.

Moss, Candida. *The Myth of Persecution: How Early Christians Invented a Story of Martyrdom.* New York: HarperOne, 2013.

Rabbi Nathan. *The Fathers According to Rabbi Nathan.* English translation of Aboth de Rabbi Nathan. Translated by Judah Goldin. New York: Schocken Books, 1974.

Nicholls, Rachel. *Walking on the Water: Reading Mt. 14:22–33 in the Light of its Wirkungsgeschichte.* Leiden: Brill, 2008.

Perkins, John. Foreword (2009) to *When Helping Hurts: How to Alleviate Poverty without Hurting the Poor . . . and Yourself,* by Steve Corbett and Brian Fikkert. Chicago: Moody Publishers, 2009, 2012.

Plato. *Euthyphro, Apology, Crito, Phaedo.* Translated by Benjamin Jowett. Amherst, NY: Prometheus Books, 1988.

———. *Republic, Books 1–5.* Translated by Chris Emlyn-Jones and William Preddy. LCL 216. Cambridge, MA: Harvard University Press, 2013.

Polizzotti, Mark. *Sympathy for the Traitor: A Translation Manifesto.* Cambridge, MA: The MIT Press, 2018.

Quash, Ben. *Found Theology: History, Imagination and the Holy Spirit.* London: Bloomsbury, 2013.

Rah, Soong-Chan. *Prophetic Lament: A Call for Justice in Troubled Times.* Downers Grove, IL: IVP Books, 2015.

Regev, Eyal. "Cherchez les femmes: Were the *yaḥad* Celibates?" *DSD* 15 (2008): 253–84.

Reveal, Judith C. "Warner, Susan Bogert and Anna Bartlett Warner." In *Women in World History: A Biographical Encyclopedia,* https://www.encyclopedia.com /women/encyclopedias-almanacs-transcripts-and-maps/warner-susan -bogert-and-anna-bartlett-warner.

Rittgers, Ronald K. *The Reformation of Suffering: Pastoral Theology and Lay Piety in Late Medieval and Early Modern Germany.* Oxford: Oxford University Press, 2012.

Rom-Shiloni, Dalit. "Socio-Ideological *Setting* or *Settings* for Penitential Prayers?" In *The Origins of Penitential Prayer in Second Temple Judaism.* Vol. 1 of *Seeking the Favor of God,* edited by Mark J. Boda, Daniel K. Falk, and Rodney A. Werline, 51–68. Atlanta: Society of Biblical Literature, 2006.

Rowe, C. Kavin. *One True Life: The Stoics and Early Christians as Rival Traditions.* New Haven, CT: Yale University Press, 2016.

Schlatter, Fredric W. "The Author of the *Opus Imperfectum in Matthaeum.*" *Vigiliae Christianae* 40, no. 4 (1988): 364–75.

Schneiders, Sandra M. *The Revelatory Text: Interpreting the New Testament as Sacred Scripture.* Collegeville, MN: Liturgical Press, 1999.

Schreiner, Susan E. *Where Shall Wisdom Be Found? Calvin's Exegesis of Job from Medieval and Modern Perspectives.* Chicago: University of Chicago, 1994.

Sherwood, Yvonne. *A Biblical Text and Its Afterlives: The Survival of Jonah in Western Culture.* Cambridge: Cambridge University Press, 2000.

Sider, Ronald J. *Rich Christians in an Age of Hunger.* Rev. ed. Downers Grove, IL: InterVarsity Press, 1984.

Sliwka, Jennifer. "Illusive and elusive: The (im)possibility of seeing in Michael Simpson's flat surface paintings." Paper presented at the Theology, Modernity, and Visual Arts colloquium, Art Institute of Chicago, May 23, 2019.

Steele, Richard B. "Transfiguring Light: The Moral Beauty of the Christian Life According to Gregory Palamas and Jonathan Edwards." *SVTQ* 52, no. 3–4 (2008): 403–39.

Steinmetz, David C. "The Superiority of Pre-Critical Exegesis." *Theology Today* 37, no. 1 (1980): 27–28.

Stevenson, Kenneth W. *The First Rites: Worship in the Early Church.* Collegeville, MN: Liturgical Press, 1989.

Stevenson, William R., Jr. *Christian Love and Just War: Moral Paradox and Political Life in St. Augustine and His Modern Interpreters.* Macon, GA: Mercer University Press, 1987.

Stewart, Kenneth. "The Doctrine of Regeneration in Evangelical Theology: The Reformation to 1800." *Journal for Baptist Theology and Ministry* 8, no. 1 (Spring 2011): 42–57.

Stinger, Charles L. *The Renaissance in Rome.* Bloomington, IN: Indiana University Press, 1998.

Sullivan, Mary Louise. *Mother Cabrini: "Italian Immigrant of the Century."* New York: Center for Migration Studies, 1992.

Sumption, Jonathan. *Pilgrimage: An Image of Mediaeval Religion.* Totowa, NJ: Rowman & Littlefield, 1975, 2002.

Swatos, William H., Jr., and Luigi Tomasi, eds. *From Medieval Pilgrimage to Religious Tourism: The Social and Cultural Economics of Piety.* Westport, CT: Praeger, 2002.

Taylor, Marion Ann, ed. *Handbook of Women Biblical Interpreters: A Historical and Biographical Guide.* Grand Rapids: Baker Academic, 2012.

Teske, Roland J. "St. Augustine and the Vision of God." In *Augustine: Mystic and Mystagogue,* edited by Joseph C. Schnaubelt, Frederick van Fleteren, and Joseph Reino, 207–308. New York: Lang, 1994.

Thompson, John L. "At the Margins of the Rule of Faith: Reflections on the Reception History of Problematic Texts and Themes." *JTI* 7, no. 2 (2013): 187–98.

———. *Reading the Bible with the Dead.* Grand Rapids: Eerdmans, 2007.

Ticciati, Susannah. *A New Apophaticism: Augustine and the Redemption of Signs.* Leiden: Brill, 2015.

————. "Response to Walter Moberly's 'Theological Thinking and the Reading of Scripture.'" *JTI* 10, no. 1 (2016): 117–23.

Tiemeyer, Lena-Sofia. "The Doubtful Gain of Penitence: The Fine Line between Lament and Penitential Prayer," in Bier and Bulkeley, *Spiritual Complaint,* 102–24.

Tizon, Al. *Whole and Reconciled: Gospel, Church, and Mission in a Fractured World.* Grand Rapids: Baker Academic, 2018.

Tolstoy, Leo. "Some Social Remedies." In *Pamphlets.* Christchurch, Hants: The Free Age Press, 1900.

Tomoioagă, F. T. "The Vision of Divine Light in Saint Gregory Palamas's Theology." *Acta Theologica* 35, no. 2 (2015): 142–53.

Torrell, Jean-Pierre. *The Person and His Work.* Vol. 1 of *Saint Thomas Aquinas,* translated by Robert Royal. Washington, DC: Catholic University of America Press, 1996.

Trautwein, Sherri. "Adams, Hannah." In Taylor, *Handbook of Women Biblical Interpreters,* 27–31.

Undheim, Sissel. *Borderline Virginities: Sacred and Secular Virgins in Late Antiquity.* New York: Routledge, 2018.

Van der Horst, Pieter W., and Silvia Castelli. "Celibacy in Early Judaism." *RB* 109, no. 3 (2002): 390–402.

Van Dijk, S. J. P. "The Medieval Easter Vespers of the Roman Clergy." *Sacris Erudiri* 19 (1969): 261–363.

Voskamp, Ann. "When the Word Becomes Words." *Christianity Today* 62, no. 10 (December 2018). https://www.christianitytoday.com/ct/2018/decem ber/voskamp-havens-when-word-becomes-words-rendille.html.

Walsh, Joseph J., ed. *What Would You Die For? Perpetua's Passion.* Baltimore, MD: Apprentice House, 2006.

Waltke, Bruce K., James M. Houston, and Erika Moore. *The Psalms as Christian Lament: A Historical Commentary.* Grand Rapids: Eerdmans, 2014.

Warner, William. *The Way of the Didache.* Lanham, MD: University Press of America, 2007.

Weigel, George, with Elizabeth Lev and Stephen Weigel. *Roman Pilgrimage: The Station Churches.* New York: Basic Books, 2013.

Weinandy, Thomas G., Daniel A. Keating, and John P. Yocum, eds. *Aquinas on Scripture: An Introduction to His Biblical Commentaries.* New York: T&T Clark, 2005.

Welch, John W. "Counting to Ten." *JBMS* 12, no. 2 (2003): 40–57.

Werline, Rodney Alan. *Penitential Prayer in Second Temple Judaism: The Development of a Religious Institution.* Atlanta: Scholars Press, 1998.

Westerholm, Stephen, and Martin Westerholm, *Reading Sacred Scripture: Voices from the History of Biblical Interpretation.* Grand Rapids: Eerdmans, 2016.

Westermann, Claus. *Praise and Lament in the Psalms.* Translated by Keith R. Crim and Richard N. Soulen. Atlanta: John Knox, 1965, 1981.

Wilken, Robert Louis. *Isaiah.* Translated and edited by Robert Louis Wilken with Angela Russell Christman and M. J. Hollerich. The Church's Bible. Grand Rapids: Eerdmans, 2007.

Williams, Rowan. "Historical Criticism and Sacred Text." In *Reading Texts, Seeking Wisdom*, edited by David F. Ford and Graham Stanton, 217–28. Grand Rapids: Eerdmans, 2003.

———. "Redeeming Sorrows." In *Religion and Morality*, edited by D. Z. Phillips, 132–48. New York: St. Martin's Press, 1996.

Wisch, Barbara. "The Matrix: 'Le Sette Chiese di Roma' of 1575 and the Image of Pilgrimage." *Memoirs of the American Academy in Rome* 56/57 (2011/2012): 271–303.

Wolterstorff, Nicholas. "A Response to Trevor Hart." In *Renewing Biblical Interpretation*, edited by Craig Bartholomew, Colin Greene, and Karl Moller, 335–41. Cumbria, UK: Paternoster; Grand Rapids: Zondervan, 2000.

Zerner, Ruth. "Dietrich Bonhoeffer and the Jews: Thoughts and Actions, 1933–1945." In *Bystanders to the Holocaust.* Vol. 8 pt. 3 of *The Nazi Holocaust*, edited by Michael R. Marrus, 1390–1405. Westport, CT: Meckler, 1989.

INDEX